This book brings together in a single coherent framework a research programme begun by the author over 40 years ago. The main model around which the analysis is built is Hicksian in character having been drawn in large part from John Hicks *Value and Capital.* The model is extended so as to include money and securities. In respect of the theory of the firm the model focuses on demand and supply plans, on inputs and outputs, on inventories, and on the dependencies between them. The stability of temporary equilibrium is discussed for linear and non-linear cases. Because the concept of structural stability is important for understanding non-linear cases, it is defined and applied to the case of economic motion generated from the temporary equilibrium analysis. The addenda focus on developments in economic theory following the publication of the main model.

Dynamic economic theory

Dynamic economic theory

Michio Morishima

CAMBRIDGE
UNIVERSITY PRESS

CAMBRIDGE UNIVERSITY PRESS
Cambridge, New York, Melbourne, Madrid, Cape Town, Singapore, São Paulo, Delhi

Cambridge University Press
The Edinburgh Building, Cambridge CB2 8RU, UK

Published in the United States of America by Cambridge University Press, New York

www.cambridge.org
Information on this title: www.cambridge.org/9780521118880

First published 1996
Reprinted 1998
This digitally printed version 2009

A catalogue record for this publication is available from the British Library

Library of Congress Cataloguing in Publication data

Morishima, Michio, 1923–
[Dōgakuteki keizai riron. English]
Dynamic economic theory / Michio Morishima.
p. cm.
Translation of the author's thesis published in Tōkyō by Kōbundō,
1950. English translation originally published: London:
International Centre for Economics and Related Disciplines,
1980. With new addenda.
Includes bibliographical references and index.
ISBN 0–521–56324–0 (hc)
1. Statics and dynamics (Social sciences) 2. Equilibrium
(Economics) I. Title.
HB145.M6712 1996
339.5–dc20 95-43037 CIP

ISBN 978-0-521-56324-6 hardback
ISBN 978-0-521-11888-0 paperback

Contents

Preface

1 To publish a translation of a book which was published nearly half a century ago in an academically local language we need convincing justifications. This volume originally entitled *Dogakuteki Keizai Riron* (*DKR*) was published in Japanese in 1950, by Kobundo, Tokyo. Soon after the war, I returned from the military service to the university and completed my undergraduate study at Kyoto University in 1946. *DKR* is a thesis written as a report on my graduate research work supported by the Ministry of Education Special Scholarship. The topic suggested by my supervisor, Professor Hideo Aoyama, was the 'mathematization of Hicks' *Value and Capital* (*VC*)', so that *DKR* is more or less parallel to it. However, there are a few substantial differences.

First, in *VC* it is assumed that output equals supply and input equals demand. This basic assumption enables us to use the production theory of the firm as the tool to explain its behaviour in the market. Moreover, this assumption implies that the stocks of input and output commodities do not change. In *DKR* I was concerned with firms whose inputs and outputs may deviate from the demands for the factors and the supplies of the products, respectively. I had, therefore, to construct a theory of the firm which could explain its production, trading, and inventory consistently.

Secondly, once this line of approach is adopted, it is clear that we cannot be satisfied with a physical input–output theory of the firm of the *VC* type. Money and securities are close substitutes for inventories of physical commodities. The theory of the firm, therefore, has to be extended so as to explain its behaviour of liquidity preference. This means that the economy should not be dichotomized into the real and monetary subeconomies. The indifference analysis for consumers' behaviour must be extended such that it can derive the demand for monetary goods, money, and securities.

Thirdly, stability was one of the most fashionable subjects of the late 1940s. In addition to those conditions for stability provided by Samuelson, Sono offered another condition. Unfortunately it was incomplete in the sense that it was not obtained from a dynamic analysis of the system. In *DKR* I 'dynamized' Sono's condition and found that stability is obtained whenever a function which resembles the Liapounoff function diminishes at every point except the equilibrium. Moreover, the structural stability was discussed. Under the assumption of this kind of stability it was shown that any stable temporary equilibrium point of a non-linear economy has its own stability zone. This led to the conclusion that provided that tatonnement starts from a point within a stability zone, the temporary equilibrium corresponding to the zone will be established when the tatonnement finally terminates.

Fourthly, *DKR* states that there are two types of stability which are important in developing dynamic theory. First, the *stability of* the temporary equilibrium *point* has to be examined. In the case of successive temporary equilibrium points all being stable, we have a sequence of equilibrium points, in terms of which economic fluctuations and development are described. Thus the stability of the equilibrium point is the unavoidable requisite for dynamic analysis. Instability has to be ruled out, in order for the economy to be workable through time without meeting any deadlock. Even though the equilibrium point is stable in each period (say, Hicks' 'week'), the second kind of stability remains to be discussed. That is to say, it has to be found out whether the actual sequence of temporary equilibria is stable or not with respect to an exogenous change in the data.

Thus we have two stability problems; the stability of the equilibrium point and the *stability of motion* or path. These have usually been associated with respectively two groups of economists: the first to general equilibrium theorists and the second to growth economists. They have often been confused, because the latter has usually been developed as the stability theory of the long-run equilibrium point, despite the fact that the existence of a long-run equilibrium point is doubtful, so we should examine the stability of the growth path rather than a long-run state of affairs. Moreover, whereas stability is the target of analysis in the first problem, instability should not be ignored in the second. In fact, in some cases such as technological innovations, they are carried out with the intention to launch the economy into a new orbit by using the power of instability working in the neighbourhood of the path of motion that the economy is following.

2 It seems to me that the four points above would justify publishing *DKR* in English nearly fifty years after its first appearance. It is of course true that in these years the theory of general equilibrium has been advanced greatly and put in a very modern form. Therefore, it would be necessary to reassess *DKR* from the contemporary advanced theory point of view. I have expressed my own present view in *Capital and Credit* (*CC*), 1992. When

comparing this, the reader will find outlined a number of shortcomings of *DKR*; it is, in fact, no more than a book which has to be criticized in *CC* together with those other books with which I disagree there.

Part II, called 'Addendum', is compiled in order to reexamine *DKR* from various points of view developed in other theorists' works in the period of 1950–90. It is a kind of survey of these works, but it is not comprehensive since it is a collection of my published or unpublished papers written for various purposes. It may, nevertheless, be useful for clarifying my views on these problems, developed after my writing of *DKR* and for connecting it to current economic theory in the West.

The Addendum consists of eight articles. The first two are concerned with what I call 'truncated' tatonnement procedures. According to the so-called 'Walrasian' tatonnement, transactions are not actually carried out until general equilibrium is established. To achieve this, it takes, generally speaking, an infinitely long time. The temporary equilibrium method of Hicks tacitly assumes that tatonnement is carried out extremely intensively in each week such that general equilibrium is realized at its end. It also assumes that transaction, consumption, and production are made instantly or within a very short time span at that point. Such an assumption (or consideration) is absent in Walras' (1954) *Elements of Pure Economics*; he assumes that tatonnement is truncated so as to make effective transactions at a point in time when general equilibrium has not yet been realized. Then individuals' or firms' endowments change, which initiates a new tatonnement. Thus, contradicting the so-called Walrasians, the real Walras is a *dis*equilibrium economist, at least in the field of dynamics.

After having established this view in Article I, Article II applies the idea of 'truncation' to the tatonnement in terms of quantities. In this system, prices are fixed, and adjustments are made to quantities. This is a system which Hicks later calls the 'fixprice' system. If we call the number of times of groping (or tatonnement) actions carried out until they are truncated 'the effective length of tatonnement', we find that it is assumed to be 1 in the usual macro-quantity adjustment mechanism, such as Marx's reproduction scheme, so that the rate of growth of output is different between sectors, unless some special assumption is made.[1] However, when the demand schedules are perfectly flexible, so that the effective length is very large, sectors of the economy grow at a uniform rate. This may be a hidden assumption behind von Neumann's theory of balanced growth equilibrium.

When *DKR* was published, there was no non-linear theory of the trade

[1] In fact, Marx made such an assumption, so that the sectoral rates of growth obtained from his 'extended reproduction scheme' converge quickly (i.e., at the beginning of the next period) to a uniform one. See Morishima, 1973, *Marx's Economics*, Cambridge University Press, pp. 117–28.

cycle, except Kalecki, 1937 and Kaldor, 1940, both lacking a complete mathematical proof of the existence of a limit cycle. However, those works which appeared soon after the publication of *DKR* belong to the field of macrodynamics and are not works of general equilibrium analysis. Their equations are of the van der Pol and Payleigh types respectively, depending upon the forms of investment function. Article III is concerned with a consolidation of their equations so as to include both elements of investment. In Article IV I try to apply the non-linear theory of oscillations to the theory of tatonnement. For this purpose I aggregate several periods, say m periods into one, and show that there are fixed points of the aggregated system. They are called fixed points of order m. Where m equals 1, fixed points give Arrow–Debreu equilibria. Where $m > 1$, they give stationary solutions only in the case in which we ignore movements within the aggregated period. They may represent cycles of m periods if they are analysed into successive states of the short periods before the aggregation. In generalizing the Arrow–Debreu existence theory in this direction we find that the tatonnement theory for general equilibrium is connected with the newly developed theory of chaos. For an appropriate combination of parameters, we may easily obtain chaotic tatonnement behaviour.

In the comparative statics and dynamics analyses, *DKR* assumes absence of complementarity. After its publication, I tried to accommodate complementary goods in the system. I could work on a special case only, that is sometimes called the Morishima case. Articles V and VI are published and unpublished works of mine in this field. In Article VII (with M. Majumdar) the tatonnement approach is compared with other approaches, such as Cournot's arbitrage theory and Debreu's neo-Edgeworthian approach. Although it is true that Debreu's work has greatly contributed to the economic interpretation of the theory of core, it is shown that this way of establishing competitive equilibrium is much more expensive, in terms of the cost of psychological pressure upon the participants in trading, than the tatonnement procedure, especially when their number and the number of commodities are large.

Finally, Article VIII is concerned with the most fundamental features of the models of general equilibrium theory, all of which assume that each market has a price which is adjusted such that its market is cleared. This is, notwithstanding, an assumption that is inadequate for treating durable goods. Each durable good has at least two markets, a commodity market where a durable good newly produced is sold and a rental market where services from the commodity are dealt with. (In addition, it has a market of used goods.) The ratio of the rental price determined in the second market to the commodity price in the first must be equal, in equilibrium, to the sum of the rate of interest (or profit) and the rate of depreciation of the durable good. But the market prices determined so as to clear the excess demands do not necessarily satisfy the equations of equal profitabilities. This dilemma is called 'the dilemma of durable goods'.

Unlike past general equilibrium models developed by Ricardo, Marx and Walras, as formulated in three of my volumes (1989, 1973 and 1977), which explicitly take account of the conditions of equal profit rates, but like most of modern general equilibrium models, such as those by La Volpe (1993, originally published in Italian in 1936), Hicks, Arrow, Debreu, etc., the *DKR* model does not confront this dilemma properly. If the conditions of equal profitability, which are equivalent to Keynes' condition that the marginal efficiency of each capital good is equal to the rate of interest, are rightly taken into account, we do not have a state of general equilibrium where demand equals supply in each of the markets of consumption goods, capital goods, capital services, and other factors of production including labour and land. The only way to avoid this collapse is to introduce Say's law, as in fact the masters of the old regime of general equilibrium mentioned above explicitly or implicitly assumed it, but it is not an acceptable solution because the law is hardly considered to be realistic. Thus the general equilibrium theorists should accept Keynes' prescription: admit the equal profitability for capital goods, deny Say's law, and be confronted with the impossibility of the full-employment–full-utilization equilibrium. This approach was adopted in my *CC*, into which *DKR* is finally merged in this way.

3 Finally, it is made clear that one of two appendices and one of three mathematical notes contained in the original Japanese version of *DKR* are replaced by my 1952 *Econometrica* paper and my 1974 paper which I wrote with Takao Fujimoto, respectively. The former replacement is made because it does not create any essential change in the argument and the same sorts of issues are dealt with more neatly in the *Econometrica* paper. Also this replacement makes the original mathematical note I redundant so that it is deleted in the present volume.

The second replacement is made because the original mathematical note III on the Frobenius theorem is now explained in a more convenient and simpler way by the paper with Fujimoto; the previous note was more or less along the lines of Frobenius' article, and was less elegant. The original mathematical notes II and III appear as I and II in the present volume.

In a summer in the middle of the 1970s *DKR*, originally published in 1950, was put into English. I dictated most of its text to Marie Williams (then my secretary) and she afterwards polished up the style. The manuscript was mimeographed in 1980 and distributed among a limited number of LSE students who belonged to my group. I also acknowledge professional comments made by Frank H. Hahn on a part of the Addendum. In 1994 a group of graduate students of Kyoto University attended a series of seminars organised by Ayumu Yasutomi for examination of *DKR*. I want to note in this place his contribution together with those made by Takanori Ida and Kohki Hirose.

Finally, I am grateful to the editors of the following publications for granting permission to reproduce in this volume the articles that were originally published by them: *Econometrica* for Appendix I, *Journal of Mathematical Economics* for Mathematical Note II, *Metroeconomica* for Article II, *Zeitschrift für nationalökonomie* for Article III, *Review of Economic Studies* for Article V and *Hommage a François Perroux* for Article VII.

M. Morishima

1 The method of dynamic analysis

1 Dynamic economic theory

What subjects should economics be concerned with and what should be their scope? These are very difficult problems which invite many controversies; but, still, it is true that economics ultimately aims to explain *all* economic phenomena. Such an aim determines how economics is to be constructed. Those phenomena which economics assumes without analysis must not be economic phenomena but are ones which should be elucidated by other disciplines. It is obvious that if economics assumes an economic fact without examination, its aim, which is to deal with all economic phenomena, will never be satisfied. Thinking in this way, those economists who supported general equilibrium theory finally dug their way into a non-economic world on which economic phenomena are finally based. When successful in the business of reducing economic relationships to non-economic ones they think that they have obtained the ultimate principles of explanation and they call those non-economic phenomena by the descriptions of the data that economists take as given. Individuals' tastes, techniques of production, endowments of factors of production, prevailing expectations about the future, and various institutions will be counted as data.

Thus, the general equilibrium theory which analyses economic phenomena on the basis of a given data complex naturally pursues the question of how economic phenomena will change if there is a change in the given data complex. That is to say that general equilibrium theory is concerned with correspondences between data and economic phenomena. However, traditional equilibrium theory usually deals only with the correspondence between a data complex at a certain point in time and economic phenomena at that same time, but not with the way in which a change in data at a point in time will subsequently affect them. That is to say, its concern was confined to intratemporal or spontaneous correspondences; it was not extended to intertemporal correspondences between data and phenomena. We call general equilibrium theory of this type a static theory of equilibrium.

If the static equilibrium theory is characterized in the above way we should not be satisfied with it. As a matter of fact a change in data at a certain point in time will easily produce a change in economic phenomena at a later period. Or, it necessarily takes time for a change in data to yield an economic consequence.[1] If we are only provided with the static theory as a tool of economic analysis we must be satisfied with a partial explanation of economic phenomena, leaving unexplained those which occur with a time lag after a change in data. The static theory can only be a perfect, ultimate principle of explanation if the economic system is an ideal, frictionless one so that there is no time lag between the cause and effect. In this way it becomes an important task for theoretical economists to construct a dynamic theory of equilibrium which deals with intertemporal relationships between data and economic phenomena.

2 Methods of determining prices: with and without an auctioneer

It is obviously unquestionable that the following are the problems which economists must handle: what kinds of goods are produced or used in the production process? What kinds of goods are bought or sold, and in what amounts? To answer these questions we must know how prices are determined. In this way price analysis has become a central problem for economists. In developing dynamic economics we must have a dynamic analysis of prices as the kernel of the whole theory. The discussion of prices must begin by asking by what mechanism and by which institutions prices are determined in the actual world.

We have two systems of price determination. One is the method of competitive buying and selling in a market with an auctioneer, and the other is bargaining between buyers and sellers themselves without an auctioneer. In the following, we shall briefly explain the characteristics of these two methods.

It will be easier to understand if we explain these two methods by taking trading at the stock exchange as a typical example of them. Let us begin with competitive buying and selling. When a session of competitive trading starts, officials of the stock exchange, the hammer striker, the recorder, and the watchman, take their respective seats on the stage. The striker tells the

[1] For example, let us consider the case where the technical level is raised by some invention. In that case we will have an increase in the supply of products but this will be realized not instantaneously but after a lapse of time during which a new factory is established and starts production, using new methods; final output is obtained only after completing the whole production process.

opening of the session. Buyers and sellers, by means of calling out and gestures, express what kinds of commodities they want to buy or sell and in what amounts; in other words, they reveal their own demand or supply functions. In this way the hammer striker will get knowledge of the market, on the basis of which he proposes a price which he thinks most appropriate. Buyers and sellers will react to the price proposed in this way, and each will search for his opposite number. When they find each other they will shake hands to show that a bargain has been made between them. The watchman tells the recorder of the bargains he observes in the hall and the recorder makes a record of all of them. In this case, however, the recorder only enters the quantities of trade of each buyer or seller; he does *not* make any record of the price at which the trading has been carried out. If, at the proposed price, all the traders find their opposite numbers, then competitive buying and selling will finish immediately, but, if there remains someone who cannot find a trader, the hammer striker will alter the price and the procedure will be repeated at the new price. Transactions which have been made at the new price are also recorded but, in this case, only quantities are noted, not prices. Continuing in this way demand and supply will be exhausted in the market and the price of the commodity will be settled at an appropriate value when no one is left in the market to demand or supply commodities. When the hammer striker finds such a situation he will strike his hammer and say that trading is finished. The price thus obtained is the effective price and is also a temporary equilibrium price.

It is important to note that all trading of a commodity which has been recorded during the process of the auction must be carried out at the temporary equilibrium price, say £1, finally established. That is to say, any agreement which has been made at the price of 90p or £1.10 before the auctioneer finds the equilibrium price, must be settled at the £1 equilibrium price. Therefore, if someone who has made a commitment to buy a commodity at a certain price does not want to carry out his commitment at the final price, then he must cancel the commitment by counter-trading with someone else before the equilibrium is established. Therefore all transactions made during the process of the auction are cleared by a single price, so that this method of trading is sometimes called the method of single-price trading. We have only one effective price at the end of the auction; all the prices proposed before are no more than trial prices before moving (groping) towards the equilibrium price and no actual trading is performed under them.

According to the second method of trading which is decided between buyers and sellers without an auctioneer, the following procedure is carried out. Suppose now person A is making a gesture to the effect that he will buy 600 units of the commodity at £1 each and person B is showing that he will sell 200 units of that commodity at the same price. Then an agreement will be made between them that they will buy or sell 200 units at £1 each. In this case person A will still remain in the market and want to buy 400 units of that commodity at £1 each. In spite of this excess demand in that market the agreement which has been made between A and B, that is, the agreement that they will trade 200 units at £1, is effective so that not only the quantity but also the price is recorded and £1 will be announced in the hall as the effective price of the commodity.

As long as no new supplier appears the excess of person A will not be satisfied. Therefore he will revise his demand and propose buying 350 units at £1.10. At this new price, if person C wants to sell 400 units, then A and C will make a trading agreement of 350 units at £1.10. Then there remains in the market person C as an excess supplier who wants to sell 50 units at £1.10. This is the second method according to which a number of effective prices are established during one session. Each bargain is cleared at the corresponding price but not the final price as it was in the case of competitive buying and selling. Any prices established by the second method are effective prices associated with actual bargaining and not provisional prices for groping towards a final effective price. Therefore this method may be called one of multi-prices.

In order that some trading agreement should be completed at a certain price, the quantities to be agreed for sale must equal the quantities to be bought. This is true, not only for auction, but also for bargaining between traders without an auctioneer. When the two methods are looked at in more detail, differences will be seen between them. First, in the case of competitive buying and selling, as long as there is an individual who remains in the market without finding a trader in spite of his desire to do business, the auction will continue until such a person disappears, i.e., the total quantity of the commodity which individuals want to sell is equated with the total quantity which individuals want to buy. On the other hand, according to the second method, without an auctioneer, the price is always effective provided that there are at least some agreements of trading which are completed at that price even though there is a discrepancy between the total quantities intended to be bought and sold. Let us denote the quantity intended to be bought at price p by $D(p)$ and the corresponding quantity intended to be sold by $S(p)$. An effective price determined by auction is a solution to $D(p) = S(p)$. But an effective price determined by the second method is not necessarily a solution to the above equation, because the quantity to be agreed for trade may differ from the quantity intended to be traded. If we want to analyse prices by the use of equilibrium conditions between demand and supply we must inevitably assume the market of price determination by auction.

Let us now assume that all prices are determined by auction. The market is open continuously throughout a 'week', an artificial period during which only one session of the auction is performed. As soon as the present auction is finished the next session, therefore next week, begins. The current session is called the present week or week 0 and subsequent weeks are week 1, week 2, etc.[2]

When we talk about a change in price we must make a strict distinction between the two types of price. First, a change in prices within a week, i.e., the problem of change in groping prices, and, secondly, a sequence of those prices which are determined at the end of each week, i.e., the problem of change in effective prices over weeks. The reason why they should be distinguished is that the second sequence always satisfies the equilibrium condition between demand and supply whereas groping prices do not satisfy it. In view of the fact that it is the effective prices under which trading is actually performed and by which firms decide their production planning, it looks as if we should concentrate our attention only on the changes in the effective prices, completely ignoring changes in groping prices.

However, if we neglect price changes within a week and do not analyse them, say, by assuming smoothness and quickness of auctioning, then we will not be able to analyse the changes in effective prices over weeks satisfactorily. The reason is as follows. As will be seen below, effective prices change when there is a change in a given data complex. We must determine in what direction an effective price will change when the data complex changes. If we grasp the dynamic economic process as a series of temporary equilibria and ignore changes in groping prices between one temporary equilibrium and another, then we can only observe changes in effective prices and cannot say anything about the direction of fluctuations.[3] If, however, we analyse the process of change in groping prices we can discuss whether or not the temporary equilibrium is stable. By doing so we can classify temporary equilibrium according to the type of stability it has – e.g., whether it is stable in Hicks' sense, or stable because gross substitutability prevails in the economy, and so on. Thus the stability problem is one of

[2] This idea comes from Hicks, but there are differences between us. First, he assumes that the market is open only on a particular day of the week – say, Monday (see Hicks, 1946, pp. 115–29). But this point is immaterial in the present context. Secondly, it is not entirely clear whether, in Hicks' economy, prices are determined by auction or bargaining between traders without an auctioneer. It seems to me that he assumes the latter at least in some part of his book (e.g., *ibid.*, pp. 117–29).

[3] What is important for us is not to obtain a simple conclusion that prices will change anyhow but to know further the direction in which a price will change. Not being provided with information concerning the direction of price fluctuations, we cannot determine whether consumption and production of a commodity will increase or decrease, so that we are only supplied with poor knowledge of the economy.

investigating the types of temporary equilibrium. If we can classify them into a number of types by investigating the dynamic process of groping we can determine the direction of change in effective prices by using our knowledge of the type of equilibrium thus obtained. In this way the analysis of groping prices is indispensable as a means of determining the direction of effective price change.[4]

3 An outline of the book and its assumptions

The book may be outlined in the following way. In chapter 2 we shall discuss the individual's demand and supply planning and the firm's production planning. We shall basically follow Hicks' approach[5] but we hope to improve on it, especially on the following two points. First, Hicks discussed demand and supply of money and securities but we consider his analysis to be incomplete and want to provide a more satisfactory solution. Secondly, for the firm Hicks assumed that output equals supply and input equals demand but output and input may differ from supply and demand respectively unless the stock of the respective commodities is kept constant. We want to reconstruct the theory of firms by removing this assumption and explicitly taking the stock adjustment into account. In chapters 3 and 4 we shall discuss fluctuations in groping prices, i.e., the process of forming temporary equilibrium prices. Hicks almost neglected these problems or at best discussed them in an inappropriate way. To remove this difficulty of Hicks' I will use Samuelson's approach to stability in order to clarify the changes in groping prices within a week. Though it is unclear, Samuelson himself seems to use his stability theory to explain changes in actual effective prices. But I do not use his theory for the purpose of explaining these changes.[6] In these chapters we discuss stability conditions of temporary equilibrium and from that point of view we classify temporary equilibria into types. Chapter 5 is devoted to discussing changes in effective prices over weeks. We are very near to Hicks in considering a time series of

[4] It was Samuelson who first pointed out explicitly how the theory of stability is closely connected with the theory of comparative statics (Samuelson, 1948, pp. 258–310). It is not clear whether he fully recognised or not that the time shape of prices determined by stability theory is only a time shape of groping prices in an auction and cannot be the one of effective prices through weeks. The present volume differs from his dynamic theory in the following two main points: (i) we conclude that Samuelson's stability theory can deal with nothing else but fluctuations in groping prices in a 'tatonnement' process in Walras' sense, and (ii) we analyse fluctuations in effective prices caused by a change in data by the method of comparative dynamics rather than by Samuelson's comparative statics.

[5] Hicks, 1946, pp. 191–244.

[6] As for the difficulties which Samuelson's stability theory would bring forth if it were interpreted as a theory of fluctuations in effective prices, see chapter 3, section 6 below.

actual prices as a series of effective prices where demand and supply are equated.[7] As was discussed before, if we do not have any classification of temporary equilibria it will be impossible to say anything about the direction in which actual prices change when there is a change in data. The mathematical analysis in chapters 3 and 4, though it may be rather unpleasant for some readers, will help us to determine the direction of change. As a change in data I will deal mainly with a creation in the stock of money which was discussed by Lange but I hope we have treated the problem in a more rigorous way then he did.[8]

In this book we make the following assumptions. All prices are determined by auction. We rule out direct bargaining between traders without an auctioneer. Also we assume that prices are determined simultaneously and in an interrelated way, not in isolation; any trader who is buying or selling some commodity in a market can simultaneously appear in another market where he buys or sells another good. Secondly, there is no monopolist; the markets are in a state of perfect competition. Thirdly, all trading agreements are specified in the quantities traded, the price and the date of delivery. The trade with instantaneous delivery is called spot trading and trade whose date of contract is different from the date of delivery of the commodity is called future trading. Future trading may be further classified as long, medium, or short-term future trading according to the deferment of the delivery date. If the delivery date is different then the same commodity is treated as different commodities so that it has different temporary equilibrium prices. Similarly, for lending and borrowing, the rate of interest will be different if the term of lending is different. We shall call the economy in which lending and borrowing are limited to within a week an economy with short-term lending, while an economy with long-term lending allows lending and borrowing over several weeks. Throughout this book usual commodities are traded in a spot market and borrowing and lending are of the short term. Therefore the economy with which we are concerned in this book may characteristically be said to be a spot economy with short-term lending. Finally, we assume no international markets so that the economy is closed.

[A postscript: What I call 'security' in this book is a proof for money lent by an agent to another for a short period, i.e., a week. If it is sold to a third agent, he succeeds to all of the rights and obligations the document specifies. I have ignored stocks and shares as well as bonds throughout the original version of this volume. However, in the present version, there is an

[7] Hicks, 1946, pp. 115ff. [It is also stated here that this type of analysis of economic fluctuations in terms of a sequence of temporary equilibria was first proposed in 1930 by E. Lindahl, 1939, before Hicks. But I was ignorant of this fact when I was writing *DKR*.]

[8] Lange, 1944.

inconsistency with this principle, because I replace appendix I of the original version by a paper which I published in *Econometrica* after this volume had appeared in Japan. This paper is concerned with an individual who makes long-term lending or borrowing by dealing in bonds. But the effects of this inconsistency are insignificant, because by redefining $p_b\bar{B}$ and p_bB in the notation of new appendix I below as $x_{1,-1}$ and $x_{1,0}$ according to the notation in the text, the budget equation (1) in the new appendix I may be rewritten

$$\Sigma p_i x_i + x_{0,0} + x_{1,0} = x_{0,-1} + (1 + r)x_{1,-1}$$

This is because the price of bonds p_b is the reciprocal of the rate of interest r, and H and M in appendix I are $x_{0,0}$ and $x_{0,-1}$ in the text.

The budget equation of this form differs from the one in the economy where borrowing and lending are of the short term only in the last term. In the latter it should be $(1 + \bar{r})x_{1,-1}$ rather than $(1 + r)x_{1,-1}$ as we have in the above, where $\bar{r}$ is the rate of interest in the last week, i.e., week -1, while r is the current rate. This is because borrowing and lending should be settled weekwise in a short lending economy, as they cannot be carried over to the succeeding week.]

2 Households' and firms' economic behaviour

1 Expectations and planning

Households and firms decide their behavioural plan depending on events which are occurring in the current period and on expectations of events which will happen in the future. Their planning is not confined to the present only; they will decide on plans for the coming several weeks simultaneously with that for the current week. In the present market, however, only that part of this long-run planning which concerns current needs is carried out. It is, of course, impossible that the remaining part, concerned with the future, is carried out in the present week; that part of the planning concerned with the next week, week 1, will become effective in the next week but it will not necessarily be carried out in the same way as was decided in the present week, week 0.

Obviously one week has elapsed between week 0 when the long-run planning was decided and week 1 when the relevant part of that planning is carried out and therefore some data will have changed. Unexpected changes may occur in the individual's tastes or in the available techniques of production; also the view of future economic events may have changed during that lapse of time. Therefore as time goes by each individual and each firm will not necessarily implement the plan as it was decided. It will be examined and revised at the beginning of each week. Thus economic plans depend on expectations about the future as well as on current events.

We classify information and expectations in the following two broad categories. The first includes information or expectations concerning the individual's own tastes (techniques of production in the case of the firm) and his (or its) endowments in current and future weeks. The second category includes information and expectations of other individuals and firms and of events in the market; in more detail, information about other people's tastes, about other firms' techniques of production and about the state of demand and supply in the market and the prices of commodities. While households and firms which are in a monopolistic (or monopsonic) position or in imperfect competition situations make their plans by taking into account how the price is affected or how other households and other firms will react, those in perfectly competitive situations decide their plans depending exclusively on given prices and price expectations. As we are confining ourselves to the analysis of a perfectly competitive economy, we shall take the second category of information and expectations as consisting of those on prices and we shall exclude from it those on other persons' and other firms' behaviour.

Like other expectations, those concerning prices are neither precise nor definite and are subject to some degree of uncertainty. As for the price of a commodity at a certain specific point in time in the future, individuals or firms expect not a single value but a number of values as possibilities. They will judge one of these values as most probable and other expected values as less probable. In the case of assessing the capital value of an individual's asset we may ignore the probability distribution and evaluate it in terms of the most probable expected price, but in most other cases the probability distribution has significance in the individual's or in the firm's decision making. That is to say that even though the most probable price remains unchanged their decision may be affected if the probability of that price or the variance of the distribution is changed. However such a change in the probability distribution can be translated into a change in the most probable value of the standard probability distribution so that they have the same effect on the behaviour of the individual or the firm. By making some adjustment to the most probable value of the price a representative expected price may be determined; we will assume that each individual or each firm decides their consumption or production plan on the basis of representative expected prices determined in this way. We can determine representative expected rates of interest in the same way. In the following we refer to these representative expected prices or rates of interest simply as expected prices or expected rates of interest.[1]

Now our economy is a spot economy with short-lending. We assume there are $n + 1$ kinds of goods. Good 0 refers to money and good 1 to securities. Goods $2, \ldots, n$ are the usual commodities; they are subdivided into consumption goods, primary factors of production, and capital goods. Consumption goods are numbered as $2, \ldots, l$, primary factors as $l + 1, \ldots, m$ and capital goods as $m + 1, \ldots, n$. Individuals and firms will make plans from week 0 to week v.[2] Let $p_{i\tau}$ be the expected price of good i in week τ and r_τ the expected rate of interest of short lending from week τ to

[1] See Hicks, 1946, pp. 115–27.

[2] The value of v may differ from one individual to another.

Table 2.1

week	interest rates	prices					
0	r_0	p_{20}	p_{30}	.	.	.	p_{n0}
1	r_1	p_{21}	p_{31}	.	.	.	p_{n1}
2	r_2	p_{22}	p_{32}	.	.	.	p_{n2}
.	.	.	.	.	.	.	.
.	.	.	.	.	.	.	.
ν	r_ν	$p_{2\nu}$	$p_{3\nu}$	.	.	.	$p_{n\nu}$

week $\tau + 1$. Current prices and current rates of interest are denoted by p_{i0} and r_0 respectively. These prices and interest rates are listed in table 2.1 on the basis of which individuals and firms will make their plans.

In table 2.1 prices and interest rates are common to all individuals and firms if they refer to the current week but otherwise they are only expected values so they may differ from individual to individual, or from firm to firm.

2 Households' planning[3]

Household planning consists of income planning and expenditure or consumption planning. The sources of income are the holding of securities or a supply of the primary factors of production. Expenditure is made on consumption goods. The household does not directly invest in capital goods, for they are out of its scope. In table 2.1 the prices of capital goods are irrelevant items for households. For a particular household let x_{i_ι} be the demand for good i in week ι and y_{j_ι} the supply of good j in the same week. Regarding supply as negative demand we often put $y_{j_\iota} = -x_{j_\iota}$. Table 2.2 represents the demand and supply planning of household a (x_{0_ι} represents the amount of money which household a wants to hold in week ι; so it should be non-negative).

In determining the value of each item of the demand and supply plan, household a does not behave at random but acts on the principle described later, satisfying the following conditions. Suppose household a holds cash in the amount $x_{0,-1}$ and securities $x_{1,-1}$ at the beginning of week 0. Let r_{-1} be the rate of interest for short lending in the previous week. Then a has financial assets of the amount

$$x_{0,-1} + (1 + r_{-1})x_{1,-1}$$

[3] This section is a summary of the first half of Morishima, 1948, pp. 34–51 (with some revisions) which was intended to be a critical essay on Hicks' analysis of the demand for money.

Table 2.2

week	money	security	commodities					
0	x_{00}	x_{10}	x_{20}	x_{30}	.	.	.	x_{m0}
1	x_{01}	x_{11}	x_{21}	x_{31}	.	.	.	x_{m1}
2	x_{02}	x_{12}	x_{22}	x_{32}	.	.	.	x_{m2}
.	.	.	.	.	.	.	.	.
.	.	.	.	.	.	.	.	.
v	x_{0v}	x_{1v}	x_{2v}	x_{3v}	.	.	.	x_{mv}

before trade in week 0. Household a will appear in the current market and buy consumption goods, sell the primary factors of production and buy or sell securities; the remaining assets, if they exist, will be held in the form of money. Therefore its current demand and supply must satisfy equation

$$x_{0,-1} + (1 + r_{-1})x_{1,-1} = x_{00} + x_{10} + \Sigma p_{i0}x_{i0} \quad (1)$$

which is referred to as a's budget equation for week 0. In week 1 it has assets of the amount

$$x_{00} + (1 + r_0)x_{10}$$

and buys or sells consumption goods, primary factors of production, or securities and holds the rest in money. The same is true for subsequent weeks. Therefore a's expected purchasing and sales must satisfy the budget equations

$$x_{0_t-1} + (1 + r_{t-1})x_{1,-1} = x_{0_t} + x_{1_t} + \Sigma p_{i_t}x_{i_t} \; (t = 1, 2, 3, \ldots, v) \quad (2)$$

The household a will decide its income and expenditure plans under the $v + 1$ budget equations (1) and (2).

The plan will be decided according to the following principle. a's private economic positions are described by tables 2.1 and 2.2, i.e., by the vector

$$X = (x_{00}, x_{10}, \ldots, x_{m0}, x_{01}, \ldots, x_{mv}; p_{20}, \ldots, p_{mv}, r_0, \ldots, r_{v-1})$$

We assume that a has the ability to decide the preference between possible alternative Xs. The preference scale is decided according to the quality of commodities which satisfy person a biologically or psychologically – i.e., the utility of commodities – and by the security or convenience which the holding of assets guarantees – i.e., the liquidity of assets. Prices are not expected in a precise way and are more or less uncertain, so each household must hold cash or securities to keep liquidity at a certain level. The magnitude of liquidity and that of utility play an important role in deciding the preference order of private economic positions.

Take two arbitrary private economic positions, X^0 and X^1. Household a will decide indices u so that

(i) $u(X^0) < u(X^1)$ if X^1 is preferable to X^0,
(ii) $u(X^0) = u(X^1)$ if they are indifferent,
(iii) $u(X^0) > u(X^1)$ if the converse to (i) is the case.

Then the economic position to which a bigger index is attached is a more preferable one. We call $u(X)$ the preference index function or, according to traditional usage, the utility function.[4]

Needless to say, household a chooses the most preferable economic position but it cannot maximize its preference index unconditionally. Its plan must satisfy budget equations so that the maximization principle must be subject to the $v + 1$ constraints (1) and (2).

With given p and r, the value of x will be determined by the first-order maximization conditions which are derived by the Lagrangean method for conditional maximization provided that the second-order maximization conditions are always satisfied. That is to say once the values of all items of table 2.1 and the value of the initial assets

$$x_{0,-1} + (1 + r_{-1})x_{1,-1} \equiv \bar{x}$$

are given, the complete values of the items of table 2.2 are determined. We thus obtain a's individual demand and supply functions

$$x_{i_t} = x_{i_t}(p_{20}, \ldots, p_{mv}, r_0, \ldots, r_{v-1}, \bar{x}) \tag{3}$$

$$y_{j_t} = y_{j_t}(p_{20}, \ldots, p_{mv}, r_0, \ldots, r_{v-1}, \bar{x}) \tag{4}$$

Here let us explain expectation functions. Price expectations are formed on a variety of information – information about exogenous variables such as long-term weather forecasts or political news, as well as information about endogenous variables provided by, say, economic White Papers, statistics of price fluctuations in the past, and current prices prevailing in the market. Among them the most important one, from the point of view of the theoretical analysis, are current prices and current rates of interest. If these change each individual will revise his expected prices and expected rates of interest. Consequently we may assume that each individual has his own expectation functions[5]

$$p_{i_t} = \phi_{i_t}(p_{20}, \ldots, p_{m0}, r_0)$$

$$r_t = \phi_t(p_{20}, \ldots, p_{m0}, r_0)$$

[4] According to the traditional view, the utility function does not contain the quantities of money and securities among its arguments. Recently, however, a view is gradually becoming dominant which considers the utility function as depending on those quantities. See D. Patinkin, 1948, Klein, 1947, pp. 192–5, Mosak, 1944 and Morishima, 1948.

[5] For the expectation function, see Lange, 1944, pp. 20–1.

Substituting these into (3) and (4) we may express demand and supply, x_{j0} and y_{j0}, as another function of p_{i0}, r_0 and $\bar{x}$ so that, after deleting the second subscript 0 referring to the current week 0, we have *a*'s individual demand and supply functions

$$x_i = x_i(p_2, \ldots, p_m, r, \bar{x})$$
$$y_j = y_j(p_2, \ldots, p_m, r, \bar{x})$$

for the current week. Those concerning future weeks, i.e., weeks $1, 2, \ldots, \nu$ will not play significant roles in the rest of this book because they are only planned by individual *a* and will never be carried out exactly as planned except in very special circumstances.

3 Firms' planning[6]

It must first be noted that firms, unlike households, have two sets of planning; demand and supply planning and production planning. Firms will supply their products, consumption goods, or capital goods, and demand producers' goods, primary factors of production, or capital goods. They will issue securities and redeem them. Let firm *A*'s supply of good *i* in week ι be denoted by y_{i_ι} and its demand for good *j* by x_{j_ι}. Regarding supply as negative demand and putting $y_{i_\iota} = -x_{i_\iota}$, then *A*'s demand and supply plan will be described in table 2.3. However firm *A* will not necessarily produce the same amount as y_{i_ι} in week ι, and put in production the same amount as x_{j_ι} in week ι. Denoting output of good *i* and input of good *j* in week ι by x'_{i_ι} and y'_{j_ι} respectively and regarding input as negative output so that $y'_{j_\iota} = -x'_{j_\iota}$, there may be a discrepancy between *A*'s production plan (described in table 2.4) and its demand and supply plan (in table 2.3). An excess of output over supply gives an increment in the stock of that product and an excess of demand over input gives an increment of the stock of the producer's goods. Writing the stock of good *i* in week ι as x''_{i_ι} we have

$$x'_{i_\iota} - y_{i_\iota} \equiv x''_{i_\iota} - x''_{i_\iota - 1} \qquad (5)$$

for product *i* and

$$x_{j_\iota} - y'_{j_\iota} \equiv x''_{j_\iota} - x''_{j_\iota - 1} \qquad (5')$$

for producer's good *j*. Considering the definition $y = -x$ both (5) and (5′) can be put in the same form

$$x_{i_\iota} + x'_{i_\iota} \equiv x''_{i_\iota} - x''_{i_\iota - 1} \; (i = 2, \ldots, n) \qquad (6)$$

[6] This section is a revised version of the second half of Morishima, 1948, which was intended to be a critical essay on Hicks' theory of the firm. The traditional theory is only concerned with the firms' production plan, its demand–supply plan being left unexamined.

Table 2.3

week	money	security	commodities					
0	x_{00}	x_{10}	x_{20}	x_{30}	·	·	·	x_{n0}
1	x_{01}	x_{11}	x_{21}	x_{31}	·	·	·	x_{n1}
2	x_{02}	x_{12}	x_{22}	x_{32}	·	·	·	x_{n2}
·	·	·	·	·	·	·	·	·
·	·	·	·	·	·	·	·	·
ν	$x_{0\nu}$	$x_{1\nu}$	$x_{2\nu}$	$x_{3\nu}$	·	·	·	$x_{n\nu}$

Table 2.4

week	commodities						
0	x'_{20}	x'_{30}	x'_{40}	·	·	·	x'_{n0}
1	x'_{21}	x'_{31}	x'_{41}	·	·	·	x'_{n1}
2	x'_{22}	x'_{32}	x'_{42}	·	·	·	x'_{n2}
·	·	·	·	·	·	·	·
·	·	·	·	·	·	·	·
ν	$x'_{2\nu}$	$x'_{3\nu}$	$x'_{4\nu}$	·	·	·	$x'_{n\nu}$

This gives relationships connecting the demand and supply plan and the production plan. As A's initial stocks for week 0, x''_{i-1} that is alternatively written as $\bar{x}_{i0}$, are given, we can derive a stock plan from its demand and supply plan and its production plan. These three plans are not independent; one of them is derived from the others.

In determining the values of the items of plans for demand, supply, and production, firm A takes into account the following conditions. The first condition is the relationship (6) mentioned above and the second is the condition of technical limitations for production. If all inputs of producers' goods and all outputs except the output of good i in week ι, $x'_{i\iota}$, are specified, then the maximum value which is technically feasible for this remaining output, $x'_{i\iota}$, will be technically determined. Conversely, if all outputs of every week are given and all inputs except the one for good j in week ι, i.e., $y'_{j\iota}$, are given then the minimum value of this remaining input $y'_{j\iota}$ which is required will be technically determined. These technical limitations may be mathematically translated into the language of implicit functions. We assume that there exists an implicit function of that sort

$$f(x'_{20}, x'_{30}, \ldots, x'_{n0}, x'_{21}, \ldots, x'_{n\nu}) = 0 \tag{7}$$

which is called the production function or production technique function.

We have thus assumed that technical limitations of production can be expressed by a single production function but in reality technical conditions are so complicated that they can hardly be described by a single function, e.g., it may be conceivable that for each ι outputs in week ι are independent of those in the subsequent weeks $\iota + 1, \iota + 2, \ldots$ and depend on inputs in some preceding weeks only. Generally speaking technical limitations can only be described by a number of implicit functions but not by any single one. However as a first approximation to reality we have accepted our present assumption which would enable us to put our analysis of the firm in a simple and clear form.

Next we must explain the concept of profit which we use in the following analysis. After retaining some amount of money, say k_ι, from firm A's proceeds in week ι the rest will be distributed among the firm's shareholders and executives as dividends or bonuses. That may be called the profit or the net income of the firm. The amount k_ι will be spent by A on producers' goods, etc. in week ι and may be called the cost which A incurs in week ι. Representing the profit in week ι by R_ι we have the definitional relationship

$$R_\iota = -\Sigma p_{i_\iota} x_{i_\iota} - k_\iota \tag{8}$$

where the summation, Σ, is taken only over all products which A supplies, excluding producers' goods which A demands. Discounting R_ι ($\iota = 1, 2, \ldots, \nu$) by the ratio

$$\beta_\iota = \frac{1}{(1 + r_0)(1 + r_1)\ldots(1 + r_{\iota-1})}$$

respectively and, summing up, we obtain

$$V = R_0 + \beta_1 R_1 + \ldots + \beta_\nu R_\nu \tag{8'}$$

which is, following Hicks, called the capitalized value of the streams of profit.

In week ι firm A has purchasing power amounting to

$$x_{0_{\iota-1}} + (1 + r_{\iota-1})x_{1_{\iota-1}} + k_\iota$$

With that sum A buys some amounts of the factors of production in the market and carries forward cash of the amount x_{0_ι} to the following week. If it remains a positive residual then the firm will make loans; otherwise it will borrow the necessary amount. Therefore A's plan must satisfy the following $\nu + 1$ budget equations

$$x_{0_{\iota-1}} + (1 + r_{\iota-1})x_{1_{\iota-1}} + k_\iota = x_{0_\iota} + x_{1_\iota} + \Sigma p_{i_\iota} x_{i_\iota} \tag{9}$$

where the summation Σ is taken only over all producers' goods which A demands, excluding products which it supplies. It is clear that k_ι has a character of working capital. The budget equations are the third set of constraints which are imposed on A.

Finally, we explain what I call the liquidity function. As was pointed out by Keynes, we can receive potential conveniences or safeties if we hold some amounts of assets and keep the right of disposing of them by our own will.[7] For example, an unexpected difficulty may occur in carrying out some trade; in that case, the greater the cash balances or the quantity of securities we hold, the more easily can we evade the difficulty. Firms which have big stocks of producer's goods can continue their production relatively easily and smoothly even if the supply of these producer's goods diminishes. The adaptability of firms to unforeseen accidents is closely related to their cash balances, holding of securities and inventories. It is also related to prices, interest rates, and their expected values; in fact it is obvious that the cash of £1,000 at price level 1 and the same amount of cash at price level 100 give different adaptabilities to firms. Therefore, we may assume that the adaptability of a firm to unforeseen events depends on

$$X = (x_{00}, x_{10}, x_{01}, \ldots, x_{1v}, x'_{20}, \ldots, x'_{nv}, p_{20}, \ldots, p_{nv}, r_0, \ldots, r_{v-1})$$

We assume that firm A can compare any two Xs and the adaptabilities these Xs provide A with and determine indices ϕ so that

(i) $\phi(X^0) < \phi(X^1)$, if X^0 gives less adaptability than X^1,
(ii) $\phi(X^0) = \phi(X^1)$, if they give the same adaptability,
(iii) $\phi(X^0) > \phi(X^1)$, if X^0 gives more adaptability than X^1.

The function $\phi(X)$ is called A's liquidity function. As is seen below, A will keep ϕ at a certain fixed level, ϕ^0, so that

$$\phi^0 = \phi(X) \tag{10}$$

In determining demand and supply plans and production plans over $v + 1$ weeks from week 0 to week v, firm A maximizes profit over the production period rather than profit in a particular week. In other words A will maximize the capitalized value of the stream of profits (8'). A will, at the same time, take its liquidity position into account. It should not be left in a position with no adaptability to unforeseen events; it should keep some degree of adaptability which is determined by the type of entrepreneur. *It is a principle of the firm's planning to maximize the capitalized value of the stream of profits subject to the condition that the value of the liquidity function be as large as a given level, ϕ^0.*

In addition to that liquidity condition, A must consider conditions (6), (7), (9), and (10). Then the problem is mathematically one of conditional

[7] Keynes, 1936, pp. 240–1.

maximization of the capitalized value of profits. Using the Lagrangean method we obtain necessary and sufficient conditions for the maximizations by means of which x in table 2.3, x' in table 2.4, and stocks of x'' are determined as functions of prices and rates of interest (including their expected values) as well as the stocks $\bar{x}_i$ and the assets $\bar{x}$ at the beginning of week 0, where

$$x_{0,-1} + (1 + r_{-1})x_{1,-1} \equiv \bar{x}$$

Each of these functions can be reduced to a function of current prices, p_{i0} and the current rate of interest, r_0, initial stocks $\bar{x}_i$, and the initial asset $\bar{x}$ only if we take expectation functions of prices and interest rates into account. Omitting the subscript referring to week 0 we can write A's current demand and supply functions as

$$x_i = x_i(p_2, \ldots, p_n, r, \bar{x}_2, \ldots, \bar{x}_n, \bar{x})$$

current output and input functions as

$$x_i' = x_i'(p_2, \ldots, p_n, r, \bar{x}_2, \ldots, \bar{x}_n, \bar{x})$$

and current stock functions as

$$x_i'' = x_i''(p_2, \ldots, p_n, r, \bar{x}_2, \ldots, \bar{x}_n, \bar{x})$$

All xs concerning the future weeks are merely planned quantities and do not play an important role in the subsequent analysis.[8]

[8] As equation (9) shows, k_ι ($\iota = 0, 1, \ldots, \nu$) play the role as funds for purchasing factors of production. If they are exogenously determined and do not respond to a change in data, then it may happen that the funds are deficient or excessive, so that the firm's demand–supply plan and input–output plan over the $\nu + 1$ weeks depend on the initial holdings of money $\bar{x}$, the initial stocks of commodities $\bar{x}_i$, and k's. On the other hand, if k_ιs are variables which are determined according to the maximization principle, then it can be shown (Morishima, 1948, pp. 46–8) that only current demands and supplies of commodities would depend on $\bar{x}$ and $\bar{x}_i$, all other variables, i.e., demands and supplies in future weeks, $\iota = 1, 2, \ldots, \nu$, and inputs, outputs and stocks of commodities in current and future weeks, $\iota = 0, 1, 2, \ldots, \nu$, not being influenced by them at all. Even this case violates the traditional (Hicksian) premises, current supply = current output and current demand = current input.

3 Stability conditions for a temporary equilibrium: the linear case

1 Excess demand functions

In the previous chapter we discussed how households or firms determine their plans of behaviour, i.e., demand and supply plans or production plans, taking prices and rates of interest as given in the market. In this chapter we examine the mechanism by which prices and rates of interest come to take equilibrium values.

Those x_i $(i = 1, 2, \ldots, n)$ which were determined in the last chapter are summed up over all households $a, b, \ldots$ and firms $A, B, \ldots$; then we have

$$E_i = \Sigma x_i = E_i(p_2, \ldots, p_n, r, \alpha) \; (i = 1, 2, \ldots, n)^1$$

where α is a parameter which is intended to represent the array of initial assets $\bar{x}$ and initial stocks $\bar{x}_j (j = 2, \ldots, n)$ of all households and all firms. If x_i takes on a positive value it represents the demand for i; if it is negative then $-x_i$ is the supply of that good. E_i is the amount of good i obtained by subtracting the total supply of good i from its total demand so that it represents the excess demand for good i which exists in the economy. Demand and supply of good i is equated when $E_i = 0$ while the market for good i is in a state of excess demand or excess supply according to $E_i > 0$ or $E_i < 0$.

As for money, excess demand is defined as the total sum of x_0, which each individual or each firm wants to hold in week 0 minus the total sum of $\bar{x} = x_{0-1} + (1 + r_{-1})x_{1-1}$ which is the cash balance of each individual or each firm at the beginning of week 0; that is to say

$$E_0 = \Sigma x_0 - \Sigma \bar{x} = E_0(p_2, \ldots, p_n, r, \alpha)$$

gives excess demand for cash balances; α is a parameter, which I have explained above, and $\bar{x}$ is independent of p and r. The total sum of $\bar{x}$ over all individuals and firms is the stock of money which exists at the beginning of

[1] The summation is taken over all individuals and firms, so that it is of course not made with respect to the subscript i standing for commodity.

week 0; it is equal to the total sum of $x_{0,-1}$, i.e., the total stock of money, M, at the end of the last week *plus* $(1 + r_{-1})E_{-1}$ where $E_{-1} = \Sigma x_{1,-1}$. If we denote Σx_0, i.e., the total desired cash balance, by L then $E_0 = 0$ represents $M + (1 + r_{-1})E_{-1} = L$ and $E_0 > 0$ or $E_0 < 0$ represents respectively that the existing stock of money falls short of or exceeds the desired cash balance. If we assume that demand and supply for securities are in equilibrium in the previous week, i.e., $E_{-1} = 0$, then the expression $E_0 = 0$ is equivalent to the expression $M = L$.[2]

2 Time element '*t*'

As we have explained previously, there are two mechanisms for determining prices and interest rates. One is a system of competitive buying and selling with an auctioneer, and the other is a system of bargaining between traders without an auctioneer. In the following we assume that all traders, households, and firms meet each other in a hall where competitive buying and selling of all commodities and securities are carried out through an auctioneer. In this spot market with short lending, individuals and firms are perfectly competitive with each other, ruling out all monopolistic behaviour. Before we proceed to the analysis of the determination of prices and interest rates we must explain about our time element t which is fundamental to our dynamic analysis.

It is usual to say that the week begins at 00.00 hours Monday and ends at 24.00 hours Sunday. A point of time within a week is expressed, for example, as 09.15 hours Wednesday. Let us use the term 'calendar time' for such an expression. Similarly the second week begins at 00.00 hours Monday and ends at 24.00 hours Sunday. It must be noted that the end of the first week, i.e., 24.00 hours Sunday, is the beginning of the second week, i.e., 00.00 hours Monday. Therefore that point of time belongs both to the first and second weeks. To avoid such overlapping we must exclude the point of time 24.00 hours Sunday from one of the weeks and include it in the other. In this way we may avoid overlapping but if we do so then either the first week has the week end and the second week has no beginning, or *vice versa*. We shall include 24.00 hours Sunday in the beginning of the second week as 00.00 hours Monday. Therefore in our economy each week has a beginning but no week has a week end.

[2] The condition for monetary equilibrium in the present week is that the cash balances L which the households and the firms want to hold in the present week equals the existing quantity of money in the same week. However, the condition we have obtained here is that L equals the quantity of money M which existed in the previous week. This means that we are assuming that the quantity of money remains unchanged from the previous to the present week. See chapter 5 for the creation (or reduction) of money.

We then have a set of points of time belonging to a week which has the power of continuum. Such a set can be made to correspond to real numbers from 0 to infinity in a one-to-one relationship, keeping the order; that is to say, the calendar time from the beginning of one week until the beginning of the next week can be made to correspond with the real number, t, from 0 to infinity. Without using calendar time we can alternatively express the point of time by the week to which it belongs and by the position of that point within the week. The latter can be expressed by the real number t and, if t tends to infinity, time is approaching the week end and *vice versa.*[3]

As soon as the market is open at the beginning of the week competitive buying and selling commence. They continue until the beginning of the next week. We will use our time element as a parameter signifying the progress of competitive trading.

3 Temporary equilibrium

Let us begin with the following fact. If demand exceeds supply in the market of commodity i at a certain point in time in the process of competitive trading then, as a result of competition among demanders, they will propose a higher price. Conversely if supply exceeds demand competition among suppliers results in a lower price. When demand is equated to supply, demanders can buy what they want to buy and suppliers can sell what they want to sell. Therefore, neither a higher price nor a lower price is proposed.

That a higher price is proposed in the process of competitive trading means that the groping price p_i increases as trading proceeds, i.e., as t increases. Therefore at the point in time at which a higher price is proposed dp_i/dt (which is written as $\dot{p}_i$ throughout the rest of the book) takes on a positive value. If lower prices are proposed $\dot{p}_i$ of course takes on a negative value. Therefore the above fact can be expressed as follows

$$\text{sign } \dot{p}_i = \text{sign } E_i \tag{1}$$

We assume that there is a function which satisfies the relationship (1) and write it as[4]

[3] Let the beginning and the end of a week be represented as τ_0 and τ_1, respectively, by the calendar time. There are infinitely many ways of correspondence which make the real numbers $\tau(\tau_0 \leqq \tau < \tau_1)$ correspond to real numbers from 0 to ∞, preserving the order. For example, $t = (\tau_0 - \tau_1)^{-1} + (\tau_1 - \tau)^{-1}$ satisfies these conditions. Suppose τ corresponds to t according to one way and to ξ according to another. Then there is one-to-one correspondence between t and ξ, and ξ tends to ∞ as t tends to ∞. So ξ too serves as a parameter to express the progress of competitive trading.

[4] As has been stated in footnote 3 above, there are many ways of making calendar time $\tau(\tau_0 \leqq \tau < \tau_1)$ correspond to real numbers from 0 to ∞. Let τ correspond to t in one way and

$$\dot{p}_i = F_i(E_i);\ F_i(0) = 0,\ F_i'(0) > 0 \tag{2}$$

As for the rate of interest, it will be bid up if the supply of securities is greater than the demand for them and conversely it will be bid down if the demand for securities is greater than the supply of them. If the demand is equated to the supply all the intended lending and borrowing can be realized so that the rate of interest will remain unchanged. In view of this fact, i.e., symbolically

$$\text{sign}\ \dot{r} = \text{sign}\ (-E_1) \tag{3}$$

we assume that there is a function satisfying (3), i.e.[5]

$$\dot{r} = F_1(E_1);\ F_1(0) = 0,\ F'_1(0) < 0 \tag{4}$$

As a result of competitive trading we will reach a state where all prices and the rate of interest will no longer fluctuate. Trade is actually carried out at these prices and this rate of interest. That is to say the values of p_i and r which establish equations

$$\dot{r} = 0,\ \dot{p}_i = 0\ (i = 2, \ldots, n) \tag{5}$$

are the prices and the rate of interest which govern trade in week 0. If (5) holds we say that the economy is in a state of temporary general equilibrium. Considering equations (2) and (4) we find that the conditions for (5), i.e., the conditions for temporary general equilibrium are n simultaneous equations

$$E_i(p_2, \ldots, p_n, r, \alpha) = 0\ (i = 1, \ldots, n) \tag{6}$$

ξ in another. If (1) holds for t, then we have

$$\text{sign} \frac{dp_i}{d\xi} = \text{sign}\ E_i$$

for ξ. However, even though (2) holds for t, equation

$$\frac{dp_i}{d\xi} = G_i(E_i)$$

does not necessarily hold for ξ. For example, let $t = \xi^2$, we then have from (2)

$$\frac{dp_i}{d\xi} = 2\xi F_i(E_i)$$

so that $\frac{dp_i}{d\xi}$ depends on ξ as well as E_i. For the sake of simplifying the analysis we assume throughout the following that τ is transformed into t for which (2) holds.

5 Concerning the response of the rate of interest there may be a different hypothesis. See chapter 4, section 7 below on that point.

Temporary equilibrium prices, p_i^0 and the temporary equilibrium rate of interest r^0 are solutions to these simultaneous equations. As α takes on a given value as a result of economic activities in the previous week only p_i and r are counted as unknowns. The number of equations is equal to the number of unknowns and therefore p_i and r are determined in such a way that equations (6) are fulfilled.

Where temporary equilibrium is established, in what situation is there an excess demand for money? This is seen in the following way. First, demands and supplies of a household must satisfy the budget equation

$$x_{00} - [x_{0,-1} + (1 + r_{-1})x_{1,-1}] = -x_{10} - \Sigma p_i x_{i0} \tag{7}$$

For an entrepreneurial or capitalist household which receives income R_0 as dividends or entrepreneurial profits we have

$$x_{00} - [x_{0,-1} + (1 + r_{-1})x_{1,-1}] = R_0 - x_{10} - \Sigma p_i x_{i0} \tag{8}$$

Finally for a firm we have an equation for profit and a budget equation. They are respectively equations (8) and (9) in the previous chapter. By eliminating k from them we obtain, for a firm

$$x_{00} - [x_{0,-1} + (1 + r_{-1})x_{1,-1}] = -x_{10} - \Sigma p_i x_{i0} - R_0 \tag{9}$$

Therefore for a society as a whole we have the sum of (7) or (8) over all households and (9) over all firms, i.e.

$$-E_0 = M + (1 + r_{-1})E_{-1} - \mathrm{L} = E_1 + \Sigma p_i E_i \tag{10}$$

This final equation holds for all possible values of prices and the interest rate throughout the process of competitive trading. Therefore it is an identity in terms of p_i and r. We refer to this identity (10) as Walras' law.[6]

From Walras' law we easily find the value of excess demand for cash balances in the state of temporary equilibrium. In other words, by (6) the right-hand side of (10) vanishes, therefore $E_0 = 0$; that is, there is neither excess demand nor excess supply of money. Particularly, where there is an equilibrium in the securities market in the previous week we have $E_{-1} = 0$ and hence $M = L$.

4 Fundamental equation

Let us now write r as p_1; then the excess demand function for each good (including money) is a function of $p_1, p_2, \ldots, p_n$. The adjustment function of the rate of interest (4) may be written as

$$\dot{p}_1 = F_1(E_1) \tag{4'}$$

[6] See Lange, 1942.

By assumption (4′) and

$$\dot{p}_i = F_i(E_i)\ (i = 2,\ldots,n) \tag{2}$$

become 0 where $E_i = 0\ (i = 1,\ldots,n)$. Expanding these functions in a Taylor series we obtain

$$\dot{p}_i = F_i^0 E_i + \ldots \tag{11}$$

where $F_i^0 = dF_i(0)/dE_i$. As has been stated in the previous section there is a price set $p_i^0\ (i = 1,\ldots,n)$ where all excess demands, E_i, vanish. Expanding E_i in a Taylor series at that point we obtain from (11)

$$\dot{p}_i = \sum_{j=1}^{n} F_i^0 E_{ij}^0 (p_j - p_j^0) + \ldots\ (i = 1,\ldots,n) \tag{12}$$

where $E_{ij} = \partial E_i/\partial p_j\ (i,j = 1,\ldots,n)$ and the superscript ^{0} applied to E_{ij} represents E_{ij}^0 as the value of the partial derivative E_{ij} at the temporary equilibrium point.

In the above expression (12) the part after the + sign, represented by the abbreviation of dots, consists of the terms which are of higher orders with respect to $(p - p^0)$. Generally speaking, price adjustment functions, if they are expanded, may contain higher-order terms with respect to $(p - p^0)$ so that $\dot{p}_i$ is not necessarily a linear function. Thus actual price adjustment functions are, in general, of non-linear types but in this chapter we confine ourselves to the case in which all $\dot{p}_i$ are linear. The reason why I devote one chapter to such a somewhat unrealistic case of linear systems is that the properties of the linear case will become useful when we examine non-linear systems later.[7] Putting

$$F_i^0 E_{ij}^0 = a_{ij}$$

then the linear price adjustment functions may be written more simply as

$$\dot{p}_i = \Sigma a_{ij}(p_j - p_j^0) \tag{13}$$

In our system if, as soon as the market is open, prices and the rate of interest are proposed by chance at the temporary equilibrium prices $p_1^0, p_2^0, \ldots, p_n^0$, the demands are equated to the respective supplies at the outset so that there is no bidding of prices up or down. Prices are kept at p_i^0 throughout the week. That is to say that if the initial values of p_i are set at p_i^0 the differential equations have stationary solutions

$$p_i(t) = p_j^0\ (i = 1,\ldots,n)$$

namely, p_i takes on a stationary value, p_i^0, regardless of the value of t.

[7] See chapter 4 below.

However we may have such a case only by chance. In general, prices proposed at the beginning of the week, denoted by $\bar{p}_i$, will be different from p_i^0. In that case there will be some commodities whose demands are not equated with their supplies at the initial prices. Therefore, prices must be adjusted. Groping prices are not stationary with respect to t and fluctuate from time to time according to the adjustment functions (13). The time shape of groping prices can be elucidated by finding the general solutions of (13). Let the characteristic equations

$$f(\lambda) = \begin{vmatrix} a_{11} - \lambda & a_{12} & \dots & a_{1n} \\ a_{21} & a_{22} - \lambda & \dots & a_{2n} \\ \dots & \dots & \dots & \dots \\ a_{n1} & a_{n2} & \dots & a_{nn} - \lambda \end{vmatrix} = |a_{ij} - \lambda\delta_{ij}| = 0$$

have roots $\lambda_1, \dots, \lambda_s$. Then by the familiar method simultaneous first-order linear differential equations (13) are solved and their solutions may be written in the form

$$p_i(t) = p_i^0 + \sum_{k=1}^{s} q_{ik}(t)e^{\lambda_k t} \tag{14}$$

where $q_{ik}(t)$ is a polynomial with respect to t. It has an order of, at most, $\mu_k - 1$ (μ_k stands for the degree of multiplicity of λ_k). Coefficients of the polynomials are determined by the value of a_{ij} and the initial value of prices. We refer to equations (14) as *the fundamental equations of fluctuations of groping prices.*[8]

Let us now explain in some detail fluctuation factors $e^{\lambda_k t}$ and $t^\mu e^{\lambda_k t}$ of the fundamental equations. In order to promote better comprehension of the time shape of fluctuations of groping prices it would be convenient to divide our explanation into the case where fluctuation factors have a real characteristic root λ_k and the case where they have a complex one.

(i) Let us first deal with the case where fluctuation factors are real. It is well known that if $e^{\lambda_k t}$ is real it traces out the curves as illustrated in figure 1.

As for the factors $t^\mu e^{\lambda_k t}$ (which is written as x for the sake of simplicity) it reduces to $x = t^\mu$ if $\lambda_k = 0$ (the graph is omitted). On the other hand, if $\lambda_k \neq 0$ we have, by differentiating x with respect to t

[8] Where (13) holds for a system of time t which is determined in an appropriate way, we have the fundamental equation of fluctuations (14). Another system of time ξ which is also a one-to-one correspondence with the calendar time τ is related to the time t by $t = \phi(\xi)$. Substituting this relationship into (14) we have the equation of fluctuations in terms of ξ

$$p_i(\xi) = p_i^0 + \Sigma h_{ik}(\xi)e^{\lambda_k \varphi(\xi)}$$

$$\dot{x} = [\mu + \lambda_k t]t^{\mu-1}e^{\lambda_k t}$$

First if $\lambda_k > 0$, x and $\dot{x}$ are positive for all $t > 0$ and tend to infinity as t tends to infinity. x traces out, therefore, a curve as is illustrated in figure 2. On the other hand, if $\lambda_k < 0$, x will become 0 when $t = 0$ and when $t = \infty$. x will take on the maximum value when $t = -\mu/\lambda_k > 0$ where $\dot{x} = 0$ (see figure 2).

(ii) Next we deal with fluctuation factors which are complex. Because

$$\lambda_k = R_k + \sqrt{-1}\, I_k$$

we have

$$e^{\lambda_k t} = e^{R_k t}(\cos I_k t + \sqrt{-1} \sin I_k t)$$

If a complex number λ_k is a characteristic root then its conjugate complex number λ'_k is also a characteristic root. It can be shown that in the fundamental equation (14) coefficient $q_{ik}(t)$ applied to $e^{\lambda_k t}$ is conjugate with the coefficient $q'_{ik}(t)$ applied to factor $e^{\lambda'_k t}$. Therefore we have

$$q_{ik}(t) = \alpha(t) + \sqrt{-1}\, \beta(t),$$
$$q'_{ik}(t) = \alpha(t) - \sqrt{-1}\, \beta(t)$$

Consequently

$$q_{ik}(t)e^{\lambda_k t} + q'_{ik}(t)e^{\lambda'_k t} = 2e^{R_k t}(\alpha(t) \cos I_k t - \beta(t) \sin I_k t) \tag{15}$$

where

$$\alpha(t) = \sum_{\mu=0}^{\bar{\mu}} \alpha_\mu t^\mu, \; \beta(t) = \sum_{\mu=0}^{\bar{\mu}} \beta_\mu t^\mu$$

(in these expressions $\bar{\mu}$ is defined as $\bar{\mu}_k - 1$). We may then write (15) as

$$\sum_0^{\bar{\mu}} 2A_\mu e^{R_k t}(\cos(I_k t + \omega_\mu))t^\mu$$

where

$$A_\mu^2 = \alpha_\mu^2 + \beta_\mu^2, \; \tan \omega_\mu = \beta_\mu/\alpha_\mu$$

It is seen that (15) is composed of

$$y = e^{R_k t} \cos(I_k t + \omega_0)$$

and

$$z = t^\mu e^{R_k t} \cos(I_k t + \omega_\mu), \; (\mu \neq 0)$$

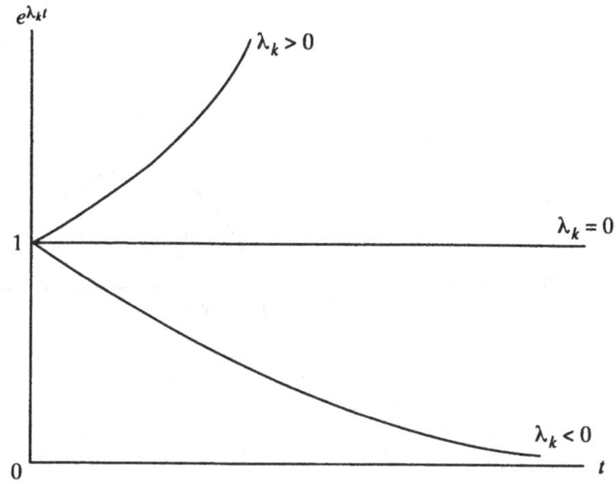

Figure 1

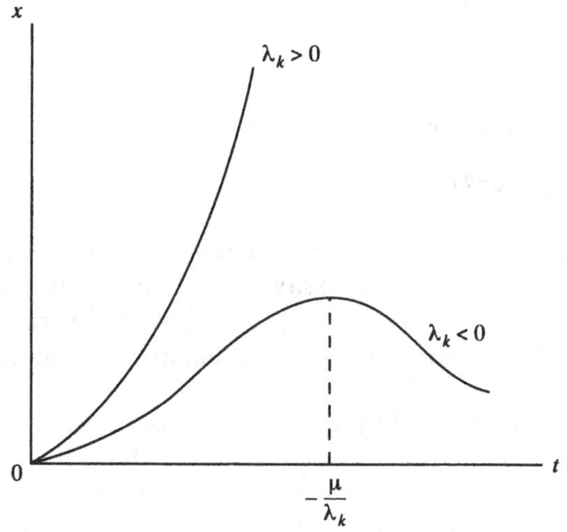

Figure 2

Therefore we may explain the behaviour of the quantity (15) through time by analysing y and z. First we examine y. Where $R_k = 0$ we find $y = \cos(I_k t + \omega_0)$ so that y is a periodic function with period $2\pi/I_k$ (see figure 3). On the other hand, where $R_k \neq 0$, y is not a periodic function in the strict sense but the time between two consecutive points of time where $y = 0$ is constantly $T_1 = 2\pi/I_k$. Therefore we call T_1 the quasi-cycle period. Let t_0 be

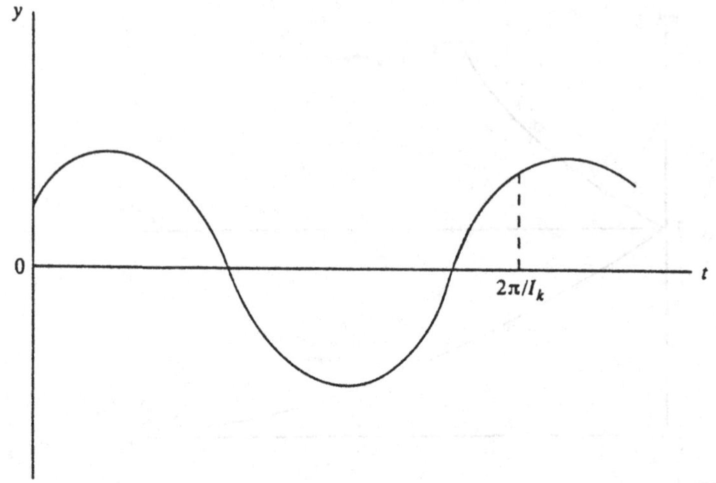

Figure 3

the first point of time where $\cos(I_k t + \omega_0) = 1$ and consider points of time

$$t = t_0, t_0 + T_1, t_0 + 2T_1, \dots$$

Then, at these points of time y will take on the values

$$e^{R_k t}, e^{R_k(t_0 + T_1)}, e^{R_k(t_0 + 2T_1)}, \dots$$

Moreover, at these points, the values of $\dot{y}$ are equal to the values of the derivative of $e^{R_k t}$ with respect to t. That is to say that the curve of y is tangent to the curve of $e^{R_k t}$ at points $t_0, t_0 + T_1, t_0 + 2T_1, \dots$. If $R_k > 0$ y traces out explosive oscillations (figure 4a), while we have damping oscillations if $R_k < 0$ (figure 4b).

From the analysis of y we can find by analogy how z behaves. The curve to which z is tangent at points $t_0, t_0 + T_1, t_0 + 2T_1, \dots$ is $t^u e^{R_k t}$. If $R_k \geqq 0$, z traces out undamped oscillations while, if $R_k < 0$, z converges.

The fundamental equation states that fluctuations in prices are the result of the above-mentioned fluctuation factors. It depends on the prices and the rate of interest initially proposed, $\bar{p}_i$, which factors are active and which factors are inactive. Also, the composition of active factors depends on them. If initial prices, $\bar{p}_i$, are set at p_i^0, no fluctuation factors are active and hence prices are stationary.

Where two fluctuation factors are compounded there appears in the market new kinds of fluctuations which are not observable when only one or other of the factors is active. This may be illustrated by the following

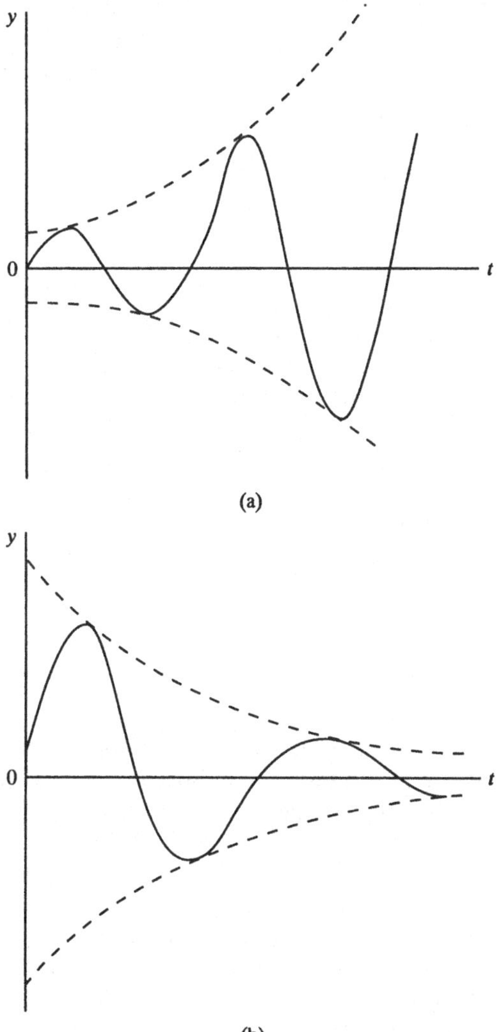

Figure 4

example. Suppose there are two factors, $e^{\lambda_1 t}$ and $e^{\lambda_2 t}$; λ_1 and λ_2 are real and negative and $\lambda_1 > \lambda_2$. They are compounded into

$$f(t) = e^{\lambda_1 t} + ce^{\lambda_2 t}$$

Let t_1 be the value of t which makes $f(t) = 0$. Then it is a solution to

$$e^{(\lambda_1 - \lambda_2)t} = -c$$

So if $c < -1$, there is only one solution, t_1, to the above equation and it is positive. Where $c = -1$ then we obtain $t_1 = 0$, while in the case of $c > -1$ there is no t_1 in the range $t \geqq 0$. Next, differentiate $f(t)$ with respect to t, then

$$df(t)/dt = \lambda_1 e^{\lambda_1 t} + c\lambda_2 e^{\lambda_2 t}$$

Let t_2 be the value of t which makes $df(t)/dt = 0$. Obviously t_2 is a solution to

$$e^{(\lambda_1 - \lambda_2)t} = -c\lambda_2/\lambda_1$$

By assumption we have $\lambda_2/\lambda_1 > 1$, so that there is only one t_2 which is positive and greater than t_1, if $c < -1$. Also, when $c = -1$, we have a positive t_2. However if $c > -1$, t_2 may or may not exist in the range $t > 0$. Thus, depending on the value of c, we have four kinds of time shapes as figures 5a–d show.

These examples illustrate that in spite of each fluctuation factor, $e^{\lambda_1 t}$ or $e^{\lambda_2 t}$ being monotonically decreasing, their compound of $f(t)$ may produce, depending on the composition, a peak at the point in time t_2. The fundamental equations for groping prices which are the aggregate of many fluctuation factors will produce various time profiles for groping prices.

5 Stability of temporary equilibrium

Let us now introduce the concept of stability of temporary equilibrium. We begin with a simple, well-known analogy from physical dynamics. Consider a frictionless pendulum. It will be in a state of equilibrium in two positions, (i) where it is at the bottom point *a* with the initial speed being zero and (ii) where it is at the top point *b* with zero initial speed (see figure 6). These two equilibria have completely different properties. If the pendulum, which was at *b*, is displaced from there by some exogenous shock it will divert from *b* further and further at a higher and higher speed. On the other hand, if it is at point *a* a small shock on the pendulum will displace it from *a*; after that it will oscillate around *a*. The smaller the shock the smaller will be the amplitude of the oscillations. Therefore if the initial shock is sufficiently small we can always confine movements of the pendulum to a small neighbourhood of *a*. Thus the point at *a* and the one at *b* produce different reactions to a given initial shock. We call *a* a stable equilibrium position and *b* unstable.

Phenomena similar to these may occur in the process of competitive buying and selling. If some small shock is administered to prices which are in a state of temporary equilibrium then they may either diverge from the temporary equilibrium point or remain in the small neighbourhood of the equilibrium point. We call the temporary equilibrium unstable in the first

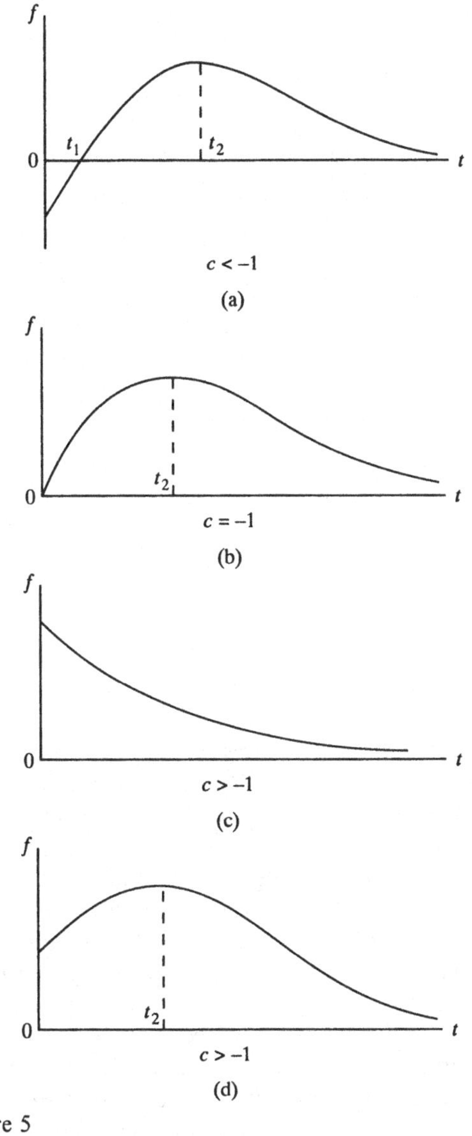

Figure 5

case and stable in the second. That is to say in more rigorous terms that we define the temporary equilibrium as stable if groping prices always remain in the small region, ε, which contains the temporary equilibrium point, provided that price movement starts from a region $\delta(\varepsilon)$ contained in ε. On the contrary, temporary equilibrium is unstable if in any $\delta(\varepsilon)$ contained in a

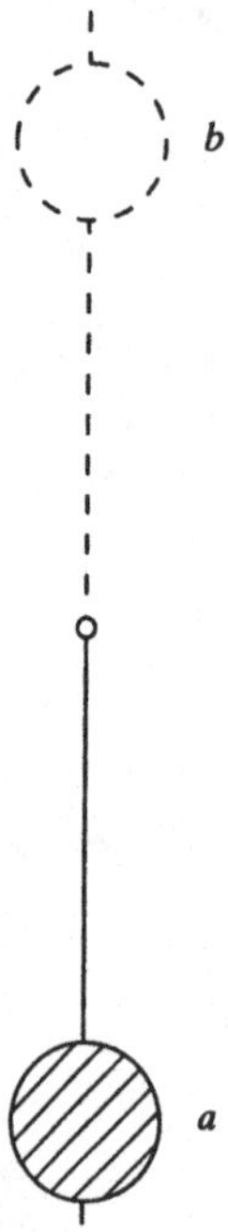

Figure 6

given region, ε, there is a point $\bar{P}$ which generates a path of groping prices which eventually move out of the region ε. To distinguish another kind of stability which will be defined later we refer to this definition of stability as stability *according to Liapounoff*.[9]

What are the conditions under which a temporary equilibrium becomes stable or unstable in the sense of Liapounoff? First we discuss the conditions for instability. If real characteristic roots are all positive and the real parts of all complex characteristic roots are all positive then each fluctuation factor will be explosive as t tends to ∞, so that groping prices $p_1(t), p_2(t), \ldots, p_n(t)$ will diverge and cannot be confined to any finite region ε however small a $\delta(\varepsilon)$, from which the path starts, is taken. (The exception is the case where the initial position is set at the point of temporary equilibrium P^0.) Therefore the equilibrium is unstable according to Liapounoff. A real number may be considered as a special complex number whose imaginary part is zero so that for real roots λ_k we have $\lambda_k = R_k$ and

9 It was Liapounoff, 1907, who contributed greatly to the theory of stability. In writing this book I have not benefited from his original work but have been acquainted with it through A. A. Andronow and C. E. Chaikin, 1949 [Yasui, 1950, has also discussed Liapounoff, 1907].

$I_k = 0$. Bearing this in mind we may write *the conditions for Liapounoff instability as*

$$R_k > 0 \textit{ for all } k$$

That is to say, all real parts are positive.

Before we proceed to find the conditions for Liapounoff stability let us classify it into two groups. Corresponding to a region ε which contains the temporary equilibrium point, we take another region contained in ε, $\delta(\varepsilon)$. Consider the case of prices always remaining in ε if the groping starts from a point in $\delta(\varepsilon)$. If there is at least one such $\delta(\varepsilon)$ then we have Liapounoff stability but such a $\delta(\varepsilon)$ may be further classified into the following two kinds. (i) $\delta(\varepsilon)$ contains the equilibrium point within it and (ii) the equilibrium point exists on the boundary of $\delta(\varepsilon)$. In the first case if the starting point of the groping is in a small neighbourhood of the equilibrium point then groping prices are always kept within ε, irrespective of the direction from the position of the initial point in relation to the equilibrium point. In this case equilibrium is said to be absolutely stable in the Liapounoff sense. On the other hand, if groping starts from some point in a region $\delta(\varepsilon)$ which contains the equilibrium point as an inside point, the path will eventually move out from ε but still will be confined to ε if it starts from any point in another $\delta(\varepsilon)$ which has the equilibrium point on its boundary as classified in (ii). In such a case the nearness of the initial point to the equilibrium point is not sufficient for confining the price movement to the ε region. It must lie in a special direction from the equilibrium point. That is to say that equilibrium is stable with respect to only those points contained in the $\delta(\varepsilon)$ of the type (ii). In this case we say that equilibrium is conditionally stable in the Liapounoff sense.

Let us first find a condition for absolute stability. If real characteristic roots are all negative and real parts of complex characteristic roots are also all negative then all fluctuation factors converge to zero when t tends to infinity; hence, if initial groping prices $\bar{p}_i$ are taken sufficiently near to the equilibrium point (i.e., if $d(\varepsilon)$ is taken to be a sufficiently small neighbourhood of the equilibrium point) then all $p_i(t)$ are always within the given ε.

On the other hand, in the case of some characteristic roots λ_k being zero or a purely imaginary number we must have the following. Let $A = (a_{ij})$ and $I =$ the $n \times n$ unit matrix. Simple elementary divisors $(\lambda_k - \lambda)^{\nu_{ik}}$ of $A - \lambda I$ which correspond to the zero or purely imaginary characteristic roots λ_k have indices ν_{ik}. If they are all 1, the fundamental equations do not contain the factors $t^{\mu}e^{\lambda_k t}(\mu \geqq 1)$ but only $e^{\lambda_k t}$ which is 1 for $\lambda_k = 0$ and $\cos(I_k t + \omega_0)$ for $R_k = 0$. Therefore, even though the matrix A has such characteristic roots, the movements of the prices are confined to a given region ε if the initial prices are taken in a sufficiently small neighbourhood, $\delta(\varepsilon)$, of the temporary equilibrium point; the equilibrium is absolutely stable according to Liapounoff. That is to say, *the conditions for absolute stability are*

$$R_k \leqq 0 \textit{ for all } k$$

where the indices of those simple elementary divisors of $A - \lambda I$ *which correspond to the characteristic roots,* $\lambda_k = 0$ *or* $R_k = 0$*, are all unities.*

Next, derive the conditions for conditional stability. Suppose the above conditions for absolute stability are only partly satisfied. First, if at least one of those simple elementary divisors which corresponds to the roots $\lambda_k = 0$ or $R_k = 0$ has an index which is 2 or greater than 2, then the fundamental equations contain a fluctuation factor t^μ or $t^\mu \cos(I_k t + \omega_0)$ with $\mu \geqq 1$. This factor diverges in a monotonic or cyclic way; that is, it is an instability factor. Secondly, if some of the characteristic roots have a positive real part, $R_k > 0$, then the corresponding fluctuation factors are instability factors. Where both stability and instability factors co-exist the region $\delta(\varepsilon)$ which includes the equilibrium point as an inner point, however small it may be, has a point within it which, if it is taken as the initial point, makes instability fluctuation factors effective in the fundamental equations. Therefore $\delta(\varepsilon)$ contains certain points, where the paths starting from them will eventually move out of the region ε. However there is a region consisting of points which nullify all instability factors; so if we take $\delta(\varepsilon)$ as such a region (that is a subset of the previous $\delta(\varepsilon)$ which contains the equilibrium point as an inner point) groping prices always fluctuate within the region ε if the groping starts from any point within the new $\delta(\varepsilon)$. The equilibrium point is thus stable, not for all points in its neighbourhood, but for some of them. We now have *the conditions for conditional Liapounoff stability:* $R_k \leqq 0$ *for some k and* $R_k > 0$ *for all other k, or all* $R_k \leqq 0$*, provided that the indices of the simple elementary divisors corresponding to the roots* $R_k = 0$ *are at least as large as* 2.

According to the above definition of Liapounoff stability, groping prices remain in the ε neighbourhood of the equilibrium prices if they are initially set at some point in $\delta(\varepsilon)$ but they do not necessarily converge to equilibrium prices. In fact the cases illustrated in figure 7 and 8 are both stable in the Liapounoff sense. The first one represents a case where the price movement starting from $\delta(\varepsilon)$ never converges to the equilibrium point, while the second generates convergence.

Thus Liapounoff stability includes both the cases of convergence to the equilibrium and of fluctuating around the equilibrium point. In particular we refer to the case of convergence, i.e.

$$\lim_{t \to \infty} p_i(t) = p_i^0$$

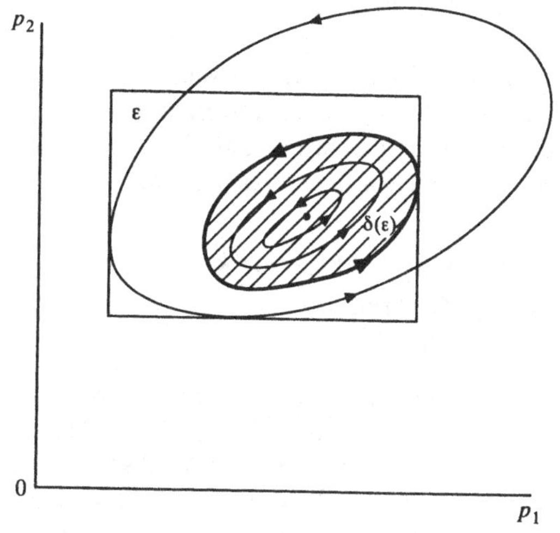

Figure 7

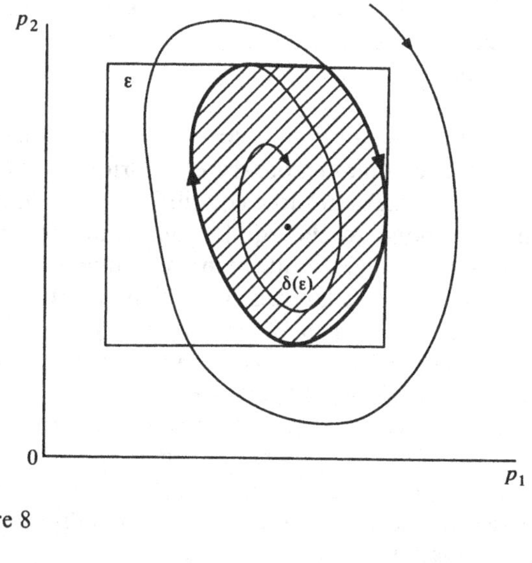

Figure 8

as the case of the equilibrium point being *strongly* stable.[10] The definition of stability in economics is given, in the tradition of Walras, Hicks, and Samuelson, in this strong form. We have said that equilibrium is stable if prices which deviate from equilibrium prices through some shock, or are

[10] It is also said to be asymptotically stable.

initially set by the auctioneer at some disequilibrium point, eventually converge to equilibrium, i.e., forces restoring or tending to equilibrium are at work in its neighbourhood.[11] Depending on whether such forces prevail throughout a small neighbourhood of the equilibrium point or in only part of it, we say that the equilibrium has absolute strong stability or conditional strong stability. *The conditions for conditional strong stability may be written as*

$$R_k < 0 \textit{ for some } k, \textit{ and } R_k \geqq 0 \textit{ for other } k$$

and those for absolute strong stability as

$$R_k < 0 \textit{ for all } k$$

Therefore if there are characteristic roots λ_k which are zero or purely imaginary the equilibrium may be conditionally strongly stable but cannot be absolutely strongly stable. Even in this case it can be absolutely stable in the sense of Liapounoff, particularly in the case of $\lambda_k = 0$. Auctioneering which started from a point in $\delta(\varepsilon)$ will end at a point P^1 in the neighbourhood of the equilibrium point P^0. The fact that $\lambda_k = 0$ implies that the matrix A is singular so that this equilibrium is not unique. We have many others in the neighbourhood of P^0; the point P^1 where the auction is ended is also an equilibrium point. We call this equilibrium point P^0 neutral if prices deviating from the equilibrium point P^0 approach another equilibrium P^1 in its neighbourhood.

As we have seen above, if the equilibrium is strongly stable or neutral, groping prices will converge to some temporary equilibrium point and commodities and securities are traded at those equilibrium prices and the rate of interest which correspond to the equilibrium point being approached. In all other cases, prices and the rate of interest either diverge or continue ceaseless oscillation. As a result, prices and the rate of interest will not be determined during that week. Therefore *to determine prices and the rate of interest by competitive trading it is requisite that the temporary equilibrium should be strongly stable or neutral.* If we have strong stability only conditionally, prices will be determined if the auction starts from some selected, particular prices. Otherwise, if it starts from other prices, they will remain undetermined. In the case of neutrality the final prices depend on the initial prices. Thus the stability conditions for temporary equilibrium are the conditions for price formation.[12]

[11] For example, see Hicks, 1946, p. 62.

[12] If the real parts of all λ_k are negative, we have $\lim_{t\to\infty} p_i(t) = p_i^0$. Since ξ tends to infinity when t tends to infinity, (14′) yields $\lim_{\xi\to\infty} p_i(\xi) = p_i^0$. This means that the stability is invariant with respect to transformation of systems of timing, say, from t to ξ.

It has also been pointed out by Samuelson, 1948, pp. 274–5, that the stability is invariant with respect to linear transformations of commodities.

6 Samuelson's theory and direct buying and selling between traders

It is well known that the problem of finding the time path of prices, p_i, and the rate of interest, r, from differential equations (2) and (4) was first discussed by Samuelson. At the beginning of the 1940s this problem attracted the attention of some other economists and we obtained some additional results. It seems to me, however, that those economists were not well acquainted with the field to which this theory can be applied. In other words, this theory determines prices and the rate of interest as a function of t but we do not know whether the functions thus obtained are meant to describe the time sequence of temporary equilibrium prices or fluctuations in groping prices before reaching a set of temporary equilibrium prices. If this theory can explain only the latter then it should not be used to explain the former. Also if the actual market does not determine prices by the method of competitive trading through an auctioneer, but determines prices by direct bargaining between traders, then it cannot explain anything about the actual market if it is merely concerned with fluctuations of groping prices.

Then what are the phenomena to which Samuelson's theory can be applied? In this section we want to show that this theory cannot be applied to analysing (i) the process of fluctuations in prices which are determined by direct bargaining between traders and (ii) the process of fluctuations in temporary equilibrium prices by auctioneering.

(i) Let $p_1, \ldots, p_n$ be prices at time t_0 and $p_1, \ldots, p_{n-1}, p_n + \Delta p_n$ be those at t_1 (we assume that only p_n is changed). Demands of person a take on the values $x_1, \ldots, x_n$ at t_0 and $x_1 + \Delta x_1, \ldots, x_n + \Delta x_n$ at t_1. The initial stock of money of a at t_0 is denoted by $\bar{x}$. First consider the case of competitive trading; at t_0 demands must satisfy[13]

$$t_0\colon \bar{x} = p_1 x_1 + \ldots + p_n x_n \tag{16}$$

Suppose now individual a has bought commodities i by the amounts x_i' at t_0. At t_1 he owns commodities $x_1', \ldots, x_n'$ but must pay money for them at prices $p_1, \ldots, p_{n-1}, p_n + \Delta p_n$ prevailing at t_1. (Remember that, in our competitive trading, payments for the trade which has been contracted during the session are made not at the prices which were prevailing when the contracts were made but at the prices currently prevailing.) Therefore, at t_1 a has money of the amount

[13] In the following, we ignore, for simplicity's sake, the problems concerning the demands for money and securities. In doing so we do not lose anything in the generality of the conclusions.

$$\bar{x} - \sum_{i=0}^{n-1} p_i x_i' - (p_n + \Delta p_n)x_n'$$

after the payment and stocks of commodities being worth

$$\sum_{i=0}^{n-1} p_i x_i' + (p_n + \Delta p_n)x_n'$$

so that his total purchasing power at t_1 is the same $\bar{x}$ as it was at t_0. The individual's demands and supplies satisfy at t_1

$$\begin{aligned} t_1\colon \bar{x} = p_1(x_1 + \Delta x_1) + \ldots + p_{n-1}(x_{n-1} + \Delta x_{n-1}) \\ + (p_n + \Delta p_n)(x_n + \Delta x_n) \end{aligned} \tag{17}$$

Therefore, we obtain from (16) and (17)

$$-x_n = p_1 \frac{\Delta x_1}{\Delta p_n} + \ldots + p_n \frac{\Delta x_n}{\Delta p_n} \tag{18}$$

a condition which induced changes in demands and supplies must satisfy when a change in price p_n alone is proposed in a market where competitive trading takes place through the auctioneer.

On the other hand, in the case of direct bargaining between traders we have quite different results. Suppose now individual a does not buy any commodities at t_0. Then a's initial cash holding at t_1 is of the amount $\bar{x}$. Therefore his demands and supplies at t_1 must satisfy (17) and therefore we obtain (18).

However if a has bought commodity n by x_n and paid the amount $p_n x_n$ at t_0 then he has cash of the amount $\bar{x} - p_n x_n$ and stock of commodity n by x_n at t_1. These stocks are evaluated at $(p_n + \Delta p_n)x_n$ because the price of commodity n is changed. Therefore the total purchasing power of a at t_1 is

$$(\bar{x} - p_n x_n) + (p_n + \Delta p_n)x_n = \bar{x} + \Delta p_n x_n$$

Therefore his demand and supply at t_1 must satisfy the following budget equation

$$\begin{aligned} \bar{x} + \Delta p_n x_n = p_1(x_1 + \Delta x_1) + \ldots + p_{n-1}(x_{n-1} + \Delta x_{n-1}) \\ + (p_n + \Delta p_n)(x_n + \Delta x_n) \end{aligned}$$

This, together with the budget equation at t_0, (16), implies the relationship

$$p_1 \frac{\Delta x_1}{\Delta p_n} + \ldots + p_n \frac{\Delta x_n}{\Delta p_n} = -\Delta x_n \tag{19}$$

Thus in the case of direct bargaining the individual's demand and supply curves satisfy condition (18) if he has bought nothing at the previous point in time while they satisfy (19) when he has bought something. *The slopes of* *his demand functions are different, depending on whether or not he bought commodities at t_0; demands and supplies depend not only on prices but also on trade in the past.*

In his stability analysis Samuelson assumes that market demand and supply functions depend on prices only

$$D_i = D_i(p_1(t), \ldots, p_n(t)),$$
$$S_i = S_i(p_1(t), \ldots, p_n(t))$$

As a commodity is demanded or supplied by different persons or firms D_i and S_i are independent of each other. If p_n only changes by Δp_n as time passes from t_0 to t_1, demand changes by

$$\Delta D_i = \frac{\partial D_i}{\partial p_n} \Delta p_n$$

This magnitude is independent of S_i at time point t_0. That is to say ΔD_i is determined irrespective of how much of commodity i is supplied at t_0 and hence how much trade in commodity i is made at t_0. Thus, if contracts at t_0 are all temporary ones that are made during the process of auction, ΔD_i is independent of them. However, if some are fixed ones at t_0 or are made in the market of direct bargaining in the past, then ΔD_i must depend on them, that is to say, on the past history of transactions until t_0. Hence we must conclude that Samuelson's theory based on the above market demand and supply functions can explain the process of competitive trading through an auctioneer, but not the process of fluctuations in prices determined by direct trading, as he ignores the history.

(ii) It can easily be shown that Samuelson's theory cannot be applied to the analysis of the time series of the temporary equilibrium process.[14] Suppose now t referred to calendar time and we are always in some state of temporary equilibrium. We then examine the time series $p_i(t)$ and $r(t)$ of temporary equilibrium prices and the rate of interest.

According to Samuelson prices will change if and only if there is a positive or negative excess demand; price remains unchanged if excess demand is zero. Therefore by Samuelson's theory, as long as $p_i(t)$ and $r(t)$ change with regard to an increase in t, there must be some excess demand or excess supply so that $p_i(t)$ and $r(t)$ cannot be temporary equilibrium prices and the rate of interest; specifically, Samuelson's theory cannot analyse fluctuations in temporary equilibrium prices.

We must now conclude that Samuelson's theory can be used only for the analysis of competitive trade through an auctioneer, i.e., the tatonnement process.

[14] Dynamic processes of temporary equilibrium prices will be discussed in chapter 5 below.

7 Hicks' and Sono's stability conditions

In this section we discuss how our stability conditions of temporary equilibrium are related to other stability conditions which may be considered as important from the viewpoint of the history of economic analysis.

7.1 *Hicks' stability condition*[15]

According to general equilibrium theory, prices are not determined in isolated markets; they are determined simultaneously in general markets where all demands and supplies meet each other. From this we think that it is natural to assume that a change in some price will at once affect other prices. In this way we have repercussions on prices.

Hicks' analysis of how price changes propagate is based on the following assumptions. First, the price of commodity p_i is determined so as to equate the demand for i with its supply. In other words, the price of commodity i has the ability to adjust the demand and supply of the same commodity; but it disturbs demands and supplies of other commodities. Therefore if there is a change in the prices of some commodities then prices of other commodities will change so that equilibrium between demand and supply of respective commodities is maintained. Secondly, Hicks assumes that no time is needed for repercussions from one price to another, that is, repercussions take place instantaneously. Therefore in Hicks the concept of repercussions is not one of intertemporal but of simultaneous relationships.

Let us classify repercussions in the following way. If a change in price p_s induces a change in only one other price, all other prices remaining unchanged, we say that there is a repercussion of order 1. If a change in prices affects two prices only, that repercussion is said to be of order 2. Repercussions of orders 3 and 4 are similarly defined until we finally obtain one of order $n-1$. Repercussions of the order $n-1$ are complete in the sense that a change in p_s induces changes in all other prices.

Let us now consider a repercussion of order m where a rise in p_s will affect $p_1, \ldots, p_m$. If we assume that the market is in a state of general equilibrium before the change, then prices p_i $(i = 1, 2, \ldots, m)$ must change so as to satisfy equations

$$\frac{dE_i}{dp_s} = 0 \; (i = 1, \ldots, m; m < s) \tag{20}$$

In this case, it may happen that the demand for commodity s exceeds its supply or that the converse is the case or that its demand is still equated

[15] Hicks, 1946, pp. 62–77, pp. 315–19, and Lange, 1944, pp. 91–4.

with its supply. If we have excess demand for commodity s then p_s will be raised by competition among demanders. Therefore p_s will be in a position far removed from the equilibrium point. We have thus an unstable movement when

$$\frac{dE_s}{dp_s} > 0 \tag{21}$$

On the contrary, if we have excess supply of commodity s, p_s will decline by virtue of competition among suppliers. Therefore p_s which was first raised will now tend to return to the direction of equilibrium prices so that

$$\frac{dE_s}{dp_s} < 0 \tag{22}$$

is the stability condition. From (20) and (22) we obtain

$$\frac{dE_s}{dp_s} = \begin{vmatrix} E_{11}^0 & \cdots & E_{1m}^0 & E_{1s}^0 \\ \cdot & \cdots & \cdot & \cdot \\ E_{m1}^0 & \cdots & E_{mm}^0 & E_{ms}^0 \\ E_{s1}^0 & \cdots & E_{sm}^0 & E_{ss}^0 \end{vmatrix} \div \begin{vmatrix} E_{11}^0 & \cdots & E_{1m}^0 \\ \cdot & \cdots & \cdot \\ E_{m1}^0 & \cdots & E_{mm}^0 \end{vmatrix} < 0$$

We say that temporary equilibrium has stability of order $m + 1$ if the market is stable when we have repercussions of prices of order m. On the other hand, if the above ratio of the determinants has the opposite sign, the market is unstable of order $m + 1$; it is said to be neutral of order $m + 1$ if we have

$$\frac{dE_s}{dp_s} = 0$$

As for the rate of interest we may make a similar analysis. Suppose a rise in the rate of interest above the equilibrium rate induces a change in prices $p_2, \ldots, p_{m+1}$. If this causes an excess demand for securities, the rate of interest, as far as we accept the loanable fund theory, will fall; it will be bid up in the converse case, i.e., if we have an excess supply. Therefore the stability condition of order $m + 1$ with respect to the rate of interest is given as

$$\frac{dE_1}{dp_1} = \begin{vmatrix} E_{11}^0 & \cdots & E_{1,m+1}^0 \\ \cdot & \cdots & \cdot \\ E_{m+1,1}^0 & \cdots & E_{m+1,m+1}^0 \end{vmatrix} \div \begin{vmatrix} E_{22}^0 & \cdots & E_{2,m+1}^0 \\ \cdot & \cdots & \cdot \\ E_{2,m+1}^0 & \cdots & E_{m+1,m+1}^0 \end{vmatrix} > 0 \tag{23}$$

On the other hand, if we accept the liquidity preference theory the stability of the rate of interest will be determined by the excess demand for money. That is, if a rise in the rate of interest induces an excess supply of money, i.e.

$$\frac{dE_0}{dp_1} < 0; \frac{dE_i}{dp_1} = 0, (i = 2, \ldots, m+1) \tag{24}$$

then the rate of interest is stable. Taking Walras' law into account we can show that (23) is consistent with (24), provided $m + 1 = n$. Therefore both liquidity preference and loanable fund theory produce the same answer concerning the stability of the rate of interest, but (23) and (24) are not consistent with each other if $m + 1 < n$. Hence there is a possibility that loanable fund theory insists on instability whereas liquidity preference theory insists on stability. Hicks regarded these two theories of interest as equivalent,[16] but as the above shows they are not equivalent if repercussions of prices are limited,[17] and therefore 'imperfect' in Hicks' sense. In the following we assume loanable fund theory.

The above stability condition of order $m + 1$ is the condition for price p_s to be stable when a change in p_s has repercussions on $p_1, \ldots, p_m$. We have a different stability of order $m + 1$ with respect to p_s if we assume that a change in p_s affects different m prices. In a similar way we obtain analogous conditions with respect to prices other than p_s. In particular, we say that the market has the perfect stability of order $m + 1$ if not only all these stability conditions of order $m + 1$ but also those of any lower order up to m are entirely satisfied. This definition of perfect stability is reduced to the one defined by Hicks in the particular case of $m + 1 = n$. The conditions for it are given as

$$E_{ii}^0 < 0, \quad \begin{vmatrix} E_{ii}^0 & E_{ij}^0 \\ E_{ji}^0 & E_{jj}^0 \end{vmatrix} > 0, \quad \begin{vmatrix} E_{ii}^0 & E_{ij}^0 & E_{ik}^0 \\ E_{ji}^0 & E_{jj}^0 & E_{jk}^0 \\ E_{ki}^0 & E_{kj}^0 & E_{kk}^0 \end{vmatrix} < 0, \ldots \tag{25}$$

for $i \neq j \neq k \neq i$, etc. However, in (25) those determinants which have the row of partial derivatives of the excess demand for securities E_1 must have the opposite sign for stability. Those determinants which satisfy conditions (25) are called 'Hicksian'.

As has been said above, Hicks' analysis of stability in multiple markets assumes that when p_s changes, other prices are instantaneously adjusted so as to equate demand and supply in the respective markets. Therefore, where this sort of assumption is inadequate, Hicks' conditions are not justifiable

[16] Hicks, 1946, pp. 153–62.

[17] Cf. chapter 4, section 7 below.

ones for stability. In the real world, Hicks' hypothesis of the repercussions of prices is seldom satisfied, so we must generalize the stability analysis of multiple markets by removing his hypothesis. It was Samuelson's theory, explained in the preceding sections, which solved this important problem. In his case a change in p_s affects p_i intertemporarily at a finite speed of adjustment $\dot{p}_i$ but not instantaneously or simultaneously at an infinite speed. All these changes occur instantly in Hick's case.

Thus, Hicks' stability conditions are valid only in special cases, so it may appear that we need not attach importance to them. However, apart from the point of view of stability, the Hicksian property of the determinants of the partial derivatives of the excess demand functions is itself not only elegant but also a useful property which plays, as will be seen later, an important role in the comparative-dynamics analysis of the economy. Consequently it would be desirable to examine the cases in which a given temporary equilibrium will be of the Hicksian type. Concerning this problem we make some investigations below.

7.1.1 *Metzler's case*

Metzler shows that if conditions

$$a_{ii} < 0, a_{ij} > 0, (i \neq j) \tag{26}$$

are satisfied for all i and j, then the necessary and sufficient conditions for the real parts R_k of the latent root, λ_k, of the characteristic equation

$$|a_{ij} - \lambda\delta_{ij}| = |A - \lambda I| = 0$$

to be all negative are

$$a_{ii} < 0, \begin{vmatrix} a_{ii} & a_{ij} \\ a_{ji} & a_{jj} \end{vmatrix} > 0, \begin{vmatrix} a_{ii} & a_{ij} & a_{ik} \\ a_{ji} & a_{jj} & a_{jk} \\ a_{ki} & a_{kj} & a_{kk} \end{vmatrix} < 0, \ldots \tag{27}$$

where $i \neq j \neq k \neq i$, etc.[18] To prove this theorem of Metzler, let us take a positive number $\bar{a}$ which is greater than the largest absolute value of $a_{ii}, i = 1, \ldots, n$, so that

$$a_{ii} + \bar{a} > 0 \ (i = 1, \ldots, n)$$

On the other hand, the characteristic equation can be rewritten in the form

$$|A - \lambda I| = |A + \bar{a}I - \rho I| = 0 \tag{28}$$

so that we obtain

$$\lambda = \rho - \bar{a}$$

[18] Metzler, 1945.

Therefore, an obvious sufficient condition for $R_k < 0$ for $k = 1,\ldots,s$, is that $|\rho_k| < \bar{a}$ for all $k = 1,\ldots,s$. On the other hand, as elements of matrix $A + \bar{a}I$ are all positive, equation (28) has a simple root, θ, which is positive and greater than the absolute value of any other root ρ_k.[19] Accordingly, if $R_k < 0$ for all k, then $\lambda = \theta - \bar{a} < 0$; therefore, in view of $|\rho_k| \leqq \theta$ for all k, we obtain $|\rho_k| < \bar{a}$ for all k. Thus, under the Metzler conditions (26) the necessary and sufficient condition for a temporary equilibrium to be absolutely strongly stable is that $|\rho_k| < \bar{a}$ for $k = 1,\ldots,s$.

Next, expanding (28), we obtain

$$(\rho - \bar{a})^n - \Sigma a_{ii}(\rho - \bar{a})^{n-1} + \Sigma \begin{vmatrix} a_{ii} & a_{ij} \\ a_{ji} & a_{jj} \end{vmatrix} (\rho - \bar{a})^{n-2} + \ldots + (-1)^n |A| = 0$$

Where conditions (27) hold, the coefficients of the above equation are all positive, so that it has no root such that $\rho_k - \bar{a} \geqq 0$. Therefore, $0 < \theta < \bar{a}$; hence $|\rho_k| < \bar{a}$ for all k.

On the contrary, suppose $|\rho_i| < \bar{a}$ for $i = 1,\ldots,n$. If all ρ_i are real, we have sign $|A|$ = sign $(-1)^n$, because

$$|A| = \prod_i (\rho_i - \bar{a})$$

If some of ρ_is are complex numbers, their conjugate numbers are also roots of the characteristic equation. Let ρ_i and $\bar{\rho}_i$ be conjugate to each other; then $(\rho_i - \bar{a})(\bar{\rho}_i - \bar{a}) > 0$. Because, thus, the total number of the complex roots, say l, is necessarily even, we have sign $|A|$ = sign $(-1)^{n-l}$ = sign $(-1)^n$.

Next, the cofactors of $|vI - \bar{a}I - A|$ are all positive as long as $v \geqq \theta$,[20] so that by putting $v = \bar{a} > 0$, we find that the cofactors of $|-A|$ are positive. Consequently

$$|A_{ii}| = \text{sign } (-1)^{n-1}$$

where A_{ii} denotes the matrix of order $n - 1$ obtained from A by deleting its ith row and ith column. Evidently, $|\rho' I - \bar{a}I - A_{ii}| = 0$ has a simple root θ' which is positive and greater than the absolute value of any other root; and we can show that $\theta' < \theta$, because otherwise we would have $|\theta I - \bar{a}I - A_{ii}| > 0$ since $\theta' \geqq \theta$. Hence $0 < \theta' < \theta$. Putting $v' = \bar{a} > \theta'$, we obtain $|v'I - \bar{a}I - A_{ii}| = |-A_{ii}|$ whose cofactors are all positive; hence sign $|A_{iijj}|$ = sign $(-1)^{n-2}$, where A_{iijj} is a matrix of order $n - 2$ obtained from A_{ii} by removing its row and column containing the element a_{jj}. Continuing with this procedure, we obtain (27). Thus, conditions (27) are necessary and sufficient for $|\rho_i| < \bar{a}, i = 1,\ldots,s$. This establishes that where

19 See Frobenius, 1908, and Mathematical Note II below.

20 Frobenius, 1908, and Mathematical Note II below.

(26) prevails, (27) is necessary and sufficient for the economy to be absolutely strongly stable.

Now in viewing $a_{ij} = F_i^0 E_{ij}^0$ $(i,j = 1,\ldots,n), F_1^0 < 0$ and $F_i^0 > 0$ $(i = 2,\ldots,n)$ we at once see that conditions (27) are equivalent to those of (25). (Note, however, that in (25) the determinants containing the row of the partial derivatives of E_1 have the opposite sign.) Hence the temporary equilibrium is Hicksian. In short, where Metzler's conditions (26) prevail, an absolutely strongly stable equilibrium point is Hicksian, and vice-versa.

7.1.2 *Samuelson's and Lange's case*[21]

Samuelson and Lange have shown that where conditions

$$a_{ij} = a_{ji}\ (i,j = 1,\ldots,n) \tag{29}$$

are satisfied, an equilibrium point is Hicksian as long as it is absolutely strongly stable. In this case, because of (29), the characteristic equation is symmetric, so that its latent roots are all real and the necessary and sufficient conditions for them to be all negative are (27). Therefore, considering the assumptions of the signs of $F_i^0, i = 1,\ldots,n$, we find that the equilibrium is Hicksian.

7.1.3 *Sono's case*[22]

Let us write $a_{ij} + a_{ji} = 2\sigma_{ij}$ and assume

$$\sigma_{ii} < 0, \begin{vmatrix} \sigma_{ii} & \sigma_{ij} \\ \sigma_{ji} & \sigma_{jj} \end{vmatrix} > 0, \ldots \tag{30}$$

As will be seen later, these are equivalent with what we call the dynamic version of Sono's stability conditions. In this place, let us first show that conditions (30) imply the absolute strong stability of the temporary equilibrium point. Let $B = (\sigma_{ij})$; we can then show that the real parts of the characteristic roots of $|A - \lambda I| = 0$ are all situated in the interval set by the maximum and minimum characteristic roots of $|B - \rho I| = 0$.[23] Therefore, where the characteristic roots of the latter equation, which are real, are all negative, the real part of each characteristic root of the former equation takes on a negative value, that is, $R_k < 0$ for all k; and the necessary and sufficient conditions for all ρ_i being negative are (30).

Next we show that (30) implies that the equilibrium is Hicksian. It is obvious that under (30)

$$\Sigma\Sigma\sigma_{ij}x_ix_j = 2\Sigma\Sigma a_{ij}x_ix_j$$

[21] Samuelson, 1948, p. 271, and Lange, 1944, p. 98.

[22] Sono, 1944.

[23] See Hirsch, 1902, and Mathematical Note I below.

is negative definite for all values of x_i except $x_i = 0, i = 1,\ldots,n$. Accordingly, taking x_i such that

$$\begin{aligned}\lambda &= a_{11}x_1 + \ldots + a_{1m}x_m,\\ 0 &= a_{21}x_1 + \ldots + a_{2m}x_m,\\ &\ldots\\ 0 &= a_{m1}x_1 + \ldots + a_{mm}x_m, \ (m \leqq n),\\ x_j &= 0, \ (j = m+1,\ldots,n)\end{aligned}$$

then we get $\lambda x_1 < 0$. Since $\lambda = \Delta x_1$, where

$$\Delta = \begin{vmatrix} a_{11} & \ldots & a_{1m} \\ \cdot & \ldots & \cdot \\ a_{m1} & \ldots & a_{mm} \end{vmatrix} \div \begin{vmatrix} a_{22} & \ldots & a_{2m} \\ \cdot & \ldots & \cdot \\ a_{m2} & \ldots & a_{mm} \end{vmatrix}$$

we obtain $\Delta < 0$ and, hence, (27). In view of the assumptions concerning $F_i^0, i = 1,\ldots,n$, we find that the equilibrium is Hicksian.

7.1.4 *The case of perfect stability*

In parallel to Hicks' definition of perfect stability explained above, we define perfect dynamic stability in the following way. Suppose now some of $\dot{p}_i$ take on the value of 0 (that is, $F_i^0 = 0$ for, say, $i = m+1,\ldots,n$) and $p_{m+1},\ldots,p_n$ are kept at their equilibrium values. The prices which can vary are only $p_1,\ldots,p_m$. In this case, the dynamic stability of equilibrium requires that the real parts of the latent roots of the characteristic equation

$$\begin{vmatrix} a_{11} - \lambda & \ldots & a_{1m} \\ \cdot & \ldots & \cdot \\ a_{m1} & \ldots & a_{mm} - \lambda \end{vmatrix} = 0$$

are all negative. If this is the case, we say that the equilibrium is dynamically stable of order *m*; these stability conditions of order *m* vary, depending on which prices are kept constant. We say that the equilibrium is perfectly dynamically stable of order *m* if it is stable for any order up to *m* for all possible combinations of prices which are kept constant. In the following, we assume the perfect dynamic stability of order *n*; so the market is invariably stable even though any prices lose their flexibility.

Let $|A_m|$ be a principal minor of $|A|$ of order *m*, and $\lambda_i^{(m)}, i = 1,\ldots,m$, the roots of the characteristic equation $|A_m - \lambda I| = 0$. Then, where all real parts of $\lambda_i^{(m)}, i = 1,\ldots,m$, are negative, we have

$$\text{sign}|A_m| = \text{sign}(-1)^m$$

because $|A_m| = \Pi\lambda_i^{(m)}$. This result is valid for all values of $m = 1,\ldots,n$, so that we obtain (27), and hence the equilibrium is Hicksian.

In the above we have seen that a stable, temporary equilibrium is Hicksian in any of the four cases, 1–4. Our argument may be summarized as follows: (i) In case 1 or 2, the equilibrium is Hicksian that is necessary and sufficient for its stability. (ii) The same property is necessary (but not sufficient) for the equilibrium to be stable in the sense of Sono or dynamically perfectly stable.[24]

7.2 *Sono's stability condition*[25]

It has been seen that Hicks' stability condition is valid only under his special assumption on the repercussion of prices. Noticing this, Sono has developed the following theory which is independent of that assumption.

The system of equilibrium prices and interest rates is represented by a point in the n-dimensional space of prices and the rate of interest. Consider a continuous curve Γ through the equilibrium point, and let $p_i = f_i(\tau), i = 1,\ldots,n$, be a parametric representation of the curve; at $\tau = 0$ we have $p_i^0 = f_i(0)$. Concerning the integral along the curve

$$G(\tau) = -\int_0^\tau \Sigma k_i E_i f_i'(\tau) d\tau \ (k_1 = -1, k_i = 1, i = 2,\ldots,n)$$

we have three possibilities: along Γ, $G(\tau)$ takes on, at the equilibrium point, (i) a minimum, (ii) a maximum, or (iii) neither a minimum nor a maximum. In the case of (i), (ii), or (iii), Sono defines the equilibrium point as stable, unstable, or neutral, respectively. (Note that $dG/d\tau = -\Sigma k_i E_i f_i'(0)$ at $\tau = 0$.) This is a classification according to the excess demands for commodities along a given curve Γ. We may make a similar classification along a different curve. Sono calls a given equilibrium point absolutely stable (or unstable) if it is classified as stable (or unstable) for all possible curves Γ; and conditionally stable (or unstable) if it is stable (or unstable) with respect to some Γs but not all Γs. As can be easily shown, the necessary and sufficient conditions for absolute stability are that the principal minors of the determinant $|s_{ij}|$, where $2s_{ij} = k_i E_{ij}^0 + k_j E_{ji}^0$, be alternatively negative and positive.

From Sono's point of view, Hicks' stability condition may be seen as follows. Assuming Hicksian repercussions of order m, we may take a curve which satisfies (20). At the equilibrium point we then have (20) and

[24] However, in the case of the kinds of commodities being less than or equal to three, the Hicksian conditions (25) are necessary and sufficient for the dynamic perfect stability. See Watanabe, 1950, pp. 60–5.

[25] Sono, 1944.

$$\frac{dG}{d\tau} = 0 \text{ and } \frac{d^2G}{d\tau^2} = -k_s \frac{dE_s}{dp_s} f_s'^2$$

Therefore if G takes on a minimum at the equilibrium point along Γ, then (22) holds, so that the equilibrium has Hicksian stability of order $m + 1$, while if G takes on a maximum, we have (21) and, hence, Hicksian instability of order $m + 1$. Thus Hicks may be considered as examining stability of the equilibrium point in terms of $G(\tau)$ which is calculated along a particular curve satisfying the conditions of Hicksian repercussions. Consequently, Hicks' stability is no more than a conditional stability; his perfect stability (or instability) is necessary but not sufficient for Sono's absolute stability (or instability).

In the above theory of stability by Sono, τ is a parameter for expressing the curve Γ, but does not represent time at all. Even if G is minimized at the equilibrium point along some Γ, it does not necessarily mean that forces to restore equilibrium work in the neighbourhood of the point of equilibrium. Moreover, his theory does not explain the path along which prices converge to (or diverge from) their equilibrium values. In other words, the definitions of stability and instability are only useful for classifying equilibrium points according to demands and supplies in their neighbourhoods and have nothing to do with dynamic stability or instability.[26] Therefore, it would be most desirable to dynamize his theory in such a way that its original form is conserved as much as possible.

Taking time t as a parameter, prices $p_i(t)$ determined in section 4 above trace out a curve $\Gamma(t)$ in the n-dimensional space. Consider an integral along Γ

$$G_\Gamma(t) = \int_0^t \Sigma\{p_i(t) - p_i^0\}^2 dt$$

Needless to say, the value of G_Γ depends on Γ. Evidently, we have

$$\frac{dG_\Gamma}{dt} = \Sigma\{p_i(t) - p_i^0\}^2$$

[26] At every point of equilibrium, excess demands are zero. Therefore, all equilibria are uniform while we look only at them. However, in the neighbourhood of each equilibrium point, excess demands for commodities may take on various values, so that we can classify equilibria into types according to the values of excess demands in the neighbourhood. If stability and instability only refer to the types of equilibrium thus classified, they have nothing to do with dynamic stability. Where stability is defined with no reference to time elements, conditions for it may be called static stability conditions. Sono's theory is a typical example of static stability theory while Hicks' is semi-static, because for him the problem of stability was a dynamic problem, although he was unable to deal with it dynamically. [The dynamization of Sono's theory below, which in its essence amounts to the modern analysis of stability by the use of the Liapounoff function has first been formulated by Morishima, 1949.]

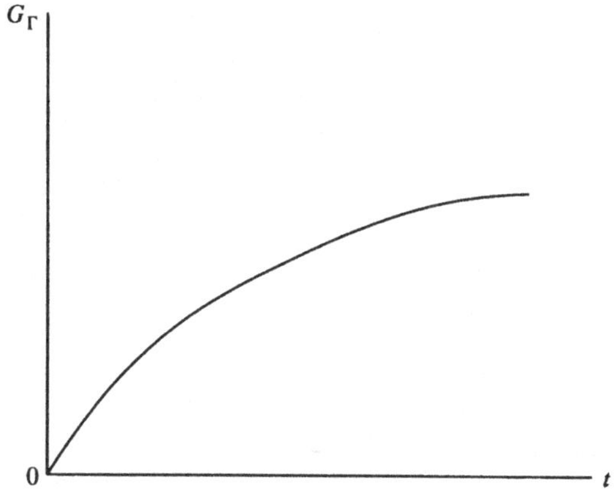

Figure 9

which is always positive unless $p_i(t) = p_i^0$ for all i. As time t is increasing at all times, the economy moves in the direction in which G_Γ is increasing. Therefore, if

$$\frac{d^2 G_\Gamma}{dt^2} < 0 \tag{31}$$

for all t, then we eventually have $\lim_{t\to\infty} \Sigma\{p_i(t) - p_i^0\}^2 = 0$ which implies $\lim_{t\to\infty} p_i(t) = p_i^0, i = 1,\ldots,n$, so that the equilibrium is strongly stable. But the converse is not true; that is, the strong stability does not imply (31) because it is possible that prices are strongly stable while dG_Γ/dt oscillates. Thus (31) is no more than a sufficient condition for strong stability; in the same way $d^2G_\Gamma/dt^2 > 0$ is a sufficient condition for instability.

For a given t a point is determined on the curve Γ and it, in turn, determines the value of G_Γ. Thus G_Γ is a function of t. Where $G_\Gamma(t)$ traces out a curve as figure 9 illustrates, then the equilibrium is strongly stable and prices converge on equilibrium ones as t tends to infinity. Thus G_Γ becomes bigger and bigger, as the economy approaches nearer and nearer to the equilibrium. Thus G_Γ takes on a maximum (or a minimum) at the equilibrium point if strong stability (or instability) prevails. (Figure 10 illustrates the case of instability.)

The curve Γ is determined when initial prices $p_i(0)$ are given, so that a different Γ is obtained for a different set of initial prices. That is, $G_{\Gamma'}$ for Γ' differs from G_Γ for Γ. An equilibrium point which is found to be strongly stable according to G_Γ may be unstable according to $G_{\Gamma'}$. An equilibrium point is said to be conditionally strongly stable if it is strongly stable only

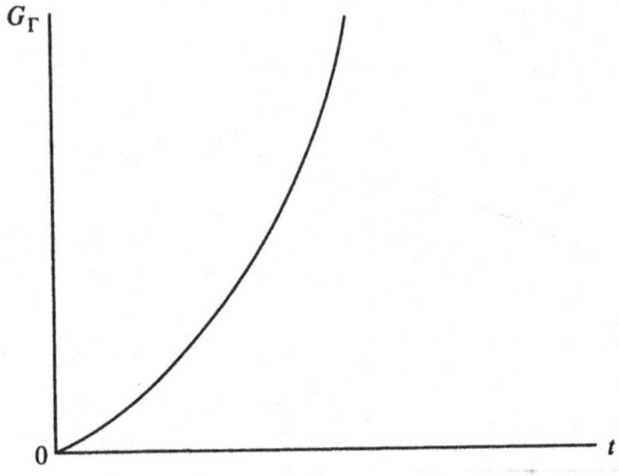

Figure 10

for some particular sets of initial prices and absolutely strongly stable if it is strongly stable for all sets. A sufficient condition for strong stability is given as

$$\frac{d^2G_\Gamma}{dt^2} = 2\Sigma\dot{p}_i\{p_i(t) - p_i^0\}$$

$$= \Sigma\Sigma(a_{ij} + a_{ji})\{p_i(t) - p_i^0\}\{p_j(t) - p_j^0\} < 0$$

This is obtained irrespective of initial prices if (30) prevails, so that (30) gives a sufficient condition for absolute strong stability. We have seen in subsection 7.1.3 above that, where (30) prevails, all the characteristic roots have negative real parts. Also, even though some F_i^0's become 0, (30) implies strong stability, provided that corresponding prices p_i are kept at their equilibrium values. In other words, (30) is a sufficient condition for perfect stability in the sense defined in subsection 7.1.4 above. Moreover, where $-F_1^0 = F_2^0 = \ldots = F_n^0 > 0$, (30) is reduced to Sono's own conditions for absolute stability.

An idea similar to Sono's has been developed by Lange.[27] He considers a functional

$$P(p_1(t), p_2(t), \ldots, p_n(t))$$

such that

$$\dot{p}_i(t) = \frac{\partial P}{\partial p_i(t)}$$

and calls it the adjustment potential. If P exists, prices and the rate of

[27] Lange, 1944, pp. 97–9.

interest change in the direction in which P increases. This is because, if P increases when p_i increases, then we have $\dot{p}_i > 0$, so that the price of good i (or the rate of interest in the case of $i = 1$) will rise; or conversely, if P decreases when p_i increases, then $\dot{p}_i < 0$, and, therefore, p_i decreases; hence, in any case, P increases. Consequently, we can define whether a point of equilibrium is stable or unstable according to whether P is maximized or minimized at that point. Lange's P plays the same role as Sono's G_Γ. However, P does not necessarily exist and may not be effective as a criterion for stability unless the above-mentioned Samuelson–Lange conditions $a_{ij} = a_{ji}, i, j = 1, \ldots, n$ are fulfilled. It is thus confirmed that Sono's theory, especially its dynamically reformulated version, is constructed in a very skillful and effectual way.

8 Stability of the canonical system — proportional changes in prices

We have so far been concerned with a system involving n variables. In this section we examine under what conditions an n-variable system can be reduced to a system with fewer variables. This problem is closely related to the problem of determining circumstances where macroeconomic theory is validated.[28]

[28] The problem of deriving macrotheory from microtheory is called the aggregation problem. It deals with the conditions under which many social demand and supply functions for individual commodities can be aggregated into a smaller number of aggregated social demand and supply functions. There are three approaches. The first deals firstly with how to aggregate individual production functions containing many variables, $f(x_1, \ldots, x_n) = 0$ and individual utility functions, $u = u(x_1, \ldots, x_n)$ into individual production functions, $F(X_1, X_2) = 0$, and individual utility functions, $U = U(X_1, X_2)$, containing a few variables. Using these production and utility functions we derive individual demand and supply functions of a few variables and then we aggregate them into social demand and supply functions. An example of this approach is Hicks' theory of groups of commodities. For the aggregation of individual production or utility functions with many variables into those with a few variables, the original individual production or utility function must satisfy the condition of separability. That is to say, to aggregate $x_1, \ldots, x_m$ into X_1 and $x_{m+1}, \ldots, x_n$ into X_2 those commodities in the first group must be separable from those in the second group, and *vice-versa* (see, for example, Okamoto and Morishima, 1950). (For the definition of separability see Sono, 1943.) According to the second approach, individual production functions or utility functions with many variables are at once aggregated into social production or utility functions with a few variables, from which social demand and supply functions are derived (Klein, 1946). The case where this procedure is possible is also the case of individual production or utility functions satisfying the conditions of separability (Nataf, 1948, Okamoto and Morishima, 1950). The third approach does not aggregate production and utility functions at all; it aggregates only social demand and supply functions. In this case the conditions for aggregation are the proportionality of prices. In the following we adopt the third approach originating from Lange, 1944 and being revised by Yokoyama, 1950.

Let us assume that in a given n-variable system

$$\dot{p}_i = \sum_1^n a_{ij}(p_j - p_j^0) \; i = 1,\ldots,n \tag{32}$$

As long as $n - m + 1$ prices, $p_m,\ldots,p_n$ are proportional to $p_m^0,\ldots,p_n^0$, their speeds of adjustment $\dot{p}_m,\ldots,\dot{p}_n$ are also proportional to $p_m^0,\ldots,p_n^0$, irrespective of the values of the other prices. Then, coefficients a_{ij} must satisfy

$$\sum_m^n a_{kj}\pi_j = \pi_k\left(\sum_m^n a_{mj}\pi_j\right) \tag{33}$$

$$a_{kh} = \pi_k a_{mh}, \; k = m,\ldots,n; \; h = 1,\ldots,m-1$$

where $\pi_k = p_k^0/p_m^0, k = m,\ldots,n$.

In the system (32) which satisfies (33), if initial values of prices $p_m,\ldots,p_n$ are proportional to $p_m^0,\ldots,p_n^0$, i.e.

$$p_m(0): \ldots : p_n(0) = p_m^0: \ldots : p_n^0 \tag{34}$$

then $p_m(t),\ldots,p_n(t)$ are proportional to $p_m^0,\ldots,p_n^0$, for all values of t, regardless of the values of the other prices. In that case, solutions $p_i(t), i,\ldots,m$, to (32) are equivalent to solutions to an m-variable system

$$\dot{p}_i = \sum_1^m b_{ij}(p_j - p_j^0) \; i = 1,\ldots,m \tag{35}$$

where $b_{im} = \sum_m^n a_{ij}\pi_j, b_{ij} = a_{ij}, i = 1,2,\ldots,m; j = 1,2,\ldots,m-1$. It can also be shown that $p_k(t), k = m,\ldots,n$, obtained from (32) are identical with $p_m(t)$ from (35) multiplied by π_k. Thus, particular solutions to (32) which satisfy (34) are equivalent to the general solutions to (35), whereas the general solutions to the former are not identical to those of the latter. Therefore, provided (34) is satisfied, the stability–instability problem in system (32) can be reduced to the same problem in (35).

In short, where in an n-variable system (32) with coefficients satisfying conditions (33), initial conditions are set so that (34) is fulfilled, we may construct an m-variable system by retaining one of the $n - m + 1$ markets where prices change proportionally and eliminating the other $n - m$ markets. The stability property of the equilibrium point remains invariant when reducing variables from n to m.

In the case of several groups of prices which vary proportionately being present, we may take one price from each group as its representative and construct a system consisting of these representatives and other prices which do not change proportionately. In this way, we may minimize the number of variables. The system with the smallest number of variables is called the canonical system of the original system from which it is derived. *Stability or instability of the temporary equilibrium is determined by the sign of the real parts of the characteristic roots of the canonical system; we need not bother about the original system which contains a tremendous number of variables.*

9 An example of the canonical system

Here, let us provide an example of the canonical system. First, it is evident that we may put the worker's budget equation

$$x_{0,-1} + (1 + r_{-1})x_{1,-1} = x_{00} + x_{10} + \Sigma p_i x_{i0}$$

in the form

$$F^S = C + (x_{00} - \bar{x}) + x_{10} \tag{36}$$

where F^S represents the worker's wage income and C his expenditure on consumption goods. If we denote the dividend (or entrepreneurial profit) which a capitalist (or an entrepreneur) receives by R_0, then this household's budget equation may be written as

$$R_0 = C + (x_{00} - \bar{x}) + x_{10} \tag{37}$$

where C, of course, stands for his consumption. On the other hand, for a firm we have

$$x_{00} - \bar{x} = -x_{10} - \Sigma p_i x_{i0} - R_0 \tag{9}$$

where $-\Sigma p_i x_{i0}$ represents the amount of money A which the firm obtains during the current week by selling its finished products to consumers or other firms *minus* its payment to other firms, A_1, for the purchase of their products *minus* its wage payment F^D. Then (9) may be put in the form

$$A - A_1 - F^D = (x_{00} - \bar{x}) + x_{10} + R_0 \tag{38}$$

Evidently, A and A_1 are the sums received or spent in the current week, respectively, but they are neither the value of output nor the value of input. In order to determine output or input we must take account of how the stock of goods has changed during the week. By (6) in chapter 2, we have for each good

output = the quantity supplied + stock in the current week
– stock in the previous week

and

input = the quantity demanded + stock in the previous week
– stock in the current week

Therefore, we have for all goods

> the value of output – the value of input ≡ total receipts from sales – total amounts of goods purchased + the value of stocks in the current week – the value of stocks in the previous week.[29]

In this expression, the left-hand side represents the net output Y of the firm, and the first two terms on the right-hand side are written as A and A_1, respectively. The value of stocks in the current week, or more precisely, the value, at the end of the week, of the firm's capital equipment which includes both its stocks of unfinished goods or working capital and its stocks of finished goods, is estimated at G, while the firm's stock (or capital equipment) at the end of the last week would be worth G_0 at the end of the current week. Then, from the above expression we obtain

$$A - A_1 = Y + G_0 - G$$

Bearing this in mind, (38) can be rewritten as

$$Y - F^D = I + (x_{00} - \bar{x}) + x_{10} + R_0 \tag{39}$$

where I represents investment, that is, the increment in the value of the stocks, $G - G_0$. Apart from the cost of maintenance of stocks, the left-hand side of (39) is identical with the profit or income of the firm defined by Keynes.[30]

In the economy as a whole, the sum of (36), (37), and (39) holds. By omitting Σ, we write Y, C, I, etc. for $\Sigma Y, \Sigma C, \Sigma I$, etc., respectively. M, L, and E represent the existing quantity of money, the cash balances which households and firms want to hold in the present week, and the excess demand for securities, respectively. Then, for the entirety of the society the identity held is

$$Y + (F^S - F^D) = C + I + (L - M) + E \tag{40}$$

In this expression the sum of $(1 + r_{-1})x_{1,-1}$ does not appear, because a temporary equilibrium was established and, hence, there was no excess demand for securities in the previous week. Whether the economy is in the state of temporary equilibrium or not, (40) is always satisfied; it is no more than a restatement of Walras' law.

Let us now reconsider how prices and the interest rate are determined. According to the loanable fund theory, as we have so far assumed, the rate of interest is lowered or raised according to whether the excess demand for

[29] More exactly, we mean by the value of stocks in the previous week the stocks of commodities at the end of the previous week evaluated at their prices in the present week.

[30] Keynes, 1936, pp. 52–5.

securities is positive or negative. On the other hand, according to the liquidity preference theory which considers that the rate of interest is regulated by the demand and supply of money, the rate of interest is raised (or lowered) when the total desired cash balances exceed (or fall short of) the existing quantity of money, and it is kept constant while the money market is in equilibrium. The adjustment function of the rate of interest may then be given as

$$\dot{r} = F(L - M);\ F(0) = 0, F'(0) > 0 \tag{41}$$

Assuming (41), by the same procedure as before, we can construct a new n-variable system which determines prices and the rate of interest. In this system securities do not appear explicitly. This system is not equivalent to our previous one in which the speed of adjustment of the rate of interest depends on the excess demand for securities, with no explicit presence of money. In the following we assume the new system having the adjustment equation (41) for the rate of interest.

Now let different kinds of labour be labelled as $2,\ldots,m-1$, and consumption and capital goods as $m,\ldots,n$. For the latter we have

$$\dot{p}_i = F_i(E_i) = F_i^0 E_i,\ i = m,\ldots,n$$

Assume now that prices of consumption and capital goods fluctuate proportionately, that is

$$p_i(t) = \pi_i p_m(t),\ i = m+1,\ldots,n$$

Taking the constants k_i so as to satisfy $\sum_m^n k_i\pi_i = 1$ and condition (42) below, we define the price index $P(t)$ as

$$P(t) = \sum_m^n k_i p_i(t)$$

We then easily find

$$P(t) = \sum_m^n k_i \pi_i p_m(t) = p_m(t)$$

On the other hand, we have $\dot{P} = H^0\left(\sum_m^n \pi_i E_i\right)$

where

$$\frac{F_m^0 k_m}{\pi_m} = \ldots = \frac{F_n^0 k_n}{\pi_n} = H^0 \tag{42}$$

We can easily show that

$$P\left(\sum_{m}^{n} \pi_i E_i\right) = PX = C + I - Y$$

Therefore, defining C', I', and Y' as $C = PC'$, $I = PI'$, and $Y = PY'$, respectively, we finally obtain

$$\dot{P} = H(C' + I' - Y') = H(X) \tag{43}$$

As we have shown in the previous section, in the n-variable system with $p_m, \ldots, p_n$ changing proportionately, we need not be concerned with all the n variables; those prices which change proportionately can be represented by one of them, p_m. As $P(t) = p_m(t)$, P is the representative of $p_m, \ldots, p_n$. Similarly, by assuming a proportional change in wages for heterogeneous labour $2, \ldots, m-1$, we have the adjustment function for the representative wage rate, or the wage unit in Keynes' terminology; that is

$$\dot{W} = G(N) \tag{44}$$

where N stands for the aggregate excess demand for employment of all kinds of labour, measured in wage units.

Under the assumptions of proportional changes in prices and in wage rates we may reduce the original n differential equations to three equations, (41), (43), and (44). In the state of temporary equilibrium, $E_i = 0, i = 0, 1, \ldots, n$, we have

$$L(P, W, r) = M,\ E(P, W, r) = 0,\ N(P, W, r) = 0,$$
$$Y'(P, W, r) = C'(P, W, r) + I'(P, W, r), \text{ or } X(P, W, r) = 0$$

Expanding (41), (43), and (44) in the Taylor series at the point of temporary equilibrium, P^0, W^0, r^0, we may solve these differential equations by the usual method and obtain solutions $P(t), W(t), r(t)$. The condition for stability is that the real parts of the latent roots of the characteristic equation

$$\begin{vmatrix} F^0L_r - \lambda & F^0L_w & F^0L_p \\ G^0N_r & G^0N_w - \lambda & G^0N_p \\ H^0X_r & H^0X_w & H^0X_p - \lambda \end{vmatrix} = 0$$

be all negative, where L_r, X_p, etc. are the values of the respective partial derivatives evaluated at the point of temporary equilibrium (P^0, W^0, r^0).

Now, as is well known, Keynes assumes the liquidity preference theory of interest and asserts that the level of national income Y is determined by $Y' = C' + I'$, given the level of P corresponding to this Y'. On the other hand, in pre-Keynesian theories which assume the quantity theory of money, the price level is determined by $L = M$ and the rate of interest by $S = I$, where $S = Y - C$ is savings. Thus the assertion of causal relationships which are the opposite of those maintained by the traditional theories is considered as the most important feature of Keynes' theory.

In the above canonical system, the liquidity preference theory is adopted and $\dot{r}$ is a function of $L - M$; the condition which makes $\dot{r}$ zero is $L = M$. The condition which makes the price level P stationary is $Y' = C' + I'$ or $X' = 0$.[31] Our example of the canonical system is a very Keynesian one.

10 Structural stability

In this section we examine how a change in the price flexibility of a good or in its degree of substitution will affect the stability of the equilibrium.

First, let us define price flexibility. If a unit of excess demand for good i induces a change in p_i, we say that p_i is flexible. The degree of flexibility of p_i is defined as the speed of price change per unit of excess demand:

$$\dot{p} = F_i(1) = F_i^0$$

It usually takes on a positive value, but in some special cases it may be 0 or negative. Where the degree of flexibility is 0, we say that p_i is inflexible or rigid; where it is negative, we say that p_i is negatively flexible.[32] According to the loanable fund theory of interest, the speed of adjustment of the rate of interest is a function of the excess demand for securities and its degree of flexibility is given by

$$\dot{r} = F_1(1) = F_1^0$$

which is usually negative.

Secondly, the degree of substitution of a good is defined as follows. Evidently the partial derivative

$$\frac{\partial E_i}{\partial p_j} = E_{ij}$$

gives the effect of a change in the price of good j on the excess demand for another good i. If, as a result of an increase in the price of good j alone, either an increase in the demand for good i or a decrease in its supply (or both) comes about and, hence, the excess demand for good i is increased, then good i is said to be a substitute for good j. If the excess demand for good i remains unchanged in spite of a rise in the price of good j, good i is

[31] This may be expressed as $S' = I'$ because $S' = Y' - C'$.

[32] Lange, 1944, p. 95.

independent of j,[1] while they are complementary to each other if a rise in the price of good j diminishes the excess demand for good i. Therefore, according to

$$E_{ij} >, =, < 0$$

good i is substitutive for, independent of, or complementary to good j. We measure the degree of substitution of good i for good j by the magnitude of E_{ij}.[33]

As has been repeatedly stated, the stability of the system is determined by the signs of the real parts of the characteristic roots λ. The values of λ are continuous functions of all a_{ij} defined as

$$a_{ij} = F_i^0 E_{ij}^0$$

The stability of the system, therefore, depends on price flexibilities and degrees of substitution of all goods. Then how does it depend on them? This will be examined below for a few interesting cases.

(I) Let us adopt the liquidity theory of interest, so that $\dot{r} = F(E_0)$. In this case if we assume that all commodities, including money but excluding securities, are substitutive for each other, we have $E_{ii}^0 < 0$, $E_{ij}^0 > 0$, so that Metzler's conditions (26) are satisfied. The necessary and sufficient condition for the system to be stable is, in this case, that the matrix (E_{ij}^0) is Hicksian.[34] How does an increase in the degree of substitution of a good affect the stability in such a system?

We can easily show

$$\frac{\partial \Delta_2}{\partial E_{ij}^0} = -E_{ji}^0 \tag{45}$$

where

$$\Delta_2 = \begin{vmatrix} E_{ii}^0 & E_{ij}^0 \\ E_{ji}^0 & E_{jj}^0 \end{vmatrix}$$

which is positive because the matrix (E_{ij}^0) is Hicksian. Because $E_{ji}^0 > 0$, (45) must be negative. Thus an increase in E_{ij}^0 gives rise to a decrease in Δ_2. If E_{ij}^0 becomes sufficiently large, Δ_2 will at last take on a negative value and the

[33] These definitions of substitution and complementarity are different from the usual ones which are given in terms of the sign of the substitution term of the Slutsky equation. In fact, we classify goods by the total effect E_{ij}^0 which includes not only the income effect but also the intratemporal substitution effects.

[34] Elements E_{ij}^0 of the matrix include E_{0j}^0 but *not* E_{1j}^0.

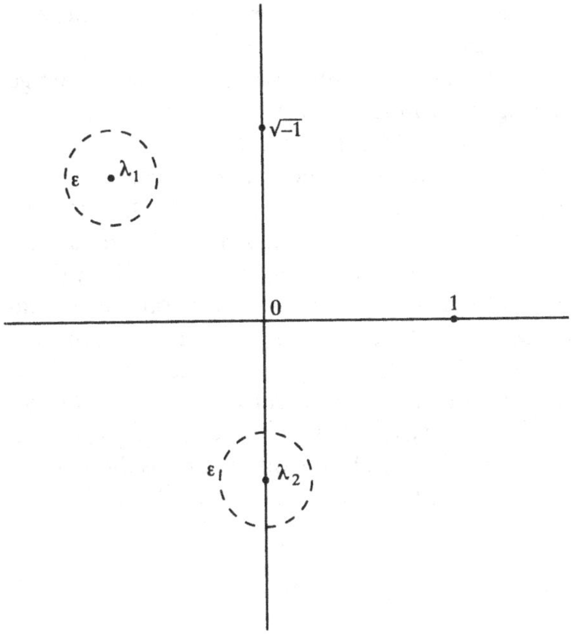

Figure 11

matrix (E_{ij}^0) ceases to be Hicksian. We must, therefore, conclude that *the system in which all commodities (excluding securities) are substitutive for each other will be unstable if the degrees of substitution of commodities are too large.*

Where the rate of interest is determined by $\dot{r} = F_1(E_1)$ so that the loanable fund theory holds, Metzler's conditions (26) are equivalent to $E_{ii}^0 < 0, E_{ij}^0 > 0, i = 2,\ldots,n, j = 1,\ldots,n$, and $E_{11}^0 > 0, E_{1j}^0 < 0, j = 2,\ldots,n$. Again the equilibrium is stable if and only if (E_{ij}^0) is Hicksian;[35] so an increase in $E_{ij}^0 (i \neq 1)$ or a decrease in E_{1j}^0 will impair the stability of the system and will finally make it unstable.

(II) The characteristic roots λ's are represented as points on the Gauss plane or the complex plane having the horizontal and the vertical coordinates as the real and the unreal axes, respectively. Figure 11 exemplifies them. We may then state: (i) that, if all characteristic roots are located on the left-hand side of the vertical coordinate, the system is absolutely stable, (ii) that, if they are all on the right-hand side, it is absolutely unstable, (iii) that, if some of them are on the left and others on the right, it is conditionally stable, and, finally, (iv) that, if some of the characteristic roots are on the vertical

[35] The elements include E_{1j}^0 but not E_{0j}^0.

coordinate and the rest on the left-hand side of it, then the system is stable in the sense of Liapounoff, though not strongly stable.

The values of the λs are continuous functions of a_{ij}, so that the λs change within their very small neighbourhoods, as long as a change in a_{ij} is sufficiently small. Therefore, if the system is absolutely strongly stable (or strongly unstable) before the change in a_{ij}, then after the change the λs remain on the left (or right) side of the vertical coordinate and, hence, the system is still absolutely strongly stable (or unstable). In such a case no stable system turns into an unstable one unless a_{ij} varies significantly. On the other hand, in the case of the system having some λs on the vertical coordinate and thus being stable in Liapounoff's sense, those λs can each shift to the right-hand side of the coordinate if a_{ij} varies infinitesimally. In other words, for a small change in a_{ij}, the system can easily turn into an unstable one. Such a kind of stability which is easily destroyed by a small variation in a_{ij} is called critical stability. The condition for it is the same as the condition for Liapounoff stability, that is

$$\text{some } R_k = 0 \text{ and other } R_k < 0$$

An obvious, sufficient condition for critical stability is that

$$|A| = 0$$

Consequently, (i) when some of $F_i^0 (i = 1, \ldots, n)$ are zero, the stability is critical, that is to say, a Liapounoff stable system in which some prices are inflexible or rigid may easily become unstable when one of the price flexibilities changes from zero to a positive magnitude, however small it may be. (ii) We obtain $|A| = 0$, when the determinant $|E_{ij}^0|$ vanishes. Therefore if there is another temporary equilibrium point in an infinitesimally small neighbourhood of a given temporary equilibrium point $(r^0, p_2^0, \ldots, p_n^0)$, i.e., the latter is a neutral equilibrium point of order n, then its stability is critical, and the system is said to be structurally unstable.

(III) Let us explain the structural stability of the system in more detail. We classify the types of fluctuations in a groping price according to the fluctuation factors which the fundamental equation of fluctuations of that price contains. As we have seen, there are five types of fluctuation factors:

(i) $e^{\lambda t}$, where λ is a real number;
(ii) $e^{Rt} \cos(It + \omega)$, where λ is a complex number and R its real part;
(iii) t^μ or $t^\mu \cos(It + \omega_\mu)$, where λ is 0 or an imaginary number; μ is a rational number such that $0 \leq \mu \leq \bar{\mu} - 1$, where $\bar{\mu}$ is the largest of the indices of simple elementary divisors corresponding to λ;
(iv) $t^\mu e^{\lambda t}$, where λ is a real number and $1 \leq \mu \leq \bar{\mu} - 1$;
(v) $t^\mu e^{Rt} \cos(It + \omega_\mu)$, where λ is a complex number and $1 \leq \mu \leq \bar{\mu} - 1$.

Fluctuations in prices which are caused by fluctuation factors (i) or (ii) are called price fluctuations of the first kind, those by (iii) of the second kind, and those by (iv) or (v) of the third kind. When the fundamental equation contains fluctuation factors (iv) or (v) as well as factors (iii), fluctuations of a mixture of the second and the third kinds will take place.

The system which will always produce fluctuations in prices of the first kind, regardless of the initial conditions, is called a system of the first type. Those in which fluctuations in prices of the second or third kind may occur, depending on the initial conditions, are said to be of the second or the third type, respectively. A mixture of the second and the third types is a system where some sets of initial prices may produce fluctuations in prices of a mixture of the second and third kinds. Because the values of the characteristic roots λ depend on the coefficients of the characteristic equation, the type of system is determined by the degrees of substitution of goods and the price flexibilities.

Provided with these classifications, let us now define the structural stability of the system in the following way. If a small variation in the degree of substitution or the price flexibility of a good changes the type of system, then the system is said to be structurally unstable, whilst a system whose type remains invariant with respect to a small change in a_{ij} is structurally stable. Given these definitions, we can at once specify the cases in which the system is structurally stable. First, as has been seen in (II), the λ which is 0 or purely imaginary can easily become a real or complex number when a_{ij} varies slightly. Thus, the system of the second type is obviously structurally unstable. Secondly, the λ which is a multiple root will be split into a number of simple roots when a_{ij} varies. For example, the double root which is real will be split by a change in a_{ij} into either two different real roots λ_1 and λ_2 or two conjugate complex roots $a + ib$ and $a - ib$. Therefore, after the change, the fundamental equations of price change do not contain the fluctuation factors of the kind (iv) or (v), so that the system is no longer of the third type. Thus the system of the third type is structurally unstable. It is evident that the mixture of the second and third types is also structurally unstable.

Finally, we consider systems of the first type. In the case of all λs being simple, their simplicity is not affected by a sufficiently small change in a_{ij}, so that after the change the fundamental equations contain the fluctuation factors (i) and (ii) only and, hence, the system remains one of the first type. It is structurally stable. On the other hand, in the case where some of the λ's are double roots with the indices of simple elementary divisors being 1, the indices may easily be greater than 1 when a_{ij} changes; therefore the fluctuation factors of the third kind may appear in the fundamental equations of price change and the system is structurally unstable.

From the above analysis we may conclude that the necessary and sufficient condition for structural stability is that *none of the characteristic roots of the system is zero or an imaginary number and all of them are simple.*

(IV) A detailed investigation is now made for a two-variable system. There are the following nine possibilities concerning the roots λ_1 and λ_2:

(1) both λ_1 and λ_2 are real and negative;
(2) they are real and positive;
(3) they are real and different in sign;
(4) they are complex numbers and their real parts are negative;
(5) they are complex numbers and their real parts are positive;
(6) they are imaginary numbers;
(7) both of them are zero;
(8) either of them is zero, while the other is negative;
(9) either of them is zero, while the other is positive.

The equilibrium is absolutely strongly stable in cases (1) and (4), absolutely unstable in (2) and (5), and absolutely stable in the sense of Liapounoff in (6) to (8), though cases (6) to (9) are usually referred to as being neutral. In case (9) the equilibrium is only conditionally stable in the sense of Liapounoff; instability movements will take place for some initial positions, whilst in case (3) the equilibrium point is conditionally stable–unstable in the strong sense and is a saddle point. An object placed at a point on the surface of a saddle eventually approaches or diverges from the equilibrium point on the saddle (i.e., the saddle point), depending on where it is put initially.

There are two cases of absolute strong stability (or instability); they are cases (1) and (4) (or (2) and (5)). In these two cases, prices fluctuate in completely different ways. Let the origin of the (p_1, p_2)-plane be the point of equilibrium and show on the plane how prices move. Possible paths in cases (1) and (4) are illustrated in figures 12a and b, respectively. (The directions of the paths, or of the arrows, in the unstable cases (2) and (5) are opposite to those of (1) and (4) respectively.)

In case (1) we call the equilibrium point a stable node or a stable point of the first kind, and in case (4) a stable focus or a stable point of the second kind. We obtain an unstable node or focus in the case of (2) or (5) respectively.

There are the following relationships between the values of the characteristic roots (i.e., the types of the equilibrium point) and the coefficients of the system. Putting

$$\alpha = -(a_{11} + a_{22}),\ \beta = \begin{vmatrix} a_{11} & a_{12} \\ a_{21} & a_{22} \end{vmatrix}$$

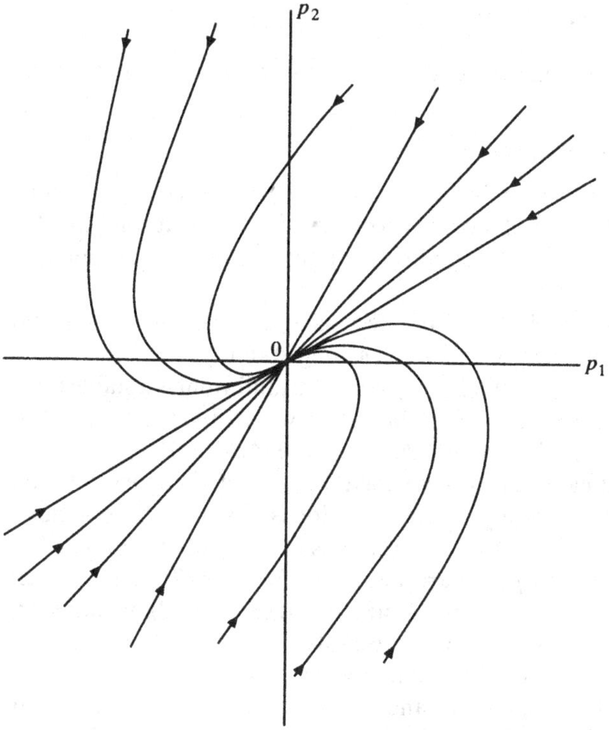

(a)

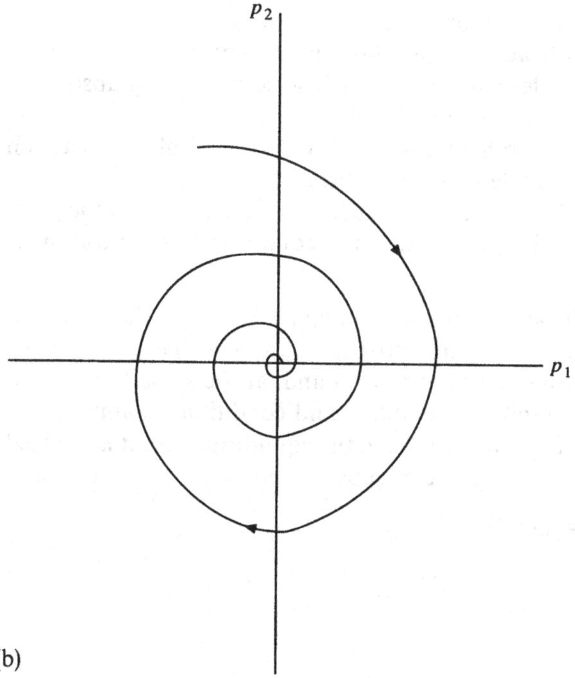

(b)

Figure 12

the characteristic equation can be written as $\lambda^2 + \alpha\lambda + \beta = 0$. Solving, we have the relationships

$$\lambda_1 + \lambda_2 = -\alpha, \ \lambda_1\lambda_2 = \beta$$

(a) If $\beta < 0$, λ_1 and λ_2 are real and opposite in sign. The converse of this proposition is also true. Hence the necessary and sufficient condition for case (3) (i.e., the case of the equilibrium point being a saddle point) is $\beta < 0$.

(b) Conditions $\alpha > 0$ and $\beta > 0$ are necessary for case (1) or (4) and necessary and sufficient for absolute strong stability.

Where $\delta = \alpha^2 - 4\beta \geqq 0$, λ is real, and the equilibrium is a stable node so that we have case (1). On the other hand, where $\delta < 0$, λ is complex, we obtain the case of a stable focus, i.e., case (4).

In the critical case of $\delta = 0$, we have $\lambda_1 = \lambda_2$, and the equilibrium which is a node can easily change to a focus when we have a small change in a_{ij}. That is to say, the system is structurally unstable.

(c) Conditions $\alpha < 0$ and $\beta > 0$ are necessary for case (2) or (5). When $\delta \geqq 0$, the equilibrium is an unstable node (i.e., case (2)), while when $\delta < 0$, it is an unstable focus (i.e., case (5)).

The system is structurally unstable when $\delta = 0$.

(d) When $\alpha = 0$ and $\beta > 0$, both λ_1 and λ_2 are imaginary numbers so that we have case (6). Paths of prices do not trace out spirals, as are shown in figure 12, but ellipses. This is a critical case between stable and unstable foci, and the equilibrium point is a neutral focus.

(e) For $\alpha > 0$ and $\beta = 0$ we have case (8). This is a critical case between stable-node and saddle-point equilibria. The equilibrium is absolutely stable in the sense of Liapounoff.

(f) For $\alpha < 0$ and $\beta = 0$ we have case (9). This is a critical case between unstable-node and saddle-point equilibria.

(g) For $\alpha = 0$ and $\beta = 0$ we have case (7). Prices remain forever at the place where they are initially put, so that the equilibrium is neutral in its perfect sense.

We may summarize the above argument in figure 13. When the combination of the coefficients of the characteristic equation (α, β) is given on the thick lines, the equilibrium point is neutral and, at the same time, it is a critical point between stability, instability, and conditional stability.

Next, let us investigate how the type of the equilibrium point is affected when a price flexibility or a degree of substitution of a good changes.

(i) First, when E_{j1}^0 changes, we have

$$\frac{\partial \alpha}{\partial E_{11}^0} = -F_1^0; \ \frac{\partial \beta}{\partial E_{11}^0} = F_1^0 F_2^0 E_{22}^0$$

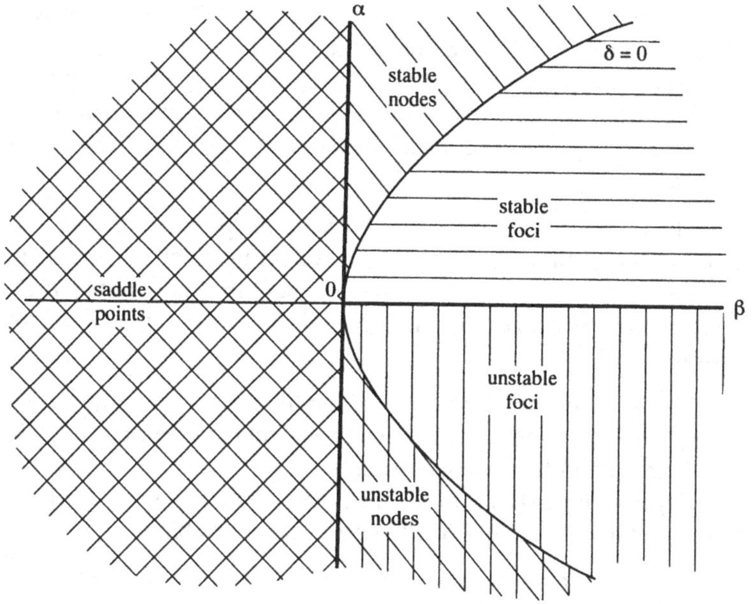

Figure 13

On the assumption that prices are flexible, i.e., $F_i^0 > 0, i = 1, 2$, we obtain $\frac{\partial \alpha}{\partial E_{11}^0} < 0$. This means that if the value of E_{11}^0 becomes larger, i.e., the excess demand curve of good 1 becomes less downwards or more upwards sloping, the equilibrium will be less stable or even unstable. As E_{11}^0 goes on increasing, the equilibrium which was stable before the change eventually becomes a saddle point, provided $E_{22}^0 < 0$, and an unstable focus or node, provided $E_{22}^0 \geqq 0$. In any case, *an excess demand curve which is sufficiently upwards sloping is a destabilizer of the system.*

(ii) Next consider the case where the degree of substitution of good 1 for good 2, E_{12}^0, increases. We then have

$$\frac{\partial \alpha}{\partial E_{12}^0} = 0; \quad \frac{\partial \beta}{\partial E_{12}^0} = -F_1^0 F_2^0 E_{21}^0$$

Assuming that prices are flexible, we find that the sign of E_{21}^0 determines the sign of $\partial \beta / \partial E_{12}^0$. An increase (or a decrease) in E_{12}^0 diminishes the value of β, provided $E_{21}^0 > 0$ (or < 0). Therefore, where the two goods, 1 and 2, are very substitutive (i.e., $E_{21}^0 > 0$ and E_{12}^0 takes on a very large positive value), the system at last becomes conditionally stable; the same result is obtained where they are very complementary (i.e., $E_{21}^0 < 0$ and E_{12}^0 takes on a negative value which is large in the absolute value). (If the system was unstable before the change, it eventually becomes conditionally stable as the two goods are highly substitutive or complementary.) We may thus conclude that *a high degree of substitution or complementarity between the two goods makes the system conditionally stable and, therefore, cannot be an absolute stabilizer.*

(iii) Finally, let us examine relationships between the price flexibilities and the stability of the equilibrium. Consider a system in which all prices are positively flexible, $F_i^0 > 0, i = 1, 2$. Suppose its equilibrium is stable. If F_1^0 goes on declining in such an economy, its equilibrium will be successively of the following types:

(a) where $E_{22}^0 < 0$, first stable, then critical and finally conditionally stable;
(b) where $E_{22}^0 = 0$, first stable, then perfectly neutral in the sense of both λ_1 and λ_2 being 0 and finally conditionally stable;
(c) where $E_{22}^0 > 0$, first stable focal, then neutral focal, unstable focal, unstable nodal, critical, and finally conditionally stable.

In the case of (a), (b), or (c), we have a critical equilibrium when the price of good 1 is rigid, i.e., $F_1^0 = 0$, and a conditionally stable one when it is negatively flexible, i.e., $F_1^0 < 0$. The price of good 1 is positively flexible before the economy reaches a critical position.[36]

[36] Critical states have been discussed by Furuya, 1949. Also, see A. A. Andronow and C. E. Chaikin, 1949, pp. 192–3 with respect to the structural stability of the canonical system.

4 Stability conditions for a temporary equilibrium: the non-linear case

1 Price movements in the linear and non-linear systems

We have so far discussed the determination of equilibrium prices and their stability in a system where the excess demand functions are assumed to be linear. But the adjustment functions of the rate of interest and prices

$$\dot{r} = F_1(E_1), \dot{p}_i = F_i(E_i)$$

which prevail in the actual world are not necessarily linear. In order to analyse a system consisting of non-linear excess demand functions, we may construct, as an approximation to it, a system of linear functions which is obtained by neglecting the higher-order terms of the original functions and use the linear theory of stability developed in the previous chapter. However, conclusions derived in this way are often wrong and may mislead us seriously, as will be explained below.[1]

Suppose an equilibrium point p^0 of a non-linear system is a stable point in the sense of Liapounoff. When the initial point of groping prices $p(0)$ is given sufficiently near to p^0, those terms of the adjustment functions which are of higher than first order are infinitesimals of higher order than their linear terms, so that adjustment speeds of prices are determined by the values of the linear terms of the respective functions. Since p^0 is a Liapounoff-stable point of equilibrium, prices are always confined within its ε neighbourhood which is a sphere of price movements where higher-order terms are infinitesimals of higher order. We may, therefore, always neglect higher-order terms of the excess demand functions and safely use the results of the linear system. Thus, *when movements of prices are confined to a sufficiently small neighbourhood of a Liapounoff stable equilibrium point, prices will fluctuate in the same way as they do in the same region in the system consisting of the linearized adjustment functions.*

On the other hand, if the equilibrium is not stable in the sense of

[1] In writing this chapter, I have greatly benefited by A. A. Andronow and Chaikin, 1949.

Liapounoff, a movement of prices which has started from a point in a neighbourhood of the equilibrium point where higher-order terms are negligible will sooner or later reach a point where they are not negligible. Fluctuations in prices can no longer be described approximately by the fundamental equations of price change for the linear system. In fact, in the linear system which is unstable, prices tend to infinity as time t tends to infinity, while in the non-linear system, as will be seen below, prices do not necessarily become infinite. This is because the higher-order terms of the adjustment functions work in such a way that they restrain the speeds of price adjustments.

Moreover we must remember the following fact. Even if the equilibrium is Liapounoff stable, prices will take on values at which the higher-order terms are not negligible, unless initial prices have been set very close to the equilibrium prices and, hence, we have to take the effects of the higher-order terms upon the movement of prices into account. Thus initial prices given at a point which is far from a Liapounoff stable equilibrium point may generate a movement which is entirely different from the corresponding one in the linear system. Suppose an equilibrium point p^0 is absolutely strongly stable. In the case of a linear system, prices will converge to p^0 for any initial price set given in the space of prices and the rate of interest, while in the case of a non-linear system we have the convergence of prices to p^0 for those initial price sets which are given sufficiently near to p^0; otherwise they may diverge to infinity or converge to another equilibrium point p^1.

We should not, therefore, blindly apply the stability results for a linear system to the corresponding non-linear system. In this chapter we investigate non-linear systems in order to make our analysis of the determination of prices more satisfactory.

2 Price fluctuations in an isolated market

Let us first consider a case of one variable, i.e., an isolated market of a commodity. Let the adjustment function of the price of that commodity be

$$\dot{p} = F(E(p))$$

Assume that the function F is analytic with respect to p in the interval $(\bar{p} - a,\ \bar{p} + a)$. Then, by Cauchy's theorem concerning the existence of a solution, there is an interval $(\bar{t} - b, \bar{t} + b)$, where $b > 0$, in which the equation has a unique solution $p = \psi(t)$ through $\bar{p}$ at $\bar{t}$, i.e., $\bar{p} = \psi(\bar{t})$. This solution is analytic with respect to t in the interval $(\bar{t} - b, \bar{t} + b)$.

This is then explained geometrically in figure 14. First the interval $(\bar{p} - a, \bar{p} + a)$ cuts off a belt which is parallel to the t-coordinate in the (t, p)-plane. The interval $(\bar{t} - b, \bar{t} + b)$ then determines a rectangle on the

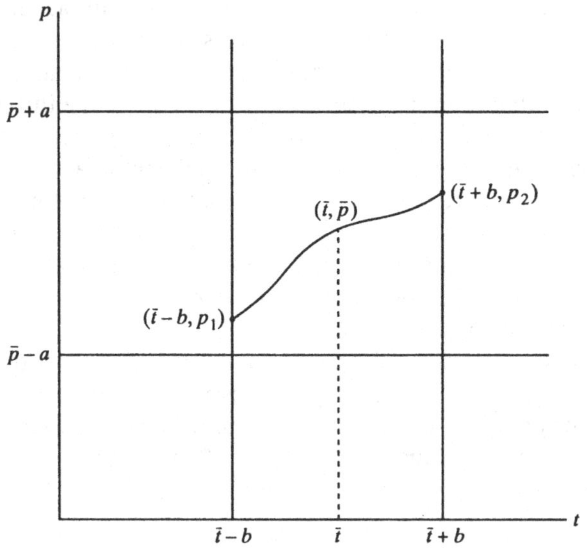

Figure 14

belt. Evidently, point $(\bar{t}, \bar{p})$ is an inner point of the rectangle. Cauchy's theorem states that in the interval $(\bar{t}-b, \bar{t}+b)$ there is a curve $\psi(t)$ through point $(\bar{t}, \bar{p})$ which is a unique solution in the interval to the original differential equation, corresponding to the initial condition $(\bar{t}, \bar{p})$. We refer to $\psi(t)$ as the integral curve. Thus we have a unique solution in the interval $(\bar{t}-b, \bar{t}+b)$; then, under what condition can we extend it to a greater interval? To reply to this question, we take up an end point $p_1 = \psi(\bar{t}-b)$ of the integral curve. If F is still analytic at p_1, then we may reapply Cauchy's theorem to the point p_1 and extend $\psi(t)$ to $\bar{t}-c$, where $c > b$. On the contrary, if p_1 is a singular point where F ceases to be analytic, we can no longer apply Cauchy's theorem, and the extension of the integral curve is impossible. The other end point $(\bar{t}+b, p_2)$ can be treated in the same way.

Thus we can extend our solution until p reaches a singular point of F. If we assume that $F(E(p))$ is analytic with respect to p everywhere in the interval $(-\infty, \infty)$, we may extend the solution until p becomes infinity. Therefore, in the case of p never becoming infinity the solution exists for all values of t in the interval $(-\infty, \infty)$. In the following we assume that F is analytic for all values of p.

Since our system is non-linear the equation $F(E(p)) = 0$ does not necessarily have a unique solution but may, in general, have $m+1$ solutions, say, $p^0, p^1, \ldots, p^m$. We arrange them so that $p^0 < p^1 < p^2 < \ldots < p^m$. Since these are equilibrium prices, each $p^i (i = 0, 1, \ldots, m)$ is a stationary solution which is valid when p is set at p^i at $t = 0$. In the (t, p)-plane, the integral curves corresponding to these stationary solutions are straight lines parallel to the t-axis, by which the space is split into horizontal belts.

Suppose now the initial point is given at an inner point in the interval (p^i, p^{i+1}). F vanishes at p^i and p^{i+1} but does not change its sign between them. Therefore, when the initial point is given within the interval (p^i, p^{i+1}) we obtain an integral curve which is monotonic. It asymptotically approaches either of the two lines p^i or p^{i+1} as $t \to \infty$, and the other as $t \to -\infty$. It is clear from the uniqueness of the solution that integral curves do not intersect each other. The price arrives at p^i or p^{i+1} only at $t = +\infty$, or $-\infty$, but never at any finite value of t.

When the initial point is given either in the interval $(-\infty, p^0)$ or in (p^m, ∞), the price becomes minus infinity at some finite value of t or $t = -\infty$ or ∞. If the price becomes minus or plus infinity as t increases (or decreases), it asymptotically approaches p^0 or p^m as t decreases (or increases). Summarizing these we obtain figure 15.[2]

3 Stability of equilibrium in an isolated market

In this section we derive stability conditions for a single commodity which is isolated from others.

(I) The condition for local stability. We assume, as before, that the adjustment function is a real analytic function of p in the interval $(-\infty, \infty)$. Expanding $\dot{p} = F(E)$ in a Taylor series, we have

$$\dot{p} = a_1(p - p^0) + a_2(p - p^0)^2 + \dots \tag{1}$$

If $a_1 \neq 0$, p^0 is a simple root of $\dot{p} = 0$, while if $a_1 = a_2 = \dots = a_{n-1} = 0$ and $a_n \neq 0$, it is an n-tuple root. We call the former a simple equilibrium point or an equilibrium point of order 1 and the latter a multiple equilibrium point or an equilibrium point of order n.

Let us first deal with the case of a simple equilibrium point. Consider a linear differential equation

$$\dot{p} = a_1(p - p^0)$$

and refer to it as the equation of the first approximation. Since $a_1 \neq 0$, the linearized system has structural stability. Since (1) can be put in the form

$$\dot{p} = a_1(p - p^0)\left[1 + \frac{a_2}{a_1}(p - p^0) + \frac{a_3}{a_1}(p - p^0)^2 + \dots\right] \tag{2}$$

the part in the square brackets on the right-hand side of this expression

[2] Andronow and Chaikin, 1949, pp. 140–4.

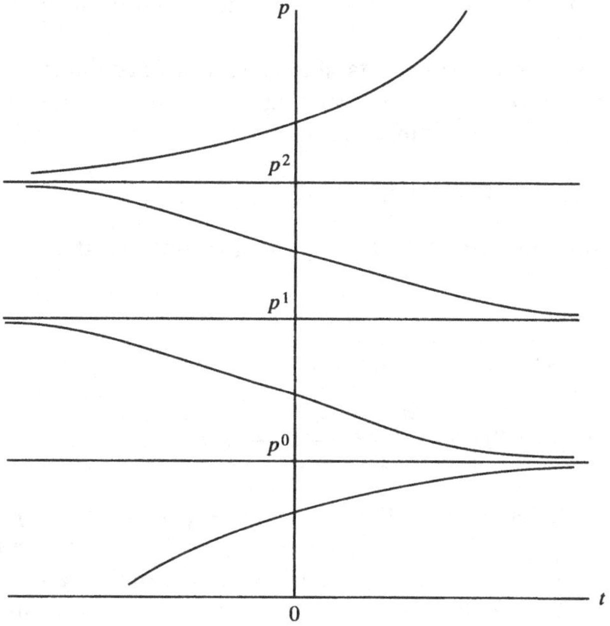

Figure 15

takes on a value which is nearly equal to 1 and, therefore, the sign of $\dot{p}$ is determined by the sign of $a_1(p - p^0)$, as long as $(p - p^0)$ is sufficiently small in absolute value. If $a_1 < 0$, p will approach p^0 as t increases. Therefore, p is confined to the region where the part in the square bracket of (2) is nearly equal to 1; and we have

$$\lim_{t \to \infty} p(t) = p^0$$

On the other hand, if $a_1 > 0$, we have the following result. For sufficiently small $|p - p^0|$, the sign of (2) is determined by the sign of $a_1(p - p^0)$. As $a_1 > 0$, p diverges from p^0 as t increases and will reach a point in the region where the higher-order terms of the adjustment function play a significant role. As has been seen in the previous section, the integral curve is a monotonic function of t, so that once p reaches such a point, it will never return to a point at which the higher-order terms are negligible. We may, therefore, conclude as follows. When the initial value of the price is given sufficiently near to the simple equilibrium point p^0, the condition of $a_1 < 0$ is necessary and sufficient for p^0 being stable. We call this the stability condition in the small domain. Thus, *whether p^0 is stable or not in the small* *domain is determined by whether it is stable or not in the linear system of the first approximation.*

Next let us be concerned with stability of a multiple equilibrium. Let p^0 be an equilibrium of order n by assuming $a_1 = a_2 = \dots = a_{n-1} = 0$ and $a_n \neq 0$. Then we have the adjustment function

$$\dot{p} = a_n(p - p^0)^n + a_{n+1}(p - p^0)^{n+1} + \dots \tag{3}$$

In this case the equation of the first approximation is written as

$$\dot{p} = a_n(p - p^0)^n \tag{4}$$

Since (3) is rewritten as

$$\dot{p} = a_n(p - p^0)^n\left[1 + \frac{a_{n+1}}{a_n}(p - p^0) + \dots\right]$$

the sign of $\dot{p}$ is determined by the sign of $a_n(p - p^0)^n$ as long as $p - p^0$ is sufficiently small. Therefore, if the first term $a_n(p - p^0)^n$ acts upon p so as to bring it nearer (or farther from) p^0, then p^0 has stability (or instability) in the small domain. This is because in the case of p being pulled nearer to p^0 because of the first term, p remains in the region where the higher-order terms can be neglected and, hence, eventually converges to p^0, while in the case of p being pushed away from p^0 because of the first term, p will move into a region where the higher-order terms are effective and, in view of the fact that the integral curve is monotonic, p will never come back to the neighbourhood of p^0.

Thus the local stability or instability of the non-linear system is determined by the stability or instability of the system of the first approximation. Then what is the condition for stability of the equilibrium of the latter system? First assume that n is an odd number. Solving (4) we have

$$p(t) = p^0 \pm \frac{1}{[a_n(1 - n)t + (p(0) - p^0)^{1-n}]^{\frac{1}{n-1}}}$$

where the sign $\pm$ is contingent on the value of $p(0)$. When a_n is positive, the first term of the part in the square brackets of the denominator is negative, while the second term is always positive, regardless of the sign of $(p(0) - p^0)$, because $n - 1$ is an even number. Therefore, as t becomes larger and reaches the value $T > 0$, where the denominator of the above expression vanishes, $p(T)$ will be $\pm\infty$. That is to say, p^0 is unstable. On the contrary, when $a_n < 0$, an increase in t gives rise to an increase in the denominator, so that we have $p(\infty) = p^0$; that is, p^0 is stable. Thus the equilibrium is locally stable or unstable according to $a_n < 0$ or >0.

Next, suppose n is an even number. Solving (4), we obtain

$$p(t) = p^0 + \frac{1}{[a_n(1-n)t + (p(0) - p^0)^{1-n}]^{\frac{1}{n-1}}}$$

When $a_n > 0$, in the above expression, the first term of the part in the square brackets takes on a negative value, while the second term is positive provided that $p(0) > p^0$. Therefore, the denominator vanishes at some $t = T > 0$, so that p^0 is unstable. On the other hand, provided $p(0) < p^0$, the second term is also negative, because $n - 1$ is an odd number. It can then easily be seen that p approaches p^0 if t tends to infinity; hence, p^0 is stable. Thus, if $a_n > 0$, the equilibrium point p^0 is unstable for $p(0) > p^0$ and stable for $p(0) < p^0$. In other words, it is unstable upwards and stable downwards. On the contrary, if $a_n < 0$, the converse is true; that is to say, the equilibrium is stable upwards and unstable downwards. We call such an equilibrium point of semi-stability or one-sided stability–instability (see p^1 in figure 15). *An equilibrium is semi-stable only when it is a multiple equilibrium point.*[3]

(II) The stability domain. An equilibrium p^0 is said to be stable in some domain A if the groping price $p(t)$ starting from any $p(0)$ in A converges to p^0. In the case of a linear system, if the equilibrium is stable, the price converges to the equilibrium point, irrespective of the value of the initial price which is arbitrarily given, so that the equilibrium is stable in an infinitely large size of domain. However, in the case of a non-linear system, even if an equilibrium is stable in a small domain, it is not necessarily stable in a larger domain. It is important to determine the stability domain of each equilibrium point.

It is well known that the differential equation, $\dot{p} = F(E(p))$, which has no t as an explicit argument of F, has the general solution of the form

$$p = \psi(t - \bar{t}, \bar{p})$$

where $p(\bar{t}) = \bar{p}$. Assuming that p^i has local stability, we have

$$\lim_{t \to \infty} \psi(t - \bar{t}, \bar{p}) = p^i \tag{5}$$

for sufficiently small $|\bar{p} - p^i|$. We also know that (5) holds, independently of the value of $\bar{t}$, as long as $|\bar{p} - p^i|$ is small. Therefore, however large the value of $\bar{t}$, $p(t)$, starting from $p(0) = \psi(-\bar{t}, \bar{p})$ converges to p^i as t tends to infinity.

[3] Samuelson, 1948, pp. 294–6. Andronow and Chaikin, 1949, pp. 147–8.

Let us define $p^* = \lim_{t \to \infty} \psi(-\bar{t}, \bar{p})$. Then the equilibrium price p^i is stable for all $p(0)$s which are nearer to p^i than p^* is to p^i.

The p^* thus defined depends on whether $\bar{p}$ is greater or smaller than p^i. If $\bar{p} > p^i$, then

$$\lim_{\bar{t} \to \infty} \psi(-\bar{t}, \bar{p}) = p^{i+1}$$

while if $\bar{p} < p_i$, then

$$\lim_{\bar{t} \to \infty} \psi(-\bar{t}, \bar{p}) = p^{i-1}$$

In these expressions, p^{i+1} denotes the smallest of those equilibria which are larger than p_i, while p^{i-1} denotes the largest of those equilibria which are smaller than p^i. We thus find that *the open interval* (p^{i-1}, p^{i+1}) *is the stability domain of* p^i. *In particular the largest equilibrium* p^m *has the stability domain* (p^{m-1}, ∞), *and the smallest* p^0 *has* $(-\infty, p^1)$; *if* p^m *and* p^0 *are both stable. These two intervals are, of course, open.*

4 The law of alteration of stability and instability

Measuring p along the vertical axis and $\dot{p}$ along the horizontal one, the adjustment function is expressed by a curve in the $(p, \dot{p})$-plane. We have an equilibrium point at $\dot{p} = 0$, so that where the curve cuts or touches the vertical axis we have an equilibrium. The system illustrated in figure 16 has six equilibrium points, $p^0, p^1, \ldots, p^5$. By the use of the results obtained in the previous section we find that these points have the stability properties shown in table 4.1.

Table 4.1 may be summarized as follows. If, above p^i, the price-adjustment curve lies on the right (or left) side of the vertical axis, then p^i is unstable (or stable) upwards. If, below p^i, the curve is on the right (or left) side of the axis, p^i is stable (or unstable) downwards. A point which is stable (or unstable) both upwards and downwards is a usual stable (or unstable) equilibrium point, while a point which is stable either upwards or downwards only is a semi-stable point.

As is easily seen, on the assumption that the curve is continuous, once the curve crosses the vertical axis from the left to the right, the curve remains on the right side of the axis until the curve meets the axis again. Consequently if the equilibrium p^i is unstable upwards, the lowest p^{i+1} among those equilibria which are higher than p^i is necessarily stable downwards. Similarly if p^i is stable upwards, p^{i+1} is necessarily unstable downwards.

Table 4.1. *Stability and instability of equilibria*

p^0	$a_1 > 0$	instability
p^1	$a_1 = 0, a_2 > 0$	downwards stability–upwards instability
p^2	$a_1 = a_2 = 0, a_3 < 0$	stability
p^3	$a_1 = a_2 = 0, a_3 > 0$	instability
p^4	$a_1 < 0$	stability
p^5	$a_1 = 0, a_2 < 0$	downwards instability–upwards stability

Thus, *of the two consecutive equilibria, if the higher one is stable* (*or unstable*) *downwards, then the lower one is unstable* (*or stable*) *upwards.* We call this rule *the law of alternation of stability and instability.*

According to Samuelson, between any two stable (or unstable) equilibrium points there is always another equilibrium point which is unstable (or stable). He refers to this rule as the separation theorem of stable and unstable equilibria.[4] The relationship between his separation theorem and our law of alternation is as follows. If we assume that each equilibrium is stable or unstable both upwards and downwards by ruling out points of one-sided stability–instability, the law of alternation is reduced to the separation theorem. Conversely, if in the separation theorem the distance between two consecutive equilibria becomes shorter and shorter and finally they coincide with each other, we have an equilibrium point of one-sided stability–instability; which Samuelson has ruled out. It can easily be seen that equilibrium points, $p^0, p^1, \ldots, p^5$ in figure 16 satisfy the law of alternation.

5 An example of non-linear systems

For the sake of facilitating the understanding of the rather abstract discussion in the last section, let us consider an example of non-linear systems. According to textbooks of economics, the supply of labour (or the supply of agricultural products) is usually upward sloping at low wage rates (or low prices) but is likely to turn back on itself when the wage rate (or the price) reaches some level (see curve SS' in figure 17). If we assume that the demand curve is downward sloping, then the isolated market of such a commodity has two equilibrium points, p^0 and p^1. Below p^0 we have an excess demand and above p^0 an excess supply; while below p^1 we have an excess supply and above p^1 an excess demand. Therefore, the

[4] Samuelson, 1948, p. 294.

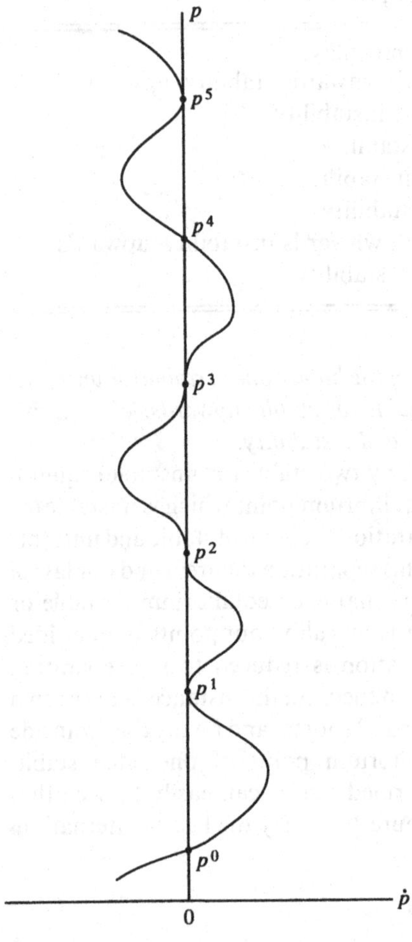

Figure 16

slope of the excess demand curve is negative at p^0 and positive at p^1. Assuming that the wage rate (or the price) is positively flexible, i.e., $dF(0)/dE > 0$, we find that p^0 is a stable equilibrium point and p^1 an unstable point. That is to say, of the two equilibria in the labour market or the market of agricultural products, the lower one is stable and the higher one is unstable.

Suppose now the demand curve shifts rightwards so that the demand and supply curves are tangent to each other at p^2. Then the demand exceeds the

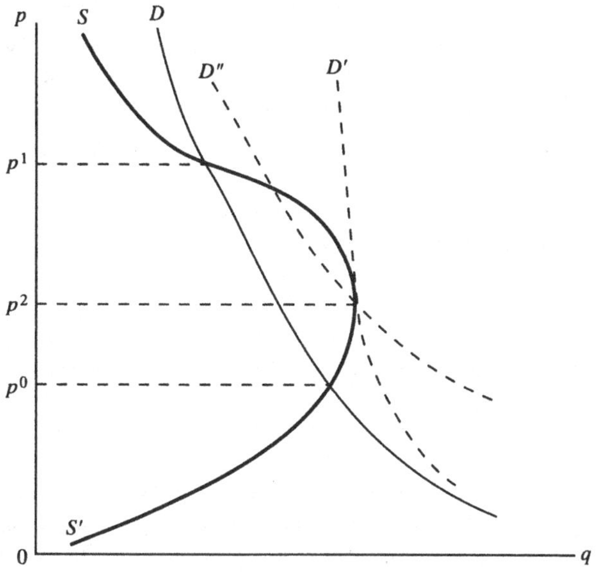

Figure 17

supply at any price above p^2 as well as below p^2. The first and the second derivatives of the excess demand curve are 0 and positive, respectively, at p^2. As the price is assumed to be flexible, p^2 is stable downwards and unstable upwards, so that we have a case of semi-stability.

At the semi-stable point of equilibrium, p^2, the first derivative of the $\dot{p}$ function vanishes and, therefore, it is a multiple equilibrium and the system is structurally unstable. Thus the multiplicity of an equilibrium point, its semi-stability and the structural instability of the system are closely related to each other. This fact would easily be understood by reasoning in the following way. Suppose now that the demand function slightly shifts to the left from the position of D'. Then it will cross the supply curves at two distinct points which are considered to coincide with each other and take on the same value at p^2 when the demand curve is placed at the critical position D'. This shows the multiplicity of p^2. Of the two equilibria, the upper one is unstable and the lower one is stable. The downwards instability domain of the upper equilibrium is the same as the upwards stability domain of the lower equilibrium. When both equilibria converge to p^2, that domain is reduced to zero. The limiting point p^2 is then unstable upwards and stable downwards, and, hence, semi-stable. Finally, if the slope of the demand curve (or the supply curve) at p^2 changes slightly, the first derivative of the $\dot{p}$ function can easily become positive or negative because it is 0 before the change. For example, suppose D' is rotated at p^2 to D''. Then the first derivative takes on a negative value and the semi-stable point p^2 becomes stable both upwards and downwards. Thus a slight change in the system (say, a rotation of the demand curve) may cause the type of the equilibrium point to change, say, from the semi-stable to the stable type; this shows the structural instability of the system.

6 A non-linear market of multiple commodities

(I) *Local behaviour*

In this section we are concerned with a more general non-linear system, i.e., a market of multiple commodities with non-linear adjustment functions of the rate of interest and prices

$$\dot{r} = F_1(E_1), \dot{p}_i = F_i(E_i), i = 2, \ldots, n \tag{6}$$

Assuming that these adjustment functions are analytic in some region of the space having prices and interest rate as coordinates, we have, by Cauchy's theorem, for t in the interval $(\bar{t} - b, \bar{t} + b)$, unique solutions to (6)

$$\begin{aligned} r &= \psi_1(t - \bar{t}, \bar{r}, \bar{p}_2, \ldots, \bar{p}_n), \\ p_i &= \psi_i(t - \bar{t}, \bar{r}, \bar{p}_2, \ldots, \bar{p}_n), i = 2, \ldots, n \end{aligned} \tag{7}$$

where $r = \bar{r}$ and $p_i = \bar{p}_i$ when $t = \bar{t}$, and $(\bar{r}, \bar{p}_2, \ldots, \bar{p}_n)$ is a point in the region where the functions (6) are analytic. If we assume, more strongly, that they are analytic everywhere in the price–interest rate space of prices and the rate of interest, unique solutions can be extended to the interval $(-\infty, \infty)$ of t. Throughout the following we make this strong assumption.

Therefore, the existence of unique solutions is assured. What form, then, do these solutions take? In other words, how do prices and the rate of interest change when t changes? Or more particularly, to what values do they converge when t tends to infinity? This is, of course, the problem of stability.

Generally speaking, a non-linear system has several sets of stationary solutions $(r^0, p_2^0, \ldots, p_n^0), (r^1, p_2^1, \ldots, p_n^1), \ldots$ each of which gives an equilibrium point. Since the adjustment functions are assumed to be analytic, they can be expanded into Taylor series. Writing $r = p_1$, and expanding them into the series from $(p_1^0, p_2^0, \ldots, p_n^0)$, (6) can then be put in the form

$$\begin{aligned} \dot{p}_i &= \sum_j a_{ij}(p_j - p_j^0) + \Sigma a_{ijk}(p_j - p_j^0)(p_k - p_k^0) + \ldots \\ &= \Sigma a_{ij}(p_j - p_j^0) + \rho_i(\ldots) \end{aligned} \tag{8}$$

where all *a*s are constant and $\rho_i(\ldots), i = 1, \ldots, n$, are polynomials of $(p - p^0)$ containing only the terms of order two or more than two.

Let us consider a linear system

$$\dot{p}_i = \Sigma a_{ij}(p_j - p_j^0) \tag{9}$$

and call it the system of the first approximation to the original non-linear system. We assume that this linear system is structurally stable. Therefore, roots λ_i of the characteristic equation $|A - \lambda I| = 0$ are neither 0 nor an imaginary number; they are, moreover, all simple. As no $\lambda_i = 0$, so that $|A| \neq 0$; therefore, the point $p^0 = (p_1^0, p_2^0, \ldots, p_n^0)$ is a simple solution to (8). The equilibrium point p^0 is a simple equilibrium point of the original non-linear system.

Let us first derive the stability conditions in the small domain. If the initial point is given sufficiently near to the equilibrium point p^0, effects of the terms $\rho_i(\ldots)$ upon fluctuations in prices are negligible, so that the p_is determined by (8) approximately equal those determined by (9). Therefore, the price movements in such a region are approximated by the solutions to (9) in the same region. Since the values of λ_i determine whether the solution to (9) approach p^0, the condition of the local stability of the non-linear system may also be given in terms of λ_i.[5] We have the following stability condition by Liapounoff.

The Liapounoff stability condition: *In a non-linear system whose first-approximation system is structurally stable, the equilibrium point p^0 is stable if and only if the linear system of the first approximation has the characteristic roots whose real parts are all negative. The equilibrium point of the non-linear system p^0 is a node, a focus or a saddle point according to whether the corresponding equilibrium point of the first approximation system is a node, a focus or a saddle point, respectively.*

This Liapounoff condition may be described, in more detail, as follows.

1′ The case of λ_i being all real and of the same sign. If all λ_i are negative, p^0 is absolutely stable in the small domain, while if all λ_i are positive p^0 is absolutely unstable. In these two cases, the equilibrium point is a node.

2′ The case in which some of the λ_is are complex numbers but their real parts and the other real characteristic roots are all of the same sign. If $R(\lambda_i) < 0$ (or >0), then p^0 is an absolutely stable (or unstable) focus.

[5] Let Λ be the diagonal matrix with diagonal elements $\lambda_1, \ldots, \lambda_n$. A matrix K transforms A to Λ; i.e., $\Lambda = KAK^{-1}$. Write $\xi = K(p - p^0)$. Then from (9)

$$\begin{aligned}\xi'\dot{\xi} &= \xi' K\dot{p} = \xi' KA(p - p_0) + \xi' K\rho(\ldots) = \xi' KAK^{-1}K(p - p^0) + \Phi(\ldots)\\ &= \xi'\Lambda\xi + \Phi(\ldots)\end{aligned}$$

where ξ' denotes the transposition of ξ. Where the real parts of complex characteristic roots λ_i and the other real characteristic roots are all negative, we have $\xi'\Lambda\xi < 0$. Also we can show that $\Phi(\ldots)$ is an infinitesimal of higher order than $\xi'\Lambda\xi$, provided that ξ is small and non-zero. Therefore, $\xi'\dot{\xi} < 0$ which implies that $\xi'\xi = (p - p^0)K'K(p - p^0)$ is always decreasing. Hence $\lim_{t\to\infty} p(t) = p^0$.

3′ The case in which the real roots and the real parts of the complex roots are not all of the same sign, some of them being positive and the rest negative. The equilibrium point p^0 is a saddle point, so that it is conditionally stable.

(II) The stability domain. In the above we have obtained the condition for an equilibrium point p^0 to be stable in the small domain. The next problem with which we are concerned is to determine the domain in which the equilibrium p^0 is stable. First let us assume that p^0 is a point which is absolutely stable in its neighbourhood. Since solutions to the differential equations to (6) are given in the form of (7) and p^0 is a locally absolutely stable point, we have

$$\lim_{t \to \infty} \psi_i(t - \bar{t}, \bar{p}_1, \ldots, \bar{p}_n) = p_i^0 \tag{10}$$

for any initial point $(\bar{p}_1, \bar{p}_2, \ldots, \bar{p}_n)$ which is sufficiently near to p^0. (10) holds true, regardless of the value of $\bar{t}$, as long as the absolute values $|p_i - p_i^0|, i = 1, \ldots, n$, are sufficiently small. For any value of $\bar{t}$, provided that the point $\bar{p}$ is fixed sufficiently near to p^0, the price movement which starts from $p_i(0) = \psi_i(-\bar{t}, \bar{p}_1, \ldots, \bar{p}_n)$ converges to p^0 as t tends to infinity. With given $\bar{p}$, we may consider, for any arbitrary finite value of $\bar{t}$, a point $p(0) = [\psi_1(-\bar{t}, \bar{p}), \ldots, \psi_n(-\bar{t}, \bar{p})]$ and define a set consisting of such points for all values of $\bar{t}$. The price movement starting from any point in the set eventually approaches p^0, so that the set gives the stability domain.

Next consider the case of absolute instability in the small domain. If p^0 is locally absolutely unstable, it is unstable within the domain of any size. This is obvious because even though $p(t)$ starting from some initial position moves in the direction of p^0 as t increases, it goes away from p^0 as soon as it reaches a sufficiently small neighbourhood of p^0; hence $p(t)$ never converges to p^0.

In the case of p^0 which is conditionally stable in the small domain, (10) holds for those $\bar{p}$s which are sufficiently near to p^0 and satisfy some conditions, but it does not hold for those $\bar{p}$s which do not satisfy those conditions, however small $|\bar{p} - p_0|$ may be. Let us take a point $\bar{p}$ sufficiently near to p^0, such that (10) holds for it. Since we have (10) for an arbitrary value of $\bar{t}$, the price movement starting from

$$p_i(0) = \psi_i(-\bar{t}, \bar{p}_1, \ldots, \bar{p}_n)$$

converges to p_i^0 as $t \to \infty$. With given $\bar{p}$ we obtain different $p(0)$ for different values of $\bar{t}$. The set of such $p(0)$'s gives the domain where the equilibrium point p^0 is conditionally stable. The domain for conditional stability differs from that for absolute stability in the respect that while $\bar{p}$ is any point which is near to p^0 in the latter case, $\bar{p}$ must be, in the former, not only near to p^0 but must also satisfy some conditions.

We thus have determined the stability domain. A non-linear system usually has several equilibria, among which absolutely or conditionally stable ones have their own stability regions. Then what properties has each point on the boundaries of the stability domain? In the case of a single market it has been seen that each of the boundary points is an equilibrium point; from this fact we have derived the law of alternation (or the separation theorem) of stable and unstable equilibria. In the case of the multiple-commodity market, however, points on the boundary are not necessarily equilibrium points. This is shown in the following way. Let $\bar{p}$ be a point which is sufficiently near to p^0. Then

$$\lim_{\bar{t}\to\infty} \psi_i(-\bar{t}, \bar{p}_i, \ldots, \bar{p}_n) \quad i = 1, \ldots, n$$

gives a point on the boundary of the stability domain of p^0. This may be $\pm\infty$ or another equilibrium point p^1. However, it is also possible that it is neither $\pm\infty$ nor an equilibrium point. For example, in the case of two goods, the equations

$$\dot{p}_1 = F_1(p_1, p_2), \; \dot{p}_2 = F_2(p_1, p_2)$$

may have a set of cyclic solutions. Let T be their period of cycle; then we have

$$p_1(t+T) = p_1(t), \; p_2(t+T) = p_2(t) \tag{11}$$

These $p_1(t)$ and $p_2(t)$ do not simultaneously produce $\dot{p}_1(t) = 0$, $\dot{p}_2(t) = 0$, so that, for any t, point $(p_1(t), p_2(t))$ cannot be an equilibrium point. (11) traces out a closed curve C on the (p_1, p_2) plane. If there is a single equilibrium point in the inside of C, it is possible that p^0 is stable in the whole inside of C; in this case the closed curve C is a boundary of the stability domain of p^0, but no point on C is an equilibrium point. That is to say, it is possible that a stable equilibrium point p^0 and another equilibrium point p^1 are separated from each other by a closed curve on which the market is always in the state of disequilibrium (see figure 18). Similarly, a price movement which starts from a point in the vicinity of an unstable equilibrium point p^0 does not converge to another equilibrium point but to a closed curve C consisting of disequilibrium points only, as t tends to infinity (see figure 19). [Also, see article III in the addendum.]

Finally, let us prove that no equilibrium point p^i can be an element of the stability domain U_j of another equilibrium point p^j, so that U_j has one and only one equilibrium point among its elements. First, it is evident that p^j is

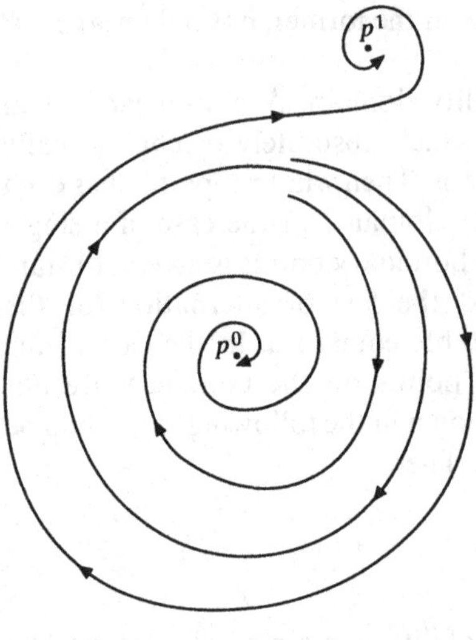

Figure 18

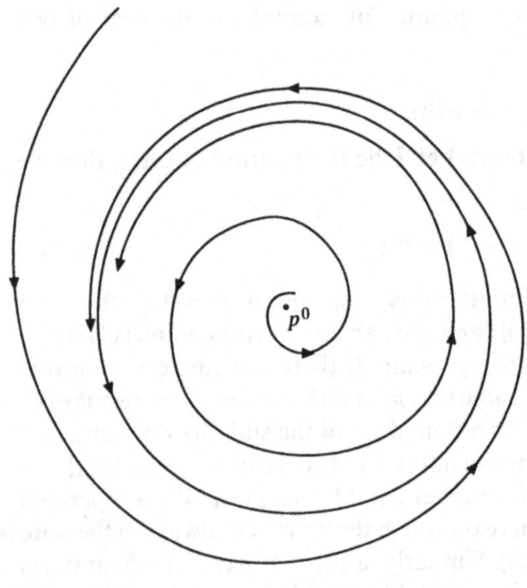

Figure 19

an element of U_j. Suppose now another equilibrium point $p^i (i \neq j)$ is also an element of U_j. Then a price movement starting from p^i must converge to p^j as $t \to \infty$. Nevertheless, p^i is an equilibrium point so that if the initial prices are given at p^i, prices must stay there. This means that p^i is not a member of the stability domain U_j, a contradiction.

Throughout the above, we have assumed that the first-approximation linear system of a given non-linear system is structurally stable. Our next task is to remove this assumption and to find conditions for a temporary equilibrium to be stable. This problem, however, is not dealt with in the present volume.

7 The loanable fund theory versus the liquidity preference theory

According to the usual view, the rate of interest is determined by the demand and supply of capital. If this capital is taken as the real capital, the rate of interest may be determined, as Böhm-Bawerk said, by the relative desire for present and future goods. That is to say, those technological and psychological elements which influence the preferences between the present and future commodities are the underlying forces which govern the rate of interest. On the other hand, if the 'capital' is taken as the money capital in the sense of the power to dispose of a given quantity of money, different theories of interest may be developed. Up to now the two major theories of interest taking the monetary approaches have been put forward. One is the loanable fund theory according to which the rate of interest is determined by demand and supply of loanable funds, i.e., borrowing and lending. The other is the liquidity preference theory according to which it is determined by demand and supply of money. According to Hicks, among these three representative theories of interest, the two monetary theories are not opposed to each other.[6] These two look *prima facie* as if they are competitive and alternative, but they are, in fact, different in expression and identical in essence. In the following we shall examine Hicks' assertion of the identity of the two monetary theories of interest. We shall differ from Hicks in concluding that the loanable fund theory *cannot* be equivalent to the liquidity preference theory; we shall also show that a synthesis of these two leads to a dynamic system which is necessarily non-linear.

(1) Hicks' proof. Hicks considers, first of all, that the rate of interest is determined, together with other prices, by the conditions of temporary general equilibrium. For him the theory of the determination of the rate of interest is no more than a part of the general equilibrium theory of the determination of prices; but the general equilibrium theory he adopts is not a dynamic theory containing intertemporal elements $\dot{p}$ and $\dot{r}$, like the one which we have so far discussed, but the classical static theory of general equilibrium. To be exact, while we start with the adjustment functions of prices and the rate of interest from which, considering the definition of temporary equilibrium in terms of $\dot{p}$ and $\dot{r}$, we derive the conditions of

[6] Hicks, 1946, pp. 153–62.

temporary equilibrium (6) of chapter 3, Hicks gives $n+1$ equations between demand and supply of goods, including money

$$E_i(r, p_2, \ldots, p_n) = 0, \; i = 0, 1, \ldots, n$$

as the conditions of temporary equilibrium, without giving any explicit consideration to adjustment functions.

These $n+1$ equations include only n unknowns $p_2, \ldots, p_n$ and r, so that at first it may be thought that the system is overdetermined. However, considering Walras' law which holds identically, irrespective of whether an equilibrium is established or not, one of the $n+1$ equations follows from the rest. Therefore, the system is not overdetermined; the equilibrium equations have solutions which give temporary equilibrium values of prices and the rate of interest. In eliminating one equation we may choose any equation, the demand–supply equation for money, the demand–supply equation for securities, or a similar equation for any other commodity.

First, if we decide to eliminate the equation for money, the temporary equilibrium values of prices and the rate of interest are determined by the demand–supply equations for commodities and securities. It is of course natural to match the price of rice with the demand–supply equation for rice, the price of wheat with the equation for wheat, and so on. By eliminating prices and equations in this way, the rate of interest and the demand–supply equation for securities finally remain to be matched with each other. Then we are naturally led to a view that the rate of interest is determined by the demand and supply of securities; this is the loanable fund theory.

On the other hand, if we eliminate the demand–supply equation for securities by Walras' law, the temporary equilibrium prices are determined by the demand–supply equations for money and commodities. Again, since it is natural to match the price of each commodity with the demand–supply equation for the same commodity, the rate of interest is bound to be matched with the equation for money. Hicks gives the equilibrium between the demand and supply of money by the equation

$$E_0 = L - M = 0$$

where L represents the total amount of cash balances which the individuals and the firms want to hold at the end of the present week, and M the existing amount of money. Thus the equilibrium condition for money states that the total desired amount of cash balances equals the total existing amount of money, so that the rate of interest is determined by the public's liquidity preference. We, therefore, have the liquidity preference theory.

Thus we obtain the loanable fund theory by eliminating the demand–supply equation for money and the liquidity preference theory by eliminating the equation for securities. In any case, it makes no difference to solutions to the system of general equilibrium equations whether we eliminate one equation or another by the use of Walras' law, so that it is a matter of convenience whether we should adopt the loanable fund theory or the liquidity preference theory. There is no significant difference between the two. They only give different descriptions of the same body, the general equilibrium theory of interest.

(2) A criticism of Hicks' proof. Let us first summarize Professor Takata's criticism of Hicks.[7] Takata's argument proceeds in the following way. Among the $n + 1$ equilibrium conditions, only n equations are independent; they can be any n equations, because we may eliminate any one equation. There can be no query about that. If we may derive from Hicks' argument that 'the rate of interest which is determined by the demand and supply of securities can equivalently be said to be determined by the demand and supply of money', then we can equally say, by the same reasoning, that 'the price of apples which is determined by the demand and supply of apples, can equivalently be said to be determined by the demand and supply of securities'. Takata says: 'If the latter statement is a nonsense, we must conclude that the former is also a nonsense.' Hicks' error is a consequence of his implicit assumption that 'the validity of a proposition of causality depends on a mathematical way of solving equations'; his argument is based on the premise that whether a causal law is valid or not can be judged by whether a certain kind of manipulation of formulae is possible or not. Thus Takata concludes that although the use of mathematical formulae are unavoidable in order to describe the state of general equilibrium, it is not understandable for Hicks to try to establish the equivalence of the two different causal relationships by showing that we may arbitrarily choose among n different sets of independent equations derived from the $n + 1$ equilibrium equations. In the following we shall annotate in detail this criticism by Takata of Hicks.

First, it must be remembered that Hicks develops his theory of interest as a part of the general equilibrium theory. As he acknowledges, 'each equation plays its part in the determination of all prices'. He is perfectly right in saying so. However, a question arises when he says that 'since it is natural to "match" the price of each commodity with the demand and supply equation for the same commodity, the rate of interest is bound to be "matched" with the equation for the demand and supply of money'. This sentence plays the most important role in Hicks' proof, but the key word in this sentence, 'match', is not well defined; its meaning is not as clear as Hicks thinks it is. Consequently we must reexamine Hicks' proof for possible meanings of the word.

According to a first possible interpretation, 'to match' may be taken as meaning 'to make to correspond'. Being interpreted in that way, Hicks'

[7] Takata, 1948.

argument cannot mean anything. 'Correspondence' and 'causal relationship' are unrelated; a correspondence between A and B does not necessarily mean that A is the cause of B or that A is the result of B.

Secondly, when we say that the price of good A is matched with the demand–supply equation for A, we may mean by it that the former is obtained by solving the latter. Taking the word 'match' in this sense, we may determine prices of $n - 1$ commodities as functions of the rate of interest by solving $n - 1$ demand–supply equations of the commodities with respect to their prices, because the prices of the commodities are matched with their demand and supply equations. Substituting these $n - 1$ functions into the demand–supply equation for money or the equation for securities, they both become functions of the rate of interest only. By solving the equation for money or the equation for securities we obtain, from either of them, an equilibrium rate of interest. Because these two equations are not independent, the two rates of interest thus obtained are equal to each other. However, this argument merely shows that the same equilibrium rate of interest is obtained, irrespective of the equation to be eliminated; it does not prove the equivalence of the loanable fund theory which asserts that the rate of interest balances the demand and supply of securities, with the liquidity preference theory which asserts that it balances the demand and supply of money. If Hicks maintains that by this reasoning he could prove the equivalence of the two theories of interest, we have to follow Takata in saying that Hicks confuses the causal relationship with the way of solving the system of equations.[8]

Next, let us turn to the third interpretation. According to Hicks, a temporary general equilibrium is defined as a state of affairs where demand is equated with supply for all goods including money and securities; the equilibrium prices and the equilibrium rate of interest are prices and the interest rate which realize such a state. This gives the definition of temporary general equilibrium and the definitions of equilibrium prices and rate of interest. We know the existence of a temporary general equilibrium; but in order to elucidate why prices and the rate of interest are settled at the temporary general equilibrium point, rather than any other point, we have to transform the conventional price theory which merely counts the number of independent equations and the number of unknowns into a kinetic causal theory of prices which can explain the process of price formation. Since we are concerned with whether the two causal theories are equivalent or not, we ourselves must reformulate Hicks' general equilibrium theory of interest as a causal theory – a theory which can analyse not only the finally realized state of temporary equilibrium but also the process

[8] A similar criticism is made by Klein, 1947, pp. 117–23.

of searching towards and reaching it; otherwise we cannot say anything about whether Hicks' theory can be a synthesis of the two causal theories or not.[9]

In the analysis of the process of forming a temporary general equilibrium the most important concept of Hicks' is the concept of repercussions of prices, i.e., the effects of a change in a price upon other prices. Considering that prices have the function of adjusting demand and supply to each other, he assumes that the price of commodity A is changed so as to clear the market of A. Because of this assumption, given other prices, the price of A is determined at a value where the demand for commodity A is equated with its supply; when prices of other commodities change, the price of A will also change so that the market for A is kept in equilibrium.

As for fluctuations in the rate of interest, there may be two possible views: first, the view that the rate of interest is adjusted so as to equilibrate the demand and supply of securities and, secondly, the view that it is adjusted so as to equilibrate the demand and supply of money. We refer to the former as kinetic (or genetical, or g-) loanable fund theory and the latter as g-liquidity preference theory. Then, to establish the equivalence of the two theories of interest we must show that the rate of interest has a function of adjusting the demand and supply of securities as long as it has a function of clearing the money market and vice versa.

Because of repercussions upon prices, an equilibrium is established in each commodity market. First, according to g-loanable fund theory, the rate of interest is changed such that excess demand vanishes in the market for securities. In this way the market for securities is equilibrated momentarily, but at the new rate of interest the equilibrium for the commodity markets will be broken and repercussions will be brought about from the rate of interest to prices. Prices of commodities A, B, ... are determined such that the demands for A, B, ... are equated to their supplies, respectively, and equilibrium is restored in the markets for A, B, ... But under this new price system there is no reason why the demand and supply of securities should be at equilibrium. The rate of interest will again be adjusted so as to equate the demand and supply of securities and this change in interest influences prices. Repeating the above process of adjustment we finally reach a state of temporary general equilibrium for all goods including securities and money.

Next, assuming g-liquidity preference theory, we consider the process of establishing a temporary general equilibrium. At the outset we assume that an equilibrium has already been established for each commodity (except securities and money). At the given rate of interest, the demand for money

[9] As for the need of genetical-causal theory of prices, see, for example, Yasui, 1940, pp. 45–58.

may exceed or fall short of its supply, and the rate of interest is adjusted so as to equilibrate the demand and supply of money. Then the money market is in equilibrium but at the new rate of interest the demand for commodities is not necessarily equal to the respective supplies. Prices must change. Repeating this process of adjustment in the rate of interest to prices and then prices to the rate of interest, the economy eventually reaches a state of temporary general equilibrium.

We can now discuss whether g-liquidity preference theory and g-loanable fund theory are equivalent or not. When a temporary equilibrium is realized in each commodity market, we have $E_i = 0, i = 2, \ldots, n$. Therefore, considering Walras' law (or Hicks' money equation) we obtain, in this case

$$E_0(r, p_2, \ldots, p_n) = -E_1(r, p_2, \ldots, p_n)$$

Loanable fund theory asserts that the rate of interest is adjusted such that $E_1 = 0$. Therefore, it changes to the value r' at which $E_1(r', p_2, \ldots, p_n) = 0$ holds. In view of the above equation, we at once find that this rate of interest also equates the demand and supply of money. Thus, providing that prices fulfill the function of equilibrating the demands and supplies of commodities, we may say that the rate of interest will clear the money market if it clears the market for securities and vice versa. From this one might think that he may conclude that we have causally proved the equivalence of the two theories of interest, but this conclusion is, in fact, not so perfectly right as it looks at first sight. In the following we shall explain this point.

In the above we assumed that given the rate of interest, repercussions occur from the rate of interest to prices. On the other hand, we may equally conceive of the case where, with given price of commodity 2, repercussions occur from the price of commodity 2 to other prices and the rate of interest. In this case, if we take g-loanable fund theory, as a result of repercussions, demands are equated with supplies for commodities $3, 4 \ldots$ and securities but not necessarily for commodity 2. Then the price of commodity 2 will change so as to equate its demand with its supply. Therefore a disequilibrium will again occur in the market for commodities $3, 4, \ldots$ and securities so that the prices of these commodities and the rate of interest have to be changed. In this way equilibrium is restored in the market for commodities $3, 4, \ldots$ and securities but at the same time the demand and supply of commodity 2 will become unequal. We have, by Walras' law, $E_0 = -p_2E_2$, in this case. Since E_0 is not zero it is clear that the rate of interest does not fulfill the function of adjusting the demand and supply of money. Therefore g-loanable fund theory and g-liquidity preference theory are not equivalent.

Thus if repercussions occur from the price of commodity 2 to other prices and the rate of interest has a function of adjusting the demand and supply of securities, then we obtain $E_0 = -p_2E_2$, since p_2 will change, with given other prices and the rate of interest, so as to establish $E_2 = 0$. It also establishes $E_0 = 0$. That is to say, p_2 has a function of adjusting the demand and supply of money. This is a situation that was referred to by Takata as the case for which, following Hicks' rhetoric, one may say that the price of apples is determined by the demand and supply of money.

(3) We have seen in the above that g-loanable fund theory and g-liquidity preference theory are not equivalent in Hicks' own system. We may then ask in what relationship do they stand in our system.

First we must explain the difference between Hicks' and our systems. As has been stated, Hicks assumes that the price of commodity A adjusts the demand and supply of A and therefore with given other prices the price of A fluctuates so as to establish the equality between the demand and supply of good A. We call this assumption Hicks' assumption of price repercussions. In our system it is assumed that the adjustment functions of prices and the rate of interest play the same role as Hicks' assumption plays in his system. Just as Hicks gave the name of 'loanable fund theory' (or liquidity preference theory) to the theory which assumes that the rate of interest has the function of adjusting the demand and supply of securities (or money) so we give the same name to the theory which assumes that the rate of change in the interest rate $\dot{r}$ depends on the excess demand for securities (or money). Then the system of determining prices and the rate of interest is given as

$$\dot{r} = F_1(E_1);\ \dot{p}_i = F_i(E_i)$$

when g-loanable fund theory is assumed, or as

$$\dot{r} = G(E_0);\ \dot{p}_i = F_i(E_i)$$

when g-liquidity preference theory is assumed.

Interpreting in this way, the two theories are not equivalent in our system too. In fact, considering Walras' law, we obtain

$$\dot{r} = G(E_0) = G(-E_1 - \Sigma p_i E_i)$$

so that $\dot{r}$ is not a function of E_1 alone. It can thus be seen that *g-loanable fund theory maintains that the rate of interest will change depending on the demand for and supply of securities only while g-liquidity preference theory maintains that the rate of interest depends not only on demand for and supply of securities but also on the flow of money spent on the demand for other commodities and received from the supply of other commodities.* In fact it maintains that the rate of interest depends on the total flow of money. Therefore in the case of $E_1 = 0$, g-loanable fund theory would conclude that the rate of interest is momentarily in a stationary state while g-liquidity preference theory would not conclude a stationary rate of interest if there is a discrepancy between the demand for and supply of other commodities, so we do not have $L = M$. Moreover, there is no assurance that the characteristic roots of the g-loanable fund system are equal to those of the g-liquidity preference system, so that even if either of the theories concluded the stability of the equilibrium point, the other may conclude instability. The equilibria whose existence the two theories maintain are the same but the two theories may disagree about the realization of them. It is now clear that they are not equivalent.

Then which of the two is right? The answer to this matter must come from the facts of the real world. If the actual mechanism is the one which is described by $\dot{r} = F_1(E_1)$, then g-loanable fund theory should be adopted; conversely if it is well described by $\dot{r} = G(E_0)$, we must accept g-liquidity preference theory. The facts may order us to adopt a third theory of interest other than these.

In this way the validity of the two theories is decided by the facts and cannot be judged by formal reasoning. What we can do, at the most, without getting involved in fact finding, is to synthesize the two theories. Let us now consider an adjustment function of the rate of interest which satisfies the following two conditions:

(i) With the money market being in equilibrium, if the demand for securities is smaller (or larger) than their supplies, the rate of interest is bid up (or down) and if they are equal to each other the rate of interest is stationary, and

(ii) with the securities market being in equilibrium, if the amount of cash balances which the public want to hold is greater (or smaller) than the existing quantity of money, then the rate of interest is bid up (or down) and it ceases to fluctuate if they become equal.

We may then conceive of the adjustment function of the rate of interest of the type

$$\dot{r} = F(E_0, E_1)$$

where $F(0,0) = 0$, $F_0(0,0) > 0$ and $F_1(0,0) < 0$ and the subscript attached to F represents a partial differentiation. A system which assumes this function for the rate of interest and $\dot{p}_i = F_i(E_i)$ for prices is one which synthesizes the two theories of interest. In this general system the rate of interest has two flexibilities, one with respect to money and the other with respect to securities.

Let us finally show that the system which synthesizes the two interest theories is necessarily a non-linear one. This is because, even though the excess demand functions of all commodities except money and securities are linear, either E_0 or E_1 must be non-linear by virtue of Walras' law

$$-(E_0 + E_1) = \Sigma p_i E_i$$

If the system is structurally stable the local stability of the temporary equilibrium is determined by the latent roots of the equation

$$|a_{ij} - \lambda\delta_{ij}| = 0$$

where $a_{1j} = F_0^0 E_{0j}^0 + F_1^0 E_{1j}^0$ and $a_{ij} = F_i^0 E_{ij}^0$. In the special case of $F_0^0 = 0$, i.e., that the rate of interest is inflexible with respect to money, we obtain g-loanable fund theory. On the other hand, if $F_1^0 = 0$, i.e., that the rate of interest is inflexible with respect to securities, we have g-liquidity preference theory.[10] This fact that the synthesized interest theory is necessarily non-linear implies that either the loanable fund theory or the liquidity preference theory is non-linear. We thus have an important field of application of the non-linear theory of stability.

[10] [For a further view concerning the problem of the loanable fund theory versus the liquidity preference theory, see section 6 of article VIII: The dilemma of durable goods, added below.]

5 Comparative dynamics

1 Method of analysis

We have so far discussed how prices and the rate of interest are determined in a particular period, the present week. We have, at the same time, also discussed the movement of prices but it was only the movement of groping prices which appears in the process of tatonnement – not the movement of temporary equilibrium prices through weeks. Effective prices, at which trade is carried out, are realized at the end of each week. In order to explain the movement of effective prices from week to week, we must not confine our investigation to the present week but extend it to future weeks. This chapter is devoted to this problem which has been left unexamined in the previous chapter, that is, to the analysis of the fluctuation of prices over weeks. This is, needless to say, a very important problem which is closely related to the problem of trade cycles or economic growth.

The problem of the fluctuations in prices over weeks consists of two subproblems. The first is the comparison of different prices of a good, in a particular week, in different circumstances. The second is the intertemporal relationship between prices in different weeks. The former is usually dealt with by comparative statics. We want to discuss the latter by using the analysis of comparative dynamics.[1]

Let us first explain how comparative statics and comparative dynamics can be applied to the analysis of the fluctuation in prices. Let us use subscript ι to signify the variables and the functions in week ι. Then the system of determining prices and the rate of interest in week ι can be represented as

$$\dot{r}_\iota = F_{1_\iota}(E_{1_\iota}), \dot{p}_{i_\iota} = F_{i_\iota}(E_{i_\iota})$$

as we assume the loanable fund theory of interest.

[1] We shall discuss the first problem in earlier sections of this chapter and then the second in section 6 below.

We assume that where $E_{i_\iota} = 0$, $i = 1,\dots,n$, the rates of adjustment of prices and the rate of interest are zero, i.e., $\dot{r}_\iota = \dot{p}_{i_\iota} = 0$. Then the temporary equilibrium prices and interest rate in week ι are obtained as solutions to simultaneous equations

$$E_{i_\iota}(r_\iota, p_{2_\iota},\dots,p_{n_\iota},\alpha_\iota) = 0,\ i = 1,\dots,n$$

Therefore, in order to show how equilibrium prices and the interest rate change from period to period, we must investigate how excess demand functions change from period to period and analyse the effects of the change in excess demand functions upon equilibrium prices. In other words, by comparing the condition for equilibrium of demand and supply in the present week

$$E_{i0}(r_0, p_{20},\dots,p_{n0},\alpha_0) = 0 \tag{1}$$

with those in the next week

$$E_{i1}(r_1, p_{21},\dots,p_{n1},\alpha_1) = 0 \tag{2}$$

we can compare the equilibrium prices for the present week and for the next week. If the equilibrium demand and supply conditions for the next week (2) prevailed in the market of the present week then the same prices as we have in the next week would prevail in the present week. In this way an intertemporal comparison of prices in different weeks can be reduced to a comparison of prices in alternative circumstances in the same week. That is to say, in addition to the system (1) that is actually prevailing in the present week, we imagine an alternative system (2) and ask how equilibrium prices of the present week would be different if the actual system were (2) rather than (1). The difference between the prices determined by the real system (1) and those determined by the imagined system (2) gives the difference in the prices and the interest rate between weeks 0 and 1. We call such an analysis comparative statics analysis which reduces the problem of comparison of prices and the interest rate at different points of time to a comparison between simultaneous, alternative states of affairs. We can thus analyse the dynamic movements of prices over weeks by the use of comparative statics. Traditionally, most economists have dealt with the problem of fluctuations in this way.

In contrast to comparative statics described above, the method of comparative dynamics deals with the same problem in the following way. The dynamic system of determining prices and the rate of interest is given by the differential equations

$$\dot{r}_0 = F_{10}(E_{10}),\ \dot{p}_{i0} = F_{i0}(E_{i0}) \tag{3}$$

for the present week and by another set of differential equations

$$\dot{r}_1 = F_{11}(E_{11}), \dot{p}_{i1} = F_{i1}(E_{i1}) \quad (4)$$

for the next week. The effective prices in the present week are given by the values which solutions to (3) take on at $t = \infty$. Similarly for the effective prices for the next week, i.e., they are the values which solutions to (4) take on at $t = \infty$.

In addition to the actual dynamic system (3) let us consider an imaginary system (4). (Equation (4) is the actual system in the next week but is an imaginary one when it is taken as a system of the present week.) If the actual dynamic system were not (3) but (4) the effective prices of the present week would take on the values which solutions to (4) approach as $t = \infty$. We may reduce the comparison between the two sets of effective prices of the present and next weeks to the comparison between the values which solutions to two mutually exclusive dynamic systems (3) and (4) take on at $t = \infty$.

By the previous method of comparative statics analysis, solutions to two sets of simultaneous equations are compared, while this method compares solutions to two sets of differential equations. Therefore this method of analysis can make not only a comparison of the effective prices which are established at the end of the week but also a comparison of the entire processes of formation of the effective prices. The comparative analysis of two mutually exclusive dynamic systems, A and B, is called comparative dynamics. By regarding the dynamic systems of price formation of the present week and the next week as if they are mutually exclusive alternative systems we may explain differences between the price formations in the two weeks by applying the method of comparative dynamics analysis.

By the use of comparative dynamics we can explain how prices fluctuate from this week to the next, from the next to the week after the next, and so on. The same problem could be dealt with by applying the method of comparative statics. But where the system is non-linear and has multiple sets of equilibrium prices and interest rates, the comparative statics analysis cannot tell which set would actually prevail in the market at its closing time. In the following we use the former method. It will be made clear in section 5 below that comparative dynamics analysis is concerned with the entire process of price formation and has much greater explanatory power than comparative statics analysis which is only concerned with the temporary equilibrium conditions of each week.

2 Analysis of parameters – with special reference to the creation of money

In comparative statics or dynamics two systems are compared which differ in the values of the parameters. At the beginning of the analysis we must specify the parameters of the system. As far as our present problem is concerned this is to make clear what factors will affect the shapes of excess demand functions.

(I) As we have seen in chapter 2, demands and supplies of households and firms are functions of current and expected prices – the interest rate is regarded as one of the prices – and the initial assets (initial holding of money and initial stocks of commodities).

Expected prices are functions of current prices (that is subjective expectation functions) so that demands and supplies ultimately depend on current prices and initial assets only. Therefore, even if current prices are the same, demands and supplies are different if the initial assets are different. This means that the demand and supply curves traced out in the prices–interest rate space will shift when the value of initial assets changes so that the latter is the parameter of the curves. More exactly, the shapes of demand and supply curves depend on the distributions of the initial stock of money among households and firms and the distribution of the initial stocks of commodities among firms.

Next we must consider expectation functions which link expected prices and the expected rate of interest to current prices and the current rate of interest respectively. These functional relationships will change if the household's or the firm's judgement of the future economic situation changes. Therefore, if the household or the firm receives new information which would give rise to a revision of their judgement or if their psychology changes, then the expected function will be modified and therefore excess demand functions will shift or change their slopes.

Let us consider the third factor. Demand and supply curves are derived, for the household, from a given order of preferences of commodities and, for the firm, from a given technology and a given order of liquidity preferences. Therefore, if the order of preferences, technology, or liquidity preferences has changed, then demand and supply curves must be affected. The change in the curves may take the form of a change in their slopes, i.e., a change in the degree of substitution, or the form of parallel movements of the curves.

As has been seen, the excess demand function of each good depends on many factors. We express the complex of these factors simply by α and write the excess demand function as

$$E_i = E_i(p_1, p_2, \ldots, p_n, \alpha);\ p_1 = r \tag{5}$$

A change in α induces a movement in the position or slopes of the excess function. The most important elements of α are initial assets and stocks while subsidiary elements include expectations, tastes, and technology.

(II) Next we must mention other important factors which change the shape of the excess demand functions. They are the economic activities of the banks and of the government. In the following we explain this in more detail.

Our analysis has so far been based on the following definitions of excess demand for commodities and excess demand for cash balances. (i) Excess demand for commodities is the difference between demand and supply made by the public, i.e., households and firms. (ii) Excess demand for cash balances is the excess of the cash balances which the public want to hold in the present week over the quantity of money which they hold at the beginning of the week. The point of temporary equilibrium of the present week is the point where these excess demands all vanish.

Clearly we have not given any consideration to the activities of banks and of the government but this does not necessarily mean that there are no banks or no government in our system; it means that they do not carry out any economic activity in the present week. Needless to say, this assumption greatly limits the applicability of our theory to reality. Therefore, we must consider an economic system which allows banks and government to be active, and derive economic laws for that system.

The most important economic activities of banks are the creation and contraction of money supply. Money supply is increased or decreased through the form of buying or selling securities by banks.

Let us first consider the creation of money. In a short-term lending spot economy, money is created by buying securities of one week's maturity. Let D_1^B be the banks' demand for securities and let S_0^B be the money created; we then have

$$S_0^B \equiv D_1^B$$

but this equality assumes that no banks sold securities in the previous week. If banks sold securities of the amount S_{-1}^B they must return to the public, in this period, money of the amount $(1 + \bar{r})S_{-1}^B$ which is the principal and interest that banks borrowed in the previous week. This implies a creation of money. Therefore the total amount of money created is the sum

$$S_0^B \equiv (1 + \bar{r})S_{-1}^B + D_1^B$$

Money supply is contracted in the following way. First, the amount D_{-1}^B which banks lent to the public or to the government in the previous week – that is, banks' demand for securities in the previous period, *plus* interest on the securities, will be returned to banks during this week. Moreover, banks can sell securities of the amount S_1^B; money will be contracted through this channel also. Therefore the total contraction of money supply in this week amounts to

$$D_0^B \equiv (1 + \bar{r})D_{-1}^B + S_1^B$$

Next we consider the activities of the government. Like ordinary households the government also demands various kinds of goods. This expenditure is usually financed by taxes, etc.; when the government's expenditure exceeds its tax revenue, government securities are issued. However, in the following we assume, for the sake of simplicity, that the government does not levy taxes at all and its expenditures are financed entirely by issuing government securities. The term of these government securities is one week, assuming a short-term lending spot economy.

The government will acquire by selling government securities S_1^G to banks. If it has issued government securities of the amount S_{-1}^G in the previous week, it must return money of the amount, $(1 + \bar{r})S_{-1}^G$ to banks. Therefore the government's net acquisition of cash in the present week amounts to $S_1^G - (1 + \bar{r})S_{-1}^G$. The government will spend this amount of money on various items. If we assume that it will entirely spend the amount of money that it acquires in the present week in buying consumption and capital goods, we have the government's budget equation

$$S_1^G - (1 + \bar{r})S_{-1}^G \equiv \sum_{2}^{n} p_i\beta_i \tag{6}$$

where β_i represents its demand for commodity i.

Let us now turn our attention to the entire economy. First of all we have the sum of the individuals' and firms' budget equations

$$-E_0 \equiv M + (1 + \bar{r})E_{-1} - L \equiv E_1 + \Sigma p_i E_i \tag{7}$$

Next we have an equation which expresses banks' creation of money ΔM

$$\Delta M \equiv S_0^B - D_0^B \equiv (1 + \bar{r})(S_{-1}^B - D_{-1}^B) + D_1^B - S_1^B \tag{8}$$

Therefore for the entire economy consisting of the public, banks, and the government, we have the sum of (6), (7), and (8). That is to say

$$\begin{aligned} M + \Delta M + (1 + \bar{r})(E_{-1} + D_{-1}^B - S_{-1}^B - S_{-1}^G) - L \\ \equiv (E_1 + D_1^B - S_1^B - S_1^G) + \Sigma p_i(E_i + \beta_i) \end{aligned} \tag{9}$$

Thus, when we allow for the activities of banks and the government, temporary market equilibrium conditions are modified. In chapter 3 above we discussed temporary equilibrium and obtained, as conditions for it, that the demand be equal to the supply for each good, that is, the excess demand must vanish in each market. However, the demand and supply in that chapter includes only the demand and supply by households and firms, those by the government and banks having been ignored, simply because we have assumed that no activities are carried out by the latter institutions. Where they carry out economic activities demand and supply must include their demand and supply also. It is then obvious that temporary market equilibrium conditions are given as commodity-wise equalities between the total demand and total supply including government's and banks' demand and supply respectively. Since temporary equilibrium held in the previous week, demand for securities was equal to their supply in the previous week so that we have $E_{-1} + D^{B}_{-1} - S^{B}_{-1} - S^{G}_{-1} = 0$. Therefore from (9) we obtain

$$M + \Delta M - L \equiv (E_1 + \beta_1) + \Sigma p_i(E_i + \beta_i) \qquad (10)$$

where $\beta_1 \equiv D^{B}_{1} - S^{B}_{1} - S^{G}_{1}$. (10) expresses Walras' law in the economy where the government and banks can carry out economic activities. Temporary market equilibrium conditions are now stated as

$$L = M + \Delta M; \ E_i + \beta_i = 0 \ (i = 1, \ldots, n)$$

Thus, equality between demand and supply is restated by including government's and banks' demand and supply. However, there are significant differences between their demand and supply and the public's. As has been repeatedly stated, the public's demand and supply are determined so that the utility or profit is maximized. In this maximization, prices and the rate of interest are taken into account and therefore the public's demand and supply are given by well-defined functions of the prices and the rate of interest. On the other hand, where the government buys a certain amount of certain goods with the intention of increasing the public's welfare or of pursuing war, the government will demand these goods of these amounts regardless of groping price. Also the creation of money is determined by the banks' lending policy and its amount may be more or less independent of the fluctuation of groping prices, when they are moderate, in the market. In this way we may regard ΔM and β_i not as functions of prices and the rate of interest but as autonomous parameters. Thus the fourth group of parameters which will change the excess demand function of commodities includes the amount of money created and the government's demand. In particular, as for the excess demand function of securities, the parameter is β_1 which is the banks' demand for securities *less* the government's and the banks' supply of securities.

3 Comparative dynamics analysis of the 'linear' model (I)[2]

Let us now make a comparative dynamics analysis of the process of price formation.[3] We begin by assuming that banks and the government carry

[2] α is a parameter which represents the given state of data.

[3] As an interesting example of comparative dynamics analysis, we may mention Okishio, 1950.

out no economic activities, i.e., $\Delta M = \beta_i = 0$ $(i = 1, \ldots, n)$. Suppose now that when the complex of parameters, α, is α^0, temporary equilibrium values take on $p_1^0, p_2^0, \ldots, p_n^0$. Expanding E_i in a Taylor series we have

$$E_i = \Sigma(E_{ij}^0 + \Delta E_{ij})(p_j - p_j^0) + E_{i\alpha}^0(\alpha - \alpha^0) + \ldots$$

where $\Delta E_{ij} = E_{ij\alpha}^0(\alpha - \alpha^0)$. Therefore we have the adjustment functions of the rate of interest and of prices

$$\dot{p}_i = F_i^0\{\Sigma(E_{ij}^0 + \Delta E_{ij})(p_j - p_j^0) + E_{i\alpha}^0(\alpha - \alpha^0)\} + \ldots, (p_1 = r)$$

In the above expressions the omitted part after the plus sign consists of the terms of higher orders with respect to $p_j - p_j^0$. We assume in the following that there are no such higher-order terms: i.e., the market is linear with respect to prices and the rate of interest. As we have discussed in chapter 4, section 7 above, we cannot make this assumption of linearity for both the money market and the securities market. In the following we adopt the loanable fund theory of the rate of interest and assume that the excess demand for securities is linear.

Let us now define

$$\Delta a_{ij} = F_i^0 \Delta E_{ij};\ \Delta a_i = F_i^0 E_{i\alpha}^0(\alpha - \alpha^0)$$

The adjustment functions of the rate of interest and prices in the linear market can then be put in the form

$$\dot{p}_i = \Sigma(a_{ij} + \Delta a_{ij})(p_j - p_j^0) + \Delta a_i \tag{11}$$

We can easily solve these linear differential equations. For this purpose we additionally define

$$H = |a_{ij} + \Delta a_{ij}| \quad i,j = 1, \ldots, n,$$
$$H_{ij} = \text{the cofactor of } a_{ij} + \Delta a_{ij} \text{ in } H$$

Let $\mu_k, k = 1, 2, \ldots, s \leqq n$ be distinct roots of the characteristic equation,

$$|a_{ij} + a_{ij} - \mu\delta_{ij}| = 0, \text{ where } \delta_{ii} = 1 \text{ and } \delta_{ij} = 0 \text{ for } i \neq j.$$

Considering α as a constant independent of t, we have the general solutions to (11)

$$p_i(t) = p_i^0 - (\Sigma \Delta a_j H_{ji})/H + \Sigma q_{ik}(t) e^{\mu_k t} \tag{12}$$

By defining $U = |E_{ij}^0 + \Delta E_{ij}|$

$$U_{ij} = \text{the cofactor of } E_{ij}^0 + \Delta E_{ij} \text{ in } U$$

we have

$$H = F_1^0 F_2^0 \ldots F_n^0 U,$$

$$\Sigma \Delta a_j H_{ji} = F_1^0 \ldots F_n^0 (\Sigma E_{j\alpha}^0 U_{ji})(\alpha - \alpha^0)$$

Then we can eliminate F_i^0 and rewrite (12) in the form

$$p_i(t) = p_i^0 - (\Sigma E_{j\alpha}^0 (\alpha - \alpha^0) U_{ji})/U + \Sigma q_{ik}(t) e^{\mu_k t} \tag{13}$$

We call this equation the fundamental equation of comparative dynamics (I). It explains how prices will change when the public's (the households' or firms') demands or supplies shift. From this equation we get the following result.

(i) Substitutions between commodities are affected when our tastes, or available techniques or elasticity of expectations change (in this last case intertemporal substitutions between commodities are affected). If we assume that in such changes only degrees of substitution of commodities vary, thus $\Delta a_{ij} \neq 0$ but Δa_is are all zero, then the second term disappears from the fundamental equation (I). Moreover if we assume Δa_{ij}s are sufficiently small, then the characteristic roots μ_ks are in a small neighbourhood of the characteristic roots λ_ks which are the latent roots of the equation $|a_{ij} - \lambda \delta_{ij}| = 0$, provided that the system is structurally stable before the change. Therefore we have

$$\text{sign } R(\mu_k) = \text{sign } R(\lambda_k)$$

Thus the stability of the original system implies stability after the change insofar as the degrees of substitutions vary to a small extent. Prices after the change will approach the temporary equilibrium prices p_i^0 of the original systems as t tends to infinity. That is to say, *in the 'linear' market, which is structurally stable, a small change in the degree of substitution will affect the time shape of groping prices but does not yield any change in the equilibrium prices finally established*, provided that the temporary equilibrium is stable in the original system.

(ii) Next we are concerned with the case where there is no change in the degree of substitution and the excess demand function makes a parallel shift. In that case we have $\Delta E_{ij} = 0$, so that obviously $\mu_k = \lambda_k$ for all k. Thus, if the temporary equilibrium in the original system is stable, then the new equilibrium after the shift is also stable. Define

$$J = |E_{ij}^0| \, i, j = , \ldots, n,$$
$$J_{ij} = \text{the cofactor of } E_{ij}^0 \text{ in } J$$

Then we can write the new equilibrium prices after the shift as

$$p_i^0 - (\Sigma E_{j\alpha}^0 (\alpha - \alpha^0) J_{ji})/J$$

For the sake of simplicity let us now consider that the demand for only one commodity, say k, is changed. First assume $k \neq 1$. Since $E^0_{j\alpha} = 0 (j \neq k)$, the difference between the new and old equilibrium prices of commodity i is given by

$$\Delta p_i = -E^0_{k\alpha}(\alpha - \alpha^0)J_{ki}/J$$

the sign of which is generally indefinite. But if we assume that the system possessed Hicksian stability before the change, then we can ascertain the sign of Δp_k. That is to say that in this case we have $J_{kk}/J < 0$. Therefore an increase (or decrease) in the demand (or supply) of good k gives rise to an increase in the equilibrium price of good k because we have $E^0_{k\alpha}(\alpha - \alpha^0) > 0$ in this case. On the other hand, if the supply (or demand) of good k is increased (or decreased), i.e., if $E^0_{k\alpha}(\alpha - \alpha^0) < 0$ then the equilibrium price of good k will decline.

As for the rate of interest we have the following result. Assume that the system has Hicksian stability before the change; then $J_{11}/J > 0$. Therefore an increase in the demand for securities – that is a decrease in the demand for cash balances – makes the equilibrium value of the rate of interest fall. In the converse case it will rise.

(iii) Let us next consider the case where a change in the parameter α induces a change in the degrees of substitution between commodities as well as a parallel shift in the excess demand function of good k ($k \neq 1$). In this case the equilibrium price of good i will be changed by the amount

$$-E^0_{k\alpha}(\alpha - \alpha^0)U_{ki}/U \tag{14}$$

Generally speaking this amount is indefinite. It may be positive or negative. However, if we assume that the system is stable in Hicks' sense *after* the change in the parameter, then (14) is of the same sign as $E_{k\alpha}(\alpha - \alpha^0)$ for $i = k$. In other words when excess demand for good k increases (or decreases), its price rises (or falls) accordingly. When $k = 1$ we have $U_{11}/U > 0$; therefore an increase (or decrease) in the demand for securities makes the interest rate fall (or rise).

For $i \neq k$ what value does (14) take on? That is to say, we now consider the effect of an increase in demand for good k upon prices of goods i other than k. We cannot give a definite answer to this problem. Even if we assume that the system is Hicksian we need an additional assumption, say, that the new system after the change in demand is a Metzler-stable system. In this case, after the increase in the parameter, $a_{ij} + \Delta a_{ij}$ becomes all positive ($i \neq j$) and the new system is stable so that all the cofactors of order $n - 1$ of the determinant $|-a_{ij} - \Delta a_{ij}|$ are positive. [This result follows from a proposition attributable to Frobenius (1908) which asserts that if $(a_{ij} + \Delta a_{ij} + \delta_{ij})$, where $\delta_{ij} = 0$ or 1 according to $j \neq i$ or $j = i$, is a positive, stable matrix, then the cofactors of the matrix $(s\delta_{ij} - (a_{ij} + \Delta a_{ij} + \delta_{ij}))$ are all positive if $s \geqq v$, where v is the largest positive characteristic root of the positive matrix. As the stability means $v < 1$, we have the result by putting $s = 1$.] On the other hand, we have the sign of $|a_{ij} + \Delta a_{ij}| = \text{sign}(-1)^n$. Therefore U_{ki}/U is negative for all i where $k = 2, \ldots, n$. Therefore *an increase (or decrease) in the demand for good k increases (or decreases) not only the price of good k but also prices of all other commodities (including the rate of interest).*

For $k = 1$, the ratio U_{1i}/U is positive irrespective of the value of i. Therefore *an increase in the demand for securities diminishes the rate of interest and all prices.* Either an increase in the demand for good k or an increase in demand for securities will give rise to a decrease in cash balances but they have opposite effects on the rate of interest and prices. It would lead to erroneous conclusions if we limit our view of how prices will change to considering a change in the demand and supply of money, ignoring how such a change in the demand and supply of money is caused – if, that is to say, we neglect the change in the demand and supply of commodities or securities which lies behind the change in the demand and supply of money. Metzler's condition

$$a_{ij} + \Delta a_{ij} > 0 \ (i \neq j)$$

implies $E_{ij}^0 + \Delta E_{ij} > 0$ for $i \neq 1$. (i) Therefore, in the system, all commodities (excluding securities) are substitutive for each other and if the rate of interest increases, the demand for commodities will increase. On the other hand, for $i = 1$ Metzler conditions imply

$$F_1^0(E_{1j}^0 + \Delta E_{1j}) > 0 \ (j \neq 1)$$

Since $F_1^0 < 0$, this implies $E_{1j}^0 + \Delta E_{1j} < 0$, that is to say, (ii) an increase in a price will diminish the demand for securities. This means that securities are gross complementary with all other commodities. When conditions (i) and (ii) are satisfied, we say that substitution relationships are dominant among commodities in Metzler's sense.

4 Comparative dynamics analysis of the 'linear' model (II) – effects of the creation of money

So far we have assumed that banks and the government carry out no economic activity in the current period and we have examined the effects of a change in the public's demand and supply functions upon equilibrium prices. In this section we conversely assume that there is no change in the public's demand and supply functions and examine the effects of banks' and the government's economic activities.

When banks and the government carry out economic activities the adjustment functions of the rate of interest and of prices are written in the form

$$\dot{p}_i = F_i(E_i + \beta_i),\ i = 1, \ldots, n$$

where $p_1 = r$. Assuming the linearity of the adjustment functions the above expression can be re-written as

$$\dot{p}_i = \Sigma a_{ij}(p_j - p_j^0) + F_i^0 \beta_i \tag{15}$$

Regarding β_i as constant we obtain as the general solutions to (15)

$$p_i(t) = p_i^0 + \Sigma q_{is}(t) e^{\lambda_s t} - \Sigma \beta_j \frac{J_{ji}}{J} \tag{16}$$

We call (16) the fundamental equation of comparative dynamics (II). If we assume that the market consisting of households and firms only (i.e., excluding banks and the government) is stable, then the real parts of the characteristic roots λ_s are all negative. The limits obtained for t tending to infinity give the temporary equilibrium prices of the system (15). They are $p_i^0 - \Sigma \beta_j J_{ji}/J$. The second term of this expression stands for the effect on equilibrium prices of a change in banks' and the government's economic activity.

As we stated before, there are two ways of increasing or contracting money supply. The first method of increasing (or contracting) money supply is for the banks to buy (or sell) securities from (or to) the public. The second is for banks to buy government securities from the government. Let us now investigate each of these two cases.

(i) When banks create money by lending to the public the government's activity is not influenced by the creation of money so we may assume that $S_1^G = \beta_i = 0$ $(i = 2, \ldots, n)$. In this case we have

$$\Delta M \equiv D_1^B - S_1^B \equiv \beta_1$$

(we assume $D^B_{-1} = S^B_{-1} = S^G_{-1} = 0$). Therefore the effect upon the equilibrium price of commodity i is given as

$$-(J_{1i}/J)\Delta M$$

If the system consisting of the public only is a Hicksian stable system we have $J_{11}/J > 0$. Therefore an increase in money ($\Delta M > 0$) gives rise to a decrease in the rate of interest and vice versa.

The effects on prices cannot be determined on the assumption that the system is Hicksian stable only. In order to ascertain the directions of price change we must assume additional conditions, e.g., the dominance of substitutes in Metzler's sense which was examined in (iii) of the previous section. We are not concerned with this case here but with another case which is considered more important than Metzler's case.

First we assume that the system is Hicksian stable. We also assume $E^0_{1i} < 0$ and $E^0_{i1} < 0, i = 2, \ldots, n$. In the case of Metzler substitutability we have $E^0_{i1} > 0$ but since an increase in the rate of interest may be considered to decrease the demand for all commodities – especially those for capital goods – we assume opposite conditions, i.e., $E^0_{i1} < 0$. The other condition $E^0_{1i} < 0$ implies that the demand for securities will decrease. This is because the demand for funds increases when there is an increase in prices. The third condition which we assume is that the system of order $n - 1$, obtained by excluding securities, is a stable one satisfying Metzler conditions.

In a system satisfying all these three conditions – I refer to it as an A system – the directions of change of prices are certain. First, from the first and third conditions we have

$$J_{11}/J > 0, J_{11ki}/J_{11} < 0 \tag{17}$$

Where J_{11ki} is a cofactor of E^0_{ki} in J_{11}, applying Laplace expansion to J_{1i} we have

$$J_{1i} = -\sum_2^n E^0_{k1} J_{11ki}$$

Considering (17) and the second condition we obtain

$$J_{1i}/J < 0, i = 2, \ldots, n$$

This implies that *a creation of money raises all prices.*

(ii) Next we examine the case where banks create money by buying government securities from the government. In this case S^B_1 is zero and $D^B_1 = S^G_1$ so that β_1 is zero. Therefore we have

$$\Delta M \equiv \sum_2^n p_i \beta_i$$

provided that $D^B_{-1} = S^B_{-1} = S^G_{-1} = 0$. If we assume that the government spends all the money it acquires on commodity $k, \Delta M = p_k \beta_k$. The temporary equilibrium value of the rate of interest and prices will shift by the amount

$$-(J_{ki}/J)\beta_k$$

In the A system in what directions will prices and the rate of interest change? First of all we immediately know that the price of commodity k will be raised. On the other hand, by the Laplace expansion we have

$$J_{ki} = E^0_{11}J_{11ki} - \sum_2^n \sum_2^n E^0_{h1}E^0_{1j}J_{11kihj}$$

where J_{11kihj} is the cofactor of E^0_{hj} in J_{11ki}. Furthermore by the third condition we have $J_{11kihh}/J_{11} > 0$ and $J_{11ki}/J_{11} < 0$. Taking the first condition and $E^0_{11} > 0$ into account we find that J_{ki} contains a term which has a sign opposite to the one of J. For $h \neq j$, what sign J_{11kihj}/J has cannot be determined, so the sign of J_{ki}/J is also uncertain but as it contains negative terms it is probable that J_{ki}/J itself is also negative. Therefore we may say that the prices of goods other than k will probably also be raised.

Next we examine the direction of the change in the rate of interest. Since

$$J_{k1} = -\sum_2^n E^0_{1i}J_{11ki}$$

we have $J_{kl}/J < 0$; this means that the rate of interest must be raised. This increase in the rate of interest is easily understandable because we have assumed that an increase in prices will induce an increase in the demand for funds.

In the above we have assumed that banks finance the entire amount of government expenditure by creating money. However in the actual world banks will sell to the public all or some of the government securities which they bought from the government. This means a contraction of money supply which produces a rise in the rate of interest and a fall in prices. *Thus an increase in prices caused by government expenditure will tend to be offset by a fall in prices due to the public's buying of government securities. In the money market we have a shortage of money due to price increases aggravated by the additional shortage of money caused by the contraction of the money supply and therefore the rate of interest will take on a very high value.*

This is a remarkable conclusion. When banks lend directly to the public we have a short-term fall in the rate of interest and a short-term increase in prices. On the other hand, when banks lend to the government both the rate of interest and prices will go up. These conclusions are obtained under a number of conditions and state that the effects of a creation of money are different when the channels of creation of money are different – through the public or through the government.

(iii) Assuming that our system is of the A type, we have examined in (i) the effects of creating money through the channel of lending to the public, and in (ii) a similar effect of an increase in money supply through the channel of lending to the government. One of the conclusions which we have obtained is that the rate of interest will be shifted if money is created by the method of either (i) or (ii) alone. Therefore in the A system if we want to keep the rate of interest constant in spite of an increase in money supply we must create money by a method combining (i) and (ii). We shall now investigate how they should be combined and how prices are affected if money is created in this way.

Let us assume that the government will buy only commodity k by the amount β_k and banks will lend to the government the amount of money which is equal to $p_k\beta_k$. In this case if banks buy securities of the amount β_1 from the public (or sell securities of the amount $-\beta_1$ to the public) then the net creation of money amounts to

$$\Delta M = \beta_1 + p_k\beta_k, (D^B_{-1} = S^B_{-1} = S^G_{-1} = 0)$$

and, as is easily seen, the equilibrium value of the rate of interest will shift by the amount

$$\Delta r = -\frac{J_{11}}{J}\beta_1 - \frac{J_{k1}}{J}\beta_k$$

If β_1 and β_k satisfy the relationship

$$\beta_1 = -\frac{J_{k1}}{J_{11}}\beta_k \tag{18}$$

then obviously we have $\Delta r = 0$. Where lending to the government and lending to the public each shift the rate of interest in the same direction, we must absorb money of the amount (18) from the public when the government makes its expenditure. That is to say, banks should not only lend to the government the entire amount $p_k\beta_k$ which it needs, but they must simultaneously sell government securities of the amount $-\beta_1$ to the public. However, where lending to the government and lending to the public affect the interest rate in opposite directions, banks must lend to the public the amount of money satisfying the relationship (18). At the same time they lend money to the government. Only in this way can the rate of interest be kept constant. In addition there is a case of $J_{11} = 0$. We exemplify later, in (iv), such a case.

Next let us consider how the equilibrium values of prices will be affected when banks adopt a monetary policy which keeps the rate of interest unchanged. As prices will shift by the amount

$$\Delta p_i = -\frac{J_{1i}}{J}\beta_1 - \frac{J_{ki}}{J}\beta_k$$

we have

$$\Delta p_i = \frac{1}{J}\frac{1}{J_{11}}(J_{1i}J_{k1} - J_{ki}J_{11})\beta_k$$

by virtue of (18). By the theorem of Jacobi we have

$$J_{11}J_{ki} - J_{1i}J_{k1} = JJ_{11ki}$$

so that we obtain

$$\Delta p_i = -\frac{J_{11ki}}{J_{11}}\beta_k \tag{19}$$

This relationship is formally equivalent to the formula which shows the effects on prices of an increase in the demand for good k in a system where no securities exist. That is to say, if banks adopt a monetary policy to keep the rate of interest constant in spite of an increase in the government's demand for good k, prices will change in exactly the same way as they could change in a system where there are no securities.

Finally let us explain the sign taken by (19). In (ii) we have examined the effect of government expenditure upon prices providing that the system is of the A type. We have there obtained the conclusion that the government's demand would probably, but not necessarily, raise prices. However, if banks adopt a monetary policy such that the rate of interest is kept unchanged in spite of an increase in government expenditure, all prices will be raised provided that the system is of the A type. This is because all J_{11ki}/J_{11} are negative since the system of order $n-1$ (excluding securities) is assumed to be a Metzler-stable system; and therefore (19) necessarily takes on a positive value where $\beta_k > 0$.

(iv) Apart from A there is another important system which we should investigate. We make the following assumptions concerning demand and supply functions. Throughout the following we assume, for the sake of simplicity, that the parameter α is fixed and not indicated explicitly in the excess demand functions.

1′ Each commodity (excluding money and securities) has an excess demand function which is homogeneous of degree zero in all prices except the rate of interest. Thus, for all θ we have

$$E_i(r, \theta p_2, \ldots, \theta p_n) = E_i(r, p_2, \ldots, p_n),\ i = 2, \ldots, n$$

2′ The amount of cash balances which the public want to hold is a homogeneous function of degree 1 in all prices, i.e.

$$L(r, \theta p_2, \ldots, \theta p_n) = \theta L(r, p_2, \ldots, p_n)$$

In the following we call a system which satisfies 1′ and 2′ a B system. What effects does a creation of money have upon prices and the rate of interest in the B system? First of all, by Walras' law we have

$$M - L \equiv E_1 + \Sigma p_i E_i$$

As M stands for the quantity of money which the public already holds at the beginning of the present week, it is a constant. Therefore in view of 1′ and 2′ the excess demand function of securities cannot be a homogeneous function in prices.[4] Therefore we have $J \neq 0$.

In a system where the temporary equilibrium values are stable, the lending of money by the banks to the public changes the equilibrium values by

$$\Delta r = -\frac{J_{11}}{J}\Delta M;\ \Delta p_i = -\frac{J_{1i}}{J}\Delta M, \text{ where } D^{\mathrm{B}}_{-1} = S^{\mathrm{B}}_{-1} = S^{\mathrm{G}}_{-1} = 0$$

Considering 1′ we have $J_{11} = 0$, as we have from 1′

$$\sum_{2}^{n} E_{ij}^{0} p_j^{0} = 0,\ i = 2, \ldots, n$$

Thus the loan to the public has no effect on the rate of interest in the B system. Moreover, from the above equation we have

$$J_{12}:J_{13}:\ldots:J_{1n} = p_2^0:p_3^0:\ldots:p_n^0$$

Consequently we have

$$p_2^0 + \Delta p_2 : p_3^0 + \Delta p_3 : \ldots : p_n^0 + \Delta p_n = p_2^0 : p_3^0 : \ldots : p_n^0$$

On the other hand, we have

$$L(r^0, p_2^0, \ldots, p_n^0) = M$$

and from 2′ we have $\pi L(r^0, p_2^0, \ldots, p_n^0) = M + \Delta M$ where we have $\pi = (p_i^0 + \Delta p_i)/p_i^0$ so that we finally obtain

$$p_i^0 + \Delta p_i : M + \Delta M = p_i^0 : M$$

Hence we can conclude as follows. *In the B system if money is created in the form of a loan to the public, all prices change at the same rate as the volume of*

[4] Let $E_i = f_i\left(r, \frac{p_2}{p_n}, \ldots, \frac{p_{n-1}}{p_n}\right)$, $i = 2, \ldots, n$ and $E_1 = p_n f_1\left(r_1, \frac{p_2}{p_n}, \ldots, \frac{p_{n-1}}{p_n}\right)$. The system of equations, $E_i = 0, i = 1, 2, \ldots, n$ has, in general, no solutions because the number of equations exceeds the number of unknowns, $r, \frac{p_2}{p_n}, \ldots, \frac{p_{n-1}}{p_n}$ by 1 (provided $p_n \neq 0$). See Patinkin, 1949, p. 20. In order for a system in which the excess demand function of commodities excluding securities and money are all homogeneous of degree zero in prices, e.g., a system assumed by the classical school, not to be overdeterminant, it is necessary that the excess demand function for securities is not homogeneous of order 1 in prices (Patinkin, 1949, p. 22).

money increases. That is to say we have the quantity theory of money proposition. In fact many modern economists have pointed out the homogeneity conditions 1′ and 2′ as implicit assumptions underlying the quantity theory of money.[5]

Thus in the B system the quantity theory of money is valid when money is created through the channel of a loan to the public. What, then, is the consequence if money is created in the form of a loan to the government? Assuming that the government spends exclusively on commodity k the amount of money thus acquired, then the rate of interest and prices will change by

$$\Delta r = -\frac{J_{k1}}{J}\beta_k, \Delta p_i = -\frac{J_{ki}}{J}\beta_k$$

respectively. Taking into account the previous homogeneity conditions and Walras' law the excess demand for securities E_1 is equal to the constant M minus some homogeneous function of degree 1 in prices (excluding the rate of interest). In view of this fact we can show

$$J_{ki} = \frac{p_i^0}{p_2^0} J_{k2} + \frac{M}{p_2^0} J_{k21i}$$

Consequently to obtain proportional change in prices, $\Delta p_i : \Delta p_2 = p_i^0 : p_2^0$, we must have

$$M = 0 \text{ or } J_{k21i} = 0, \ i = 3, \ldots, n$$

but M is not equal to zero and the condition $J_{k21i} = 0$ does not follow from homogeneity conditions only. Therefore in the B system prices do not necessarily change proportionately.

From the above we have the following conclusions. First, in the B system, an increase in money created in the form of a loan to the public produces a change in prices at the same rate as in money, while a creation of money in the form of a loan to the government does not necessarily produce a proportional change in prices. This means that, although the quantity theory of money holds if money is created to lend to the public, it does not necessarily hold if it is created to lend to the government. *Thus the validity of the quantity theory of money depends on the channel through which money is created.* The crude quantity theorist who does not pay any attention to this point may be in serious danger of reaching misleading conclusions. Secondly, in the B system, the excess demand function for labour is

[5] As far as the quantity theory of money is taken as a short-term theory, we have to consider that it presumes conditions 1′ and 2′. However, they are not necessary conditions for the quantity theory to be valid in the long-run. See section 9 below.

homogeneous of degree zero. Considering the fact that the demand and supply of labour are decided by different persons, we must assume that in the B system both the demand and the supply functions of labour are homogeneous of degree zero in prices. When money is created in the form of a loan to the public, the rate of interest is constant and prices will increase proportionately in the B system. Therefore there is no change in the demand and supply for labour so that this creation of money is not effective as a short-run policy for promoting employment. On the other hand, if the money is created in order to lend to the government, the rate of interest will change and prices will not necessarily change proportionately. A change in relative prices will induce a change in the demand for labour. Thus we may conclude that *in the B system the effectiveness of a short-run monetary policy to reduce unemployment depends on the channel of money creation.*

These conclusions are no more than common sense but, still, they are remarkable conclusions from general equilibrium analysis. For the canonical system which we have obtained in chapter 3, section 9, we can make a similar comparative dynamic analysis. It is interesting economically but is left to the reader as an exercise.

5 The relationship between comparative dynamics and comparative statics

Let us consider how the above comparative dynamic analysis differs from comparative statics analysis which is traditionally used, and let us decide what is the merit of the former over the latter. First of all it is clear that comparative statics analysis can only explain the shift in the temporary equilibrium point which is caused by a change in a parameter. Paying no attention to the adjustment functions of prices which give intertemporal relationships in the process of forming prices and concentrating on the temporary equilibrium conditions only, the comparative statics analysis examines how the temporary equilibrium value P changes to P' when the parameter complex changes from α to α'. It cannot explain the course along which prices approach P' as α shifts to α'.

More exactly, we must say as follows. Comparative statics analysis only sees that the equilibrium point P corresponds to the parameter complex α and P' to α', and completely neglects whether P or P' is realized at α or α' respectively. In fact if P is an unstable equilibrium point when the parameter complex is α then P will not be realized if tatonnement starts from a point other than P, in spite of the fact that P corresponds to α. Provided that the system is structurally stable, an unstable equilibrium point P at α will remain unstable even after α changes to α'. That is to say, P' is also unstable so that it will also not be realized. The comparative statics formula that $P \to P'$ as $\alpha \to \alpha'$ is valid as the formula for a shift in the mathematical solutions to the temporary equilibrium equations, but is not valid as a formula for describing the change in the prices actually realized. This is the first difficulty of comparative statics analysis.

Let us now assume that the equilibrium point is always stable. Then we can avoid the above difficulty but still we have the following one. If we take the comparative statics analysis as an analysis which explains the whole process of price formation, i.e., not only the shift in equilibrium prices which is realized at the end of the week but also the shift in prices during the formation process, its formula that $P \to P'$ as $\alpha \to \alpha'$ implies that P shifts to P' instantaneously at an infinitely high speed as α shifts to α'. This means that the real parts of the characteristic roots are all $-\infty$. Therefore we can say that in the particular case where the characteristic roots have the real part of $-\infty$, comparative statics can explain how the whole process of price formation is affected by a change in the parameter complex, but otherwise it can only explain the shift in the goal which is reached at the end – not the change in the process of reaching it. In order to recognize comparative statics analysis as a perfect theory of price change we must make an extreme and unrealistic assumption that the real parts of the characteristic roots are all $-\infty$.

As is always assumed in comparative statics analysis, we have assumed in sections 3 and 4 of our comparative dynamics analysis that a change in a parameter is a persistent magnitude from the beginning to the end of the week. That is to say, as far as that week is concerned the change is a permanent one but an actual change in a parameter is not necessarily of that type. It is possible that it may be an intermittent change or a transient or instantaneous one. For example, at the beginning of a certain week we may have a temporary change in taste which returns to the old state of taste during the process of tatonnement. Or we may have the case where banks change their lending policy several times within one 'week' and the amount of money created changes in the process of tatonnement. [A famous example of this is Mr. Lamont's drastic U-turn in British monetary policy, from sticking to the European exchange mechanism to quitting it, that he made on 16 September 1992.] In this way the change in a parameter may depend on time t. In that case the analysis of effects of a change in the parameter must be essentially dynamic; so the problem becomes one which is amenable to comparative dynamics analysis and cannot be solved by comparative statics.

Let us now assume that banks lend money to the public. Assume that the amount of money created in this way is a known function of t

$$\Delta M = \beta_1(t)$$

Then we obtain

$$\begin{aligned}\dot{p}_1 &= F_1^0(\Sigma E_{1j}^0(p_j - p_j^0) + \beta_1(t)),\\ \dot{p}_i &= F_i^0(\Sigma E_{ij}^0(p_j - p_j^0))\end{aligned} \tag{20}$$

where p_i^0 is the equilibrium price of commodity i when $\beta_1(t) = 0$. In solving these simultaneous differential equations we determine the constant B_{ij} so as to satisfy the conditions

$$\begin{aligned}\lambda_j B_{ij} &= \sum_{h=1}^{n} a_{ih} B_{hj},\ i,j = 1,\ldots,n,\\ -J_{1i}/J &= \sum_{j=1}^{n} B_{ij},\ i = 1,\ldots,n\end{aligned} \tag{21}$$

Consider $p_i(t)$ determined as

$$p_i(t) = p_i^0 - \frac{J_{1i}}{J}\beta_1(t) + \sum_j B_{ij}\left(\dot{\beta}_1 \frac{1}{\lambda_j} + \ddot{\beta}_1 \frac{1}{\lambda_j^2} + \ldots\right) \tag{22}$$

then it can be easily shown that (22) is a particular solution to (20). This is because we have

$$\dot{p}_i = -\frac{J_{1i}}{J}\dot{\beta}_1 + \sum_j B_{ij}\left(\ddot{\beta}_1 \frac{1}{\lambda_j} + \dddot{\beta}_1 \frac{1}{\lambda_j^2} + \ldots\right) \tag{23}$$

from (22); on the other hand, considering (21), we have

$$\begin{aligned}\sum_j a_{ij}(p_j - p_j^0) + F_i^0\beta_i &= \sum_j\sum_h a_{ih}B_{hj}\left(\dot{\beta}_1 \frac{1}{\lambda_j} + \ddot{\beta}_1 \frac{1}{\lambda_j^2} + \ldots\right)\\ &= -\frac{J_{1i}}{J}\dot{\beta}_1 + \sum_j B_{ij}\left(\ddot{\beta}_1 \frac{1}{\lambda_j} + \dddot{\beta}_1 \frac{1}{\lambda_j^2} + \ldots\right)\end{aligned} \tag{24}$$

where $\beta_i = 0$ for $i \neq 1$. Therefore (23) equals (24) so that (20) is satisfied.

Now it is well known that the general solution to simultaneous linear differential equations is the sum of a particular solution to them and the general solutions to simultaneous homogeneous linear differential equations, which are obtained by removing the terms $F_1^0\beta_1$, which are independent of the unknown functions. By applying this general rule we find that the general solutions to (20) are given as

$$p_i(t) = p_i^0 - \frac{J_{1i}}{J}\beta_1(t) + \Sigma q_{is}e^{\lambda_s t} + \sum_j B_{ij}\left(\dot{\beta}_1 \frac{1}{\lambda_j} + \ddot{\beta}_1 \frac{1}{\lambda_j^2} + \ldots\right) \tag{25}$$

from which we obtain the following results:

(i) When $\lim_{t\to\infty} \beta_1(t) = 0$ so that $\dot{\beta}_1(\infty) = \ddot{\beta}_1(\infty) = \ldots = 0$ the rate of interest and prices which will be realized at the end of the week will be p_i^0. In other words, a change in the parameter β_1 will induce a change in the time shape of p_i but does not cause any change in the temporary equilibrium prices.

(ii) When $\lim_{t\to\infty} \beta_1(t) \neq 0$ but $\dot{\beta}_1(\infty) = \ddot{\beta}_1(\infty) = \ldots = 0$ the rate of interest and prices will be at the end of the week

$$p_i^0 - \frac{J_{1i}}{J}\beta_1(\infty)$$

(iii) When $\beta_1(t)$ does not converge, $p_i(t)$ also does not.

The case of an intermittent or transient change in $\beta_1(t)$ is a special case of (i); while a permanent change in $\beta_1(t)$ is a special case of (ii). Taking $\beta_1(t)$ in an appropriate way we can fix $p_1(t)$ at the value p_1^0 for all t. That is to say, *the banks can maintain the rate of interest at a particular value from the beginning to the end of the week by adopting an appropriate policy.*

It is obvious that we can carry out an analysis similar to the above for any change in any other parameter. *Thus the comparative dynamics analysis can explain the effect of a non-constant change in a parameter. This is the most decisive advantage of comparative dynamics over comparative statics.*

[We have so far confined ourselves to the case of the economy being linear. However, where excess demand functions are non-linear, we may have multiple general equilibria. Some of them may be stable, separated by an unstable equilibrium or a limit cycle. If the economy is 'structurally unstable', a point which has belonged to a stability domain of an equilibrium point before a change in a parameter may easily turn out to belong to a stability zone of another equilibrium after the change, as has been pointed out previously, so that the results of comparative dynamics are considerable and significant. On the other hand, comparative static analysis that is powerless to identify which equilibrium is actually realized, tends to conclude as if the results of the comparative statics were obtained for any arbitrarily chosen equilibrium.]

6 Intertemporal relationships

We have seen that the method of comparative dynamics can be used for analysing a price change in the short run, i.e., how effective prices in the current week differ from those in the previous week. In the same way we compare the parameter complex in week τ with those in week $\tau - 1$. We can analyse how prices in week τ differ from those in $\tau - 1$. Taking τ as $0, 1, 2\ldots$ successively, we can trace out fluctuations in effective prices; if τ is taken to be sufficiently large we have a long-run analysis of price fluctuations. In

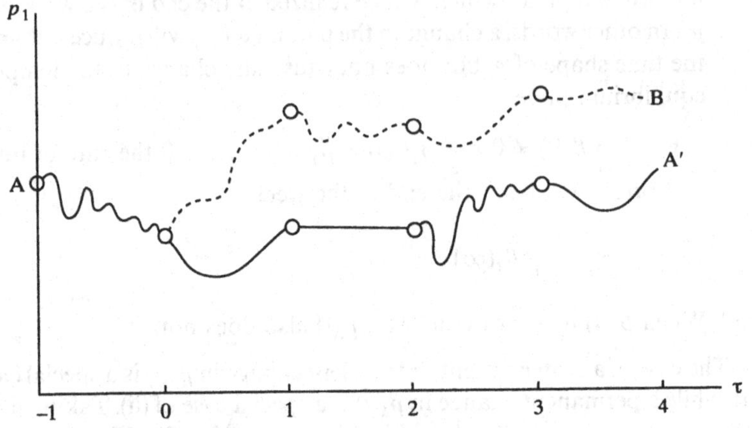

Figure 20

figure 20 the sequence of white circles gives the time series of effective prices. Continuous curves linking one white circle to the next give the time shape of groping prices for forming prices at the end of the week that are represented by the second white circle.

In this way we can trace out the time shape of effective prices but, however detailed we carry out this type of analysis we cannot analyse the fluctuations in effective prices according to their causes. The parameter complex in each week can take on any value. Therefore any kinds of time shapes of effective prices have equal probability of occurring. We cannot say from the above analysis that our time shapes will be of the form AA′ but not of the form AB. In order to know how given prices will change in one specific direction to the exclusion of others we must carry out not only a short-run comparative dynamics analysis but also a further analysis which clarifies the interrelationship between a parameter complex in one period and a parameter complex in the next.

In section 2 above we have listed the elements which are regarded as parameters in the analysis of price formation in a particular week. These elements are classified into two classes. The first includes those elements whose values in a particular period are determined by their performance in the market in the directly previous week. The second class consists of the elements whose values in a particular week are not related to their performance in the market in the previous week or, at most, are related to it in a very loose way. The values of the elements in the first class are determined by the past so that they cannot be changed at our will but those in the second class can change suddenly from week to week in an unexpected way.

The following will belong to the second class: (i) expectations, tastes, and liquidity preferences of individuals and firms, and technology used by the firms and (ii) lending by banks to the public, i.e., β_1 and government demand β_i. In the following we assume that expectations, tastes, liquidity preferences and technology can be expressed simply by a single index α and we denote the value of α in week τ by α_τ. Also we write β_i in week τ by $\beta_{i\tau}$.

On the other hand, the quantity of money and the total stock of commodities which the public has at the beginning of week τ and their distribution to each individual and each firm are elements of the first class. This is seen in the following way. At the beginning of week τ the total quantity of money held by the public is $\bar{M}_\tau = \Sigma x_{0\tau-1} + (1 + r_{\tau-1})\Sigma x_{1\tau-1}$, where the summation symbol Σ stands for the summation over all individuals and firms excluding banks and the government. If money was created by $\Delta M_{\tau-1}$ in week $\tau - 1$ in the form of government expenditure then we have $\Sigma x_{0\tau-1} = \bar{M}_{\tau-1} + \Delta M_{\tau-1}$. Since banks did not lend to the public we have $\Sigma x_{1\tau-1} = 0$. Therefore in such circumstances we would obtain $\bar{M}_\tau = \bar{M}_{\tau-1} + \Delta M_{\tau-1}$. Next if money is created by the amount $D^B_{1\tau-1}$ in week $\tau - 1$ in the form of short-term loans to the public we have $\Sigma x_{0\tau-1} = \bar{M}_{\tau-1} + D^B_{1\tau-1}$. As we have $\Sigma x_{1\tau-1} = -D^B_{1\tau-1}$ we therefore obtain $\bar{M}_\tau = \bar{M}_{\tau-1} - r_{\tau-1}D^B_{1\tau-1}$. Thus the total quantity of money held by the public in week τ depends on whether money was created at all in the previous week $\tau - 1$ *and* how it was created.[6]

Next we consider the total stocks of commodities held at the beginning of week τ. The total stock of commodity i at the beginning of week τ, $\bar{X}_{i\tau}$, is the sum of the total stock of commodity i at the beginning of week $\tau - 1$, $\bar{X}_{i\tau-1}$, and its increments during the week $\tau - 1$. Thus the increased amount of stock in week $\tau - 1$ depends on prices, the level of technology and liquidity preferences, and expectations in week $\tau - 1$ as well as the initial stock of commodities and initial amount of money in the same week. Therefore we have

$$\bar{X}_{i\tau} = \bar{X}_{i\tau}(\{p_{j\tau-1}\}, \{\bar{X}_{j\tau-1}\}, \bar{M}_{\tau-1}, \alpha_{\tau-1}) \tag{26}$$

[6] The quantity of money $\bar{M}_\tau$ which the public holds at the beginning of week τ is not necessarily equal to the quantity of money $L_{\tau-1}$ which the public had at the end of week $\tau - 1$. If lending and borrowing are carried on in week $\tau - 1$, either between the public or between the government and banks, the quantity of money involved is transferred in the transition from week $\tau - 1$ to week τ as a result of settling lending and borrowing. But the transaction is confined to the public or to the government and banks so that the total quantity of money held by the public does not change. On the other hand, lending and borrowing may take place between the public and banks. Money will then be transferred from the public to banks or *vice versa* in the transition from week $\tau - 1$ to week τ, so that the quantity of money held by the public may increase or decrease. If banks are entirely inactive or if they lend only to the government, the quantity of money held by the public at the end of week $\tau - 1$ is equal to $\bar{M}_\tau$ while if banks lend to the public $L_{\tau-1}$ is not necessarily equal to $\bar{M}_\tau$. When the public decides its planning in week τ, $\bar{M}_\tau$, but not $L_{\tau-1}$, plays the role of a parameter.

This shows that the stocks of commodities in week τ are completely determined by the past so that they are elements of the first class.[7]

Strictly speaking excess demand in week τ, $E_{j\tau}$, depends not only on $\bar{M}_\tau$ and $\{\bar{X}_{i\tau}\}$ but also on their distributions among individuals and firms, but in the following we neglect the effect of distribution for the sake of simplicity. Then from the above analysis we know that the total excess demand function (including the demand by the government) for each commodity in week τ can be written as

$$E_{j\tau}(\{p_{j\tau}\}, \{\bar{X}_{i\tau}(\{p_{k\tau-1}\}, \{\bar{X}_{k\tau-1}\}, \bar{M}_{\tau-1}, \alpha_{\tau-1})\}, \bar{M}_\tau, \alpha_\tau) + \beta_{j\tau} \qquad (26')$$

where $p_{1\tau} = r_\tau$.[8]

Assuming these, we can now discuss the time shape of effective prices. We simplify the problem by further assuming that the government and banks do not carry out any economic activity in any week, i.e.

$$\beta_{i\tau} = 0,\ i = 1, \ldots, n;\ \tau = -1, 0, 1, \ldots \qquad (27)$$

We also assume that there are no changes in expectations, tastes and technology, i.e.

$$\alpha_{-1} = \alpha_0 = \alpha_0 = \alpha_1 = \ldots \qquad (28)$$

[7] We have classified goods into three kinds, consumption goods, capital goods and primary factors of production. However, in the analysis of the production process there must be additional kinds of commodities which are unfinished consumption or capital goods or, in other words, goods in process. We must distinguish goods in process according to their degree of completion. Let us now classify them into w kinds and represent goods in process by $x_{n+1}, x_{n+2}, \ldots, x_{n+w}$. Technical relationships are different, depending on how much of the goods in process are available. Therefore the production functions given in chapter 2 must contain as their parameters stocks of goods in process, $\bar{x}_{n+i0}$ $(i = 1, \ldots, w)$, which are available at the beginning of the present week. In other words

$$f(x'_{20}, \ldots, x'_{nv}, \bar{x}_{n+10}, \ldots, \bar{x}_{n+w0}) = 0$$

In this way, to the list of parameters of the firm's demand and supply functions are added initial stocks of goods in process. They appear as parameters of excess demand functions of the present week as well as of the desired stocks of commodities which are held at the beginning of week 1. Initial stocks of goods in process in week τ depend on initial stocks of commodities (including goods in process) at the beginning of week $\tau - 1$ and the input and output of commodities during week $\tau - 1$. Therefore, they are the functions of $p_{j\tau-1}$, $\bar{X}_{j\tau-1}$, $\bar{M}_{\tau-1}$ and $\alpha_{\tau-1}$. Thus relationship (26) does hold for $i = n+1, \ldots, n+w$, too. In (26) j attached to $\bar{X}_{j\tau-1}$ refers to all $j = 1, \ldots, n+w$. In the following when I refer to the stock of commodities it includes the initial stock of goods in process. However, it must be remembered that there is no market for goods in process so they have no prices. Therefore in (26) the suffix attached to p runs from 1 to n only while the suffix attached to $\bar{X}$ runs from 2 to $n + w$.

[8] The subscripts of E and p take on the values, $1, 2, \ldots, n$, those of $\bar{X}$ the values, $2, 3, \ldots, n + w$.

Then we obtain from (27)

$$\bar{M}_{-1} = \bar{M}_0 = \bar{M}_1 = \ldots \tag{29}$$

Since $p_{i,-1}$ and $\bar{X}_{i,-1}$ are determined at the end of the previous week we find in view of (26′) that $\bar{X}_{i0}$ is determined at the beginning of the present week. We thus have all the parameters for determining temporary equilibrium prices p_{i0} in the present week. Once they are determined each $\bar{X}_{i1}$ is determined by (26). Therefore the temporary equilibrium prices p_{i1} in the next week will be determined. Repeating the same procedure we obtain $p_{i2}, p_{i3}, \ldots$. Thus the sequential relationship of temporary equilibrium prices is determined by taking the intertemporal relationship of parameters (26) into account. Therefore we cannot now say that any time shape of effective prices has an equal probability of occurrence.

In the above we have derived the time shape of effective prices on the assumptions (27)–(29). Under these assumptions of stationarity, effective prices may in general fluctuate. However, if we have

$$p_{i\tau} = p_{i\tau+1} = \ldots, \ i = 1, \ldots, n \tag{30}$$

we say that the economy is in a stationary state after week τ. In that case the temporary equilibrium in week τ is called perfect equilibrium or equilibrium over the week. Under the assumptions (27)–(29) the sufficient conditions for week τ to be in a state of perfect equilibrium are

$$\bar{X}_{i\tau+1} = \bar{X}_{i\tau}, \ i = 2, \ldots, n + w$$

In other words, stocks of each commodity must be in a stationary state after week τ. It must be noted that in deriving this result we have assumed that the shapes of the functions (26) and (26′) are the same for all weeks.

7 A change in tastes – comparative dynamics over weeks (I)

We have so far seen that the time shapes of effective prices are determined when tastes and technologies are unchanged and the government and banks do not carry out economic activities. In this section we analyse the effects of a change in tastes or technology upon the time shapes of effective prices while in section 9 below we analyse the similar effects of the economic activities of the government or banks. Let us now suppose a sequence of temporary equilibrium prices before the changes in tastes and technology are given as

$$p_{i,-1}, p_{i0}, p_{i1}, p_{i2}, \ldots \tag{31}$$

Also suppose that only parameter α_0 which represents tastes in the present week changes, with all the αs for the future weeks being kept constant. Then what effect will such a temporary change in α have upon the sequence of temporary equilibrium prices?

To discuss this problem we make, in addition to the general assumption that the system is linear, the following assumptions for simplicity. (i) Temporary equilibrium is stable in any week. (ii) A change in α_0 will cause the excess demand function for each commodity in the present week to shift and has no effect upon the degrees of substitution between commodities. (iii) A change in $\bar{X}_{i\tau}$ will cause the excess demand function for each good in week τ to shift but has no effect on the degrees of substitution. This last assumption is true for $\tau = 1, 2, \ldots$. Finally, (iv) the degrees of substitution of each good are the same throughout all weeks.

Provided with these assumptions we may solve the problem formally in the following way. A change in parameter α_0, written as $\Delta\alpha_0$, gives rise to a change in temporary equilibrium prices in the present week by the amount

$$\Delta p_{i0} = -\sum_j \frac{J_{ji}}{J} E^0_{j\alpha} \Delta\alpha_0 \tag{32}$$

Considering (26) such a change in temporary equilibrium prices in the present week together with $\Delta\alpha_0$, produces a total effect

$$\Delta\bar{X}_{i1} = \sum_j \frac{\partial \bar{X}_{i1}}{\partial p_{j0}} \Delta p_{j0} + \frac{\partial \bar{X}_{i1}}{\partial \alpha_0} \Delta\alpha_0, \ i = 2, \ldots, n + w \tag{33}$$

upon $\bar{X}_{i\tau}$. Therefore we find that temporary equilibrium prices in the first week will change by the amount

$$\Delta p_{i1} = -\sum_j \frac{J_{ji}}{J} \left(\sum_k \frac{\partial E_{j1}}{\partial \bar{X}_{k1}} \Delta\bar{X}_{k1} \right) \tag{34}$$

In the second week, $\bar{X}_{k2}$ is changed from the value before the change in tastes in the present week by the amount

$$\Delta\bar{X}_{k2} = \sum_i \frac{\partial \bar{X}_{k2}}{\partial p_{i1}} \Delta p_{i1} + \sum_h \frac{\partial \bar{X}_{k2}}{\partial \bar{X}_{h1}} \Delta\bar{X}_{h1} \tag{35}$$

As a result temporary equilibrium prices in the second week will change by

$$\Delta p_{i2} = -\sum_j \frac{J_{ji}}{J} \left(\sum_k \frac{\partial E_{j2}}{\partial \bar{X}_{k2}} \Delta\bar{X}_{k2} \right)$$

Repeating in this way we find that temporary equilibrium prices in week τ will change by

$$\Delta p_{i\tau} = -\sum_j \frac{J_{ji}}{J} \left(\sum_k \frac{\partial E_{j\tau}}{\partial \bar{X}_{k\tau}} \Delta\bar{X}_{k\tau} \right), \ i = 1, \ldots, n \tag{36}$$

where a change in initial stocks in week $\tau, \Delta\bar{X}_{k\tau}$, is given by

$$\Delta\bar{X}_{k\tau} = \sum_i \frac{\partial\bar{X}_{k\tau}}{\partial p_{i\tau-1}} \Delta p_{i\tau-1} + \sum_h \frac{\partial\bar{X}_{k\tau}}{\partial\bar{X}_{h\tau-1}} \Delta\bar{X}_{h\tau-1}, \; k = 2,\ldots,n+w \tag{37}$$

Let us now give a substantial explanation of the above formal derivation of the effects of $\Delta\alpha_0$ upon the time sequence of temporary equilibrium prices.[9] Throughout the following we assume that temporary equilibrium is Hicksian-stable and that the substitution relationship is dominant in each week.

Interpreting $\Delta\alpha_0$ as a change in tastes in the present week we assume that it induces a general increase in the demand for consumption goods. By the assumption of equilibrium being Hicksian-stable an increase in the demand for consumption good s raises its price. At the same time that increase in demand brings about rises in the prices of other commodities as well, if we assume the substitution relationship being dominant. In this way the price of good s will increase as a result of a simultaneous increase in the demand for consumption goods. Similarly the price of other consumption goods will also increase. As the substitution relationship is dominant, prices of the primary factors of production and capital goods will increase but since those goods for which demand directly increases are consumption goods, the price increases in primary factors of production and capital goods are more moderate than in the case of consumption goods. These are explanations of the formula (32).

Such a general increase in prices in the present week has an effect upon the stock of each commodity. Because of the increase in demands and the rise in prices, the supply of consumption goods will increase but the output of consumption goods cannot be increased quickly so that the supply of consumption goods has to be increased by decreasing the stock of consumption goods. Thus in the case of i being a consumption good (33) takes on a negative value. Next we consider producers' goods. Price increases of consumption goods in the present week give a stimulus to the firm producing consumption goods. As price increases in producers' goods are more gradual than those of consumption goods, the firms will want to expand the production of consumption goods. Then inputs are increased so that the demand for producers' goods too is increased. Therefore the stocks of producers' goods will generally decrease. As for the stock of goods in process, we may say as follows. As a result of expansion in production, goods in process will be increased but as only a short time has elapsed since the expansion of production, an increase in the stock of goods in process

[9] The time shapes of fluctuations which are described verbally below are no more than one of those which are most probable among possible time shapes.

may be regarded as almost negligible. Summarising the above, for consumption goods i we have $\Delta \bar{X}_{i1} < 0$; for producers' goods i we have the same kind of inequality and for goods in process we have $\Delta \bar{X}_{i1} > 0$ but the quantity is negligible. These explain (33).

In such circumstances where stocks do not increase for producers' goods significantly or decrease for products, what will happen to excess demand in week 1? First, because of the negligible increase in the available amount of products, the firms will become more bullish in supplying products. Therefore the supply prices of products will rise. On the other hand, a decrease in firms' stock of producers' goods will stimulate their outside demand for producers' goods and therefore their prices will rise. In this way in week 1 excess demand is increased in both products and producers' goods and we have a general increase in temporary equilibrium prices in week 1. This explains (34).

I have already explained above that initial stocks of products are decreased in week 1 but, since not enough time has elapsed, output will not increase, so we may assume that output is constant. Because of the price increase in week 1, supply in week 1 will probably increase. Therefore, at the beginning of week 2 we generally have decreased amounts of stocks of products. As for producers' goods, stocks decrease at the beginning of week 1. A rise in prices will give rise to an expansion in production and, hence, in input so that the firms increase their demand for producers' goods; they also put the stocks of producers' goods which they hold into the process of production. Consequently the initial stock at the beginning of week 2 will be smaller than the amount before the change. These are explanations of (35).

When the initial stock of products in week 2 diminishes, the supply prices of the products will be raised while a decrease in the initial stock of producers' goods will raise the demand price for them. Therefore in week 2 excess demand curves for all goods shift to the right. Consequently, temporary equilibrium prices will generally rise in week 2. Following this process successively we will have a general price increase in future weeks which is relatively near to the present week.

However, after a lapse of a considerable time the situation would be completely changed. As a result of an expansion in production, inputs will increase in each week and these increased inputs will gradually ripen into goods in process so we have increased amounts of stocks of goods in process. Therefore we have an increase in $\bar{X}_{h\tau}, h = n + 1, \ldots, n + \omega$. The goods in process will finally ripen into finished products. As this stage the supply of products will increase so that the price of products will decline. At the same time, because substitution relationships are dominant, prices of producers' goods will also decline since the decline in the prices of products whose supplies were originally increased is greater than the decline in the prices of producers' goods which occur as a result of repercussions of prices through chains of substitution relationships. Producers' goods are now relatively expensive so a reduction in production will be brought about, but we still have a huge stock of goods in process. Therefore, by applying small amounts of labour to goods in process we can easily produce commodities at the reduced level of production. Hence the demand for labour will decrease and the temporary equilibrium value of wages has to decline.

We have so far interpreted $\Delta\alpha_0$ as representing a change in tastes. In the case of $\Delta\alpha_0$ representing a change in technology or a change in expectations we may analyse their effects in exactly the same way as above. The only difference would be that in the case of, for example, technological change, that which changes first is not the demand for consumption goods but the supply of products or the demand for producers' goods. In this way the starting point of repercussions is different but once it induces a change in temporary equilibrium prices in the present week and a change in the initial stocks of commodities in the first week, then the subsequent process of repercussions is exactly the same as in the case of a change in tastes. That is, a change in the initial stock of commodities induces a change in temporary equilibrium prices which in turn induces a change in the initial stock of commodities in the following week which leads to a further change in temporary equilibrium prices in the relevant week, and so on. A change in tastes may often be a temporary one but a change in technology is not temporary but persists over a considerable period. Therefore, in the case of a change in technology, there will be effects which are compounded of those changes in $\alpha_0, \alpha_1, \alpha_2, \ldots$.

8 The stability condition of fluctuations in effective prices

Now we derive the stability condition of the time shapes of effective prices. There are two kinds of stability theories: the first is the stability theory of the equilibrium point, which, of course, examines whether a given equilibrium point is stable or not, while the second is the stability theory of motion which investigates whether a given series of fluctuations is stable or not. In the former, we derive the condition for prices which start to fluctuate from a non-equilibrium initial position and do not diverge far from the equilibrium point, while in the latter we derive the condition for a path of motion that does not diverge in the presence of a disturbance far from the original undisturbed path. These two stability theories are different from each other, but they should be synthesised at the root; that is, the former is a special case of the latter. This can be understood easily if we consider that an equilibrium point gives a stationary solution, so that the condition for prices not to diverge from a given equilibrium point can be restated as the condition for prices not to diverge from a given particular motion which is stationary. In the previous chapters we have derived conditions for stability of a temporary equilibrium point. They all belong to the stability theory of the equilibrium point. We now have to examine the stability of fluctuations in effective prices in the form of the stability theory of motion. Because a perfect equilibrium point which is stationary does not necessarily exist except in some special cases, fluctuations in effective prices cannot in general be examined in the framework of the stability theory of point.

Let us first define the concept of Liapounoff stability in the stability theory of motion. For an arbitrary $\varepsilon > 0$, take a sufficiently small $\delta(\varepsilon)$ such that $\varepsilon > \delta(\varepsilon) > 0$. If $|\Delta p_{i\tau}| < \varepsilon$ for all τ as long as $|\Delta p_{io}|$ is taken to be smaller than $\delta(\varepsilon)$, the original motion of prices (31) is said to be Liapounoff stable. Let a sequence of white circles stand for the original motion and a sequence of black dots for the motion after a hypothetical displacement in week 0 (see figure 21). If the displacement is taken to be very small, so that the white circle and the black dot at $\tau = 0$ are sufficiently near to each other, then the black dots are very close to the corresponding white circles, for all τ, in the case of Liapounoff stability. On the contrary the original motion is Liapounoff unstable if the black dots are far apart from the corresponding white circles for large values of τ, however close the white circle and the black dot may be for $\tau = 0$. Where the original motion is Liapounoff stable, the motion after a small hypothetical displacement can be approximated by the original motion; otherwise a small displacement causes a big change in the motion (see figure 22).

Let us now assume

$$\frac{\partial \bar{X}_{k2}}{\partial p_{i1}} = \frac{\partial \bar{X}_{k3}}{\partial p_{i2}} = \ldots = \frac{\partial \bar{X}_{k\tau}}{\partial p_{i\tau-1}} = \ldots,$$

$$\frac{\partial \bar{X}_{k2}}{\partial \bar{X}_{i1}} = \frac{\partial \bar{X}_{k3}}{\partial \bar{X}_{i2}} = \ldots = \frac{\partial \bar{X}_{k\tau}}{\partial \bar{X}_{i\tau-1}} = \ldots, \tag{38}$$

$$\frac{\partial E_{j2}}{\partial \bar{X}_{k2}} = \frac{\partial E_{j3}}{\partial \bar{X}_{k3}} = \ldots = \frac{\partial E_{j\tau}}{\partial \bar{X}_{k\tau}} = \ldots$$

Substituting (36) which holds for week $\tau - 1$, into (37) for week τ, we then obtain

$$\Delta \bar{X}_{k\tau} = \Sigma b_{kh} \Delta \bar{X}_{h\tau-1} \tag{39}$$

where b_{kh} represents the effect which a change in the initial stock of good h in week $\tau - 1$ gives directly, or indirectly through a change in prices and the

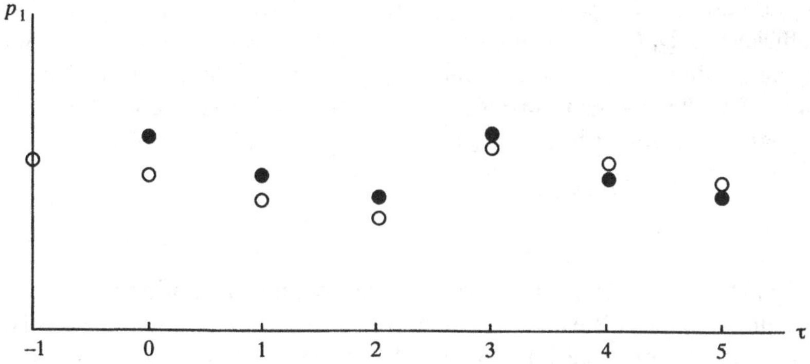

Figure 21

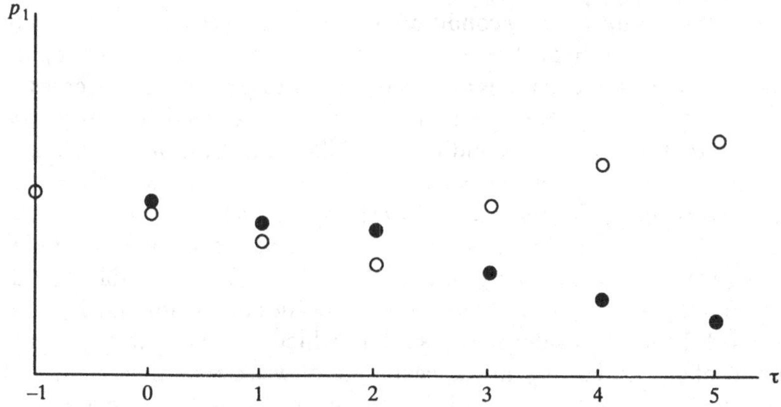

Figure 22

rate of interest in week $\tau - 1$, upon the initial stock of good k in week τ.[10] By the assumption of (38), each b_{kh} remains unchanged over the weeks. General solutions to simultaneous, linear difference equations (39) are written as

$$\Delta \bar{X}_{k\tau} = \Sigma Q_{kj}(\tau)\rho_j^\tau, \ \tau = 1, 2, 3, \ldots$$

where $\rho_1, \rho_2, \ldots, \rho_m$ are distinct roots of the characteristic equation

$$|b_{ij} - \rho\delta_{ij}| = 0$$

and $v_1, v_2, \ldots, v_m$ are the multiplicities of the respective roots; the $Q_{kj}(\tau)$ is a

10 $$b_{kh} = \frac{\partial \bar{X}_{k\tau}}{\partial \bar{X}_{h\tau-1}} - \sum_i \sum_j \frac{\partial \bar{X}_{k\tau}}{\partial p_{i\tau-1}} \frac{J_{ji}}{J} \frac{\partial E_{j\tau-1}}{\partial \bar{X}_{h\tau-1}}$$
$$(k, h = 2, \ldots, n + w)$$

polynomial in τ of degree one less than the multiplicity v_j of the root ρ_j. The coefficients of $Q_{kj}(\tau)$ are determined by the initial stocks of week 1. Now we can easily obtain the conditions under which the original series of effective prices after the change in tastes are Liapounoff stable. The conditions for $\Delta\bar{X}_{k\tau}$ and $\Delta p_{i\tau}$ not to become $\pm\infty$ as $\tau \to \infty$ are: for all $i = 1,\ldots,m$

$$|\rho_i| \leqq 1 \text{ if } v_i = 1,$$

$$|\rho_i| < 1 \text{ if } v_i \neq 1$$

In particular, where $|\rho_i| < 1$ for all i, we say that the motion is strongly Liapounoff stable. [We also see: even in the case of Liapounoff instability, that is $|\rho_k| > 1$ for some k, the path of $\Delta\bar{X}_{i\tau}$ converges in a relative sense to the one traced out by the particular component $Q_{ij}(\tau)\rho_j^{\tau}$ with ρ_j which is the maximum among $\rho_1, \rho_2, \ldots, \rho_m$ in absolute value.]

When the strong stability condition is fulfilled it is clear that the path of motion after a hypothetical displacement will converge to the original path of motion. In the same case it is also seen that the original path converges to a perfect equilibrium point and prices eventually become stationary, provided that the following condition is fulfilled. *First, the government and banks do not carry out any economic activity in any week. Secondly, there is no change in the utility functions, liquidity preference functions, or expectations functions in any week.* This tendency towards a perfect equilibrium point can be proved in the following way. In the original path the public has, at the beginning of week 1, the stock of commodities of the amount $\bar{X}_{i0}$ and prices will be p_{i1}. Consider now a state in which the public has the same amount of stocks, i.e., $\bar{X}_{i0}$ at the beginning of week zero, then p_{i1} would prevail in week 0, so that the initial stock for week 2 of the original path of motion would appear as the initial stock in week 1. Corresponding to this fact, prices for week 2 of the original path would prevail in week 1 and so on in the following weeks.

Thus if we consider hypothetically that initial stocks, $\bar{X}_{i,-1}$ of week 0 change to $\bar{X}_{i0}$, then the price will change, in week τ, from $p_{i\tau}$ to $p_{i\tau+1}$ so that the price path will move in week τ by $\Delta p_{i\tau} = p_{i\tau+1} - p_{i\tau}$. In this expression the left-hand side represents the movement of prices in week τ which is caused by the hypothetical displacement in the initial stock of commodities. On the right-hand side the first term represents the prices in week $\tau + 1$ and the second term represents those in week τ. Therefore the expression means that a shift in the price path is exactly the same as the difference between prices in the two successive years of the original path. Such a peculiar shift occurs under the two assumptions which I specified above. By the strong-stability conditions we have $\lim_{t\to\infty} \Delta p_{i\tau} = 0$ which means that two paths converge to each other. It also means that $\lim_{t\to\infty} (p_{i\tau+1} - p_{i\tau}) = 0$, that is to say that the original price movement eventually becomes stationary. In the case of the previous italicized assumptions being satisfied strong stability implies eventual realization of perfect equilibrium. If these assumptions are not fulfilled even though the initial stocks of commodities in week 0 are taken as $\bar{X}_{i0}$, prices would not be p_{i1}, so that strong stability is not a condition for convergence towards a stationary state.

The stability condition for temporary equilibrium which we have derived previously is the condition for whether or not, in a specific week, equilibrium prices can be found by auction; in other words, it is a condition for whether or not buyers and sellers in the auction can find a compromise by changing prices. The time element t introduced there is just a measure representing the progress of the auction. Prices discussed there are groping prices. We should not confuse this stability of temporary equilibrium with stability of the economy through actual time. When we speak of the stability of the economy in everyday conversation we are not talking about whether or not temporary equilibrium prices can be found in the market; we are discussing whether the sequence of effective prices is stable or unstable. Therefore the stability condition for the sequence of effective prices has more realistic significance than the stability condition of temporary equilibrium.

When we have derived the stability condition of temporary equilibrium, the initial stocks of commodities are all taken as constant. Factors which determine stability are the buyers' and sellers' response to groping prices (i.e., E_{ij}^0) and their ability to change groping prices (i.e., F_i^0). Intertemporal relationships between initial stocks of commodities have no part in that theory. On the other hand, factors which determine stability of effective prices (i.e., coefficients b_{ij}) show how a change in the initial stock of good j in week τ influences, directly and indirectly through the change in effective prices in the same week, initial stocks of commodity i in week $\tau + 1$. We must emphasize to those economists who consider that the stability conditions of temporary equilibrium are the stability conditions for the economy, that *the factors which determine economic stability are the intertemporal relationship between the initial stock or, more roughly speaking, that the rate of accumulation of capital is the criterion for economic stability.*[11] We must perhaps add that the stability of temporary equilibrium in each week is necessary for the stability of the sequence of effective prices but has no other implication for the latter.

[11] This has not yet been pointed out by Samuelson, Lange and other economists who have recently been concerned with the problem of economic stability.

9 Long-run effects of money creation – comparative dynamics over weeks (II)

We have previously analysed the effects of our creation of money in a particular week upon prices and the rate of interest in the same week. In this section we shall examine the long-run effects of money creation, that is, the effects of money creation in a particular week upon prices and the rate of interest in subsequent weeks. As usual we can divide our investigations into the case of money created in the form of a loan to the public and the case of money created for financing government expenditure. In the following analysis we continue to assume the previous assumptions on p. 118, (i)–(iv), with the exception of (ii) which is now replaced by the assumption (ii′) that a change in the initial quantity of money $\bar{M}$ has no influence on the degree of substitution of commodities and shifts only the excess demand functions of each commodity in the next week and all subsequent ones. Also we assume:

$$\frac{\partial E_{j1}}{\partial \bar{M}_1} = \frac{\partial E_{j2}}{\partial \bar{M}_2} = \ldots = E^0_{jm}.$$

(I) Let us first deal with the case where money is created in the present week by the amount $\Delta M = \beta_1$ in the form of lending to the public. It is evident that the short-run effects of the creation of money, i.e., its effects upon temporary equilibrium prices and the interest rate are given by

$$\Delta p_{io} = -\frac{J_{1i}}{J}\beta_1$$

Now, when money is created in the present week by ΔM in the form of short-term lending to the public, the public will hold, at the beginning of the next week, money of the amount $\bar{M} - r\beta_1$, where r represents the temporary equilibrium rate of interest in the present week after the creation of money, i.e., $p_{10} + \Delta p_{10}$. If we assume that no money is created in the next week nor in all the subsequent weeks, the quantity of money is kept at the level $\bar{M} - r\beta_1$ throughout these weeks. Thus, when money is created in week 0 only, the creation ΔM is merely temporary; in week 1 and afterwards, money is, on the contrary, decreased by $r\beta_1$.

Such a decrease in the quantity of money has an effect upon price p_{i1} in week 1

$$\sum_j \frac{J_{ji}}{J} E^0_{j\bar{M}}(r\beta_1) \tag{40}$$

On the other hand, a change in temporary equilibrium prices in the present week gives rise to a change in the initial stocks of commodities in week 1

$$\Delta \bar{X}_{i1} = \sum_j \frac{\partial \bar{X}_{i1}}{\partial p_{j0}} \Delta p_{j0}$$

which, in turn, changes prices in week 1 by the amounts

$$-\sum_j \frac{J_{ji}}{J}\left(\sum_k \frac{\partial E_{j1}}{\partial \bar{X}_{k1}} \Delta \bar{X}_{k1}\right) \tag{41}$$

The total change in prices in week 1 will be given by the sum of (40) and (41). In week 2, $\bar{X}_{i2}$ will change by the amount

$$\Delta \bar{X}_{i2} = \sum_j \frac{\partial \bar{X}_{i2}}{\partial p_{j1}} \Delta p_{j1} + \sum_k \frac{\partial \bar{X}_{i2}}{\partial \bar{X}_{k1}} \Delta \bar{X}_{k1} + \frac{\partial \bar{X}_{i2}}{\partial \bar{M}_1}(-r\beta_1)$$

which, together with a decrease in the initial quantity of money at the beginning of week 2, produces a change in prices

$$\Delta p_{i2} = -\sum_j \frac{J_{ji}}{J}\left(\sum_k \frac{\partial E_{j2}}{\partial \bar{X}_{k2}} \Delta \bar{X}_{k2} - E^0_{j\bar{M}} r\beta_1\right)$$

Proceeding in this way successively, we have in week τ

$$\Delta p_{i\tau} = -\sum_j \frac{J_{ji}}{J}\left(\sum_k \frac{\partial E_{j\tau}}{\partial \bar{X}_{k\tau}} \Delta \bar{X}_{k\tau} - E^0_{j\bar{M}} r\beta_1\right) \tag{42}$$

where

$$\Delta \bar{X}_{k\tau} = \sum_i \frac{\partial \bar{X}_{k\tau}}{\partial p_{i\tau-1}} \Delta p_{i\tau-1} + \sum_h \frac{\partial \bar{X}_{k\tau}}{\partial \bar{X}_{h\tau-1}} \Delta \bar{X}_{h\tau-1} + \frac{\partial \bar{X}_{k\tau}}{\partial \bar{M}_{\tau-1}}(-r\beta_1) \tag{43}$$

Assuming, in addition to (38), that

$$\frac{\partial \bar{X}_{k2}}{\partial \bar{M}_1} = \frac{\partial \bar{X}_{k3}}{\partial \bar{M}_2} = \ldots = \frac{\partial \bar{X}_{k\tau}}{\partial \bar{M}_{\tau-1}} = \ldots \tag{44}$$

and substituting (42) which holds for week $\tau - 1$ into (43) for week τ, we obtain

$$\Delta \bar{X}_{k\tau} = \Sigma b_{kj} \Delta \bar{X}_{j\tau-1} + C_k(-r\beta_1) \tag{45}$$

where the b_{kj}s are the same as the ones in (39) and the C_ks are the coefficients which represent the effects which a change in the initial quantity of money give directly, or indirectly via a change in prices and the rate of interest, upon the initial stocks of commodities k.[12] Under our assumptions the values of the b_{kj}s do not change over weeks.

[12] $$C_k = \frac{\partial \bar{X}_{k\tau}}{\partial \bar{M}_{\tau-1}} - \sum_i \sum_j \frac{\partial \bar{X}_{k\tau}}{\partial p_{i\tau-1}} \frac{J_{ji}}{J} E^0_{j\bar{M}} \quad (k = 2, \ldots, n + w)$$

If we assume that the system is strongly Liapounoff stable, then $|b_{kj} - \delta_{kj}| \equiv B \neq 0$. Let B_i be the determinant obtained by replacing the ith column of B by $C_2, \ldots, C_{n+w}$; then (45) may be written as

$$\Delta \bar{X}_{k\tau} + \frac{B_k}{B}(-r\beta_1) = \sum_j b_{kj}\left[\Delta \bar{X}_{j\tau-1} + \frac{B_j}{B}(-r\beta_1)\right]$$

Therefore we have

$$\Delta \bar{X}_{k\tau} = \frac{B_k}{B} r\beta_1 + \sum_j Q_{kj}(\tau)\rho_j^{\tau}$$

When τ tends to infinity, the second term of the above expression converges to 0, so that the stocks of commodities k become in the long-run larger or smaller by the amounts $\frac{B_k}{B}(r\beta_1) k = 2, \ldots, n + w$, than their stocks before the creation of money in the present week. Let us call these effects the long-run effects of the creation of money upon the stocks of commodities. Because of these long-run effects, prices became higher or lower, in the limit of $\tau \to \infty$, by

$$\begin{aligned} \Delta p_{i\infty} &= -\sum_j \frac{J_{ji}}{J}\left[\sum_k \frac{\partial E_{j\infty}}{\partial \bar{X}_{k\infty}}\left(-\frac{B_k}{B}\right) + E_{jM}^0\right](-r\beta_1) \\ &= -\sum_j \frac{J_{ji}}{J} \tilde{E}_{jM}^0(-r\beta_1) \end{aligned} \tag{46}$$

than the prices before the creation of money. Such changes in prices in an infinitely far future week are called the long-run effects of the creation of money upon prices. In the following such a future week is referred to as week ∞. Apparently $\tilde{E}_{jM}^0$ represents the part within the first pair of brackets of (46).

(II) In the above we examined the effects of money creation in the form of a loan to the public. In the following we discuss the other alternative which is money creation for the purpose of financing government expenditure. Suppose now that the government demands commodity k by the amount β_k in the present week so that money of the amount $p_k\beta_k$ is created for this purpose. Unless the government returns the borrowed money to the banks, by increasing taxes, or the banks sell the government bonds issued to the public, the created money $p_k\beta_k$ circulates among the public forever. [It is true that the government may return to the banks the amount of money obtained by issuing new government bonds, but there is no change in the total amount that government borrows from the banks, because its new borrowing exactly equals the amount it returns. It is also true that when the banks sell to the public some amount of the government bonds they hold, the amount of money circulating in the market decreases, but the government bonds the public now holds play the role of quasi-money.] The government demand, β_k, gives rise to a change in temporary equilibrium prices in the present week which in turn induces a change in the stocks of commodities to be held at the end of the week. In the next week we have an increased initial quantity of money held by the public which generates a change in the demands and supplies of commodities. The induced change in the initial stocks of commodities will also affect the supply side. These altogether will result in a change in prices in the next week; price changes and changes in the initial stock of money will yield fluctuations in the stocks of commodities at the end of the next week. In the week after the next a change in the initial stocks of money and commodities shift demand and supply curves which in turn give rise to a change in prices; and so on in every succeeding week. The time shape of the change in stocks will be described by

$$\Delta \bar{X}_{k\tau} = -\frac{B_k}{B}\Delta M + \sum_j Q_{kj}(\tau)\rho_j^\tau$$

Under the assumption of strong Liapounoff stability $\Delta \bar{X}_{k\tau}$ converges to $-\frac{B_k}{B}\Delta M$ as τ tends to infinity. Correspondingly prices will tend to

$$\Delta p_{i\infty} = -\sum_j \frac{J_{ji}}{J}\tilde{E}^0_{j\bar{M}}\Delta M \tag{47}$$

(III) Here, let us discuss the quantity theory of money as a long-run theory of prices. Suppose now as a result of a creation or contraction of money supply in the present week, money of the amount ΔM, which may be positive or negative, is added to the initial stock of money in week 1. This stimulates changes in prices and initial stocks successively from week to week. In the long run, initial stocks of commodities will change by $-\frac{B_k}{B}\Delta M$. Therefore a change in the initial quantity of money, ΔM in week 1, will induce a change in excess demand in week ∞ by the amount

$$\tilde{E}^0_{j\bar{M}} = E^0_{j\bar{M}} + \sum_k \frac{\partial E_{j\infty}}{\partial \bar{X}_{k\infty}}\left(-\frac{B_k}{B}\right)$$

provided prices and the rate of interest in week ∞ are unchanged. On the other hand, a change in price i in week ∞ produces a change in excess demand in the same week by the amount E^0_{ji}.

Let us assume that in week ∞ excess demand for securities is homogeneous of degree 1 in the variables of the initial quantity of money in week 1 and of prices (excluding the rate of interest) in week ∞. Let us also assume that in week ∞ excess demand for commodities (excluding money and securities) is homogeneous of degree zero with respect to the initial quantity of money in week 1 and to prices (excluding the rate of interest) in week ∞. Then we have[13]

$$\begin{aligned} E_{1\infty} &= \tilde{E}^0_{1\bar{M}}\bar{M} + E^0_{12}p_{2\infty} + \ldots + E^0_{1n}p_{n\infty}, \\ 0 &= \tilde{E}^0_{j\bar{M}}\bar{M} + E^0_{j2}p_{2\infty} + \ldots + E^0_{jn}p_{n\infty} \end{aligned} \tag{48}$$

If we take $\bar{M}$ as the quantity of money and $p_{j\infty}$ as the temporary equilibrium prices before the creation of money then we have $E_{1\infty} = 0$. Therefore we have

$$-\tilde{E}^0_{j\bar{M}} = \frac{1}{\bar{M}}\left(\sum_{2}^{n} E^0_{jk}p_{k\infty}\right), j = 1, 2, \ldots, n$$

Substituting these relationships into (46) and (47) we then obtain

$$\frac{\Delta p_{2\infty}}{p_{2\infty}} = \ldots = \frac{\Delta p_{n\infty}}{p_{n\infty}} = \frac{-r\beta_1}{\bar{M}}; \ \Delta p_{1\infty} = 0,$$

and

$$\frac{\Delta p_{2\infty}}{p_{2\infty}} = \ldots = \frac{\Delta p_{n\infty}}{p_{n\infty}} = \frac{\Delta\bar{M}}{\bar{M}}; \ \Delta p_{1\infty} = 0$$

respectively, so that we obtain the propositions of the long-run quantity theory of money. That is to say, if we have a change in the initial quantity of money ΔM in week 1 as a result of a creation or contraction of money supply in the present week – this change in the initial quantity of money is kept intact throughout the subsequent weeks – we obtain a proportional

[13] In this case the excess demand function for securities in week ∞ may be written as

$$p_{n\infty}f_{1\infty}\left(r_{\infty}, \frac{p_{2\infty}}{p_{n\infty}}, \ldots, \frac{p_{n-1\infty}}{p_{n\infty}}, \frac{\bar{M}}{p_{n\infty}}\right)$$

while the excess demand function for each commodity in week ∞ as

$$f_{i\infty}\left(r_{\infty}, \frac{p_{2\infty}}{p_{n\infty}}, \ldots, \frac{p_{n-1\infty}}{p_{n\infty}}, \frac{\bar{M}}{p_{n\infty}}\right) \ (i = 2, \ldots, n)$$

The temporary equilibrium prices and interest rate in week ∞ are obtained by solving n equations, $f_{i\infty}(\ldots) = 0, i = 1, \ldots, n$. These equations have n unknowns, $r_{\infty}, \frac{p_{2\infty}}{p_{n\infty}}, \ldots, \frac{p_{n-1\infty}}{p_{n\infty}}, \frac{\bar{M}}{p_{n\infty}}$, so that they are not overdeterminant. As $\bar{M}$ is given, $p_{n\infty}$ is determined. Thus, we obtain not only relative prices but also absolute ones.

change in prices in the long run. Moreover, if prices are converging to a stationary state before the change in the quantity of money, they will also converge to a stationary state after the change. These results are obtained irrespective of the form of the creation of money, either as a loan to the public, or in order to finance government expenditure, provided that the equations (48) hold. The only difference caused by the difference in the form of money creation is that in the case of a short-term loan to the public, the initial quantity of money will decrease in week 1 so that prices in week ∞ will decline proportionately; while in the case of money being created to finance government expenditure an increase is induced in the initial quantity of money in week 1 and therefore prices in week ∞ will rise proportionately.

We have already seen that the conditions for the quantity theory of money to be valid as a short-run theory are (i) that the demand for cash balances in the present week is a homogeneous function of degree 1 in prices of the present week and (ii) that the excess demand functions for commodities in the present week are homogeneous of degree zero in prices of the present week. We then obtained the conclusion that under these assumptions the quantity theory of money holds true in the short run if money is created in the form of a loan to the public but it does not hold if it is created in the form of a loan to the government. Contemporary mathematical economists such as Don Patinkin and others usually reformulate the quantity theory of money under these assumptions (i) and (ii) and confine their investigations to the short-run analysis though it may not have been deliberately intended. Thus, if we confine our investigation to the short-run analysis, the quantity theory is true only in the case of money being created for a loan to the public. On the other hand, if we assume (48) the theory holds true in the long run irrespective of the channels of money creation. Do we consider that it holds in the short run? Or in the long run? In the case of the latter being answered in the affirmative, we have to say that the quantity theory of money assumes (48) or similar equations for sufficiently distant future weeks, but not (i) and (ii) for the current week.

(IV) Finally, a remark on the effects of money creation in the present week upon prices. First, if money is created by β_1 in the present week to lend to the public, the long-run effects on prices are given by (46) while if the same amount of money as β_1, which is denoted by ΔM, is created to lend to the government, we have the effects (47). Comparing them we can easily find that the signs of (46) are opposite to those of (47). In the case of short-run effects these two money creations often produce effects of the same signs while in the case of long-run effects they are opposite in sign. This is the first point which we should take into account when we decide monetary policies.

Secondly, comparing the absolute values of (46) and (47) the latter is as large as the former times $1/r$. Suppose now that r is 2 per cent. Then the long-run effects upon prices of money creation of one million pounds to lend to the government is 50 times larger than the corresponding effects of money creation of the same amount to lend to the public in absolute value. If the existing quantity of money before was 30 million pounds, then prices, $p_{i\infty}$, will increase by $p_{i\infty}/30$ in the former case while they will decline by $p_{i\infty}/1{,}500$ in the latter, provided the quantity theory of money holds. (Therefore we may safely ignore long-run effects on prices of a creation of money to lend to the public for one week.) This is the second point which we must consider when we decide monetary policy.

Therefore we can conclude as follows. If we are only concerned with short-term economic difficulties it is better to stimulate private producers by lending money for a short period rather than stimulating them by increasing government demand; the public will find a way out from its difficulties and this monetary policy minimizes the ill effects which would result in the long run. On the other hand, not only short-run difficulties but also recovery from a persistent stagnation (or a recovery from deadly war damages) may be our concern. In that case we should stimulate private producers by increasing government demand; then, inflation in prices will occur; this will not only stimulate producers for a long while but also contribute to reducing the real value of government debt.

10 The stability theory of economic motion and the theory of growth

[This is a supplement added to this English version of *DKR*. Since the publication of the original Japanese version the stability theory of equilibrium has been developed from Samuelson's and Metzler's stage to Arrow's and Hurwicz's one: also the theory of growth developed by Solow and others has been highlighted in academic circles. However these are not synthesized though they are closely related. The former has not been concerned with accumulation of stocks, whilst the latter has not addressed the issue of fluctuations in prices, but dealt mainly with quantitative expansion of the economy. Each of these theories has followed its own self-contained course of development, entirely independent from the other. As has been stated before and has been demonstrated in this volume, the stability theory of prices and the stability theory of motion are synthesized. The former is, in fact, contained within the latter as its necessary component. In the following we shall see that the same relationship has to be observed between the stability theory of prices and the theory of economic growth, by showing that the standard theory of economic growth is nothing other than a special case of my theory of economic motion.

The basic concepts of the growth theory are GNP, Y, the aggregate investment, I, and savings, S. As it is assumed that a portion of Y is saved, we have $S = sY$, where s is the savings ratio. Since Y is produced by capital and labour, K and N respectively, and investment is an increment of capital during the period, $I_\tau = K_{\tau+1} - K_\tau$, if we ignore depreciation, we may put the temporary equilibrium condition $I_\tau = sY_\tau$, for every τ in the following form

$$K_{\tau+1} = K_\tau + sf(N_\tau, K_\tau)$$

where $f(.)$ is the aggregated production function. Assuming that full employment of labour is realized in every period, we have $N_\tau = H_\tau$, where H_τ stands for the supply of labour which is usually assumed to grow exponentially: $H_\tau = H_0 G^\tau$. Then we have

$$K_{\tau+1} = K_\tau + sf(H_0 G^\tau, K_\tau) \tag{49}$$

that is the basic equation of Solow's type of growth theory; of course, a number of modifications and complications and, therefore, sophistications have been introduced into it. Obviously the equation (49) implies that the economy grows because of the quantity adjustment being made.

As K_τ represents the aggregate value of the stocks of commodities $\bar{X}_{i\tau}$ at the beginning of period τ, we may write $K_\tau = \Sigma p_{i\tau}\bar{X}_{i\tau}$. Then from (49) follows

$$\Sigma p_{i\tau+1}\bar{X}_{i\tau+1} = \Sigma p_{i\tau}\bar{X}_{i\tau} + sF(H_0 G^\tau, \Sigma p_{i\tau}\bar{X}_{i\tau}) \tag{50}$$

which corresponds to equation (26) of the text and may be regarded as its aggregated form. This shows not only the equivalence of the growth theory and the theory of economic motion but also that the theory of changes in equilibrium prices from period to period is an indispensable element of the theory of growth, even though most of the growth theorists usually ignore it. Thus the quantity adjustment and the price adjustment have to be synthesized to form a complete theory of growth.

In fact, our equations (39) are very similar to the Solow–Samuelson equations[14]

$$X_i(t+1) = H^i[X_1(t), X_2(t), \ldots, X_n(t)],\ i = 1, \ldots, n$$

which can be rewritten in the form

$$X_i(t+1) = \Sigma b_{ij} X_j(t),\ i = 1, \ldots, n \tag{51}$$

because the H^i's are all homogeneous of degree 1 in $X_1(t), \ldots, X_n(t)$, so that $b_{ij} = \partial H^i / \partial X_j$. They are different in the following ways. First our ΔXs are

[14] Solow and Samuelson, 1953.

displacements of stocks of commodities from the stocks along a given path of economic motion, while their Xs are outputs of commodities. Secondly, our coefficients, b, are not necessarily positive because they include indirect effects through changes in prices, while their equations evidently rule out price effects and their coefficients b are positive because they include only the direct effects of inputs upon outputs. Thirdly, Solow and Samuelson assume that H is homogeneous of degree 1, so that (51) has balanced growth solutions which are unique. They show that the balanced growth is stable, but in our case the given path of economic motion is not necessarily a path of balanced growth. Moreover, it is not necessarily stable. Depending on the values of b_{ij} the given economic motion may be stable or unstable.

In the case of the stability theory of temporary equilibrium it is important to obtain stability. Otherwise we cannot find out equilibrium prices by the tatonnement procedure. On the other hand, in the case of the stability theory of economic motion, instability rather than stability is a far more important concept for understanding the explosive development of the economy in the modern world. By carrying out an innovation in week 0, the structure of the economy in the current week may be greatly affected, so that it is possible that the initial prices which have so far belonged to a stability region of a certain set of temporary equilibrium prices may belong to a stability region of a new set of equilibrium prices which is very remote from the previous price set before the innovation.[15] Then this would have a big impact on the economy in the succeeding weeks and will create a powerful take-off. It is unfortunate that in spite of this perspective, which would closely fit economic historical observations in the past, most of the neoclassical-growth theorists have made great efforts to show that the steady path of growth equilibrium is globally stable.

Finally, some comments on Hahn's and Negishi's stability theory of the non-tatonnement process and von Neumann's theory of growth.[16] First, Hahn and Negishi have jointly or independently written papers on the non-tatonnement process, a process during which transactions are actually carried out while there remains excess demand or supply in the market, and, therefore, individuals' holdings of commodities may increase or diminish at every point in time when transactions are made. Their basic model is simple: no consumption and production but transactions are made throughout the process. However it seems to be not very difficult to extend the model so as to accommodate both consumption and production within it.

The model consists of two sets of adjustment equations: the price adjustment functions and the endowment adjustment functions. Provided

[15] I have emphasized that this would happen especially in the case of the economy being non-linear.

[16] Hahn and Negishi, 1962, and von Neumann, 1945–6.

with a number of reasonable assumptions, Hahn and Negishi have shown that the economy eventually approaches a state where no further adjustment is needed in prices and endowments. This is of course a state of general equilibrium, so that its stability is established. It is evident that the Hahn–Negishi process is not a tatonnement process for groping equilibrium prices, during which no transaction is carried out at all; it gives an effective path of economic motion.

Therefore, the equilibrium to be realised at the end of the actually effective process is not a short-run temporary equilibrium but a long-run stationary one. Their path, especially when the economy was extended so as to permit consumption and production, would be a theoretical description of the actual course of economic development. Assessing their stability theorem from this point of view, we must first point out that the actual economy would never approach a stationary equilibrium. For it to exist, parameters such as tastes, technology, liquidity preferences, expectations and so on must remain constant for an infinitely long period. This is impossible, so that we have no stationary equilibrium. Then the only meaningful stability argument is to do with the motion of the economy. In such a theory stability is not its unique focus. It is often very important to identify the kinds of parameters whose displacement in a certain direction would generate a movement diverging from the originally prescribed motion of the economy. Instability is also a focus.

Von Neumann's growth theory was first published in 1937 in German and translated into English in 1945–6, but it was in the 1960s and afterwards when it greatly attracted economists' attention. From the economic point of view, however, it is not complete and contains unsatisfactory assumptions. For example, it does not allow for consumers' choice, but assumes capitalists invest all their income automatically, and so on. All these defects with an economic model can be removed,[17] but still it has to assume that capitalists consume a constant proportion of their income and the rest is automatically reinvested. Evidently this last assumption implies Say's law.[18] In the actual world where Say's law does not hold, we cannot obtain von Neumann's equilibrium, because of the dilemma of durable goods, which I discuss in the Addendum, Article VIII. As will be seen there, the approach I have taken in this volume is also unsatisfactory. Unlike von Neumann but like Hicks, 1946, I do not assume Say's law but I allow that the rates of profits may differ from one capital good to another and from one firm to another. The model is unable to examine how they are equalized in a competitive economy.]

[17] See Morishima, 1964 and 1969.

[18] Note that the previous Solow model also assumes the law.

Appendix I
Consumer behaviour and liquidity preference [1952][1]

Consumer's behaviour in a non-monetary economy has been analysed completely by the traditional theory developed by Slutsky, Allen, and Hicks, but we have no established theory of consumer's behaviour in a monetary economy. In fact, many theorists (e.g., Professors P. A. Samuelson (1948), C. E. Leser (1943) and D. Patinkin (1948)) tried to expand the traditional theory in order to be able to analyse consumer's demand for money, but they have not yet settled the problem of the substitution between cash and bonds, which is one of the most important problems in a monetary economy. In this appendix we shall analyse consumer's behaviour in a monetary economy.

1 Fundamental notions

1.1 *Budget equation* We shall adopt the following notation: x_i represents the consumer's demand for the ith consumption good in the present period ($i = 1, 2, \ldots, n-1$), and y represents his supply of labour in the present period, which is treated as negative demand, writing x_n for $-y$. Let M and H be the quantities of cash held by the consumer at the beginning and end of the period, respectively. For simplicity, assume that all bonds are perpetuities paying 1 dollar per period. $\bar{B}$ and B express the number of bonds held at the beginning and end of the period respectively. $\bar{B}$ and B can take on

[1] This new appendix I, written soon after the work on *DKR* was finished and published in *Econometrica*, 1952 (later included in Morishima *et al.*, 1973) replaces the original one in which the utility is maximized subject to $v + 1$ budget constraints concerning the present and future weeks. The key element for the change is the idea of 'probability of the future living standard' introduced in section 1.2. It would be obtained by using the future budget constraint; but this problem of formation of the probability need not be discussed explicitly once it is assumed. The change makes the argument simpler and enables me to remove original mathematical note 1 discussing the maximization under multiple constraints, as it is no longer necessary.

negative values. That is, when $B > 0$ the consumer is a lender, and when $B < 0$ he is a borrower. Needless to say, the budget equation of the consumer takes the form

$$\sum_{i=1}^{n} p_i x_i + H + p_b B = M + (1 + p_b)\bar{B} \equiv I \tag{1}$$

where p_i is the current price of the ith good and p_b is the price of bonds, which is equal to the reciprocal of the rate of interest, r.

1.2 *Probability of the future living standard* Here we shall introduce the notion of the probability of the future standard of living. First, assume that the consumer is able to place any two future living standards in one of the following mutually exclusive categories: (a) the living L^0 preferred to the living L^1, (b) L^1 preferred to L^0, (c) L^0 and L^1 equally preferred. We attach to each living standard a positive real number ξ, and the rule of numbering is as follows:

$$\begin{aligned}
&\xi(L^1) < \xi(L^0) \text{ when (a) is the case,}\\
&\xi(L^0) < \xi(L^1) \text{ when (b) is the case,}\\
&\xi(L^1) = \xi(L^0) \text{ when (c) is the case,}
\end{aligned}$$

and $\xi = 0$ for the lowest living standard. The numbers $\xi(L^0), \xi(L^1), \ldots$ are called indices of the future living standard or, briefly, living standard indices.

Next, we assume that the consumer knows the probability that, when he holds the amount H of cash and the amount B of bonds at the prices $p_1, p_2, \ldots, p_n, p_b$, his future living standard will be at least as high as the given level ξ; denote it by

$$q(\xi) = q(H, B, p_1, \ldots, p_n, p_b, \xi) \tag{2}$$

which is called the probability of the future living standard or, briefly, the living standard probability.[2] Of course, we have

$$q(\xi) \geqslant 0, q(0) = 1$$

and $q(\xi)$ is a non-increasing function of ξ; i.e., when $\xi > \xi', q(\xi) \leqslant q(\xi')$.

1.3 *Utility function* Let X be a combination composed of a bundle of

[2] If some of x's are durable consumption goods, then $q(\xi)$ depends also on the current demand for durable consumption goods. But, if all of x's are not durable, $q(\xi)$ is independent of them. We assume, in this appendix, that all of x's are non-durable. [This probability is obviously not objective but subjective, more or less congenial to Keynes' and Hicks' view of probability used in social science (see Keynes, 1921 and Hicks, 1979). The latter says probability in social science is 'a matter of rational judgement based on information, or on evidence'.]

commodities, proposed with certainty, and a probability distribution of the future living standard, i.e.

$$X = [x_1, x_2, \ldots, x_n, q(\xi)]$$

We postulate that the consumer is able to place any two combinations in one of the following mutually exclusive categories: (I) X^0 preferred to X^1, (II) X^1 preferred to X^0, (III) X^0 and X^1 equally preferred.[3] We attach to each X a positive real number u, and the rule of numbering is as follows:

$$u(X^1) < u(X^0) \text{ when (I) is the case,}$$
$$u(X^0) < u(X^1) \text{ when (II) is the case,}$$
$$u(X^0) = u(X^1) \text{ when (III) is the case,}$$

The numbers $u(X^0), u(X^1), \ldots$ are called utility indices, and $f(u)$ is also a utility index when and only when the function $f(u)$ is a monotonically increasing function of u.[4] Taking into account (2), the consumer's utility function takes the form

$$u = u[x_1, \ldots, x_n, q(H, B, p_1, \ldots, p_n, p_b; \xi)] \tag{3}$$

where u is a function of all x's and a functional of $q(\xi)$.

1.4 *Separability postulate* In his paper originally issued in 1943, Dr M. Sono, 1961, defined 'separability of goods' as follows. Goods $X_1, X_2, \ldots, X_l$ are said to be separable from each of goods $X_{l+1}, X_{l+2}, \ldots, X_m$, when and only when the marginal rates of substitution between $X_1, X_2, \ldots, X_l$ are independent of quantities of $X_{l+1}, X_{l+2}, \ldots, X_m$, viz.

$$\frac{\partial}{\partial x_i}\left(\frac{g_j}{g_1}\right) = 0 \ (j = 2, \ldots, l;\ i = l + 1, \ldots, m) \tag{4}$$

where $g = g(x_1, x_2, \ldots, x_m)$ is a usual utility function and subscripts attached to g denote partial differentiation. If $X_1, \ldots, X_l$ are separable from each of $X_{l+1}, \ldots, X_m$ from the point of view of a particular consumer, then we can prove that his utility function has the following properties:

Property I

The indifference relations between $X_1, \ldots, X_l$ are not disturbed by quantities of $X_{l+1}, \ldots, X_m$; that is to say, if two bundles of goods $(\bar{x}_1, \bar{x}_2, \ldots, \bar{x}_l, x'_{l+1}, \ldots, x'_m)$ and $(\bar{\bar{x}}_1, \bar{\bar{x}}_2, \ldots, \bar{\bar{x}}_l, x'_{l+1}, \ldots, x'_m)$ satisfy the condition

[3] In his excellent paper, Professor Marschak, 1950, postulated complete ordering of probability space. Our postulate is the one of complete ordering of commodity-probability space.

[4] The following discussions are unaltered by the substitution of $f(u)$ for u.

$$g(\bar{x}_1,\ldots,\bar{x}_l,x'_{l+1},\ldots,x'_m) = g(\bar{\bar{x}}_1,\ldots,\bar{\bar{x}}_l,x'_{l+1},\ldots,x'_m)$$

then the condition

$$g(\bar{x}_1,\ldots,\bar{x}_l,x_{l+1},\ldots,x_m) = g(\bar{\bar{x}}_1,\ldots,\bar{\bar{x}}_l,x_{l+1},\ldots,x_m)$$

holds for any values of $x_{l+1},\ldots,x_m$.

Proof: From the separability conditions (4), we obtain

$$\frac{g_{1i}}{g_1} = \frac{g_{2i}}{g_2} = \ldots = \frac{g_{li}}{g_l} = v_i \ (i = l+1,\ldots,m)$$

where $g_{ji} = \partial^2 g/\partial x_j \partial x_i$. Therefore

$$\frac{\partial}{\partial x_i}\left\{\sum_{j=1}^{l} g_j dx_j\right\} = \sum_{j=1}^{l} g_{ji} dx_j = v_i \left\{\sum_{j=1}^{l} g_j dx_j\right\} \ (i = l+1,\ldots,m)$$

Consequently, if $\sum_{j=1}^{l} g_j dx_j = 0$, then $\partial/\partial x_i \left\{\sum_{j=1}^{l} g_j dx_j\right\} = 0 \ (i = l+1,\ldots,m)$. Q.E.D. (See Sono, 1961, pp. 243–4.)

Property II
The utility function g can be written in the form

$$g = G[h(x_1,\ldots,x_l),x_{l+1},\ldots,x_m] \tag{5}$$

and Sono has called h the proper utility function of $X_1,\ldots,X_l$, *or eigentliche Nutzenfunktion von* $X_1,\ldots,X_l$.

Proof: Let a particular bundle of goods $X_{l+1},\ldots,X_m$ be $(a_{l+1},\ldots,a_m)$ and write

$$g(x_1,\ldots,x_l,a_{l+1},\ldots,a_m) = h(x_1,\ldots,x_l)$$

If $h(\bar{x}_1,\ldots,\bar{x}_l) = h(\bar{\bar{x}}_1,\ldots,\bar{\bar{x}}_l)$, then it follows from Property I that

$$g(\bar{x}_1,\ldots,\bar{x}_l,x_{l+1},\ldots,x_m) = g(\bar{\bar{x}}_1,\ldots,\bar{\bar{x}}_l,x_{l+1},\ldots,x_m)$$

for any $x_{l+1},\ldots,x_m$. Therefore, the value of g is uniquely determined when values of $x_{l+1},\ldots,x_m$ and h are determined. Consequently, g is a function of $x_{l+1},\ldots,x_m$ and h. Q.E.D. (See Sono, 1961, p. 245.)

Conversely, we can easily prove that, if the consumer's utility function takes the form (5), then $X_1,\ldots,X_l$ are separable from $X_{l+1},\ldots,X_m$ from his viewpoint. Therefore, we may say that $X_1,\ldots,X_l$ are separable from $X_{l+1},\ldots,X_m$ when and only when the indifference relations between $X_1,\ldots,X_l$ are not disturbed by quantities of $X_{l+1},\ldots,X_m$.

Now, we shall introduce the above notion of separability into our system.[5] First, we may assume very reasonably that all of the real goods $x_1, x_2, \ldots, x_n$ are separable from $H, B, p_1, \ldots, p_n, p_b$, because the marginal rate of substitution between any two real goods (say, coffee and tea) is determined by the consumer's 'tastes' for them and may be assumed to be independent of the probability distribution of the future living standard.[6] Hence, by Property II, our utility function (3) takes the form

$$u = U[\phi(x_1, \ldots, x_n), q(H, B, p_1, \ldots, p_n, p_b; \xi)] \tag{6}$$

where ϕ is called the proper utility function of real goods. Next we shall consider the effect of a change in x_i $(i = 1, \ldots, n)$ on the marginal rate of substitution between cash and bonds. Since cash and bonds are desired by a consumer, not as consumption goods, but as means of securing his future subsistence, then the marginal rate of substitution between them is determined by (a) his expectation of the purchasing power of money in the future, (b) his expectation of the future price of bonds, and (c) his willingness to bear risks. On the assumption of perfect competition, (a) and (b) are independent of the individual demand for goods; and on the assumption that all real goods are non-durable, (c) is independent of the x's. Thus we have

$$\frac{\partial}{\partial x_i}\left(\frac{U_B}{U_H}\right) = 0 \; (i = 1, 2, \ldots, n)$$

i.e.

$$\frac{U_{Bi}}{U_B} = \frac{U_{Hi}}{U_H} \; (i = 1, 2, \ldots, n)$$

where

$$U_H = \frac{\partial U}{\partial H} = \int_0^\infty U'[\phi, q(\xi); \mu] \frac{\partial q(\mu)}{\partial H} d\mu$$

$$U_B = \frac{\partial U}{\partial B} = \int_0^\infty U'[\phi, q(\xi); \mu] \frac{\partial q(\mu)}{\partial B} d\mu$$

$$U_{Hi} = \frac{\partial^2 U}{\partial H \partial x_i} = \frac{\partial \phi}{\partial x_i} \int_0^\infty U'_\varphi[\phi, q(\xi); \mu] \frac{\partial q(\mu)}{\partial H} d\mu = U_{iH} \tag{7}$$

$$U_{Bi} = \frac{\partial^2 U}{\partial B \partial x_i} = \frac{\partial \phi}{\partial x_i} \int_0^\infty U'_\varphi[\phi, q(\xi); \mu] \frac{\partial q(\mu)}{\partial B} d\mu = U_{iB} \tag{8}$$

[5] The separability postulate was introduced first into the field of the consumer's demand for cash by Professor Takuma Yasui, 1944.

[6] By this assumption we must exclude goods demanded for their ostentatious value (diamonds, etc.) from our real goods because the desire for diamonds (the marginal rate of substitution for rice of a given quantity of diamonds) depends on the price of diamonds.

and U' is the functional derivative of U with respect to q at the point μ and U'_φ is the one of $\partial U/\partial\phi$ with respect to q at the point μ.

2 The subjective equilibrium and stability conditions

2.1 *Equilibrium conditions* Since the consumer's behaviour is to select the most preferable plan under the condition of his budget equation, our first problem is to maximize (6) subject to (1). If $p_1, p_2, \ldots, p_n, p_b$ and I are assumed to be constant, we derive the following equation as the necessary conditions of a maximum or the subjective equilibrium conditions

$$\frac{U_1}{p_1} = \frac{U_2}{p_2} = \ldots = \frac{U_n}{p_n} = \frac{U_B}{p_b} = U_H = \lambda \tag{9}$$

where $U_i = \partial U/\partial x_i = (\partial U/\partial\phi)(\partial\phi/\partial x_i)$ and λ is a Lagrange multiplier. In other words, our equilibrium conditions are as follows: (1) The marginal rate of substitution of any real commodity for cash is equal to the price of that commodity. (2) The marginal rate of substitution of bonds for cash is equal to the price of bonds ($=1/r$).

2.2 *Stability conditions* I shall call a point which satisfies (1) and (9) an equilibrium point. In order that U should be a true maximum at an equilibrium point, d^2U must be negative definite under the constraint $\sum_{i=1}^{n} p_i dx_i + dH + p_b dB = 0$. Now let

$$U_{ij} = \frac{\partial^2 U}{\partial x_j \partial x_i} = \frac{\partial U}{\partial\phi}\frac{\partial^2\phi}{\partial x_j \partial x_i} + \frac{\partial^2 U}{\partial\phi^2}\frac{\partial\phi}{\partial x_i}\frac{\partial\phi}{\partial x_j} = U_{ji} \tag{10}$$

$U_{HH} = \partial^2 U/\partial H^2$, $U_{BB} = \partial^2 U/\partial B^2$, $U_{BH} = \partial^2 U/\partial H\partial B = \partial^2 U/\partial B\partial H = U_{HB}$, and let each of U^0_{ij}, U^0_{iH}, U^0_{iB}, U^0_{HH}, U^0_{BB}, and U^0_{BH} be respectively the values that U_{ij}, U_{iH}, U_{iB}, U_{HH}, U_{BB}, and U_{BH} assume at the equilibrium point. Write

$$D = \begin{vmatrix} 0 & p_1 & \cdots & p_n & 1 & p_b \\ p_1 & U^0_{11} & \cdots & U^0_{1n} & U^0_{1H} & U^0_{1B} \\ \cdot & \cdot & \cdots & \cdot & \cdot & \cdot \\ p_n & U^0_{n1} & \cdots & U^0_{nn} & U^0_{nH} & U^0_{nB} \\ 1 & U^0_{H1} & \cdots & U^0_{Hn} & U^0_{HH} & U^0_{HB} \\ p_b & U^0_{B1} & \cdots & U^0_{Bn} & U^0_{BH} & U^0_{BB} \end{vmatrix}$$

and denote the principal minor of D of order k by D^k. Then the necessary and sufficient secondary conditions for a maximum are

$$(-1)^k D^k < 0 \; (k = 3, 4, \ldots, n+3) \tag{11}$$

Next let us postulate that $d^2u < 0$ for all values of $x_1, \ldots, x_n$, $H, B, p_1, \ldots, p_n, p_b, dx_1, \ldots, dx_n, dH$, and dB such that $du = 0$; i.e.

$$(-1)^k \Delta^k < 0 \; (k = 3, 4, \ldots, n+3) \tag{12}$$

identically in $x_1, \ldots, x_n, H, B, p_1, \ldots, p_n, p_b$, where Δ^k represents the principal minor of order k of the $n+3$ by $n+3$ determinant

$$\begin{vmatrix} 0 & U_j \\ U_i & U_{ij} \end{vmatrix} \; (i,j = 1, 2, \ldots, n, H, B)$$

We call (12) the subjective stability conditions, which we may express by saying that the marginal rate of substitution between goods (including cash and bonds) must diminish for substitutions in every direction.

Then, by the stability conditions, a point that satisfies the necessary conditions for a maximum (9) also satisfies the secondary conditions for a maximum (11). Therefore, the equilibrium point gives us a true maximum of the utility function, and the consumer makes the plan that corresponds to the equilibrium point.

2.3 *A restatement of the traditional theory of consumer's behaviour* The traditional method of economic analysis has separated the real economic phenomena and the monetary phenomena from each other, and the analysis of the monetary phenomena has been handed over to the monetary specialists. Following this tradition, the traditional consumer theory, developed by Slutsky, Allen, and Hicks, has analysed only the real plan of a consumer. Therefore it must be taken as only a part of the whole theory of consumer's behaviour.

In the following we shall demonstrate that the traditional theory is identical with the part of our consumer theory that is concerned with the real plan of a consumer.

First, when we put $U_i = (\partial U/\partial \phi)(\partial \phi/\partial x_i)$ in equation (9) and eliminate $\partial U/\partial \phi$ between the conditions, they reduce to

$$\frac{\partial \phi/\partial x_1}{p_1} = \frac{\partial \phi/\partial x_2}{p_2} = \ldots = \frac{\partial \phi/\partial x_n}{p_n} \tag{13}$$

where each $\partial \phi/\partial x_i$ depends only on $x_1, x_2, \ldots, x_n$.

Secondly, considering (10) and assuming $\partial U/\partial \phi > 0$, we have from (12)

$$(-1)^k J^k < 0 \; (k = 3, 4, \ldots, n+1) \tag{14}$$

where J^k is the principal minor of order k of the determinant

$$J = \begin{vmatrix} 0 & \dfrac{\partial \phi}{\partial x_j} \\ \dfrac{\partial \phi}{\partial x_i} & \dfrac{\partial^2 \phi}{\partial x_j \partial x_i} \end{vmatrix} \qquad (i,j = 1,\ldots,n)$$

Next let us denote the solutions of (1) and (9) by $x_1^0, x_2^0, \ldots, x_n^0, H^0, B^0$ and rewrite our budget equation (1) as

$$\sum_{i=1}^{n} p_i x_i = E \tag{15}$$

where $E \equiv I - H^0 - p_b B^0 =$ the consumer's net expenditure on real commodities.

We can now easily prove that the solutions of (13) and (15) are $x_1^0, x_2^0, \ldots, x_n^0$, and, because of (14), they give us a true maximum of ϕ under the constraint (15). That is, if $x_1, \ldots, x_n$ are separable from $q(\xi)$, the values of the x's for which ϕ is a maximum under (15) are identical with the values of the x's for which U is a maximum under (1).

Since (13) and (14) are regarded as the traditional equilibrium conditions and the traditional stability conditions respectively, we may say that $x_1^0, x_2^0, \ldots, x_n^0$ indicate the traditional equilibrium point.

Consequently, we may restate the traditional consumer theory as follows:

1 The traditional budget condition is not (1) but (15), where H^0 and B^0 are taken as determined by the monetary consumer theory.
2 The traditional theory presumes that $x_1, x_2, \ldots, x_n$ are separable from $q(\xi)$, that is, the preference relations between real commodities are not disturbed by any change in $H, B, p_1, \ldots, p_n, p_b$. Hence it follows that there exists the proper utility function ϕ of real commodities.
3 According to the theory, a consumer's behaviour is said to be rational when he maximizes his proper utility function of real commodities under his budget condition (15). Therefore, the amounts of real commodities bought by a rational consumer are determined by the condition that ϕ is a maximum subject to (15).

3 The effect of a change in price

3.1 Now suppose that p_k varies, other prices, interest rate, and I remaining unchanged. Let the reciprocal determinant of D be $\begin{vmatrix} D_0 & D_i \\ D_j & D_{ij} \end{vmatrix}$ $(i,j = 1,\ldots,n,H,B)$, and write $Z_i = D_i/D$ $(i = 0,1,\ldots,n,H,B)$, $Z_{ij} = D_{ij}/D$ $(i,j = 1,\ldots,n,H,B)$. Then, differentiating (1) and (9) with respect to p_k, we get the solutions

$$\frac{\partial x_i}{\partial p_k} = -x_k Z_i + \lambda Z_{ki} - \sum_{j=1}^{B} U^0_{j[k]} Z_{ji} \tag{16}$$

$$\frac{\partial H}{\partial p_k} = -x_k Z_H + \lambda Z_{kH} - \sum_{j=1}^{B} U^0_{j[k]} Z_{jH} \tag{17}$$

$$\frac{\partial B}{\partial p_k} = -x_k Z_B + \lambda Z_{kB} - \sum_{j=1}^{B} U^0_{j[k]} Z_{jB} \tag{18}$$

where $U^0_{j[k]}$ is the value which $\partial U_j/\partial p_k$ assumes at the equilibrium point ($j = 1, \ldots, n, H, B$) and the summation of each equation runs from 1 to B.

In each of (16), (17), and (18) the first term represents the effect of the deficiency (or excess) of I, which would arise if the consumer did not change his plan in spite of an increase (or a decrease) in p_k, and the other terms represent the effect due to the disturbances in the subjective equilibrium conditions caused by the change in p_k. Especially the last term expresses the effect that arises when the change in p_k shifts the marginal rates of substitution. We call these equations the generalized Slutsky equations.

3.2 Here we shall consider the relation between the generalized Slutsky equation (16) and the traditional one that Professor Hicks calls 'the fundamental equation of value theory'.[7]

First, by Laplace's theorem of expansion of the determinant, it follows that

$$\sum_1^n p_j Z_j + Z_H + p_b Z_B = 1 \tag{19}$$

$$p_i Z_0 + \sum_1^n U^0_{ij} Z_j + U^0_{iH} Z_H + U^0_{iB} Z_B = 0 \ (i = 1, \ldots, n) \tag{20}$$

$$\sum_1^n p_j Z_{ij} + Z_{iH} + p_b Z_{iB} = 0 \ (i = 1, \ldots, n, H, B) \tag{21}$$

$$p_t Z_i + \sum_1^n U^0_{tj} Z_{ij} + U^0_{tH} Z_{iH} + U^0_{tH} Z_{iB} = \begin{cases} 0 & (t \neq i) \\ 1 & (t = i) \end{cases}$$

$$(t; i = 1, \ldots, n, H, B; p_H = 1, \ p_B = p_b) \tag{22}$$

Next consider the determinant

$$V = \begin{vmatrix} 0 & p_j \\ p_i & \phi^0_{ij} \end{vmatrix} \qquad (i, j = 1, \ldots, n)$$

[7] The following analysis is substantially identical with the partition analysis of Lewis, 1938.

where ϕ_{ij}^0 represents the value that $\partial^2\phi/\partial x_j\partial x_i$ assumes at the point $(x_1^0,\ldots,x_n^0)$, and denote $V_0/V, V_i/V, V_{ij}/V$ by X_0, X_i, X_{ij} where V_0, V_i, V_{ij} are respectively the cofactors of $0, p_i, \phi_{ij}^0$ in V. Then, since $U_{ij}^0 = (\partial U/\partial\phi)\phi_{ij}^0 + (\partial^2 U/\partial\phi^2)\phi_i^0\phi_j^0$, it follows (by Laplace's theorem) that

$$\sum_1^n p_j X_{ji} = 0 \tag{23}$$

$$p_t X_i + \left(\frac{\partial U}{\partial\phi}\right)^{-1}\sum_{j=1}^n U_{tj}^0 X_{ij} = \begin{cases}0 & (t \neq i)\\ 1 & (t = i)\end{cases} \quad (t; i = 1,\ldots,n) \tag{24}$$

and considering (7), (8), and $U_{j[k]} = (\partial\phi/\partial x_j)(\partial^2 U/\partial p_k\partial\phi)$, we can prove that

$$\sum_{j=1}^n U_{jH}^0 X_{ji} = 0,$$
$$\sum_{j=1}^n U_{jB}^0 X_{ji} = 0 \tag{25}$$

Therefore Z_i, Z_{ki}, Z_{Hi} $(i, k = 1,\ldots,n)$ are transformed as follows

$$\sum_{j=1}^n U_{j[k]}^0 X_{ji} = 0 \tag{26}$$

$$\begin{aligned}
Z_i &= X_i - \left(\sum_1^n p_t Z_t + Z_H + p_b Z_B\right)X_i + Z_i && \text{[from (19)]}\\
&= X_i - (Z_H + p_b Z_B)X_i\\
&\quad + \left(\frac{\partial U}{\partial\phi}\right)^{-1}\sum_{t=1}^n\left(\sum_{j=1}^n U_{jt}^0 X_{ji}\right)Z_t && \text{[from (24)]}\\
&= X_i - (Z_H + p_b Z_B)X_i\\
&\quad + \left(\frac{\partial U}{\partial\phi}\right)^{-1}\sum_{j=1}^n\left(p_j Z_0 + \sum_{t=1}^n U_{jt}^0 Z_t\right)X_{ji} && \text{[from (23)]}\\
&= X_i - (Z_H + p_b Z_B)X_i\\
&\quad - \left(\frac{\partial U}{\partial\phi}\right)^{-1}\sum_{j=1}^n (U_{jH}^0 Z_H + U_{jB}^0 Z_B)X_{ji} && \text{[from (20)]}\\
&= X_i - (Z_H + p_p Z_B)X_i && \text{[from (25)] (27)}
\end{aligned}$$

$$\begin{aligned}
Z_{ki} &= -(Z_{kH} + p_b Z_{kB})X_i - \left(\sum_{j=1}^n p_j Z_{kj}\right)X_i + Z_{ki} && \text{[from (21)]}\\
&= -(Z_{kH} + p_b Z_{kB})X_i
\end{aligned}$$

$$+\left(\frac{\partial U}{\partial \phi}\right)^{-1}\sum_{t=1}^{n}\left(\sum_{j=1}^{n}U_{jt}^{0}X_{ji}\right)Z_{kt} \qquad \text{[from (24)]}$$

$$=\left(\frac{\partial U}{\partial \phi}\right)^{-1}X_{ki}-(Z_{kH}+p_bZ_{kB})X_i$$

$$+\left(\frac{\partial U}{\partial \phi}\right)^{-1}\left[\sum_{j=1}^{n}\left(p_jZ_k+\sum_{t=1}^{n}U_{jt}^{0}Z_{kt}\right)X_{ji}-X_{ki}\right] \qquad \text{[from (23)]}$$

$$=\left(\frac{\partial U}{\partial \phi}\right)^{-1}X_{ki}-(Z_{kH}+p_bZ_{kB})X_i$$

$$-\left(\frac{\partial U}{\partial \phi}\right)^{-1}\sum_{j=1}^{n}(U_{jH}^{0}Z_{kH}+U_{jB}^{0}Z_{kB})X_{ji} \qquad \text{[from (22)]}$$

$$=\left(\frac{\partial U}{\partial \phi}\right)^{-1}X_{ki}-(Z_{kH}+p_bZ_{kB})X_i \qquad \text{[from (25)]} \quad (28)$$

$$Z_{Hi}=Z_{Hi}-\left(\sum_{j=1}^{n}p_jZ_{Hj}+Z_{HH}+p_bZ_{HB}\right)X_i \qquad \text{[from (21)]}$$

$$=-(Z_{HH}+p_bZ_{HB})X_i$$

$$+\left(\frac{\partial U}{\partial \phi}\right)^{-1}\sum_{j=1}^{n}\left(\sum_{t=1}^{n}U_{tj}^{0}X_{ti}\right)Z_{Hj} \qquad \text{[from (24)]}$$

$$=-(Z_{HH}+p_bZ_{HB})X_i$$

$$+\left(\frac{\partial U}{\partial \phi}\right)^{-1}\left[\sum_{t=1}^{n}p_tX_{ti}Z_H+\sum_{j=1}^{n}\left(\sum_{t=1}^{n}U_{tj}^{0}X_{ti}\right)Z_{Hj}\right] \qquad \text{[from (23)]}$$

$$=-(Z_{HH}+p_bZ_{HB})X_i$$

$$-\left(\frac{\partial U}{\partial \phi}\right)^{-1}\sum_{t=1}^{n}(U_{tH}^{0}Z_{HH}+U_{tB}^{0}Z_{HB})X_{ti} \qquad \text{[from (22)]}$$

$$=-(Z_{HH}+p_bZ_{HB})X_i \qquad \text{[from (25)]} \quad (29)$$

Similarly, we have

$$Z_{Bi}=-(Z_{BH}+p_bZ_{BB})X_i\ (i=1,\ldots,n) \qquad (30)$$

Now, substituting (27), (28), (29), and (30) into (16) and considering (26), equation (16) can be written in the form

$$\frac{\partial x_i}{\partial p_k}=-x_kX_i+\lambda' X_{ki}-\left(\frac{\partial H}{\partial p_k}+p_b\frac{\partial B}{\partial p_k}\right)X_i$$

where $\lambda' = (\partial U/\partial \phi)^{-1}\lambda$.

In this expression the first and the second terms are, respectively, the traditional income effect and the traditional substitution effect (Hicks, 1946, p. 309), and the third term is the indirect income effect, which arises when a change in p_k changes H and B.

Since I is constant, we have $(\partial H/\partial p_k) + p_b(\partial B/\partial p_k) = -\partial E/\partial p_k$. In the traditional Slutsky equation, the third term is neglected by the assumption of constancy of E. As $H + p_b B - I(\equiv -E)$ is saving, the traditional assumption that E is constant, is equivalent to the p_k-elasticity of saving being equal to zero.

3.3 By a similar procedure, we can transform (17) and (18) into

$$\frac{\partial H}{\partial p_k} = -\frac{\partial E}{\partial p_k}(p_b U^0_{HB} - U^0_{BB})/W + p_b(p_b U^0_{H[k]} - U^0_{B[k]})/W \qquad (31)$$

$$\frac{\partial B}{\partial p_k} = -\frac{\partial E}{\partial p_k}(U^0_{BH} - p_b U^0_{HH})/W - (p_b U^0_{H[k]} - U^0_{B[k]})/W \qquad (32)$$

where W is the determinant

$$\begin{vmatrix} 0 & 1 & p_b \\ 1 & U^0_{HH} & U^0_{HB} \\ p_b & U^0_{BH} & U^0_{BB} \end{vmatrix}$$

In each of (31) and (32), the first term represents the income effect that arises when a change in p_k changes the net expenditure E, and the second term represents the substitution effect that arises when a change in p_k shifts the marginal rate of substitution between cash and bonds. Since the second term of (31) and that of (32) are opposite in sign, H and B must change in opposite directions so far as the substitution effect is concerned. Hence we can say that cash and bonds are substitutive.

Now we make the very realistic assumptions that the marginal rate of substitution of bonds for cash decreases when B is increased and that it increases when H is increased, i.e.

$$\frac{\partial}{\partial B}\left(\frac{U_B}{U_H}\right) < 0, \frac{\partial}{\partial H}\left(\frac{U_B}{U_H}\right) > 0$$

Then we have

$$U_{BB}U_H - U_{HB}U_B < 0, \ U_{HH}U_B - U_{BH}U_H < 0$$

Therefore, at the equilibrium point we have

$$U^0_{BB} - U^0_{HB}p_b < 0, \ U^0_{HH}p_b - U^0_{BH} < 0$$

Next, by our stability conditions, $W > 0$, and from (9)

$$\frac{\partial}{\partial p_k}\left(\frac{U_H^0}{U_B^0}\right) = (U_{H[k]}^0 p_b - U_{B[k]}^0)/\lambda p_b^2$$

Consequently, we have the following rules:

	Income effect on:			Substitution effect on:	
$\frac{\partial E}{\partial p_k}$	H	B	$\frac{\partial}{\partial p_k}\left(\frac{U_H^0}{U_B^0}\right)$	H	B
+	−	−	+	+	−
0	0	0	0	0	0
−	+	+	−	−	+

3.4 According to Sono, we will say that the *i*th consumption good is a proper superior good (or a proper inferior good) if X_i is positive (or negative) and a general superior good (or a general inferior good) if Z_i is positive (or negative). Needless to say, if a good is superior (or inferior) in the Hicksian sense, then it is a proper superior good (or a proper inferior good) and vice versa. What relation exists between the proper and the general superiority–inferiority of goods? Since

$$1 - Z_H - p_b Z_B = 1 - (\partial H/\partial I) - p_b(\partial B/\partial I)$$

it follows from (27) that

$$\frac{Z_1}{X_1} = \frac{Z_2}{X_2} = \ldots = \frac{Z_n}{X_n} = 1 - \frac{\partial H}{\partial I} - p_b\frac{\partial B}{\partial I}$$

Hence, if $1 > (\partial H/\partial I) + p_b(\partial B/\partial I)$, i.e., if it is the case that when the consumer's initial assets are increased by one unit of cash, less than the entire unit will be devoted to the acquisition of cash and bonds, then the above two definitions are consistent, i.e., a proper superior good is a general superior good and a proper inferior good is a general inferior good. But, if $1 < (\partial H/\partial I) + p_b(\partial B/\partial I)$, then the two definitions are inconsistent, i.e., a proper superior good is a general inferior good and a proper inferior good is a general superior good (Sono, 1961, p. 249).

3.5 Next we shall define substitute and complementary goods as follows: if $\lambda' X_{ki}$ is positive (or negative), x_k and x_i are called proper substitute (or proper complementary) goods; and if λZ_{ki} is positive (or negative), x_k and x_i are general substitute (or general complementary) goods. Of course, our proper substitutive–complementary relation is identical with the one defined by Hicks. In the following, we shall be concerned with the relationship between the proper and the general substitutive–complementary relations.

Since the determinant D is symmetrical, we have $Z_{Hk} = Z_{kH}$, $Z_{Bk} = Z_{kB}$. Therefore, it follows from (28), (29), and (30) that

$$\lambda Z_{ki} - \lambda' X_{ki} = \lambda(Z_{HH} + 2p_b Z_{HB} + p_b^2 Z_{BB})X_i X_k$$

where the part in the parentheses on the right-hand side is necessarily negative, because $\sum_{i=1}^{B} \sum_{j=1}^{B} h_i h_j Z_{ij}$ is a negative definite quadratic form by the familiar properties of the substitution term (Hicks, 1946, pp. 310–11). Consequently, we have the following relations (Sono, 1961, pp. 261–5).

1 The case in which both x_k and x_i are proper superior goods or proper inferior goods. If x_k and x_i are proper complementary goods, they are necessarily general complementary goods, but if they are proper substitutes they are not necessarily general substitutes. If x_k and x_i are general substitutes, they are necessarily proper substitutes, but if they are general complementary goods they are not necessarily proper complementary goods.
2 The case in which one of x_k and x_i is a proper superior good and the other is a proper inferior good. If x_k and x_i are proper substitutes, they are necessarily general substitutes, but if they are proper complementary goods they are not necessarily general complementary goods. If x_k and x_i are general complementary goods, they are necessarily proper complementary goods, but if they are general substitutes they are not necessarily proper substitutes.
3 For any good, $\lambda Z_{kk} < \lambda' X_{kk}$.

4 A proportional change in all prices

4.1 In order to analyse the effect of a proportional change of all current prices, we introduce the following assumption: the probability that, when a consumer holds the amount H of cash and the amount B of bonds at the prices $p_1, \ldots, p_n, p_b$, his future living standard will be at least as high as the given level ξ, is equal to the probability that, when he holds the amount εH of cash and the amount εB of bonds at the prices $\varepsilon p_1, \ldots, \varepsilon p_n, p_b$, his future living standard will be at least as high as ε. This case is not identical with, but closely related to, the Hicksian case of unit elasticity of price expectation.

Then, from this assumption it follows that the probability distribution of the future living standard is not changed when $H, B, p_1, \ldots, p_n$ are changed proportionally. Therefore, U is homogeneous of order zero in $H, B, p_1, \dots, p_n$, or

$$\frac{\partial U}{\partial H}H + \frac{\partial U}{\partial B}B + \sum_{k=1}^{n} \frac{\partial U}{\partial p_k}p_k = 0 \tag{33}$$

identically in $x_1, \dots, x_n$, H, B, $p_1, \dots, p_n, p_b$.

Differentiating (33) partially with respect to x_j, we have

$$U_{jH}H + U_{jB}B + \sum_{k=1}^{n} U_{j[k]}p_k = 0 \tag{34}$$

that is to say, the marginal utility of the jth real commodity is homogeneous of order zero in $H, B, p_1, \dots, p_n (j = 1, 2, \dots, n)$. Differentiating (33) partially with respect to H

$$-U_H = U_{HH}H + U_{HB}B + \sum_{k=1}^{n} U_{H[k]}p_k \tag{35}$$

Similarly

$$-U_B = U_{BH}H + U_{BB}B + \sum_{k=1}^{n} U_{B[k]}p_k \tag{36}$$

That is, the marginal utility of cash and that of bonds are homogeneous of order -1 in $H, B, p_1, \dots, p_n$.

4.2 Now assume

$$\frac{dp_1}{p_1} = \frac{dp_2}{p_2} = \dots = \frac{dp_n}{p_n} = d\theta$$

Then we have

$$\begin{aligned} dx_i &= \sum_{k=1}^{n} \frac{\partial x_i}{\partial p_k} dp_k = \left(\sum_{k=1}^{n} \frac{\partial x_i}{\partial p_k} p_k \right) d\theta \\ &= \left[-\left(\sum_{k=1}^{n} p_k x_k \right) Z_i + \lambda \sum_{k=1}^{n} p_k Z_{ki} \right. \\ &\quad \left. - \sum_{j=1}^{B} \left(\sum_{k=1}^{n} U^0_{j[k]} p_k \right) Z_{ji} \right] d\theta \qquad \text{[from (16)]} \\ &= \left[-(I - H - p_b B) Z_i + \lambda \left(\sum_{k=1}^{n} p_k Z_{ki} + Z_{Hi} + p_b Z_{Bi} \right) \right. \\ &\quad \left. + \sum_{j=1}^{B} (U^0_{jH} H + U^0_{jB} B) Z_{ji} \right] d\theta \end{aligned}$$

[from (34), (35), (36), and (9)]

$$= \left[-IZ_i + \left(Z_i + \sum_{j=1}^{B} U_{jH}^0 Z_{ji} \right) H + \left(p_b Z_i + \sum_{j=1}^{B} U_{jB}^0 Z_{ji} \right) B \right] d\theta \qquad \text{[from (21)]} \quad (37)$$

But, since $Z_i + \sum_{j=1}^{B} U_{jH}^0 Z_{ji} = p_b Z_i + \sum_{j=1}^{B} U_{jB}^0 Z_{ji} = 0$ $(i = 1, \ldots, n)$, the last two terms of (37) vanish and, considering (27), we have

$$\begin{aligned} dx_i &= -I(1 - Z_H - p_b Z_B) X_i d\theta \\ &= -I\left(1 - \frac{\partial H}{\partial I} - p_b \frac{\partial B}{\partial I}\right) X_i d\theta \end{aligned} \qquad (38)$$

The demand for cash balances is changed as follows

$$\begin{aligned} dH &= \left(\sum_{k=1}^{n} \frac{\partial H}{\partial p_k} p_k \right) d\theta \\ &= \left[-IZ_H + \left(Z_H + \sum_{j=1}^{B} U_{jH}^0 Z_{jH} \right) H + \left(p_b Z_H + \sum_{j=1}^{B} U_{jB}^0 Z_{jH} \right) B \right] d\theta \end{aligned}$$

But, since $Z_H + \sum_{j=1}^{B} U_{jH}^0 Z_{jH} = 1$ and $p_b Z_H + \sum_{j=1}^{B} U_{jB}^0 Z_{jH} = 0$, we have

$$dH = [-IZ_H + H] d\theta = H\left[1 - \frac{I}{H}\frac{\partial H}{\partial I}\right] d\theta \qquad (39)$$

Similarly

$$dB = [-IZ_B + B] d\theta = B\left[1 - \frac{I}{B}\frac{\partial B}{\partial I}\right] d\theta \qquad (40)$$

4.3 Since it is realistic to assume that all of $H, \partial H/\partial I, \partial B/\partial I$ are non-negative, we can deduce from (38), (39), and (40) the following laws:

1 If $I \equiv$ the initial assets of the consumer $= 0$, then $dx_i = 0$ $(i = 1, \ldots, n)$, and $dH = Hd\theta, dB = Bd\theta$; that is to say, the demand for any consumption good and the supply of labour are unchanged in spite of the proportional change in all prices, and the demand for cash balances and the demand for bonds are changed in the same proportion as prices.
2 Let $I > 0$; then we can say the following: if $(\partial H/\partial I) + p_b(\partial B/\partial I) < 1$, the demand for a proper superior real commodity decreases and the demand

for a proper inferior real commodity increases when all prices rise proportionally. If $(\partial H/\partial I) + p_b(\partial B/\partial I) > 1$, the reverse is the case and, if $(\partial H/\partial I) + p_b(\partial B/\partial I) = 1$, the demand for each real commodity is not changed.

If $\partial H/\partial I = 0$, the demand for cash balances is increased in the same proportion as prices; if $0 < (I/H)(\partial H/\partial I) < 1$, it increases less than proportionally when $d\theta > 0$; and, if $(I/H)(\partial H/\partial I) > 1$, it decreases when $d\theta > 0$. The demand for cash balances does not change in spite of the proportional change in prices when $(I/H)(\partial H/\partial I) = 1$.

If $B > 0$ (i.e., if the consumer is a lender), the number of bonds held by him at the end of the period is changed as follows: If $\partial B/\partial I = 0$, it is increased in the same proportion as prices; but, if $0 < (I/B)(\partial B/\partial I) < 1$, it increases less than proportionally when $d\theta > 0$; and, if $(I/B)(\partial B/\partial I) > 1$, it decreases when $d\theta > 0$. The number of bonds B is unchanged in spite of the proportional change in prices when $(I/B)(\partial B/\partial I) = 1$.

If $B < 0$ (i.e., if the consumer is a borrower), the number of bonds issued by him $(-B)$ increases proportionally or more than proportionally when $d\theta > 0$ because $(I/-B)[\partial(-B)/\partial I]$ is non-positive.

3 Last, let $I < 0$. If $(\partial H/\partial I) + p_b(\partial B/\partial I) < 1$, then the demand for a proper superior real commodity increases and the demand for a proper inferior real commodity decreases when $d\theta > 0$. If $(\partial H/\partial I) + p_b(\partial B/\partial I) > 1$, the reverse is the case. If $(\partial H/\partial I) + p_b(\partial B/\partial I) = 1$, the demand for each real commodity is unchanged.

If $\partial H/\partial I = 0$, the demand for cash balances is increased in the same proportion as prices. But, if $\partial H/\partial I > 0$, then $(I/H)(\partial H/\partial I) < 0$. Therefore, the demand for cash balances increases more than proportionally when $d\theta > 0$. If the consumer is a borrower, the number of bonds issued by him $(-B)$ is changed as follows: If $\partial(-B)/\partial I = 0$, it is increased in the same proportion as price; if $(I/-B)[\partial(-B)/\partial I] < 1$, it increases less than proportionally when $d\theta > 0$; and, if $(I/-B)[\partial(-B)/\partial I] > 1$, it decreases when $d\theta > 0$. The amount, $(-B)$, is unchanged in spite of the proportional change in all prices when $(I/-B)[\partial(-B)/\partial I] = 1$. But, if the consumer is a lender, the number of bonds held by him at the end of the period increases proportionally or more than proportionally when $d\theta > 0$, because $(I/B)(\partial B/\partial I)$ is non-positive.

4.4 Consider an exchange economy in which there are v consumers (denoted by $1, 2, \ldots, v$) and no firm. Then, from section 4.3 it follows that, if $I^j = 0$ $(j = 1, \ldots, v)$, or, if $\partial H^j/\partial I^j = 0$ and $p_b \partial B^j/\partial I^j = 1$ $(j = 1, \ldots, v)$, then the market demand for each commodity is homogeneous of degree zero in $p_1, \ldots, p_n$ and the market demand for cash balances is homogeneous of degree one in the same variables. But, since the sum of $\bar{B}^j$ is zero for the entire community (credits and debts cancel), we have $\sum_{j=1}^{\nu} I^j = M$, where $M \equiv \sum_{j=1}^{\nu} M^j \equiv$ the total quantities of money > 0. Therefore, at least one of I^j is necessarily positive. For such individuals, the conditions that the demand for each real commodity be homogeneous of degree zero in $p_1,\ldots,p_n$ and that the demand for cash balances be homogeneous of degree one in the same variables are thus

$$\frac{\partial H^j}{\partial I^j} = 0 \text{ and } p_b \frac{\partial B^j}{\partial I^j} = 1 \; (j = 1,\ldots,\nu) \tag{41}$$

i.e., that, if the jth consumer's initial assets are increased by one unit of cash, the entire unit is devoted to the acquisition of bonds ($j = 1,\ldots,\nu$).

In his paper Patinkin (1949–50, p. 50) arrived at the conclusion that the conditions under which the market demand for real commodities can be homogeneous of degree zero in $p_1,\ldots,p_n$, are the two trivial ones in which (a) every individual has no initial stocks of money and bonds – an assumption that, as proved above, cannot hold for every consumer in the economy – or (b) the partial derivatives of each of the functions x_i with respect to the argument I is identically zero, i.e.

$$\frac{\partial x_i^j}{\partial I^j} = Z_i^j = 0 \; (i = 1,\ldots,n;\, j = 1,\ldots,\nu) \tag{42}$$

– an assumption that was rejected by Patinkin because the many economic studies show that the income effect is usually non-zero.

Assume, however, that goods $x_1,\ldots,x_n$ are separable from money and bonds; then we have the relation (27). Hence the assumption (42) is reduced to (41) or

$$\frac{\partial x_i^j}{\partial E^j} = X_i^j = 0 \; (i = 1,\ldots,n;\, j = 1,\ldots,\nu) \tag{43}$$

Assumption (43) is, of course, contradicted by many economic studies, but it seems to me that assumption (41) may be satisfied in some economic systems.

4.5 According to Lange (1949, p. 22) 'a proportional rise of all current prices (except interest rates) results in no change in the real demand for cash balances when the elasticities of expectation are all unity', that is to say, if all elasticities of expectation are unity, then

$$\frac{dH}{H} = \frac{dp_i}{p_i} \; (i = 1,\ldots,n) \tag{44}$$

Therefore, in order for Lange's analysis to be valid, either I or Z_H must be zero when all elasticities of expectation are unity [see (39)]. But I is, of course, independent of elasticities of expectation and $Z_H(= \partial H/\partial I)$ is not necessarily equal to zero, on the assumption that the elasticities of expectation are all unity or that the probability distribution of the future living standard is unchanged when $H, B, p_1, \ldots, p_n$ are changed proportionally. Therefore, it is not a sufficient condition for (44) that all elasticities of expectation be unity.

5 Analysis of the monetary effect

5.1 In the present section we shall consider the monetary effect which was first introduced into economics by Lange (1940, p. 15ff). He treated it as a social phenomenon and left its individualistic analysis incomplete; but, since the social monetary effect is to be deduced from the individual monetary effect as a total sum of the latter, we must analyse the individual monetary effect beforehand.

Any demand for a good implies a supply of money in exchange for the good, and any supply of a good implies a corresponding demand for money. Therefore, if we denote the stream of money demanded by a consumer during the present period by M_D and the stream of money offered by him during the same period by M_S, then we have

$$M_D \equiv p_n y,\ M_S \equiv \sum_{1}^{n-1} p_i x_i + p_b(B - \bar{B})$$

Since $y \equiv$ the supply of labour $= -x_n$, his excess demand for money is given as follows

$$M_D - M_S \equiv -\sum_{1}^{n} p_i x_i - p_b(B - \bar{B})$$

Taking into account the budget equation (1), we write this in the form

$$M_D - M_S \equiv H - M - \bar{B}$$

If our consideration is restricted to a proportional change of all prices, we can define the real excess demand for money as

$$e \equiv (H - M - \bar{B})/P$$

where P is a price index of goods in general, which is defined by

$$p_i = w_i P\ (w_i = \text{constant} > 0)\ (i = 1, \ldots, n)$$

Imitating Lange's definition of the monetary effect, we define the individual monetary effect as follows: from the viewpoint of a particular consumer, the monetary effect is positive when his real excess demand for money diminishes as all prices fall proportionally and increases as all prices rise proportionally. It is negative when the reverse is the case, and it is absent or zero when his real excess demand for money remains unchanged. Therefore, the sign of the monetary effect coincides with the sign of

$$\frac{de}{dP} = \frac{\dfrac{dH}{dP}P - (H - M - \bar{B})}{P^2}$$

Since $dH/dP = \sum_{i=1}^{n} (\partial H/\partial p_i)w_i$, it follows from (39) that

$$\frac{de}{dP} = \frac{M}{P^2}\left(1 - \frac{\partial H}{\partial I}\right) + \frac{\bar{B}}{P^2}\left[1 - (1 + p_b)\frac{\partial H}{\partial I}\right]$$

Therefore, putting $\alpha = \partial H/\partial I$ and $\beta = 1/(1 + p_b)$, the signs of the monetary effect are as follows:

	$\alpha < \beta$	$\beta < \alpha < 1$	$1 = \alpha$	$1 < \alpha$
$\bar{B} > 0$	+	?	−	−
$\bar{B} = 0$	+	+	0	−
$\bar{B} < 0$	?	+	+	?

5.2 Consider an exchange economy in which there are v consumers and no firm. Then the total excess demand for money on the market is given by

$$\sum_{j=1}^{v} (M_D^j - M_S^j) = \sum_{j=1}^{v} (H^j - I^j)$$

and the sign of the social monetary effect coincides with the sign of

$$\frac{dE^R}{dP} = \sum_{j=1}^{v} \frac{de^j}{dP} = \sum_{j=1}^{v} \frac{I^j\left(1 - \dfrac{\partial H^j}{\partial I^j}\right)}{P^2}$$

where E^R is the total real excess demand for money on the market. Hence, if we denote the average of the $\partial H^j/\partial I^j$ $(j = 1, \ldots, v)$ by

$$A \equiv \frac{\sum_{j=1}^{v} I^j \dfrac{\partial H^j}{\partial I^j}}{\sum_j I^j}$$

we have

$$\frac{dE^R}{dP} = \frac{\sum^{\nu} I^j(1-A)}{P^2} = \frac{M(1-A)}{P^2}$$

where M is the total quantity of money > 0. Consequently, if the average of the $\partial H^j/\partial I^j$ is less than unity, the social monetary effect is positive, and, if A is larger than unity, it is negative. The social monetary effect is zero when $A = 1$.

In particular, if the $\partial H^j/\partial I^j$ are the same for all consumers, we find

$$\frac{dE^R}{dP} = \frac{M\left(1 - \dfrac{\partial H^j}{\partial I^j}\right)}{P^2}$$

Consequently, the sign of the social monetary effect depends only on $\partial H^j/\partial I^j$ and is independent of the distribution of I^j. Since it is realistic to assume that $\partial H^j/\partial I^j$ is non-negative and less than 1,[8] it is very probable that the social monetary effect is positive.

6 The effect of a change in interest rate

6.1 In this section we shall examine the effect of a change in the interest rate with constant prices.

Differentiating (1) and (9) partially with respect to r and solving

$$\frac{\partial x_i}{\partial r} = \frac{1}{r^2}(B - \bar{B})Z_i - \frac{1}{r^2}\lambda Z_{Bi} - \sum_{j=1}^{B} U^0_{j(r)} Z_{ji} \tag{45}$$

$$\frac{\partial H}{\partial r} = \frac{1}{r^2}(B - \bar{B})Z_H - \frac{1}{r^2}\lambda Z_{BH} - \sum_{j=1}^{B} U^0_{j(r)} Z_{jH} \tag{46}$$

$$\frac{\partial B}{\partial r} = \frac{1}{r^2}(B - \bar{B})Z_B - \frac{1}{r^2}\lambda Z_{BB} - \sum_{j=1}^{B} U^0_{j(r)} Z_{jB} \tag{47}$$

where $U^0_{j(r)}$ is the value which $\partial U_j/\partial r$ assumes at the equilibrium point ($j = 1, \ldots, n, H, B$).

Now, substituting the relations (27), (28), (29), and (30) into (45), equation (45) can be written in the form

$$\frac{\partial x_i}{\partial r} = \frac{1}{r^2}(B - \bar{B})X_i - \frac{1}{r^2}(B - \bar{B})(Z_H + p_b Z_B)X_i$$

[8] For, if the consumer's initial assets are increased by one unit of cash, less than the entire unit will be devoted to the acquisition of cash.

$$+\frac{1}{r^2}\lambda(Z_{BH}+p_bZ_{BB})X_i+\sum_{j=1}^{B}U^0_{j(r)}(Z_{jH}+p_bZ_{jB})X_i$$

$$-\left(\frac{\partial U}{\partial \phi}\right)^{-1}\sum_{j=1}^{n}U^0_{j(r)}X_{ji} \tag{48}$$

But, since $\partial U_j/\partial r = (\partial\phi/\partial x_j)(\partial^2 U/\partial r\partial\phi), j = 1,\ldots,n$, it follows from (23) that

$$\sum_{j=1}^{n}U^0_{j(r)}X_{ji}=0$$

Hence the last term in equation (48) vanishes. Consequently, together with (46) and (47), equation (48) leads to

$$\frac{\partial x_i}{\partial r}=-\left[\frac{\partial H}{\partial r}+p_b\frac{\partial B}{\partial r}-\frac{1}{r^2}(B-\bar{B})\right]X_i \tag{49}$$

As $H + p_b(B - \bar{B}) - M - \bar{B}$ is saving (denoted by S) and M and $\bar{B}$ are independent of r, the part in the brackets on the right-hand side of (49) is equal to $\partial S/\partial r$. Hence

$$\frac{\partial x_i}{\partial r}=-\frac{\partial S}{\partial r}X_i \tag{50}$$

From (50) we have the following laws:

(a) If saving increases when the interest rate rises, the demand for a proper superior real commodity decreases and the demand for a proper inferior one increases.
(b) If saving is unchanged in spite of a change in interest rate, the demand for any real commodity is unchanged.
(c) If saving decreases when the interest rate rises, the reverse of (a) is the case.

6.2 By a similar procedure, we can transform (46) and (47) into

$$\frac{\partial H}{\partial r}=\frac{\partial S}{\partial r}(p_bU^0_{HB}-U^0_{BB})/W$$

$$+p_b(p_bU^0_{H(r)}-U^0_{B(r)}-p_b^2\lambda)/W \tag{51}$$

$$\frac{\partial B}{\partial r}=\frac{\partial S}{\partial r}(U^0_{BH}-p_bU^0_{HH})/W$$

$$-(p_bU^0_{H(r)}-U^0_{B(r)}-p_b^2\lambda)/W \tag{52}$$

In each of (51) and (52), the first term represents the income effect that arises when a change in interest rate changes the saving of the consumer, and the second term represents the substitution effect that arises when the equilibrium condition $U_H = U_B/p_b$ is disturbed by a change in interest rate.

First, ignore the substitution effect on cash and bonds. Since both of $(p_b U^0_{HB} - U^0_{BB})/W$ and $(U^0_{BH} - p_b U^0_{HH})/W$ are assumed to be positive (see section 3.3), we can say the following:

(i) If saving increases when the interest rate rises, the demand for cash balances and the number of bonds held at the end of the period are increased.
(ii) If saving is unchanged in spite of a change in interest rate, they are constant.
(iii) If saving decreases when interest rate rises, the reverse of (i) is the case.

Next examine the substitution effect. It is realistic to assume that the marginal rate of substitution of bonds for cash is increased when r is increased, that is

$$\frac{\partial}{\partial r}\left(\frac{U_B}{U_H}\right) > 0$$

For it seems realistic to assume that, if the rate of interest rises, the quantity of bonds that would just compensate the consumer for the loss of a marginal unit of cash will be decreased. Hence we have

$$p_b U^0_{H(r)} - U^0_{B(r)} < 0$$

at the point $(H^0, B^0, p_1, \ldots, p_n, r)$. Therefore, we arrive at the conclusion that, if we neglect the income effect, a rise in interest rate leads to a decrease in the demand for cash balances and to an increase in the number of bonds held at the end of the period.

6.3 Assuming that the utility function of the jth consumer takes the form of $u^j(x^j_1, \ldots, x^j_n, B^j/rp, M^j/p)$ (where $p = \Sigma c_i p_i =$ the price index), Patinkin has arrived at the conclusion (1949–50, p. 49) that the individual demand functions can be written as follows

$$\left.\begin{aligned} x^j_i &= f^j_i\left(\frac{p_1}{p}, \ldots, \frac{p_n}{p}, r, \frac{I^j}{p}\right), \\ B^j &= pf^j_B\left(\frac{p_1}{p}, \ldots, \frac{p_n}{p}, r, \frac{I^j}{p}\right), \\ H^j &= -\sum_1^n p_i x_i - \frac{B_j}{r} + I^j \end{aligned}\right\} \qquad (53)$$

where $I^j = (\bar{B}^j/r) + \bar{B}^j + M^j$. But it can be easily shown that his conclusions are erroneous. Since, if we let $B^j/rp = x^j_{n+1}$ and $H^j/p = x^j_{n+2}$, then we have as the budget restraint

$$\sum_{i=1}^{n} \frac{p_i}{p} x_i^j + x^j_{n+1} + x^j_{n+2} = \frac{I^j}{p} \tag{54}$$

and as the equilibrium conditions

$$\frac{u_i^j(x_1^j, \ldots, x^j_{n+2})}{u_k^j(x_1^j, \ldots, x^j_{n+2})} = \frac{p_i}{p} \quad (i = 1, \ldots, n; k = n+1, n+2) \tag{55}$$

Hence from (54) and (55), we have

$$x_i^j = f_i^j\left(\frac{p_1}{p}, \ldots, \frac{p_n}{p}, \frac{I^j}{p}\right) \quad (i = 1, \ldots, n+2)$$

Consequently, the individual demand functions must take the forms

$$x_i^j = f_i^j\left(\frac{p_1}{p}, \ldots, \frac{p_n}{p}, \frac{I^j}{p}\right) \quad (i = 1, \ldots, n),$$

$$B^j = prf^j_{n+1}\left(\frac{p_1}{p}, \ldots, \frac{p_n}{p}, \frac{I^j}{p}\right),$$

$$H^j = pf^j_{n+2}\left(\frac{p_1}{p}, \ldots, \frac{p_n}{p}, \frac{I^j}{p}\right) \tag{56}$$

Now let us assume an exchange economy in which the partial derivative f each of the functions (56) with respect to its $(n + 1)$th argument I^j/p is the same for all consumers. Then, since the sum of $\bar{B}^j = 0$, the market demand functions take the forms

$$\left.\begin{aligned} X_i &= F_i\left(\frac{p_1}{p}, \ldots, \frac{p_n}{p}, \frac{M}{p}\right), \\ B &= prF_{n+1}\left(\frac{p_1}{p}, \ldots, \frac{p_n}{p}, \frac{M}{p}\right), \\ H &= pF_{n+2}\left(\frac{p_1}{p}, \ldots, \frac{p_n}{p}, \frac{M}{p}\right) \end{aligned}\right\} \tag{57}$$

where $X_i = \sum_{j=1}^{\nu} x_i^j$, $B = \sum_{j=1}^{\nu} B^j$, $H = \sum_{j=1}^{\nu} H^j$, $M = \sum_{j=1}^{\nu} M^j$. Therefore, from the revised Patinkin functions (57) it follows that all of (a) the demand for each real good, (b) the value of the bond demanded, $p_b B$, and (c) the demand for cash balances are independent of the rate of interest. This conclusion is clearly contradicted by many economic theories. Moreover, in such an economy the rate of interest is indeterminate because each of the monetary equilibrium conditions $H = M$ and $B = 0$ [or $F_{n+1}(p_1/p, \ldots, p_n/p, M/p) = 0$] is independent of the rate of interest. Consequently, we must reject Patinkin's analysis.

In Patinkin's analysis it is assumed that the individual is concerned only with the real value of the bonds he holds and that therefore his utility function is homogeneous of degree zero in B^j and r. But, when the consumer holds the amount B^j of bonds, he is, of course, paid B^j dollars per period; and when he holds the amount εB^j of bonds, he gains εB^j dollars per period. Hence, if $\varepsilon > 1$, the situation $(x_1^j, \ldots, x_n^j, H^j, \varepsilon B^j, p, \varepsilon r)$ is, clearly, preferred to the situation $(x_1^j, \ldots, x_n^j, H^j, B^j, p, r)$, though in these situations the real value of bonds is the same. Consequently, we must say that the consumer's utility function is not homogeneous of degree zero in B^j and r.

If the utility function takes the form

$$u^j = U^j\left(x_1^j, \ldots, x_n^j, \frac{B^j}{p}, \frac{H^j}{p}, r\right)$$

then the individual demand functions do not take the forms of (56), but the ones of (53).

Appendix II
Entrepreneur behaviour and liquidity preference

1 The basic idea

Although a dynamic analysis of the behaviour of the firm has carefully been made by Hicks, 1946, it is only concerned with its production plan. In the actual world, the production plan is only a part of the whole plan which the firm makes. It includes in addition to the production plan, the demand–supply plan of the factors of production and the products, and the inventory or stock plan of these commodities. Besides, the firm will make a demand–supply plan concerning money and securities, that is, its financial plan. The purpose of this appendix is to analyse the plans systematically by a single principle of the behaviour of the firm. Especially, the problem of the demand for money is one of the central points of interest in the following analysis.

2 Subjective equilibrium conditions of the firm

We use the following notation. Let y_{i0} be the supply of product i of the firm in the present week 0, $i = 2, 3, \ldots, m$; y_{i_ι} the expected supply of the same product in week ι in the future, x_{j0} the demand for material, capital good or factor, j, used for production in week 0, x_{j_ι} the expected demand for the same good or factor in week ι, $j = m + 1, \ldots, n$. (Throughout the following we refer to materials, capital goods, and factors of production simply and categorically as the factors of production.) These supplies and demands may differ from outputs and inputs of these commodities actually produced or carried out in the respective weeks. Let x'_{i0} be the output of product i in week 0, x'_{i_ι} its expected output in week ι, y'_{j0} the current input of the factor of production j, y'_{j_ι} its expected input in week ι.

Let $x''_{h,-1}$ be the stock of commodity h at the beginning of week 0 (that is, the end of week, -1), x''_{h0} and x''_{h_ι} the stocks of the same commodity that firm intends to hold at the end of week 0, or week ι, respectively, where

$h = 2, 3, \ldots, n$. We then obtain the following identities, the first of which holds for each product i

$$x'_{i_\iota} - y_{i_\iota} \equiv x''_{i_\iota} - x''_{i_\iota - 1} \quad i = 2, \ldots, m$$

and the second for each factor of production j

$$x_{j_\iota} - y'_{j_\iota} \equiv x''_{j_\iota} - x''_{j_\iota - 1} \quad j = m + 1, \ldots, n$$

Regarding supply as a negative quantity of demand, and input as a negative quantity of output, we put $x_{i_\iota} = - y_{i_\iota}$, $i = 2, 3, \ldots, m$, and $x'_{j_\iota} = - y'_{j_\iota}$, $j = m + 1, \ldots, n$. Then the above identities are re-written in the form

$$x_{i_\iota} + x'_{i_\iota} \equiv x''_{i_\iota} - x''_{i_\iota - 1} \quad i = 2, \ldots, n; \ \iota = 0, 1, \ldots, v \tag{1}$$

In the following we use this convention of treating demand and supply, and output and input, as quantities belonging to the same categories but with different signs and uniformly express them by single characters, x and x', respectively.

Now, let us assume that the firm makes a production plan, x', extending from week 0 to week v, which is subject to a production function expressing various technological restrictions

$$f(x'_{20}, x'_{30}, \ldots, x'_{nv}, z, z', z'', \ldots) = 0 \tag{2}$$

where z, z', z'', etc. are quantities of goods in process at various stages that the firm has at the beginning of week 0. They are given and, therefore, constant. Next let x_{0_ι}, $\iota = 0, 1, \ldots, v$, be the amount of money the firm holds in week ι. The demand for securities in week ι is denoted by x_{1_ι}, $\iota = 0, \ldots, v$, and $x_{1,-1}$ is the initial holding of the securities at the beginning of week 0. Then the net revenue of the firm in week 0 and the expected net revenue in week ι are written as

$$R_0 = - \Sigma p_{i0} x_{i0} - x_{00} + x_{0,-1} - x_{10} + (1 + r_{-1}) x_{1,-1}$$

and

$$R_\iota = - \Sigma p_{i_\iota} x_{i_\iota} - x_{0_\iota} + x_{0_\iota - 1} - x_{1_\iota} + (1 + r_{\iota - 1}) x_{1_\iota - 1}$$

respectively, where p_{i0} are prices in week 0, p_{i_ι} expected prices in week ι, r_{-1}, r_0 the rates of interest in the last and the present week, respectively, and r_ι the expected rate of interest in week ι.[1] On the assumption that firm maximizes the capitalized value, or the present discounted value, of the stream of the net revenues over $v + 1$ weeks, we may consider that the firm decides the production plan such that it maximizes

[1] The expressions R_0 and R_ι follow, by eliminating k_0 and k_ι, from (8) and (9) of chapter 2.

$$\sum_{0}^{\nu} \beta_{\iota} R_{\iota} \tag{3}$$

where β's are the discounting factors

$$\beta_{\iota} = \frac{1}{(1+r_0)(1+r_1)\ldots(1+r_{\iota-1})}$$

Hicks assumes that demand for factors of production equals their input, and supply of products their output. This means that the left-hand side of (1) vanishes, so that $x''_{i_\iota} = x''_{i_\iota - 1}$, $\iota = 0, 1, \ldots, \nu$, that is to say, the inventories are stationary. Moreover, he assumes that there is no restriction to the amounts, $k_0, k_1, \ldots$ which the firm spends on the factors of production. Footnote 1 implies that we also accept this assumption. Once it is granted, the production plan and the financial plan are independent from each other. It is obviously a gross simplification that any realistic theory should avoid. I have nonetheless accepted it because of the simplicity it brings about in analysis. We may alternatively take k as given and follow *mutatis mutandis* the same course of analysis, though we must deal with a maximization problem subject to multiple constraints: production constraint, liquidity constraint, and the budget constraints due to shortages of k.

Now we turn to the financial plan. As I have just mentioned, the following assumes flexible k, so that our analysis is very partial and cannot deal with the distortion in the plan that is created by virtue of the limited availability of k. Effects of such k upon the firm's production, inventory and finance plans will be examined later in section 8.

With this proviso, let us compare our model with Keynes' analysis of the demand for money. According to him, the firm demands money by the three motives, transaction, precaution, and speculation motives. This means that money functions so as to satisfy the people behaving with these motives; in short, it has liquidity in the sense that it provides the holder of money with a certain adaptability or manoeuvrability when he suffers from some difficulty, or meets with an accident, or finds a business opportunity. However, money is not the only commodity which has liquidity. As there is no absolute criterion for liquidity, assets of any kind more or less have certain amounts of liquidity as far as they secure the owner a certain amount of purchasing power. Let ξ be the degree of adaptability which the entrepreneur secures. We assume that he knows the probability that, when he is provided with a stream of money $(x_{00}, x_{01}, \ldots, x_{0\nu})$, securities $(x_{10}, \ldots, x_{1\nu})$, and stocks of commodities $(x''_{20}, \ldots, x''_{n\nu})$, the adaptability of his business in the future will be at least as high as the given degree ξ. This probability $Q(\xi)$ depends on interest rates $r_0, r_1, \ldots, r_{\nu-1}$ and prices $p_{20}, \ldots, p_{n\nu}$, so that we may write: $Q(\xi) = Q(X; \xi)$, where

$$X = (x_{00}, \ldots, x_{0\nu}, x_{10}, \ldots, x_{1\nu}, x''_{20}, \ldots, x''_{n\nu}, p_{20}, \ldots, p_{n\nu}, r_0, \ldots, r_{\nu-1})$$

We also assume that the entrepreneur is able to compare any two states X^0 and X^1 with respect to their respective probability distributions $Q(X^0, \xi)$ and $Q(X^1, \xi)$ and can say which of these is more preferable than the other from the point of view of his business. We attach to each $Q(X; \xi)$ a positive index ϕ, such that $\phi(Q(X; \xi))$ describes his preferences. We call this the liquidity functional of the firm.

It is well known that Keynes, 1936, defines the liquidity preference function in a macroeconomic form as $M = L(r)$,[2] where r is the current rate of interest and M is the amount of money held in the economy. Our ϕ is compared with Keynes' $M = L(r)$ in the following way. First, putting his function in an implicit form, $\tilde{L}(M, r) = 0$, we compare it with a functional expression of the implicit form

$$\tilde{\phi}(x_{00}, \ldots, x_{1\nu}, x''_{20}, \ldots, x''_{n\nu}, p_{20}, \ldots, r_{\nu-1}; \xi, \gamma) = 0 \tag{*}$$

or

$$\tilde{\phi}(x_{00}, \ldots, x_{1\nu}, x''_{20}, \ldots, x''_{n\nu}, p_{20}, \ldots, r_{\nu-1}; \xi) = \gamma \tag{4}$$

In (*) γ plays the role of a parameter. That is to say, in accordance with the value of γ which the firm intends to retain, the shape of the firm's indifference super-surface of liquidity, $\phi(\ldots, \gamma) = 0$, is different. This corresponds to Keynes' macroeconomic liquidity preference function, $\tilde{L}(M, r) = 0$, showing the relationship between the rate of interest and the amount of money to be held by the individual businesses. It is an aggregate expression of individual agents' decisions of money holdings, each of which brings about a level of liquidity that the corresponding agent intends to retain. It is, therefore, clear that, more explicitly, $\tilde{L}$ too has to have Γ as a parameter, that is the aggregate of individual γs. Thus

$$\tilde{L}(M, r, \Gamma) = 0 \tag{**}$$

From (*) and (**) it is evident that the latter is an extension of the former. There is no significant difference between my and Keynes' liquidity preference functions.

On the basis of what has been said above, we now consider a firm which maximizes the capitalized value of the stream of the net revenues (3) subject to the production function (2) and the liquidity functional (4). In the last γ is regarded as given. Moreover, the firm's demand and supply, input and output, and accumulation of inventories are connected with each other by (1). Hence the problem is formulated as: maximize (3) subject to (1), (2), and (4). Then the first-order conditions for maximization are written

[2] Keynes, 1936, p. 168.

$$\mu f_{i_\iota} = \beta_\iota p_{i_\iota}, \; i = 2, \ldots, n; l = 0, 1, \ldots, \nu \tag{5}$$

and

$$\begin{aligned} \lambda\phi_{0_\iota} &= \beta_\iota - \beta_{\iota+1}, \\ \lambda\phi_{1_\iota} &= 0 \\ \lambda\phi_{i_\iota} &= \beta_\iota p_{i_\iota} - \beta_{\iota+1} p_{i_\iota+1} \; i = 2, \ldots, n; l = 0, 1, \ldots, \nu - 1, \\ \lambda\phi_{j_\nu} &= \beta_\iota p_{j_\nu}, \text{ with } p_{j_\nu} = 1 \text{ for } j = 0 \text{ or } 1 \end{aligned} \tag{6}$$

where $f_{i_\iota} = \partial f/\partial x'_{i_\iota}$, $\phi_{0_\iota} = \partial\phi/\partial x_{0_\iota}$, $\phi_{1_\iota} = \partial\phi/\partial x_{1_\iota}$, $\phi_{i_\iota} = \partial\phi/\partial x''_{i_\iota}$, and μ and λ are Lagrangean multipliers. (5) and (6) are referred to as the subjective equilibrium conditions of the firm.

The following explanations may be given to these conditions. Conditions (5) are the conditions for the production plan. It is found that these are equivalent to Hicks' three propositions. (i) The marginal rate of substitution between two products is equal to the ratio of their expected discounted prices. (ii) The marginal rate of substitution between two factors is equal to the ratio of their expected discounted prices. (iii) The marginal rate of transformation of a factor into a product is equal to the ratio of their expected discounted prices.[3]

Conditions (6) determine demands for and supplies of money, security, and inventories of various physical commodities. These may be stated in the following way. Suppose that an increase in the demand for money by one unit in week ι gives rise to an increase in liquidity ϕ by the amount $\sum_{\mu=\iota}^{\nu} \phi_{0_\mu}$ if it is held until the end of week ν. Then we may define the marginal rate of substitution between the acquisition of money in the present week 0 and the one in week ι in the future as $\sum_{\iota}^{\nu} \phi_{0_\mu} \Big/ \sum_{0}^{\nu} \phi_{0_\mu}$. Similarly, if one unit of commodity i is increased in week ι and retained thereafter until week ν, it results in an increase in the liquidity by $\sum_{\iota}^{\nu} \phi_{i_\mu}$. Then the marginal rate of substitution between the ith inventory and the acquisition of money is defined as $\sum_{\iota}^{\nu} \phi_{i_\mu} \Big/ \sum_{0}^{\nu} \phi_{0_\mu}$ in the current week, while it is defined as $\sum_{\iota}^{\nu} \phi_{i_\mu} \Big/ \sum_{\tau}^{\nu} \phi_{j_\mu}$ between inventory i in week ι and inventory j in week τ. We obtain from (6) the following four propositions. (i) The marginal rate of substitution between the present money and the money to be acquired in the future is equal to the rate of discount β_ι over the weeks of postponement in acquisition. (ii) The marginal rate of substitution between the present

[3] Hicks, 1946, p. 197.

money and the present inventory i is equal to the present price of commodity i. (iii) The marginal rate of substitution between two inventories in the (same or different) future weeks is equal to the ratio between their expected discounted prices. (iv) Bonds are held up until the point at which they cease to make a contribution to liquidity.

From (2) and (5) we obtain x'_i as functions of p and r. (4) and (6) give x_{0_ι}, x_{1_ι} and x''_{i_ι} as functions of p and r. Considering (1) we obtain, x_{i_ι} as functions of p and r, since both x'_{i_ι} and x''_{i_ι} are functions of the same variables. These give demand and supply functions of the firm.

3 Subjective stability conditions

Let us now call a point satisfying (1), (2), (4), (5), and (6) a subjective equilibrium point. In order for the point to give a maximum of the capitalized value of the net revenues, it must fulfil the sufficient conditions for the problem of conditional maximization. These consist of: (i) at the subjective equilibrium point the quadratic form $-\mu d^2 f$ is negative definite subject to $df = 0$, and (ii) at the same point $\lambda d^2\phi$ is negative definite subject to $d\phi = 0$. If we denote the partial derivatives of f and f_{i_ι} by f_{i_ι} and $f_{i_\iota j_\tau}$, respectively, and those of ϕ and ϕ_{i_ι} by ϕ_{i_ι} and $\phi_{i_\iota j_\tau}$, respectively, all of them being evaluated at the subjective equilibrium point, then the sufficient conditions for the maximum, that is referred to as the subjective stability conditions, may be stated as: let π be an integer not less than 3. (i) For all such π, the principal minors of order π of the matrix

$$\begin{bmatrix} 0 & f_{j_\tau} \\ f_{i_\iota} & -\mu f_{i_\iota j_\tau} \end{bmatrix} \quad i,j = 2,\ldots,n;\ \iota,\tau = 0,1,\ldots,v \tag{7}$$

are positive or negative if π is odd or even, respectively. (ii) Similar conditions hold for the matrix

$$\begin{bmatrix} 0 & \phi_{j_\tau} \\ \phi_{i_\iota} & \lambda\phi_{i_\iota j_\tau} \end{bmatrix} \quad i,j = 0,\ldots,n;\ \iota,\tau = 0,1,\ldots,v \tag{7'}$$

Let us now denote the determinant of the matrix (7) by F, the cofactor of $-\mu f_{i_\iota j_\tau}$ in F by $F_{i_\iota j_\tau}$ and the ratio $F_{i_\iota j_\tau}/F$ by $X_{i_\iota j_\tau}$. As Hicks has shown,[4] the following four rules are obtained from the stability conditions (i):

(a) $X_{i_\iota j_\tau} = X_{j_\tau i_\iota}$,
(b) $X_{i_\iota i_\iota} < 0$,

(c) $\sum_{\iota=0}^{v} \sum_{i=2}^{n} \beta_\iota p_{i_\iota} X_{j_\tau i_\iota} = 0$,

[4] Hicks, 1946, pp. 310–11, p. 321.

(d) $\sum_{\iota=0}^{\mu}\sum_{i=2}^{s}\sum_{\tau=0}^{\mu}\sum_{j=2}^{s} q_{i_\iota}q_{j\tau}X_{i_\iota j\tau} < 0, \begin{cases}\mu \leqq \nu \\ s < n\end{cases}$ or $\begin{matrix}\mu < \nu \\ s \leqq n\end{matrix}$

where (d) holds for every set of qs that are not all zero.

By exactly the same procedure, we have the following four rules, (a′)–(d′), from the stability conditions (ii). In these expressions $Y_{i_\iota j\tau} = H_{i_\iota j\tau}/H$, where H is the determinant of the matrix (7′) above and $H_{i_\iota j\tau}$ is the cofactor of $\lambda\phi_{i_\iota j\tau}$ in H.

(a′) $Y_{i_\iota j\tau} = Y_{j\tau i_\iota}$,
(b′) $Y_{i_\iota i_\iota} < 0$,

(c′) $\sum_{\iota=0}^{\nu}\sum_{i=0}^{n} \phi_{i_\iota} Y_{j\tau i_\iota} = 0$,

(d′) $\sum_{\iota=0}^{\mu}\sum_{i=0}^{s}\sum_{\tau=0}^{\mu}\sum_{j=0}^{s} q_{i_\iota}q_{j\tau}Y_{i_\iota j\tau} < 0, \begin{cases}\mu \leqq \nu \\ s < n\end{cases}$ or $\begin{matrix}\mu < \nu \\ s \leqq n\end{matrix}$

where (d′) holds for every set of q such that they are not all zero.

4 Effects of a change in a price upon the production plan

Effects on the production plan are obtained from (2) and (5). First, where a price of good i only changes in week ι, we have

$$\frac{\partial x'_{i_\iota}}{\partial p_{i_\iota}} = -\beta_\iota X_{i_\iota i_\iota} \tag{8}$$

and

$$\frac{\partial x'_{j\tau}}{\partial p_{i_\iota}} = -\beta_\iota X_{i_\iota j\tau} \tag{8′}$$

Then, in view of rule (b), we have from (8): (i) If the price of a product i rises in week ι, its output in the same week is increased. (ii) If the price of a factor of production i rises in week ι, its input in the same week is diminished.

Next, suppose commodities i and j are both products or both factors of production. We say that commodity i in week ι is *substitutive* for commodity j in week τ if $X_{i_\iota j\tau} > 0$, while they are *complementary* if $X_{i_\iota j\tau} < 0$. If one of i and j is a product and the other a factor of production, we say that commodity i in week ι and j in τ are *covariant* if $X_{i_\iota j\tau} > 0$, while they are *contra-variant* if $X_{i_\iota j\tau} < 0$. We obtain the following four propositions from (8′). (iii) When the price of a product i in a particular week ι rises, then it gives rise to a decrease or an increase in the output of product j in week τ, according as it is substitutive for or complementary with commodity i in ι.

(iv) When the price of a factor i in week ι rises, then it brings about an increase or a decrease of the input of factor j in week τ, which is substitutive for or complementary with factor i in ι. (v) An increase in the price of output i in week ι induces an increase in the input j in week τ if i and j are covariant between these weeks, while it diminishes the input of j in week τ if they are contra-variant. (vi) A proposition similar to (v) is obtained between the factor of production whose price is increased and the output of a product which is covariant or contra-variant with this factor.

We have so far been concerned with an increase in the current or expected price of a single commodity in a particular, present or future, week. In the case of a proportional change of current and expected prices in all weeks, $\iota = 0, 1, \ldots, \nu$, of a single commodity i, that is to say, when

$$\frac{dp_{i0}}{p_{i0}} = \frac{dp_{i1}}{p_{i1}} = \ldots = \frac{dp_{i\nu}}{p_{i\nu}} = d\theta$$

we have

$$dx'_{i_\iota} = -\sum_{\tau=0}^{\nu} \beta_\tau p_{i\tau} X_{i\tau i_\iota} d\theta \tag{9}$$

and

$$\sum_{\iota=0}^{\nu} \beta_\iota p_{i_\iota} dx'_{i_\iota} = -\left(\sum_{\iota=0}^{\nu}\sum_{\tau=0}^{\nu} \beta_\iota p_{i_\iota} \beta_\tau p_{i\tau} X_{i\tau i_\iota}\right) d\theta \tag{10}$$

We cannot determine whether (9) takes on a positive or a negative value, while we find that the part in the parentheses of (10) is definitely negative because of (d). Therefore, we get the following two propositions. (vii) When the prices of a product increase in every week in the same proportion, then its output definitely increases in at least one week. (viii) When the prices of a factor increase in every week in the same proportion, then the input of that factor must increase in one of the weeks.

When current and expected prices of all products and all factors of production increase proportionately, we have from (c) that $dx'_{i_\iota} = 0, i = 2, \ldots, n;\ \iota = 0, 1, \ldots, \nu$. That is to say, there is no change in the production plan. This means that any output and any input in every week are functions being homogeneous of degree zero in the variables of current and expected prices.

5 Effects of a change in the rate of interest upon the production plan

Suppose the rate of interest in every week changes quasi-proportionately in the sense that

$$\frac{dr_0}{1+r_0} = \frac{dr_1}{1+r_1} = \ldots = \frac{dr_{v-1}}{1+r_{v-1}} = d\theta$$

Then outputs and inputs will change according to the formula

$$dx'_{j\tau} = \left(\sum_{\iota=0}^{v} \sum_{i=2}^{n} \iota\beta_{\iota}p_{i_{\iota}}X_{i_{\iota}j\tau} \right) d\theta \tag{11}$$

As we have from (c) in section 3 equation $\tau \sum_{\iota=0}^{v} \sum_{i=2}^{n} \beta_{\iota}p_{i_{\iota}}X_{i_{\iota}j\tau} = 0$, (11) may be put in the form

$$dx'_{j\tau} = -\sum_{\iota=0}^{v} \sum_{i=2}^{n} (\tau - \iota)\beta_{\iota}p_{i_{\iota}}X_{i_{\iota}j\tau} d\theta \tag{11'}$$

Therefore, it is evident that this does not contain the term $X_{j\tau j\tau}$ which is negative. Under the assumption that the remaining $X_{i_{\iota}j\tau}$ are all positive, we have from (11′)

$$dx'_{j0} > 0 \text{ and } dx'_{jv} < 0$$

if $d\theta > 0$. That is to say, a quasi-proportional increase in the rates of interest gives rise to an increase in the current output j and a decrease in the output j in the final week v. In the case of j being a factor of production, the same increase in the interest rates induces an increase in the current input j $(-dx'_{j0} > 0)$ and a decrease in the input j in the final week v $(-dx'_{jv} < 0)$. If we further assume that the series of $dx'_{j\tau}$, $\tau = 0, 1, \ldots, v$ is monotone, the series of output changes is monotonically declining when $d\theta > 0$, while that of input changes is monotonically decreasing in the same case. Thus we may describe effects on the production plan in the following way. A quasi-proportional increase in the rates of interest induces outputs and inputs in no distant weeks to increase more or less in parallel, while those in the remote future weeks change in the opposite directions. These are the phenomena which Hicks has called 'tilting of outputs and inputs streams due to interest changes'.

6 Criteria for formation of behavioural plans of the firm

In this section we compare our formulation of behaviour of the firm with Hicks' and Keynes' theorizing. Let us first begin with Hicks.

Hicks defines surplus of the firm as the value of net outputs, that is the value of outputs minus the value of inputs. The firm has a stream of surpluses from week 0 to week v, whose capitalized present value is obtained by adding up the discounted values of surpluses over all these weeks. He assumes that the firm's principle for making its behavioural plan is to maximize this capitalized value over the whole planning period. It does not maximize the surplus of a particular week at the sacrifice of surpluses in other weeks. In making an optimum plan, the firm of course takes the technological constraint for production into account. Thus it maximizes the capitalized value

$$\sum_{\iota=0}^{\nu}\sum_{i=2}^{n}\beta_\iota p_{i_\iota}x'_{i_\iota} \tag{12}$$

subject to the production function (2). We then obtain (5) as the necessary conditions for maximum.

This means that, as far as the production plan is concerned, there is no difference between the two types of the firms: (i) the firm dealt with in this appendix and the text which maximizes the capitalized value of the entrepreneurial net revenues subject to the technological and liquidity preference constraints, and (ii) the Hicksian firm which maximizes the capitalized value of the surpluses from the production, subject to the technological constraint only. This is because it is assumed that there is no difficulty in obtaining the amounts k_ι, $\iota = 0, 1, \ldots, \nu$, which the firm wants to spend on producers' goods in weeks ι, $\iota = 0, 1, \ldots, \nu$. By this assumption it is clear that *k*s do not impose any restriction upon the production plan, so that it is free and independent of the inventory and financial plans. Whilst our formulation enables us to analyse other aspects of the behaviour of the firm, i.e., the demand–supply, inventory, and financial plans, these are all ignored or at least not mathematically examined by Hicks.

Keynes formulates the activity of the firm in the following way. By taking (1) into account, (12) may be written

$$-\sum_{\iota=0}^{\nu}\sum_{i=2}^{n}\beta_\iota p_{i_\iota}x_{i_\iota} + \sum_{\iota=0}^{\nu}\sum_{i=2}^{n}\beta_\iota p_{i_\iota}(x''_{i_\iota} - x''_{i_{\iota}-1}) \tag{13}$$

The first term of (13) gives the firm's total supply of products over its total demand for producers' goods. In Keynes' notation, it is equal to the difference between the discounted value of the firm's proceeds A^ι in week ι, $\iota = 0, 1, \ldots, \nu$, and the discounted value of its purchases, $A_1^\iota + F^\iota$, over the same span of time. A_1^ι represents the amount that the firm pays to all other firms in week ι and F^ι is the wages paid in the same week. In the second term of (13) $\sum_{i=2}^{n} p_{i_\iota}x''_{i_\iota}$ is the total amount of stocks which the firm holds at the end of week ι, that is G^ι in Keynes' notation, while $\sum_{i=2}^{n} p_{i_\iota}x''_{i_{\iota}-1}$ represents the value which the stocks of commodities at the end of the previous week $\iota - 1$ would have if they are not consumed for production during week ι and are, therefore, evaluated at the full prices of the week. Clearly, this is the same as Keynes' G_0^ι. Hence the second term of (13) represents the capitalized value of the series of $G^\iota - G_0^\iota$ from $\iota = 0$ to $\iota = \nu$. Ignoring maintenance costs and using Keynes' terminology, it may be said that $A_1^\iota - G^\iota + G_0^\iota$ represents 'the expected user cost in week ι'. Thus, it is clear that (13) expresses

$$\sum_{\iota=0}^{\nu} \beta_\iota (A^\iota - U^\iota - F^\iota) \tag{14}$$

where U^ι stands for the user cost and the part in the parentheses is the same as Keynes' profit or income of the firm in week ι.

According to him, the firm is considered to maximize the capitalized value of the stream of profits over the planning period. It maximizes (14) subject to (2). Evidently (12) and (14) are identical, so that Hicks and Keynes are essentially the same. Keynes' theory of the firm too, like Hicks', can only deal with its production plan, all other plans concerning demand and supply, inventory, and financial matters being left unexamined.

7 Analysis of demand for stocks, money and security: Part I

What are the impacts of a change in prices upon stocks and demand for money and security? Differentiating (4) and (6), we get

$$\sum_{\iota=0}^{\nu}\sum_{i=0}^{1} \phi_{i_\iota} dx_{i_\iota} + \sum_{\tau=0}^{\nu}\sum_{j=2}^{n} \phi_{j\tau} dx''_{j\tau} = -\Delta\phi,$$

$$\phi_{i_\iota} d\lambda + \lambda \sum_{\mu=0}^{\nu}\sum_{k=0}^{1} \phi_{i_\iota k\mu} dx_{k\mu} + \lambda \sum_{\sigma=0}^{\nu}\sum_{h=2}^{n} \phi_{i_\iota h\sigma} dx''_{h\sigma} = -\Delta\phi_{i_\iota},$$

$$\phi_{j\tau} d\lambda + \lambda \sum_{\mu=0}^{\nu}\sum_{k=0}^{1} \phi_{j\tau k\mu} dx_{k\mu} + \lambda \sum_{\sigma=0}^{\nu}\sum_{h=2}^{n} \phi_{j\tau h\sigma} dx''_{h\sigma}$$

$$= \beta_\tau dp_{j\tau} - \beta_{\tau+1} dp_{j\tau+1} - \Delta\phi_{j\tau}$$

where $i = 0, 1$; $j = 2, \ldots, n$; $\Delta\phi = \sum_{\iota=0}^{\nu}\sum_{i=2}^{n} \frac{\partial\phi}{\partial p_{i_\iota}} dp_{i_\iota}$ and $\Delta\phi_{i_\iota} = \sum_{\sigma=0}^{\nu}\sum_{h=2}^{n} \frac{\Delta\phi_{i_\iota}}{\partial p_{h\sigma}} dp_{h\sigma}$. Solving the above equations we have

$$dx_{k\mu} = -\Delta\phi Y_{k\mu} - \sum_{\iota=0}^{\nu}\sum_{i=0}^{n} \Delta\phi_{i_\iota} Y_{i_\iota k\mu}$$

$$+ \sum_{\iota=0}^{\nu}\sum_{i=2}^{n} (\beta_\iota dp_{i_\iota} - \beta_{\iota+1} dp_{i_\iota+1}) Y_{i_\iota k\mu} \tag{15}$$

where $k = 0, 1$, and

$$dx''_{j\tau} = -\Delta\phi Y_{j\tau} - \sum_{\iota=0}^{\nu} \sum_{i=0}^{n} \Delta\phi_{i_\iota} Y_{i_\iota j\tau}$$

$$+ \sum_{\iota=0}^{\nu} \sum_{i=2}^{n} (\beta_\iota dp_{i_\iota} - \beta_{\iota+1} dp_{i_\iota+1}) Y_{i_\iota j\tau} \tag{16}$$

where $j = 2, \ldots, n$. $Y_{j\tau}$ is the cofactor of $\phi_{j\tau}$ in H divided by H. Effects of a change in prices upon the demand for money and security are given by (15) and similar effects upon the stocks of commodities by (16).

Let us now explain the structure of these equations. First, a change in prices affects the level of liquidity which is provided by given quantities of stocks of commodities. It also affects the purchasing power of money and security and, hence, the degree of liquidity, of which the holdings of certain amounts of money and security assure the firm. Therefore, if it keeps unchanged the demand for money and security and the stocks of commodities to be held, notwithstanding the change in prices, then the firm receives a degree of liquidity after the change, that is higher or lower than the degree it intends to keep before the change. As the firm is assumed to keep the degree at a constant level which is suitable for the type of entrepreneur, the demands for money, security, and inventories have to be adjusted. These effects are represented by the first terms of (15) and (16) which are referred to as the general liquidity effects. Secondly, the change in prices disturbs relative magnitudes of marginal liquidities of money, security, and inventories and, therefore, causes changes in the demands for them. The firm will increase the demands for those goods whose marginal liquidities become relatively larger than those of other goods after the change in prices. Through these channels the demand for money, security, and inventories are changed. These are represented by the second terms of (15) and (16) and referred to as the relative liquidity effects.

In addition, there is a third set of effects. Suppose now that the general level of liquidity and the relative marginal liquidities are not affected in spite of a change in prices. Even in such circumstances, it is true that the equilibrium conditions for inventories of commodities are disturbed by the change in prices. These disturbances have a repercussion upon money and security though their maximum conditions have no direct effect of the price change. The effects created in this way are called substitution effects; the third terms of (15) and (16) stand for them. The total effects are obtained by adding up these three effects.

Let the prices of a single commodity i change in every week proportionately. If we neglect general and relative liquidity effects, we have

$$dx''_{i\tau} = \sum_{\iota=0}^{\nu} (\beta_\iota p_{i_\iota} - \beta_{\iota+1} p_{i_\iota+1}) Y_{i_\iota i_\tau} d\theta$$

where $d\theta = dp_{i_\iota}/p_{i_\iota}$. Taking (d′) of section 3 into consideration, we have, for $d\theta > 0$

$$\sum_{\tau=0}^{\nu} (\beta_\tau p_{i\tau} - \beta_{\tau+1} p_{i\tau+1}) dx''_{i\tau} < 0 \tag{17}$$

which may be put in the following alternative form

$$p_{i0} dx''_{i0} + \sum_{\iota=1}^{\nu} \beta_\iota p_{i_\iota} (dx''_{i_\iota} - dx''_{i_\iota-1}) < 0$$

Consequently, either dx''_{i0} or one of $dx''_{i_\iota} - dx''_{i_\iota-1}$, $\iota = 1, \ldots, \nu$, must be negative. Even though some of them are positive, it is highly probable that many of them are negative because the above expression means that the sum of them takes on a negative value. On the other hand, as has already been shown, (10) takes on a positive value, so that by the same way of reasoning we may conclude that it is highly likely that most of dx'_{i_ι}, $\iota = 0, 1, \ldots, \nu$, take on positive values. From (1) we have

$$dx_{i_\iota} = -dx'_{i_\iota} + (dx''_{i_\iota} - dx''_{i_\iota-1}),\ \iota = 0, 1, \ldots, \nu$$

from which we may conclude that it is very probable that $dx_{i_\iota} < 0$. These results lead us to the following propositions: (ix) when the prices of a particular commodity rise in every week proportionately, then it is very likely that the supply of that commodity increases in every week. (x) When the prices of a factor of production rise in every week at the same proportion, the demand for that factor is likely to diminish in every week. Of course, these propositions are subject to the proviso to the effect that general and relative liquidity effects may reverse the relations asserted by the propositions.

Let us now make an additional specification of the liquidity preference function. That is, we assume that it is homogeneous of degree zero in the holdings of money and security and the prices of commodities. We have thus, for arbitrary positive value of t

$$\begin{aligned}&\phi(x_{00}, \ldots, x_{1\nu}, x''_{20}, \ldots, x''_{n\nu}, p_{20}, \ldots, p_{n\nu}, r_0, \ldots, r_{\nu-1}) \\ &= \phi(tx_{00}, \ldots, tx_{1\nu}, x''_{20}, \ldots, x''_{n\nu}, tp_{20}, \ldots, tp_{n\nu}, r_0, \ldots, r_{\nu-1})\end{aligned}$$

Then this implies that (i) the marginal liquidities of money and security are homogeneous of order -1 in variables of $x_{00}, \ldots, x_{1\nu}$ and $p_{20}, \ldots, p_{n\nu}$ and that the marginal liquidities of the stocks of commodities are homogeneous of order 0 in the same variables. These homogeneity properties imply the following conditions due to Euler

$$\left.\begin{aligned}&\sum_{\iota=0}^{\nu}\sum_{i=0}^{1}\phi_{i_\iota}x_{i_\iota}+\sum_{\tau=0}^{\nu}\sum_{j=2}^{n}\phi_{(j\tau)}p_{j\tau}=0,\\&\sum_{\mu=0}^{\nu}\sum_{k=0}^{1}\phi_{i_\iota k_\mu}x_{k\mu}+\sum_{\tau=0}^{\nu}\sum_{j=2}^{n}\phi_{i_\iota(j\tau)}p_{j\tau}=-\phi_{i_\iota},\ i=0,1\\&\sum_{\mu=0}^{\nu}\sum_{k=0}^{1}\phi_{i_\iota k_\mu}x_{k\mu}+\sum_{\tau=0}^{\nu}\sum_{j=2}^{n}\phi_{i_\iota(j\tau)}p_{j\tau}=0,\ i=2,\ldots,n\end{aligned}\right\}\qquad(18)$$

where $\phi_{(j\tau)}=\dfrac{\partial\phi}{\partial p_{j\tau}}$ and $\phi_{i_\iota(j\tau)}=\dfrac{\partial\phi_{i_\iota}}{\partial p_{j\tau}}$. When all current and expected prices of all commodities change proportionately, we obtain by substituting (18) into (15) and (16)

$$dx_{k\mu}=x_{k\mu}\frac{dp}{p}$$

$$dx''_{j\tau}=0$$

since we have (c′) of section 3. These imply the following propositions. (xi) The demand for money and the demand for security are homogeneous of degree 1 in all prices, current and expected, of all commodities. (xii) The demand for inventory of any commodity is homogeneous of degree zero in prices, the demand for and the supply of any commodity other than money and security are homogeneous of degree zero.

8 Analysis of demand for stocks and money: Part II

Let us next examine effects of a change in the rate of interest on the demand for inventory and the demand for money. Following the same procedure as that adopted in the previous section, we can derive the equations, each of which consists of three terms representing general and relative liquidity effects and substitution effects. Suppose the current and future rates of interest increase quasi-proportionately. Then we have

$$\frac{dr_0}{1+r_0}=\frac{dr_1}{1+r_1}=\ldots=\frac{dr_{\nu-1}}{1+r_{\nu-1}}=d\theta\qquad(19)$$

Neglecting general and relative liquidity effects, a quasi-proportional change (19) gives rise to a change in the demands for money and security of the amount:

$$dx_{k\mu}=\sum_{\iota=0}^{\nu}[(\iota+1)\beta_{\iota+1}-\iota\beta_\iota]Y_{0\iota k\mu}d\theta$$

$$+\sum_{\iota=0}^{\nu}\sum_{i=2}^{n}[(\iota+1)\beta_{\iota+1}p_{i_{\iota}+1}-\iota\beta_{\iota}p_{i_{\iota}}]Y_{i_{\iota}k\mu}d\theta$$

and a change in inventories of the amount

$$dx''_{j\tau}=\sum_{\iota=0}^{\nu}[(\iota+1)\beta_{\iota+1}-\iota\beta_{\iota}]Y_{0_{\iota}j\tau}d\theta$$

$$+\sum_{\iota=0}^{\nu}\sum_{i=2}^{n}[(\iota+1)\beta_{\iota+1}p_{i_{\iota}+1}-\iota\beta_{\iota}p_{i_{\iota}}]Y_{i_{\iota}j\tau}d\theta,\ j=2,\ldots,n$$

If we denote

$$I_{\iota}=\sum_{i=2}^{n}p_{i_{\iota}}(x''_{i_{\iota}}-x''_{i_{\iota}-1})$$

$$M_{\iota}=x_{0_{\iota}}-x_{0_{\iota}-1}$$

then we see that I_{ι} equals $G^{\iota}-G_{0}^{\iota}$, so that it is the gross investment defined by Keynes.[5] It is obvious that M_{ι} is the acquisition of cash in week ι. Let us suppose that the rates of interest make a quasi-proportional change (19), with all prices $p_{i_{\iota}}$ remaining unchanged. Then

$$\sum_{\iota=0}^{\nu}\beta_{\iota}[dM_{\iota}+dI_{\iota}]=0$$

by virtue of (c′) in section 3. Where $d\theta>0$

$$\sum_{\iota=0}^{\nu}\iota\beta_{\iota}[dM_{\iota}+dI_{\iota}]>0$$

because of (d′) of the same section. Hence, on the assumption of the series $\{dM_{\iota}+dI_{\iota}\}$ $\iota=0,1,\ldots,\nu$, being monotone, it is seen that the series is increasing. Therefore, $dM_0+dI_0<0$ as $d\theta>0$. Although this does not mean that each of dM_0 and dI_0 is negative, it is likely that both of them are negative. Following Keynes, we denote the current holding of money x_{00} by L. As the initial holding of money in week 0 is constant (that is, $dx_{0,-1}=0$), we have $dM=dx_{00}=dL$. Hence we obtain the following propositions. (xiii) A quasi-proportional increase in the rates of interest causes a decrease in the current demand for cash balance. (xiv) The same change in the interest rates results in a decrease in the current investment. Where general and relative liquidity effects are negligible, either of these propositions must hold necessarily, and it is also likely that both of them are true. This is a microeconomic base of Keynes' hypothesis $\frac{\partial L}{\partial r}<0$ and $\frac{\partial I}{\partial r}<0$.

[5] Keynes, 1936, pp. 62–3.

9 A shortage in the 'working capital' k

We are concerned with the type of firms which reserve an amount of money k_ι in each week in order to buy the producers' goods, etc. and have so far assumed that these k are not constant but adjusted flexibly so as to obtain a maximum of the capitalized value of the entrepreneur's net revenues. Then k does not explicitly appear as I have made it clear in footnote 8 of chapter 2. In fact, k has no place in this appendix so far. We are now concerned, in this section, with the case that the amount of k available in week 0, k_0, is not variable but constant, though in weeks in the future the entrepreneur expects that k_ι, $\iota = 1, \ldots \nu$, adjust themselves to the optimum plan 'perfectly'.

Let us compare this new case with the previous one of k being all flexible. Let the equilibrium values of k, x, x', etc. in the previous case be denoted by k^0, x^0, x'^0, etc. Then we have, from (9) and (5′) in the text

$$[x^0_{0\iota-1} + (1 + r_{\iota-1})x^0_{1\iota-1}] + k^0_\iota = x^0_{0\iota} + x^0_{1\iota} + \Sigma p_{i\iota}x^0_{i\iota},$$
$$\iota = 0, 1, \ldots, \nu \tag{20}$$

and

$$x^0_{i\iota} = y'^0_{i\iota} + x''^0_{i\iota} - x''^0_{i\iota-1},\ i = 2, \ldots, n;\ \iota = 0, 1, \ldots, \nu \tag{21}$$

respectively, where the summation Σ is taken only over all producers' goods. The actual k^*_0 differs from the optimum k^0_0 and we assume $k^*_0 < k^0_0$.

Next let x^*, x'^*, y'^*, etc. be the actual subjective equilibrium values of x, x', y', etc. obtained when the actual and expected k are set at k^*_0 and k^*_ι, $\iota = 1, \ldots, \nu$, defined below. Then we have

$$[x^*_{0\iota-1} + (1 + r_{\iota-1})x^*_{1\iota-1}] + k^*_\iota = x^*_{0\iota} + x^*_{1\iota} + \Sigma p_{i\iota}x^*_{i\iota} \tag{20′}$$

$$x^*_{i\iota} = y'^*_{i\iota} + x''^*_{i\iota} - x''^*_{i\iota-1} \tag{21′}$$

Therefore, from (20) and (20′), and (21) and (21′), respectively we get

$$(x^0_{0\iota-1} - x^*_{0\iota-1}) + (1 + r_{\iota-1})(x^0_{1\iota-1} - x^*_{1\iota-1}) + (k^0_\iota - k^*_\iota)$$
$$= (x^0_{0\iota} - x^*_{0\iota}) + (x^0_{1\iota} - x^*_{1\iota}) + (\Sigma p_{i\iota}x^0_{i\iota} - \Sigma p_{i\iota}x^*_{i\iota}) \tag{22}$$

$$(x^0_{i\iota} - x^*_{i\iota}) = (y'^0_{i\iota} - y'^*_{i\iota}) + (x''^0_{i\iota} - x''^*_{i\iota}) - (x''^0_{i\iota-1} - x''^*_{i\iota-1}),$$
$$i = m + 1, \ldots, n \tag{23}$$

(22) may be rewritten in the following way. First, for $\iota = 0$, we have $x^*_{0-1} = x^0_{0-1}$ for money and similarly for security. Hence the first two parts in the parentheses vanish for $\iota = 0$, so that we have

$$k^0_0 - k^*_0 = (x^0_{00} - x^*_{00}) + (x^0_{10} - x^*_{10}) + (\Sigma p_{i0}x^0_{i0} - \Sigma p_{i0}x^*_{i0}) \tag{24}$$

For $\iota > 0$, as we have stated above, we make the following assumption that each k_ι^* adjusts itself to the optimum plan with flexible k 'perfectly': that is, if actually planned values of holdings of money and security, $x_{0_\iota-1}^*$ and $x_{1_\iota-1}^*$ are less (or more) than the respective optimum values, $x_{0_\iota-1}^0$ and $x_{1_\iota-1}^0$, then there is a deficiency (or an excess) of the amounts of money and security to be carried over from the previous week. We say that the adjustment is 'perfect' if k_ι^* is decided such that it exceeds (or falls short of) k_ι^0 by the amount of deficiency (or excess) just mentioned. Under this assumption of perfect adjustment, the left-hand side of (22) vanishes, so that (22) is reduced to

$$0 = (x_{0_\iota}^0 - x_{0_\iota}^*) + (x_{1_\iota}^0 - x_{1_\iota}^*) + (\Sigma p_{i_\iota} x_{i_\iota}^0 - \Sigma p_{i_\iota} x_{i_\iota}^*), \ \iota = 1, \ldots, \nu \quad (25)$$

We assume that in this case equality $x_{i_\iota}^0 = x_{i_\iota}^*$ holds for all $i = 0$, 1 and $i = m + 1, \ldots, n$. Thus each part in the parentheses of (25) vanishes, and the planning with rigid k_0^* catches up with the optimum planning with flexible k_0 in week 1 and thereafter. Then for each $\iota = 1, \ldots, \nu$, the left-hand side of (23) may be written as

$$(x_{i0}^0 - x_{i0}^*) = (y_{i0}'^0 - y_{i0}'^*) + (x_{i0}''^0 - x_{i0}''^*) \quad (26)$$

$$0 = (y_{i_\iota}'^0 - y_{i_\iota}'^*) + (x_{i_\iota}''^0 - x_{i_\iota}''^*) - (x_{i_\iota-1}''^0 - x_{i_\iota-1}''^*) \quad (27)$$

where $i = m + 1, \ldots, n$; $\iota = 1, \ldots, \nu$. Note that the first equation of (23) reduces to (26) because $x_{i,-1}''^0 = x_{i,-1}''^*$. We then assume that the plan with k_0^* catches up the optimum plan with flexible k_0 in week 1 and thereafter, not only in the demand–supply plan, but also in the input and inventory plan for producers' goods. Thus

$$\left.\begin{aligned} y_{i_\iota}'^0 &= y_{i_\iota}'^*, \\ x_{i_\iota}''^0 &= x_{i_\iota}''^*, \end{aligned}\right\} \quad i = m + 1, \ldots, n; \ \iota = 1, \ldots, \nu \qquad \begin{aligned} (28) \\ (29) \end{aligned}$$

Where $k_0^0 > k_0^*$, one of the parts in the parentheses of (24) should be positive with the possibility of two or all three being positive. If the part of the last parentheses is positive, the left-hand side of (26) should be positive for one of $i = m + 1, \ldots, n$. Then at least one of the two parts on the right-hand side of (26) should be positive. Therefore, we start our examination from the case in which

$$x_{00}^0 > x_{00}^*, x_{10}^0 > x_{10}^*, x_{i0}''^0 > x_{i0}''^*, \text{ for } i = m + 1, \ldots, n \quad (30)$$

Then $x_{i0}''^0 < x_{i0}''^*$ for at least one $i = 2, \ldots, m$; otherwise, because of (29) we have

$$\begin{aligned} \gamma &= \phi(x_{00}^0, \ldots, x_{1\nu}^0, x_{20}''^0, \ldots, x_{n\nu}''^0, p, r) \\ &> \phi(x_{00}^*, \ldots, x_{1\nu}^*, x_{20}''^*, \ldots, x_{n\nu}''^*, p, r) \end{aligned}$$

which contradicts the constraint imposed upon the degree of liquidity such that it should be as large as γ even though k_0 is set at k_0^*. If $x_{i0}''^0 > x_{i0}''^*$ for all $i = 2, \ldots, m$, then one of the inequalities of (30) should reverse its sense. This means that if k_0 is fixed at a value lower than k_0^0, then some of $x_{i0}, i = 0, 1$ and $x_{i0}'', i = 2, \ldots, n$ decrease but some others of them must increase in order to compensate the decrease in ϕ due to decreases in some of $x_{i0}, i = 0, 1$, and $x_{i0}'', i = 2, \ldots, n$. Thus a suitable adjustment in the portfolio is incurred.

Secondly, where $k_0^* < k_0^0$, the firm can buy smaller amounts of producers' goods which imply a decrease in the input of these goods in production unless the inventories of producers' goods are decreased accordingly. With smaller amount of inputs the firm can only carry out production on a smaller scale. Consequently it has to be satisfied with a production plan of second best compared with the one in the case with flexible k. We may now conclude the analysis of effects of a deficiency of the 'working capital' k_0 by stating the following two propositions: (xv) to overcome the shortage of k_0 a reorganization of the firm's portfolio is inevitable, in order to continue to obtain the same level of liquidity, in spite of a loss of purchasing power due to a decrease in k_0. (xvi) The firm must reduce the scale of production as its purchasing power is decreased.

Mathematical note I
The Hirsch theorem*

Theorem

Let a_{ij} be real and let $b_{ij} = (a_{ij} + a_{ji})/2$, $A = (a_{ij})$, $B = (b_{ij})$. Then the real part α of the root, $\sigma = \alpha + i\beta$, of the equation $|\sigma I - A| = 0$ is between the largest value M and the smallest value m of the n roots $\lambda_1, \lambda_2, \ldots, \lambda_n$ of the equation $|\lambda I - B| = 0$.

Proof: As σ satisfies

$$|\sigma I - A| = 0 \tag{1}$$

there are $x_1, \ldots, x_n$, such that

$$\sigma x_j = \Sigma a_{ji} x_i, \; j = 1, 2, \ldots, n \tag{2}$$

at least one of x_i being not zero.

Let $\bar{x}_i$ be conjugate of x_i. Multiplying (2) by $\bar{x}_j$ and adding, we obtain

$$\sigma \Sigma x_j \bar{x}_j = \Sigma\Sigma a_{ji} x_i \bar{x}_j \tag{3}$$

Let σ and $\bar{\sigma}$ be conjugate. Then it is clear that

$$\bar{\sigma} \bar{x}_j = \Sigma a_{ji} \bar{x}_i, \; j = 1, 2, \ldots, n \tag{4}$$

Therefore,

$$\bar{\sigma} \Sigma \bar{x}_j x_j = \Sigma\Sigma a_{ji} \bar{x}_i x_j \tag{5}$$

By adding (3) and (5)

$$\alpha \Sigma x_j \bar{x}_j = \Sigma\Sigma[(a_{ji} + a_{ij})/2] x_i \bar{x}_j \tag{6}$$

Applying an appropriate linear transformation to (6), we get

$$\alpha \Sigma X_j \bar{X}_j = \Sigma \lambda_j X_j \bar{X}_j$$

*Hirsch, 1902, 'Sur les racines d'une équation fondamentale', *Acta Mathematica*, vol. 25.

Hence

$$\alpha = [\Sigma\lambda_j X_j \bar{X}_j]/[\Sigma X_j \bar{X}_j]$$

In view of the fact that all λ_j are real and $X_j\bar{X}_j > 0$, we immediately have $m \leqq \alpha \leqq M$.

Mathematical note II
The Frobenius theorem and its extensions*

1 Introduction

The Frobenius theorem concerning non-negative square matrices is the key theorem in the analysis of linear economic models. It asserts a number of propositions, among which the following one is most basic: any non-negative, square and indecomposable matrix A has a positive characteristic root λ with which a positive eigenvector X is associated. This proposition, proved by Frobenius (1908) in an elementary way, was later proved by Wielandt (1950) in a simpler way by applying Brouwer's fixed-point theorem[1] [Wielandt's proof is familiar among economists through Debreu and Herstein (1953)]. Then Karlin (1959) and Nikaido (1969) proved the theorem in elementary ways that avoided the fixed-point theorem. A recent proof by Arrow and Hahn (1971) is the same as Karlin's. The proof given by Murata (1972) is somewhat similar to the original one by Frobenius.

Later, a non-linear extension of the theorem was discussed by Solow and Samuelson (1953) and then by Morishima (1964). In this they slightly generalized Wielandt's method. In fact, in their articles, Brouwer's fixed-point theorem was again used to establish the existence of a positive eigenvalue and a positive eigenvector.

This note provides two alternative proofs of the theorem in the non-linear case. They are related to Karlin's and Nikaido's proofs. However, one of them, discussed in section 3, uses the Kuhn–Tucker (1950) theorem explicitly, while the other in section 4 is elementary and seems useful in the classroom for students of economics, as it is simple and enables one to dispense with the Kuhn–Tucker theorem as well as the fixed-point theorem.

*The original version of this Note has appeared as Morishima and Fujimoto (1974).

[1] Before Wielandt, Rutmann (1938, 1940) extended the Frobenius theorem to the case of linear operations in Banach spaces by using Schauer's fixed-point theorem.

2 Assumptions

We use the following notation for vector comparisons: For two vectors X^1 and X^2, (a) $X^1 \leqq X^2$ means $X_i^1 \leqq X_i^2$ for all elements; (b) $X^1 \leqslant X^2$ means $X^1 \leqq X^2$ and $X^1 \neq X^2$; and (c) $X^1 < X^2$ means $X_i^1 < X_i^2$ for all i.

Let $H(X)'$ be[2]

$$(H_1(X), H_2(X), \ldots, H_n(X))$$

which is a vector function from R^n (the n-dimensional Euclidean space) to itself. In addition to continuity and differentiability of $H(X)$, we assume:

(A.1) – Homogeneity. $H(\alpha X) = \alpha H(X)$ for any number α.
(A.2) – Non-negativeness. $H(X) \geqq 0$ for all $X \geqq 0$.
(A.3) – Monotonicity. $H(X^1) \leqq H(X^2)$ for all X^1 and X^2 such that $X^1 \leqq X^2$.
(A.4) – Indecomposability. For any non-negative vector Y' having some zero elements, it holds that at least one of Y's zero elements is converted into a positive member by the transformation $Y'(\partial H/\partial X)$.

It is easy to see that if A is a constant square matrix that is non-negative and indecomposable, then $H(X) \equiv AX$ satisfies these four assumptions.

3 A proof using the Kuhn–Tucker theorem

In this section we apply the Kuhn–Tucker theorem to establish the following generalized Frobenius theorem. (A.1)–(A.4) are all assumed.

Theorem

(i) *There are a positive number* λ^* *and a positive vector* X^* *fulfilling* $H(X^*) = \lambda^* X^*$.
(ii) X^* *is unique up to the proportionality factor.*
(iii) *If* $\lambda \neq \lambda^*$, *then there is no* $X \geqslant 0$ *such that* $H(X) = \lambda X$.
(iv) *If* $|\lambda| > \lambda^*$ *then there is no* $X \neq 0$ *such that* $H(X) = \lambda X$.

Proof: (i) Let us first consider a problem to minimize λ subject to

$$H(X) \leqq \lambda X, \quad (1)$$

$$e'X \leqq 1, \quad (2)$$

$$e'X \geqq 1, \quad (3)$$

$$X \geqq 0 \quad (4)$$

[2] Throughout this Note, an accent applied to a vector denotes the transposition of that vector.

where e' is a row vector whose elements are all unity. We write $S = \{X \mid X \geqq 0, e'X = 1\}$. It is obvious that for a given $X > 0$ in S, the minimum λ that satisfies (1) is given as

$$\lambda(X) \equiv \max_i H_i(X)/X_i \tag{5}$$

Take any $X^0 > 0$ in S and put $\lambda^0 = \lambda(X^0)$. Define

$$C^0 = \{X \mid X \in S, H(X) \leqq \lambda^0 X\}$$

$X \in C^0$ implies $X > 0$, because otherwise we would have a contradiction.[3]

Since C^0 is bounded and closed and (5) is continuous on C^0, it takes on a smallest value λ^* at a point X^* in C^0. Therefore, $X^* > 0$. It is then seen that the λ^* thus determined (i.e., the minimum of λ in C^0 subject to (1)) gives a solution to our minimizing problem (i.e., the minimum of λ subject to (1)–(4)), because it is evident that in $S - C^0$, there is no X such that $H(X) < \lambda^* X (\leqq \lambda^0 X)$. Moreover, from (5), $|\delta\lambda(X)/\partial X| < \infty$ if $X > 0$;[4] consequently there is no singular point such as an outward cusp in C^0. Hence we can apply the Kuhn–Tucker theorem to our minimizing problem.

Consider a Lagrangian function

$$L = \lambda - Y'(\lambda X - H(X)) - \mu(1 - e'X) - \nu(e'X - 1) \tag{6}$$

which is minimized with respect to λ and X and maximized with respect to Y, μ, and ν. At the minimum point, λ^*, X^*, the following conditions are fulfilled

$$1 - Y'X \geqq 0, \tag{7}$$

$$-\lambda Y' + Y'(\partial H/\partial X) + \mu e' - \nu e' \geqq 0, \tag{8}$$

$$-\lambda X + H(X) \leqq 0, \tag{9}$$

$$e'X \leqq 1, \tag{10}$$

$$e'X \geqq 1 \tag{11}$$

together with the additional conditions

$$Y' \geqq 0, \mu \geqq 0, \nu \geqq 0 \tag{12}$$

$$\lambda(1 - Y'X) = 0 \tag{13}$$

[3] Let Y be defined as a vector such that $Y_i = 0$ if $X_i > 0$ and $Y_i > 0$ if $X_i = 0$. Then from $H(X) \leqq \lambda^0 X$, we obtain $Y'(\partial H/\partial X)X \leqq \lambda^0 Y'X = 0$, as H is homogeneous of degree one in X. On the other hand, the extreme left-hand side of this expression is positive, because assumption (A.4) implies that at least one $Y'(\partial H/\partial X)_i$ must be positive for some $X_i > 0$, a contradiction.

[4] This holds almost everywhere. At points where $\lambda(X)$ is not differentiable, it has both right-hand and left-hand derivatives and they never take on $\pm\infty$.

$$(-\lambda Y' + Y'(\partial H/\partial X) + \mu e' - \nu e')X = 0 \tag{14}$$

$$Y'(-\lambda X + H(X)) = 0 \tag{15}$$

$$\mu(1 - e'X) = 0 \tag{16}$$

$$\nu(1 - e'X) = 0 \tag{17}$$

We have already seen that $X^* > 0$. Assumptions (A.2)–(A.4) imply that $H(X) > 0$ if $X > 0$. Therefore the minimum λ^* is positive by (5), and the corresponding Y is non-negative and non-zero by (12) and (13). It is also seen that the homogeneity of degree one of $H(X)$, together with (10), (11), (14), and (15) implies $\mu = \nu$ and that (8) holds with equality as $X^* > 0$.

Next, we show that $Y > 0$. Suppose the contrary; this is, some elements of Y are zero. Then (8) reduces to $(Y'(\partial H/\partial X))_i = \mu - \nu$ for those i whose Y_i's are zero. On the other hand, assumption (A.4) implies that $(Y'(\partial H/\partial X))_i$ is positive for at least one i with $Y_i = 0$. Therefore, $\mu - \nu > 0$, a contradiction. Hence, $Y > 0$, from which we obtain $\lambda^* X^* = H(X^*)$ by taking (9) and (15) into account.[5]

The statements (ii)–(iv) are proved in the following way. As λ^* is the solution to the above minimization problem, it is clear that if $\lambda < \lambda^*$, the statement (iii) trivially holds for $\lambda < \lambda^*$. Suppose now that for λ such that $|\lambda| \geqq \lambda^*$, there is $\bar{X} \neq 0$ which satisfies $H(\bar{X}) = \lambda \bar{X}$. Let $R = \{i \mid \bar{X}_i \neq 0\}$ and $\alpha = \min_{i \in R} X_i^* / |\bar{X}_i|$. Then $Z \equiv X^* - \alpha |\bar{X}| \geqq 0$, where $|\bar{X}|$ represents a vector $(|\bar{X}_1|, \ldots, |\bar{X}_n|)'$. Evidently, $\alpha > 0$. By assumptions (A.2) and (A.3), we have

$$H(|\bar{X}|) \geqq |H(\bar{X})| = |\lambda \bar{X}| = |\lambda| |\bar{X}|$$

Therefore

$$\begin{aligned} H(Z + \alpha|\bar{X}|) &= H(X^*) = \lambda^* X^* = \lambda^*(Z + \alpha|\bar{X}|) \\ &\leqq \lambda^* Z + \alpha|\lambda||\bar{X}| \leqq \lambda^* Z + H(\alpha|\bar{X}|) \end{aligned} \tag{18}$$

If $Z \geqq 0$, then $Z_i = 0$, by definition, for at least one i. From (18) we have

$$H(Z + \alpha|\bar{X}|) - H(\alpha|\bar{X}|) \leqq \lambda^* Z \tag{19}$$

Define $T = \{i \mid Z_i = 0\}$. From (19) we have $(\partial H/\partial X)_{ij} = 0$ for $i \in T, j \notin T$. Then by choosing Y such that $Y_j = 0$ for $j \notin T$ and $Y_j > 0$ for $j \in T$, we have a contradiction to assumption (A.4). Hence $Z = 0$, which implies $|\lambda| = \lambda^*$ because of (18); and $\bar{X}$ must equal either $(1/\alpha)X^*$ or $-(1/\alpha)X^*$ because of assumption (A.4) and (18). This establishes the statements (ii), (iii), and (iv) of the theorem.

[5] Because of the homogeneity we have $\lambda^* X^* = (\partial H(X^*)/\partial X)X^*$. Also, because $\mu = \nu$ and $X^* > 0$, we have $Y'(\partial H(X^*)/\partial X) = \lambda^* Y'$ from (8) and (14). Thus X^* and Y' are the column and the row eigenvectors of $\partial H(X^*)/\partial X$ associated with λ^*.

Remark 1 In the above we can get rid of differentiability of $H(X)$ (assumption (A.4)). Since $H(X)$ is continuous and monotonic with respect to each variable, it has right-hand and left-hand derivatives, $\partial H^+/\partial X$ and $\partial H^-/\partial X$, respectively, everywhere. (In fact, it is differentiable almost everywhere.) We can then replace (A.4) by similar assumptions concerning $\partial H^+/\partial X$ and $\partial H^-/\partial X$, respectively, and apply the Kuhn–Tucker theorem, regarding these derivatives as if they were derived from different constraints.

4 An elementary proof

In this section, we are concerned with a slightly more general case that $H(X)$ is continuous but not necessarily differentiable. An elementary proof will be given on the following new assumption of indecomposability which plays the equivalent role as assumption (A.4) has played.

(A.4)′ – Indecomposability. For any non-empty subset of indices $R = \{i_1, i_2, \ldots, i_m\} \subset \{1, 2, \ldots, n\}$, the relations $X_i^1 = X_i^2$ for $i \in R$ and $X_h^1 < X_h^2$ for $h \notin R$ imply that there exists at least one $i \in R$ such that $H_i(X^1) \neq H_i(X^2)$.

The other three assumptions, (A.1)–(A.3), are kept throughout. Define sets:

$$\begin{aligned}
C(\lambda) &= \{X \mid X \in S, H(X) \leqq \lambda X\}, \\
D(\lambda) &= \{X \mid X \in S, H(X) < \lambda X\}, \\
E(\lambda) &= \{X \mid X \in S, H(X) \leqslant \lambda X\}, \\
C^+(\lambda) &= \{X \mid X \in S, X > 0, H(X) \leqq \lambda X\}.
\end{aligned}$$

Then we have

Lemma 1

$C(\lambda) = C^+(\lambda)$ *for any* $\lambda > 0$.

Proof: Obviously $C(\lambda) \supset C^+(\lambda)$. Suppose $C(\lambda) \neq C^+(\lambda)$ for some λ. Then $C(\lambda)$ has an X^*, at least one of whose elements is zero. Put $R = \{i \mid X_i^* = 0\}$ and decrease each $X_h^*, h \notin R$, by a sufficiently small amount, so that R remains unchanged. Then, because of assumptions (A.3) and (A.4)′, at least one $H_i, i \in R$, becomes negative after the decrease. This contradicts (A.2); hence $C(\lambda) = C^+(\lambda)$.

Lemma 2

If $D(\lambda)$ *is empty for some* $\lambda > 0$, *then* $E(\lambda)$ *is empty as well for the same* λ.

Proof: Suppose $E(\lambda)$ is not empty for some $\lambda > 0$. Then there must be an X^0 which satisfies $H_i(X^0) \leqq \lambda X_i^0$, for the given λ, with equality for at least one i. As $C(\lambda) = C^+(\lambda)$ and $C(\lambda) \supset E(\lambda)$, we have $C^+(\lambda) \supset E(\lambda)$; hence $X^0 > 0$.

Next define $R = \{i \mid H_i(X^0) = \lambda X_i^0\}$ and diminish each $X_h^0, h \notin R$, by a sufficiently small amount so that $X_h^0 > 0$ and $H_h(X^0) < \lambda X_h^0$, for all $h \notin R$, after (as well as before) the decrease. By assumptions (A.3) and (A.4)′, there must be at least one $i \in R$ whose H_i diminishes. Thus the number of strict inequalities in $H(X^0) \leqq \lambda X^0$ can be increased. Repeating this procedure, we finally find that there is a strictly positive X at which $H(X) < \lambda X$. This implies that $D(\lambda)$ is not empty.

We can now prove the generalized Frobenius theorem.

Proof: Let us first note the following properties of $C(\lambda)$.

(a) $C(\lambda)$ is not empty for sufficiently large λ, because any $X > 0$ in S satisfies $H(X) \leqq \lambda X$ if λ is taken as $\lambda \geqq \max_i H_i(X)/X_i$.
(b) If $\lambda^1 < \lambda^2$, then $C(\lambda^1) \subset C(\lambda^2)$.
(c) $C(0)$ is empty. If it is not, any $X \in C(0)$ should be positive by virtue of Lemma 1. On the other hand, $H(X) = 0$ as $\lambda = 0$. Put $R = \{1\}$ and decrease each X_h, $h \notin R$, by a sufficiently small amount so that X remains positive. By assumption (A.4)′, $H_1(X)$ has to be negative; a contradiction to (A.2).

Now because of the above properties (a)–(c) of $C(\lambda)$, there must be a λ^* such that $C(\lambda)$ is empty for $\lambda < \lambda^*$ and not empty for $\lambda > \lambda^*$. By the continuity of $H(X)$, $C(\lambda^*)$ is not empty.[6] Hence $\lambda^* > 0$ by (c). As $C(\lambda)$ is empty for $\lambda < \lambda^*$, $D(\lambda^*)$ is empty *a fortiori* and, therefore, $E(\lambda^*)$ is so by Lemma 2. Thus any $X^* \in C(\lambda^*)$ satisfies $H(X^*) = \lambda^* X^*$, and $X^* > 0$ by Lemma 1.

Thus (i) of the theorem is proved. An argument similar to the one in the last part of section 3 establishes the other propositions (ii)–(iv) of the theorem.

Remark 2

The proof in section 3 is very similar to the proof in section 4. The only difference lies in the fact that the former uses the Kuhn–Tucker theorem to show that $H(X) \leqq \lambda X$ holds with strict equality at the minimum λ, while the latter has an advantage that it allows a clear geometrical interpretation of the theorem in low (two or three) dimensional cases.

[6] Take any decreasing sequence $\{\lambda_\nu\}$ that converges to λ^*. Let $\{X^\nu\}$ be a corresponding sequence of vectors $X^\nu \in C(\lambda_\nu) \subset S$. By the Bolzano–Weierstrass theorem, there is a subsequence of $\{X^\nu\}$ which converges to an X^* in S. Then by the continuity of $H(X)$, we have $H(X^*) \leqq \lambda^* X^*$. Hence $X^* \in C(\lambda^*)$.

Remark 3

It is clear from the proof that if $H^1(X) \leqq H^2(X)$ for any $X \geqq 0$, then λ_1^*, the Frobenius eigenvalue of H^1, is not greater than λ_2^* of H^2.

Remark 4

In the case of $H(X)$ being not necessarily indecomposable, the generalized Frobenius theorem can be proved in the following way as Arrow and Hahn (1972) did for the linear case: First consider $H(X) + \varepsilon UX$ where ε is a positive number and U is an $n \times n$ matrix with all elements being unity. Corresponding to any decreasing sequence $\{\varepsilon_v\}$ which converges to zero, we have a decreasing sequence $\{\lambda_v^*\}$ of the Frobenius eigenvalue and a sequence $\{X^{v*}\}$ of the Frobenius eigenvector. Obviously, $\lambda_v^* > 0$ and $X^{v*} > 0$ for all v, because the modified system is indecomposable. Then the same argument as the one in footnote 2 above establishes the existence of λ^* and X^* such that $H(X^*) = \lambda^* X^*$. However, note that $\lambda^* \geqq 0$ and $X^* \geqq 0$, if $H(X)$ is decomposable. See Morishima (1964, pp. 199–202).

Addendum

Introduction

After *DKR* was published in Japanese in 1950, a great theoretical development has been made in the three main areas of the general equilibrium theory, concerning existence, uniqueness and stability of general equilibrium. The existence theorem is an achievement of efforts in the first half of the 1950s, while its second half and the first half of the 1960s were devoted to uniqueness and stability, mainly to the latter. In this addendum I sketch the theoretical development after *DKR* in my own way and show how I see it from my present arrival point.

The existence problem has been solved by formulating Walras' economy in terms of inequalities, rather than equations. This inequality approach is not entirely foreign to Walras, who supports the scarcity theory of value asserting that the price is zero for a 'free (or non-scarce) good', that is a commodity for which supply exceeds demand in equilibrium. Walras is concerned with an economy in which an exchange is actually made, though some goods may be free, and distinguishes this general equilibrium (which may be called an essential equilibrium) from the more general one in which goods may all be free and, therefore, not traded. Thus the former equilibrium is described by inequalities

$$0 \leqq D_i \leqq S_i \text{ for all } i \tag{1}$$

with

$$D_i = S_i > 0 \tag{2}$$

for at least one non-free good, while the latter imposes (1) only and disregards (2) completely. Arrow and Debreu and all other contemporary economists are concerned with the latter equilibrium that may, therefore, be named an AD equilibrium, while Walras examines the existence of the former (essential) equilibrium.[1] He shows an example of an AD equilibrium which does not satisfy (2), so that no trade is made there.

Arrow and others noticed this but its implications were carelessly left unexamined. The essentiality of equilibrium is very important, however, because the general equilibria of exchange, of production, of capital formation, and of circulation of money reduce to the general equilibria of no exchange, no production, of no capital formation, and of no money in circulation, respectively, in the case of them being inessential. Finally, F. H. Hahn appeared and discussed the case in which the general equilibrium of money may possibly be reduced to the one of barter exchange. All other inessentiality are still unexamined.

According to the contemporary advanced theory of general equilibrium the most basic tool for finding an equilibrium is a mapping of a set of all prices into itself. It is utilized to distinguish a fixed point in the price space from others. In Walras' theory the work of 'tatonnement' plays the same role, so that it is the most important thought apparatus in his whole theory. It does not only examine whether an equilibrium is stable or not, but is also useful for the purpose of finding out a point where no adjustment is needed, that is a fixed point. When the tatonnement accomplishes these purposes and establishes the existence and stability of a general equilibrium, we say in ordinary language that the price mechanism works. Walras is concerned with examining such a well-behaved economic system, and my *DKR* as well as Hicks' *Value and Capital* follow this tradition of the general equilibrium theory.

Samuelson's theory of stability may be taken as a modern formulation of Walras' theory of tatonnement. However, the latter's theory, as far as its original form is concerned, is very different from the former's. Contrary to the commonly accepted view, Walras is a partial equilibrium economist in the theory of price formation. Each market determines its own price in isolation from all other markets and then all these partial equilibrium prices influence excess demand functions of all commodities. After the shift in demand and supply functions the markets are reopened, in each of which the price is determined again in the manner of partial equilibrium analysis. Walras' theory of stability investigates whether the partial equilibrium prices thus determined and revised finally approach a set of general equilibrium prices. According to this kind of interpretation of Walras, the main part of Article I below was written when Arrow and Hurwicz's stability analysis, which may be taken as an elaboration of Samuelson's approach, was very popular in the late 1950s.

While tatonnement continues, no economic activities, transactions, and

[1] M. Morishima, 1977, pp. 17–18.

production, are carried out. This is one of the premises and rules of the Walrasian game. If this is strictly observed, the participants have all to starve to death because it takes an infinitely long time to complete the whole process of tatonnement. Therefore, the tatonnement must be terminated prematurely and transactions, as well as production necessary for them, must be carried out. These activities are, of course, not equilibrium ones, so that after they have been carried into effect, tatonnement starts again and continues until it is truncated at a certain point in time. Thus the actual dynamic path that the economy traces out is seen by Walras as a sequence of disequilibria obtained by truncating the tatonnement process at various points of time. Thus, entirely contrary to the conventional view of Walras, he is a disequilibrium economist, and his dynamic path depends on the degree of truncation of the tatonnement process. Where the degree is zero, transactions and production are carried out instantly at the prices proposed arbitrarily, so that Walras' path is of a purely disequilibrium nature. There is no tendency towards equilibrium at all. Where the degree is not zero and positive, some amount of effort has been spent on finding an equilibrium and the resulting path may be regarded as an approximate of the equilibrium path. Where the degree is low, the approximation is poor and preserves the character of the pure disequilibrium path, whilst at the other extreme of the degree of truncation of tatonnement being infinitely high and rapidly repeated infinitely many times within a period of limited length, i.e., within a single market day, Walras would obtain an equilibrium path like Hicks', that is a sequence of temporary equilibria. The actual Walras lies between these two extremes. Article II deals with this problem. But the tatonnement in this article is made in terms of quantities, rather than prices.

With excess demand functions being linear, the stability theory or the tatonnement analysis, is simple. Where they are non-linear, however, a number of complications may arise inevitably if we want to establish stability of equilibrium. In *DKR*, I have been concerned with a simple case of excess demand functions being non-linear but analytical. I have shown that if such a system is 'structurally stable' at a general equilibrium point, in addition to its local stability, then the equilibrium has a stability domain; a path starting from any point in it eventually approaches equilibrium. If the domain has no boundary and is, therefore, infinitely large, the equilibrium has global stability. On the other hand, where the domain is surrounded by a boundary, the tatonnement, if it starts from a point on the boundary, may trace out a limit cycle. Whether such a cycle exists or not is more difficult to examine than the problem of existence of an equilibrium point. Even for the world of one variable only, we know a very few number of cases with limit cycles, such as those of van der Pol type, Rayleigh type, and others. In

Article III I have extended both the well-known non-linear differential equations of the van der Pol type and that of the Rayleigh type to a more general equation which may be called a mixed van der Pol–Rayleigh type and has shown that under certain conditions there is a solution tracing out a limit cycle.

The equation of the van der Pol type is extended by N. Levinson and O. K. Smith (1942) so as to include a small portion of the Rayleigh elements. The original version of Article III, which appeared in the *Zeitschrift für Nationalökonomie* is concerned with an extension of the oscillation theory in the opposite direction: that is, an extension of the equation of the Rayleigh type so as to include some small portion of the van der Pol type equation. The present version of Article III includes a new section which provides conditions under which a limit cycle exists for any mixture of the two equations, so that it completely synthesizes the van der Pol and Rayleigh oscillations.

Price adjustments in the process of tatonnement may be formulated in terms of either differential equations, as has been done in *DKR*, or difference equations. I have taken up the latter case in one of the chapters of my *Walras' Economics*. Then, the idea of higher-order fixed points naturally came up. At the point of general equilibrium no adjustment is made to any price, so that the point of equilibrium prices is a fixed point as it does not move to another point, once prices are set at that point. Then we may conceive of a fixed point of higher order. That is to say, the prices initially set at a point p^0 move to a different point p^1, according to the difference equations of price adjustment, from there to p^2, and so on, and finally from p^{m-1} reached in this way the prices may return to the original point p^0. If so, p^0 is said to be a fixed point of order m. Even though the fixed point of order 1, that is the general equilibrium point, is unique, this does not rule out the possibility that there may be fixed points of higher order. Moreover, once a fixed point of order m, say p^0, exists, then each of $p^1, p^2, \ldots, p^{m-1}$ is a fixed point of the same order. This means the non-uniqueness of the fixed points of a higher order.

Then, in *Walras' Economics,* I have been concerned with a two-commodity economy with (1) prices being normalized such that their sum equals 1 and (2) excess demand functions satisfying the weak axiom of revealed preferences between the equilibrium point and any other point of normalized prices. This setup assures the uniqueness and global stability of general equilibrium. Nevertheless it is true that the stability part of this story is only valid where we formulate the adjustment of prices in differential equations. In the case of a difference equation version being taken, we obtain an entirely different picture. My numerical example there has shown that the fixed points of order 1 and order 2 are both unstable. It also has shown that a tatonnement which started from a vicinity of the fixed point of order 1 (or order 2) eventually converges to a cycle of order 8.[2]

This numerical result depends on the values of the slope of the excess demand function of commodity 1 with respect to its normalized price, dE_1/dp_1, that takes on the value of $-8/3$ in my case. Using α as a parameter and writing $dE_1/dp_1 = -(1+\alpha)/\alpha$, then the α corresponding to $-8/3$ is 0.6. We can see that for all values of $\alpha > 0$ my excess demand functions satisfy the weak axiom of revealed preference between the equilibrium point and any non-equilibrium point. However, of course, the time path of tatonnement prices are different for different values of α. When it is small, that is E_1 is very elastic with respect to p_1, the equilibrium is stable; for α is in a medium range, it either traces out a chaotic path or approaches a limit cycle of some order. In fact, as α becomes large, the path converges to a limit cycle whose order decreases from 16 to 8 and then to 4 and 2. Finally we observe a convergence to the general equilibrium point when α increases and reaches the value of 1. These are results obtained in Article IV and enable us to conclude that the theory of chaos has a relevance to the general equilibrium theory whenever the adjustment mechanism is formulated in terms of difference equations.

We may note, in spite of this general conclusion, that there is another parameter upon which the time path of the tatonnement price depends. This is the coefficient v applied to the excess demand in the difference equation of the adjustment of the prices. It is fixed at 1 throughout the above numerical analysis, although the price caller can regulate its value freely in the process of tatonnement. If we may assume that he is skilful enough in selecting the value of v so as to avoid limit cycles and chaotic motions, we may then believe that the tatonnement will let the economy finally settle at a general equilibrium in spite of the possibility of the perverse movements discussed above.

To carry out various comparative statics analyses that lead to useful results the absence of complementarity is often assumed in this volume. After this work, therefore, I was concerned with cases where complementarity is present. Let E_i be the excess demand for commodity i and p_i its price. I have examined the following particular cases: (2) the M case with complementarity–substitutability relationships satisfying

$$\operatorname{sign}\left(\frac{\partial E_i}{\partial p_k}\right) = \operatorname{sign}\left(\frac{\partial E_i}{\partial p_j}\frac{\partial E_j}{\partial p_k}\right) \tag{2}$$

[2] See Morishima, 1977, pp. 41–5. I published it two years after the appearance of Li and Yorke, 1975, from which the theory of chaos has thereafter developed. But unfortunately I did not know its existence.

and (2) the anti-M case fulfilling

$$\operatorname{sign}\left(\frac{\partial E_i}{\partial p_k}\right) = -\operatorname{sign}\left(\frac{\partial E_i}{\partial p_j}\frac{\partial E_j}{\partial p_k}\right) \tag{3}$$

in either case the sign condition, (2) or (3), being assumed to hold for all distinct non-numeraire commodities i, j, k.[3] In the M case, which has been discussed by both Hicks and me, we have the following law of comparative statics: an increase in the demand for commodity i gives rise to an increase (or decrease) in the prices of those commodities which are substitutes for (or complementary with) i. Article V, however, does not discuss this comparative statics property at all,[4] but only deals with its stability.

Article VI is concerned with deriving comparative statics and comparative dynamics laws concerning the system of generalized gross substitutes or generalized M or quasi-Frobenius according to the terminology there. As we mainly deal with the case of no complementarity being present, an extension of the economy so as to allow for complementarity would be desirable, although I acknowledge that the extension made in Article VI is still far from the satisfactory stretch of generality. The 'theorems' gathered there will make us familiar about the structure of the system.

The Edgeworth method of establishing an equilibrium by making bargains directly between buyers and sellers was revived, extended, and modernized by G. Debreu, 1962 and 1970. His works greatly contributed to the development of the core in game theory. The result of the development of this theory is roughly summarized in the following way. When the number of agents becomes large, many feasible bargains between them are dominated and, therefore, eliminated by a bargain which is better, or at least not worse, for all the participants, because the original bargain is blocked by them. The elimination of inferior bargains by blocking obviously gives rise to a shrinking of the core; thus, when the number of participants tends to infinity, the core eventually contains, under certain conditions, only those bargains each of which is a general equilibrium. Thus the Edgeworth–Debreu approach is an alternative way of reaching the Walrasian general equilibrium.

Article VII with Professor M. Majumdar deals with this new tatonnement by the core theorists and shows that no large economy will ever adopt this tatonnement and stick to the original Walrasian method. This is because in order to block a bargain those participants who are involved in the work of blocking have to make an enormous number of calculations, in the case of a number of commodities and, especially, when the number of

[3] See Morishima *et al.*, 1973, pp. 66–7.

[4] M. Morishima, 1952a.

independent agents is large; so that the degree of the burden we assume for each agent is much bigger than the one needed for constructing markets (or exchanges) for Walrasian competitive buying and selling. The whole idea of establishing a general equilibrium by blocking and eliminating inferior bargains will be blocked by the Walrasian idea of obtaining equilibrium prices by auctions. The observation that no *large* economy of the Edgeworth–Debreu type exists in the world supports and corresponds to this conclusion.

Comparing with Walras,[5] there is a fatal weak point which is common to all general equilibrium models formulated by contemporary economists, such as Hicks', Arrow–Debreu's, Arrow–Hahn's, and Malinvaud's. All these implicitly assume that enough funds are provided for each firm, so that there is no firm which cannot attain its maximum profits because of a shortage of funds. This assumption is never fulfilled in the actual world, where firms whose rates of profits are below the average lose funds as they move out from them to firms which realize a higher rate of profits; and the funds available in the economy are re-distributed among firms until their rates of profits are all equalized. In spite of Walras' precedent in specifying general equilibrium as a state of affairs in which the rate of profits is equalized through all capital goods as well as through all firms, Hicks and his followers have entirely ignored this problem and have been concerned with a world where firms do not compete with each other with respect to the rate of profits of their businesses and their capital assets.

In *DKR* I have taken the effects of a shortage of funds upon production explicitly into consideration, but this is not enough to rescue the general equilibrium theory from its fatal difficulty. I have failed to notice that this problem of equal rates of profits is inseparably related with the problem of the impossibility of full employment of labour. The durable capital goods (machines, equipment, etc.) used by the firms are subjects of dealing in two markets. First, capital goods are dealt with in the market of new capital goods, while market or efficiency prices of capital services are determined in the rental market of capital services or set in the 'internal market' of those factories where capital goods have been installed, determining rental prices for accounting purposes. The ratio of the price of those capital services which a unit of capital good yields per period to the price of the capital good per unit gives the rate of profits of that good, that is called the marginal efficiency of capital by Keynes.

This rate has to be equalized through all capital goods. Where this condition is imposed, as has been done by Walras and Keynes, we have to

[5] Walras determines the production coefficients so as to minimize the unit cost, with given output, rather than maximize profits. Output then adjusts itself to the demand for it (see Morishima, 1977, pp. 384–5).

meet the problem which I call the 'dilemma of durable goods' in Article VIII. Then we must conclude, as Keynes did, that the general equilibrium model involving capital goods constitutes a system of overdeterminacy, so that the full employment of labour is impossible as Keynes has insisted, or, as Walras has done so, we have to smuggle Say's law into the system. This law is very unrealistic, especially in the later stage of development of the capitalist economy, so that the model cannot provide a reasonable picture of the economy. The modern works by the above mentioned theorists, including my *DKR*, have made the worst choice; that is to say, they do not impose the condition of equal rates of profits and ignore the dilemma of durable goods; and by doing so they have mistakenly concluded that general equilibrium with full employment is possible, and they have left competition among firms in the rate of profits completely unexamined. As the result of this, modern general equilibrium theory remained poor in the analysis of financial capital as well as physical, real capital.[6]

The 'dilemma of durable goods' plays, of course, a most critical role in capital theory, but it is related to the problem of monetary equilibrium also. Obviously money is a durable good, so that it has two markets: the lending–borrowing market and the holding-of-money market corresponding to the rental and stock markets of money, respectively. The single 'price' variable of money, that is, the rate of interest cannot establish equilibrium in the two markets simultaneously. This is the problem of the loanable fund theory versus the liquidity preference theory discussed in chapter 4, section 6. Then not only these two monetary equilibrium equations have to be satisfied simultaneously, but also the rate of interest established in this way must be consistent with the rate of interest determined for other durable commodities. To overcome the dilemma that would be brought forth an entirely new approach would be necessary for settling the crux.

[6] With respect to this point, see Morishima, 1992, Introduction. It is true, as one may point out, that the rates of profits are all equalized with each other in the state of balanced growth equilibrium by von Neumann. But his equilibrium too has a conflict with the full employment of labour, as will be shown later in Article VIII.

Article I
Walras' own theory of tatonnement

I Introduction

It seems to be a generally supported view that the theory of stability has smoothly developed from Walras, through Hicks, to Samuelson who is the originator of the mathematical framework of contemporary stability theory. In terms of the terminology used in this volume, Samuelson concentrates his interest upon the stability of the equilibrium point, while Hicks' object is to deal with economic motion through weeks. Walras is nearer to Hicks than Samuelson in the sense that he is also concerned with economic motion or path rather than with a stationary or static point but differs from Hicks because the path examined is a sequence of temporary equilibria in the case of Hicks, while it is, as will be shown in section III below, a disequilibrium path in the case of Walras.

Arrow and Hahn, in their now classic work (1971, pp. 4–5), who regard Walras' stability theory or theory of tatonnement as 'rather clumsy', criticize it in the following way. Walras considers that the markets carry out tatonnement in some definite order. In the first market the price is adjusted so that supply and demand are equal, regarding other prices as given. This change in the price will affect supply and demand in all other markets. Then the tatonnement is repeated in the second and subsequent markets one by one. Arrow and Hahn consider that Walras' idea of sequential tatonnement does not literally mean that markets come into equilibrium in some definite order, but it is rather a trick for the purpose of simplifying exposition, or in their own words, it is '*a convenient way of showing* how the market system in fact could solve the system of equilibrium relations' (italics by M.M.). 'The dynamic system, more properly expressed,' in their words, should regard the price changes on the different markets '*as occurring simultaneously*' (italics by M.M.). According to this line of thought Samuelson's idea of simultaneous tatonnement has become the standard of stability analysis, after Arrow and Hurwicz's powerful, highly advanced analysis.

Nevertheless we observe that Samuelson's simultaneous tatonnement is also no more than a device for simplifying exposition. Furthermore it seems that the actual world is nearer to Walras than Samuelson, because, for administrative reasons, simultaneous tatonnement of many prices is very difficult; we must organize several exchanges each of which deals with a number of specified commodities. These exchanges are independent from each other and the prices of commodities delegated to different exchanges are transmitted from one market to others, not instantly but with some delay usually, however short the time lag may be. Moreover, in any exchange competitive buying and selling for the determination of prices are arranged in some definite order. It is true that there is no economic rationale for the order chosen. It is a mere institutional arrangement. But, however arbitrary it may look, the economy works within this organizational framework.

The essential point of Walras' theory of tatonnement does not lie in the formula which deals with the prices of commodities according to a prescribed, definite order. Rather it lies in a partial equilibrium analytic way of price determination in which the price of a commodity to be determined is isolated so long as a tatonnement for that commodity is being carried out. His problem is to find out whether the collection of prices determined in this manner will eventually approach the point of general equilibrium, or not. Thus, the Walrasian process is formulated as a process of communication of a 'stop and go' or 'closed and open' type. During any session of tatonnement all dealers in the market concentrate their attention on the price for which they are haggling with each other, no communication being made between markets. After that round of tatonnement the results are made known to all economic agents. A new tatonnement is made on the basis of the prices determined in the previous round. This repeated tatonnement finally leads the markets to a close vicinity of the general equilibrium point, provided some conditions for stability are satisfied. Walras has speculated that as long as the condition that the effect of a change in the price of a commodity upon its own excess demand function dominates the effects of all other prices upon the same excess demand holds for each commodity, successive rounds of tatonnement will eventually establish general equilibrium prices. In section II, which is a reproduction of my unpublished paper, 1958, I discuss this type of Walrasian tatonnement process and show its stability under the condition that all commodities are 'gross substitutes' for each other.[1]

[1] The gross substitute case is a special case of the dominant diagonal case mentioned above. It was Walras' own conjecture that stability is obtained where excess demands are dominant diagonal.

II General equilibrium as a limit of sequences of partial equilibria

Suppose there are $n + 1$ goods of which the last is the *numeraire*, good $n + 1$. Let p_i be the price of the ith good (in terms of the *numeraire*), Q_i a vector of prices such that $Q_i = (p_1, p_2, \ldots, *, \ldots, p_n)$, where the asterisk means that the ith element is omitted. Assume that the excess demand function, E_i, of the ith good is a function not only of the price of the ith good itself but also of the prices of all other goods. Then we may write

$$E_i = E_i(p_i, Q_i),\ i = 1, 2, \ldots, n$$

Assume further that each excess demand function is continuous and single valued. Recent work[2] has shown that there exists at least one set of equilibrium prices such that $E_i(p_i, Q_i) = 0$ $(i = 1, 2, \ldots, n)$ with $P = (p_1, p_2, \ldots, p_n) \geqslant 0$.

Now let p_{it} be the price of the ith good in period t, where the excess demand for any good (at the prices $p_{1t}, p_{2t}, \ldots, p_{nt}$) may be either positive, zero, or negative. The basic assumption underlying any theory of stability of economic equilibrium is that positive excess demand for a good makes its price rise and negative excess demand makes it fall unless its price is already 0. Usually, this assumption is formulated by a system of n *differential* equations

$$dp_{it}/dt = h_i E_i(p_{it}, Q_{it}),\ h_i > 0$$

or in a system of n *difference* equations

$$p_{it+1} - p_{it} = k_i E_i(p_{it}, Q_{it}),\ k_i > 0$$

Here, however, we assume that the price of the ith good in period $t + 1$ is determined in the following way. The market for the ith good adjusts p_i in such a way as to make the excess demand for i equal to zero, regarding Q_{it} as constant. Among the values of p_i which fulfil this condition we distinguish two groups: those larger or equal to p_{it}, and those smaller or equal to it. If $E_i(p_{it}, Q_{it}) \geqslant 0$, the market selects as the price in the next period the minimal one of the first group, and if $E_i(p_{it}, Q_{it}) \leqq 0$, it selects the maximal one of the second group. This may be put as follows

$$p_{it+1} = \begin{cases} \inf\limits_{p_i}\{p_i: E_i(p_i, Q_{it}) = 0, p_i \geqq p_{it}\} \text{ if } E_i(p_{it}, Q_{it}) \geqq 0, \\ \sup\limits_{p_i}\{p_i: E_i(p_i, Q_{it}) = 0, p_i \leqq p_{it}\} \text{ if } E_i(p_{it}, Q_{it}) \leqq 0 \end{cases}$$

[2] For example, Arrow and Debreu, 1954, Nikaido, 1956, and Uzawa, 1957. See also references in footnote 1 of Arrow and Hurwicz, 1958.

We shall find that these dynamic equations lead to more powerful conclusions than the differential or difference equations of the usual type.

III Gross substitutability

In this section we shall be concerned with the following two cases: first, the case where all goods *excepting* the *numeraire* are gross substitutes (for all values of the price vector); and secondly, the case where all goods other than the *numeraire* are gross substitutes for each other, at least one of them being also a gross substitute for the *numeraire*.[3] In the first case there may be two or more equilibrium points, while the second case admits of only one equilibrium position (as will be shown below). We shall use the following assumption.

Assumption 1

When the price of the ith good is sufficiently low (or high), the excess demand for the ith good is positive (or negative), however low (or high) the prices of the other goods may be; i.e., there exists a set of sufficiently low (or high) prices, $(p_1, p_2, \ldots, p_n)$, such that for all $i = 1, 2, \ldots, n$

$$E_i(p_i, Q_i) > 0 \text{ (or } <0)$$

This means that there are upper and lower boundaries to the movement of prices if it starts from a vicinity of the general equilibrium prices. We can now prove

Theorem 1

In a system in which all goods excepting the numeraire are gross substitutes (for all values of the price vector), and which has two or more equilibrium positions, there will always be a minimal and a maximal equilibrium point (in the sense of vector comparison).

This theorem is clear from the proof of theorem 2 below.

The following definition is needed for theorem 2. Let $P_0 = (p_{10}, p_{20}, \ldots, p_{n0})$ be the initial point of price motion; then by the usual definition,[4] an equilibrium point, say $P^0 = (p_1^0, p_2^0, \ldots, p_n^0)$, is said to be *globally stable* if $\lim_{t \to \infty} p_{it} = p_i^0$ $(i = 1, 2, \ldots, n)$ for all P_0. This definition may be generalized into a definition of stability: *Let* $\bar{P}^0$ *and* $\underline{P}^0$ *be the maximal and minimal equilibrium points respectively, and let E be a region defined as:*

[3] Usually, it is assumed that all goods are gross substitutes for each other. But this is unnecessarily restrictive for stability. The existence of at least one good that is a gross substitute for the numeraire is sufficient.

[4] See Arrow and Hurwicz, 1958, p. 3.

$E = \{P: \underline{P}^0 \leqq P \leqq \bar{P}^0\}$. The system is said to be globally stable whenever for any region D containing E there exists a T, dependent on D, such that $P_t = (p_{1t}, p_{2t}, \ldots, p_{nt})$ remains in D for all $t > T$.

The following theorem can now be proved

Theorem 2

If all goods other than the numeraire are gross substitutes (for all values of the price vector), the system is globally stable in the sense of the preceding definition.

Proof: Let $\bar{p}_{io}$ be greater than p_{io}, and $\underline{p}_{io}$ smaller than p_{io}. If we take that each $\bar{p}_{io}$ is sufficiently high and that each $\underline{p}_{io}$ is sufficiently low, it follows immediately from assumption 1 that

$$E_i(\bar{p}_{io}, \bar{Q}_{io}) < 0 \quad i = 1, 2, \ldots, n$$

and

$$E_i(\underline{p}_{io}, \underline{Q}_{io}) > 0 \quad i = 1, 2, \ldots, n$$

where $\bar{Q}_{io} = (\bar{p}_{10}, \ldots, *, \ldots, \bar{p}_{no})$ and $\underline{Q}_{io} = (\underline{p}_{10}, \ldots, *, \ldots \underline{p}_{no})$.

Now define

$$\bar{p}_{i1} = \sup_{p_i}\{p_i: E_i(p_i, \bar{Q}_{io}) = 0, p_i < \bar{p}_{io}\}$$

$$\underline{p}_{i1} = \inf_{p_i}\{p_i: E_i(p_i, \underline{Q}_{io}) = 0, p_i > \underline{p}_{io}\}$$

Since $\bar{Q}_{io} > Q_{io} > \underline{Q}_{io}$, the assumption of gross substitutability yields

$$\bar{p}_{i1} > \sup_{p_i}\{p_i: E_i(p_i, Q_{io}) = 0, p_i < \bar{p}_{io}\}$$

and

$$\underline{p}_{i1} < \inf_{p_i}\{p_i: E_i(p_i, Q_{io}) = 0, p_i > \underline{p}_{io}\}$$

On the other hand, by definition we have

$$p_{i1} = \begin{cases} \sup_{p_i}\{p_i: E_i(p_i, Q_{io}) = 0, p_i \leqq \bar{p}_{io}\} \text{ if } E_i(p_{io}, Q_{io}) \leqq 0, \\ \inf_{p_i}\{p_i: E_i(p_i, Q_{io}) = 0, p_i \geqq \underline{p}_{io}\} \text{ if } E_i(p_{io}, Q_{io}) \geqq 0 \end{cases}$$

so that it is obvious that p_{i1} is contained on the closed interval $\left(\inf_{p_i}\{p_i: E_i(p_i, Q_{io}) = 0, p_i > \underline{p}_{io}\},\ \sup_{p_i}\{p_i: E_i(p_i, Q_{io}) = 0, p_i < \bar{p}_{io}\}\right)$. Hence we obtain

$$\bar{p}_{i1} > p_{i1} > \underline{p}_{i1}$$

Next, since $E_i(\bar{p}_{i1}, \bar{Q}_{io}) = 0, \bar{p}_{i1} < \bar{p}_{io}, E_i(\underline{p}_{i1}, \underline{Q}_{io}) = 0$ and $\underline{p}_{i1} > \underline{p}_{io}$ $(i = 1, 2, \ldots, n)$, the assumption of gross substitutability leads to

$$E_i(\bar{p}_{i1}, \bar{Q}_{i1}) < 0 \; (i = 1, 2, \ldots, n),$$

$$E_i(\underline{p}_{i1}, \underline{Q}_{i1}) > 0 \; (i = 1, 2, \ldots, n)$$

where $\bar{Q}_{i1} = (\bar{p}_{11}, \ldots, *, \ldots, \bar{p}_{n1})$ and $\underline{Q} = (\underline{p}_{11}, \ldots, *, \ldots, \underline{p}_{n1})$. Therefore, by the same way as the above, we obtain

$$\bar{p}_{i2} > p_{i2} > \underline{p}_{i2}$$

where

$$\bar{p}_{i2} = \sup_{p_i}\{p_i: E_i(p_i, \bar{Q}_{i1}) = 0, p_i < \bar{p}_{i1}\},$$

$$\underline{p}_{i2} = \inf_{p_i}\{p_i: E_i(p_i, \underline{Q}_{i1}) = 0, p_i > \underline{p}_{i1}\}$$

and

$$p_{i2} = \begin{cases} \sup_{p_i}\{p_i: E_i(p_i, Q_{i1}) = 0, p_i \leqq p_{i1}\} \text{ if } E_i(p_{i1}, Q_{i1}) \leqq 0, \\ \inf_{p_i}\{p_i: E_i(p_i, Q_{i1}) = 0, p_i \geqq p_{i1}\} \text{ if } E_i(p_{i1}, Q_{i1}) \geqq 0 \end{cases}$$

Proceeding in this way we find

$$\bar{p}_{io} > \bar{p}_{i1} > \ldots > \bar{p}_{it} > p_{it} > \underline{p}_{it} > \ldots > \underline{p}_{i1} > \underline{p}_{io}$$

so that the sequences $\bar{p}_{it}$ and $\underline{p}_{it}$ converge and approach limits $\bar{p}_i$ and $\underline{p}_i$ respectively. We can easily show that $\bar{p}_i$ and $\underline{p}_i$ satisfy $E_i(\bar{p}_i, \bar{Q}_i) = 0$ and $E_i(\underline{p}_i, \underline{Q}_i) = 0$ $(i = 1, 2, \ldots, n)$, where $\bar{Q}_i = (\bar{p}_1, \ldots, *, \ldots, \bar{p}_n)$ and $\underline{Q}_i = (\underline{p}_1, \ldots, *, \ldots, \underline{p}_n)$; hence $\bar{P} \equiv (\bar{p}_1, \ldots, \bar{p}_n)$ and $\underline{P} \equiv (\underline{p}_1, \ldots, \underline{p}_n)$ are constellations of equilibrium prices.

Thus any time path of prices starting from an *arbitrary* initial position of prices eventually remains in a region $\{P: \underline{P} - \varepsilon e \leqq P \leqq \bar{P} + \varepsilon e\}$ where ε is a sufficiently small positive number and $e = (1, 1, \ldots, 1)$. Hence every equilibrium point must be $\leqq \bar{P}$ and $\geqq \underline{P}$, and since $\bar{P}$ and $\underline{P}$ themselves are equilibrium points, we find $\bar{P} = \bar{P}^0$ and $\underline{P} = \underline{P}^0$.

Corollary 1

Suppose $E_i(p_{io}, Q_{io}) \leqq 0$ for all $i = 1, 2, \ldots, n$ or $E_i(p_{io}, Q_{io}) \geqq 0$ for all $i = 1, 2, \ldots, n$. Then the price set $P_t = (p_{1t}, \ldots, p_{nt})$, approaches an equilibrium price set as t tends to infinity.

Corollary 2

In particular, if the equilibrium is unique, the tatonnement prices approach the equilibrium prices.

Next we shall prove:

Theorem 3

If in addition to the previous assumptions, one good is a gross substitutive for the numeraire (for all values of the price vector), the (unique) equilibrium point must be globally stable.

Proof: First, we shall prove uniqueness of equilibrium. Since $E_i(\pi_1, \pi_2, \ldots, \pi_{n+1})$ is a homogeneous function of degree zero in non-normalized prices $\pi_1, \pi_2, \ldots, \pi_{n+1}$, Euler's theorem yields

$$\sum_{j=1}^{n+1} a_{ij} = 0 \quad i = 1, 2, \ldots, n$$

where $a_{ij} = \frac{\partial E_i}{\partial \pi_j} \pi_j$. Now let $A =$ the $n \times n$ Jacobian of a_{ij}'s $(i, j = 1, 2, \ldots, n)$, $\alpha > \max |a_{ii}|$ and $B = [\alpha I + A]$. Then all elements of B are positive, so that the absolute value of any latent root of B, say $|\lambda_k|$, is less than any row sum of B. Thus we obtain

$$\alpha + \sum_{j=1}^{n} a_{ij} = \alpha - a_{in+1} > |\lambda_k| \; (k = 1, \ldots, n)$$

By virtue of our additional assumption there exists a good i such that $a_{in+1} > 0$. Consequently we find $\alpha > |\lambda_k|$. Since $det(B - \lambda I) = det(A + (\alpha - \lambda)I) = 0$, we must have $det\, A = \prod_k (\lambda_k - \alpha)$. Hence it follows from $\alpha > |\lambda_k|$ that

$$\text{sign of } det\, A = \text{sign } (-1)^n$$

It can be proved[5] that the maximal latent root of B is greater than that of $B_i = [\alpha I + A_i]$, where A_i is a principal minor matrix of A of order $i (i < n)$; so that $\alpha > |\lambda_k^i|$, where λ_k^is are latent roots of B_i. Taking $det\, A_i = \prod_k (\lambda_k^i - \alpha)$ into account, we find

$$\text{sign of } det\, A_i = \text{sign } (-1)^i \; (i = 1, 2, \ldots, n - 1)$$

Since $a_{ij} \equiv \frac{\partial E_i}{\partial \pi_j} \pi_j = \frac{\partial E_i}{\partial p_j} p_j$, we find that the principal minors of determinant $\left| \frac{\partial E_i}{\partial p_j} \right|$ are alternately negative and positive. Hence by Samuelson's

[5] Frobenius, 1908 and Mathematical Note II.

Theorem (Samuelson, 1953–4, pp. 16–17) the equilibrium is unique.
Corollary 2 is now applicable, and the proof is completed.

IV Gross complementarity in a special pattern

We shall be concerned with a case[6] which was examined by myself (1952a, 1957) and also in the following works: Arrow and Hurwicz (1957), McManus (1958), and Arrow and McManus (1958). Let a system be divided into three sets of goods; the first set, say S_1, consists of goods i ($i = 1, 2, \ldots, m$), the second, say S_2, of goods j ($j = m+1, \ldots, n$), and the third of only the *numeraire*, i.e., good $n+1$. Assume that any two goods in the same set are gross substitutes and that any good in the first set and any good in the second set are gross complements, i.e., the excess demand for a good in the first (or second) set will be increased if the price of another good in the same set is raised, and will be decreased if the price of a good in the second (or first) set is raised. We now replace assumption 1 by the following assumption for all goods other than the *numeraire*.

Assumption 2

When the price of a good i in a set is sufficiently low (or high), the excess demand for good i is positive (or negative) however low (or high) the prices of the other goods in the same set, and however high (or low) the prices of goods in the other set may be.

Now let

$$u_i = \begin{cases} p_i & \text{if } i \in S_1 \\ -p_i & \text{if } i \in S_2 \end{cases}$$

and let

$$\begin{aligned} W_i &= (u_1, \ldots, *, \ldots, u_m) \\ X &= (u_1, \ldots, u_m) \\ Y_i &= (u_{m+1}, \ldots, *, \ldots, u_n) \\ Z &= (u_{m+1}, \ldots, u_n) \end{aligned}$$

where each asterisk means that the ith element is omitted. Then we may write as follows

$$E_i(p_i, Q_i) = E_i(u_i, W_i, -Z) \text{ if } i \in S_1$$

$$-E_i(p_i, Q_i) = -E_i(-u_i, X, -Y_i) \text{ if } i \in S_2$$

[6] I called this case a generalized p-Frobenian system. See Morishima, 1957, p. 207. [Also the title of Article VI below shows this.]

Furthermore, let

$$F_i = \begin{cases} E_i & \text{if } i \in S_1 \\ -E_i & \text{if } i \in S_2 \end{cases}$$

we have

$$F_i = F_i(u_i, V_i) \text{ for all } i = 1, 2, \ldots, n$$

where

$$V_i = \begin{cases} [W_i, Z] & \text{if } i \in S_1 \\ [X, Y_i] & \text{if } i \in S_2 \end{cases}$$

It can be shown that, if any element in V_i is increased, F_i is also increased, and we find from assumption 2 that there exists a sufficiently small (or large) vector $(u_1, u_2, \ldots, u_n)$ such that for all $i = 1, 2, \ldots, n$

$$F_i(u_i, V_i) > 0 \; [\text{or } < 0]$$

Now it is clear that the system $F_i = F_i(u_i, V_i)$ $(i = 1, 2, \ldots, n)$ has the same properties as the system in section II, so that we can derive equivalents to theorems 1 and 2 and corollaries 1 and 2 (*mutatis mutandis*).

If in addition, we assume that either of the two sets contains a good whose excess demand is increased even if the prices of all goods in the other set are raised at double the rate of the price increase of the *numeraire*, we can prove that equilibrium is unique.[7] Hence we obtain a theorem corresponding to theorem 3, though certain modifications are necessary.

[7] Let

$$A = \begin{bmatrix} a_{11} & \cdots & a_{1m} & -a_{1m+1} & \cdots & -a_{1n} \\ \cdots & \cdots & \cdots & \cdots & \cdots & \cdots \\ a_{m1} & \cdots & a_{mm} & -a_{mm+1} & \cdots & -a_{mn} \\ -a_{m+11} & \cdots & -a_{m+1m} & a_{m+1m+1} & \cdots & a_{m+1n} \\ \cdots & \cdots & \cdots & \cdots & \cdots & \cdots \\ -a_{n1} & \cdots & -a_{n1} & a_{nm+1} & \cdots & a_{nn} \end{bmatrix}$$

Suppose α is greater than $\max |a_{ii}|$. Since all elements of $B = [\alpha I + A]$ are positive, the absolute value of any latent root of B, say $|\lambda_k|$, is less than any row-sum of B. Thus we find that $\alpha + \sum_{h=1}^{m} a_{ih} - \sum_{j=m+1}^{n} a_{ij}$ $(i = 1, \ldots, m)$ and $\alpha - \sum_{h=1}^{m} a_{ih} + \sum_{j=m+1}^{n} a_{ij}$ $(i = m+1, \ldots, n)$ are greater than $|\lambda_k|$. Since excess demand for the ith good is a homogeneous function of degree zero, we have $\sum_{j=1}^{n+1} a_{ij} = 0$; so that $\alpha + \sum_{h=1}^{m} a_{ih} - \sum_{j=m+1}^{n} a_{ij} = \alpha - 2 \sum_{j=m+1}^{n} a_{ij} - a_{in+1} > |\lambda_k|$

(*continued on the next page*)

V Walras' dynamics by means of the 'continuous market'

As is generally admitted, the theory of tatonnement plays the role of an infrastructure for the realization of a state of general equilibrium in Walras' economics. However, it brings about another service that is not generally noticed yet. By the use of it his general equilibrium is put in motion. That is to say, it is a most important mechanism in his dynamic theory.

It is a generally supported view of Walras that his *Elements* only provides a static theory. But the final part of the book, Part VII, is entitled 'Conditions and Consequences of Economic Progress' where Walras develops a theory which examines how the economy works, changes, and moves through time. However sketchy, only heuristic, and not well organized it is, we can clearly and firmly grasp the essence of his dynamic theory from that part. In section 322 Walras writes:

> Finally, in order to come still more closely to reality, we must drop the hypothesis of an annual market period and adopt in its place the hypothesis of a continuous market. Thus, we pass from the static to the dynamic state. For this purpose, we shall now suppose that the annual production and consumption, which we had hitherto represented as a constant magnitude for every moment of the year under consideration, change from instant to instant with the basic data of the problem . . . [They] are thus like so many stems, where one shoot is constantly pruned, only for another shoot to grow again.[8] Every hour, nay, every minute, portions of these different classes of circulating capital are disappearing and reappearing. Personal capital, capital goods proper and money also disappear and reappear, in a similar manner, but much more slowly. Only landed capital escapes this process of renewal. Such is the continuous market, which is perpetually tending towards equilibrium without ever actually attaining it, because the market has no other way of approaching equilibrium except by groping, and, before the goal is reached, it has to renew its efforts and start over again, all the basic data of the problem, e.g. the initial quantities possessed, the utilities of goods and services, the technical coefficients, the

$(i = 1,\dots,m)$ and $\alpha - \sum_{h=1}^{m} a_{ih} + \sum_{j=m+1}^{n} a_{ij} = \alpha - 2\sum_{h=1}^{m} a_{ih} - a_{in+1} > |\lambda_k|$ $(i = m+1,\dots,n)$.

By assumption, at least one of $2\sum_{j=m+1}^{n} a_{ij} + a_{in+1}$ $(i = 1,\dots,m)$ and $2\sum_{h=1}^{m} a_{ih} + a_{in+1}$ $(i = m+1,\dots,n)$ is positive. Hence $\alpha > |\lambda_k|$.

Since $det(B - \lambda I) = det(A + (\alpha - \lambda)I)$, we get $det\, A = \Pi(\lambda_k - \alpha)$. Therefore we find that sign of $det\, A = \text{sign}(-1)^n$.

Let λ_k^i be a latent root of $[\alpha I + A_i]$, where A_i is a principal minor matrix of A of order $i(i < n)$. It can be shown that each $|\lambda_k^i|$ is less than α; so that it follows from $det\, A_i = \prod_k(\lambda_k^i - \alpha)$ that the sign of $det\, A_i = \text{sign}(-1)^i$ $(i = 1, 2,\dots, n-1)$.

[8] This sentence has wrongly been translated by W. Jaffé as: '[They] are like so many shoots that are continually being pruned at one end while they are constantly growing at the other.' This mistranslation might have given rise to the neglect of Walras' contribution to dynamics by the contemporary English-speaking Walrasians.

excess of income over consumption, the working capital requirements, etc., having changed in the meantime.

In this long quotation from Walras, the ever-growing stems Walras introduces for the purpose of metaphor stand for the tatonnement process that continues forever and takes an infinitely long time to reach a general equilibrium. Where the basic data change, a shoot of the stems is pruned, and they start to grow towards the directions of a new equilibrium that corresponds to the new data complex. In this case, too, the new equilibrium will never be realized and the shoot tracing the path of tatonnement is switched to another shoot at the point of time at which a change happens in the basic data.

Although Walras explicitly gives no comment on the truncation of the tatonnement process, we should apply a similar notion as above to transactions and production activities that are carried out in the midst of the tatonnement process. Where these have been done, they give rise to a change in the data, and a new shoot grows. Obviously these transactions and production activities are not necessarily equilibrium ones but those which are executed in a state of disequilibrium. In this way Walras uses the mechanism of tatonnement to establish a disequilibrium theory of economic progress and contrasts distinctly with Hicks' *VC* and La Volpe (1936) who are concerned with a dynamic motion that is in temporary or momentary equilibrium at any point of the path. In this kind of theory we must assume, as Hicks does, that tatonnement is completed in a finite period of time,[9] or as La Volpe does, that temporary or momentary equilibrium is realized at any moment, instantly without tatonnement. In any case, I must say, Walras surprisingly skilfully dispatches the idea of tatonnement which he originally invented for the purpose of establishing a general equilibrium, in order to generate a sequence of disequilibria from the process of tatonnement.

[9] The conversion of the ordinary calendar time during a market day, Hicks' Monday, to such a tatonnement time that takes on the value of infinity at the end of the market day, as I have introduced the time 't' in chapter 3 of the text, is essential in order to apply the differential equation approach to stability to the analysis of tatonnement on Monday.

Article II
Tatonnement in quantities: truncation, equilibration, growth

This section was originally published in the form of an independent article as Morishima, 1956, which may, however, be regarded as an example of the negative counterpart of the text of this volume. In the text we are concerned with an economy in which equilibration is made in terms of prices, while quantities are assumed to depend on prices, whereas in this article it is made in terms of quantities, all prices being implicitly assumed to be kept constant. The problem of price adjustment versus quantity adjustment later became a topic of general equilibrium analysis in the 1960s and the early 1970s.

As far as we measure the time t in an ordinary way by calendar time, the equilibrium to be established at $t = \infty$ is no more than a kind of utopia which is never realized at an actual point in time. Therefore, where we formulate a tatonnement process in terms of differential or difference equations, we should either transform the calendar time into a tatonnement time which tends to infinity at a certain point of the calendar time, as we have done so in the text, or we should truncate the tatonnement process at a certain point of the calendar time, as Walras did in his *Elements*. I have taken the latter option in this article, though, where I discuss the case of the degree of flexibility of demand schedules being infinity, I have implicitly assumed that infinitely many rounds of tatonnement can be carried out in a finite span of the calendar time.

In the following I formulate the model in terms of Marx's concepts, constant and variable capital, surplus value, the rate of profits, the rate of exploitation, etc. But the connection to Marx is not important, especially when the article is read as a continuation of *DKR*. Its keywords should be: quantity adjustment, truncation of tatonnement process, sequence of temporary equilibrium and steady growth, rather than surplus value, exploitation, etc.

1 Introduction

The Leontief system may be regarded as a simplification of the general equilibrium system of Walras as well as a generalization of the macro-economic system of Keynes. It is mathematically represented by a system of linear equations whose coefficient matrix is non-negative. In the recent years a number of mathematical theorems regarding non-negative matrices have been discovered or rediscovered by Arrow, 1951, Chipman, 1950, 1951, Debreu and Herstein, 1953, Georgescu-Roegen, 1951, Goodwin, 1950, Hawkins and Simon, 1949, Metzler, 1945, 1950, Solow, 1952, and others. It should not be thought, however, that the Leontief model is the only possible economic model to which the theorems of non-negative matrices may be applied. There is another important model of similar nature; that is, the reproduction scheme of Marx.[1]

In this article we shall try to formulate Marx's reproduction scheme in terms of a number of linear equations and show that the coefficient matrix of these equations is non-negative. As we shall indicate, each of the column sums in the matrix of Marx's reproduction scheme is greater than one, whereas that in the Leontief system is usually assumed as less than one. Thus Marx's system is intrinsically an expanding (hence, dynamic) system. This corresponds to his view that the capitalist economy is dynamic or accumulative and presents a good contrast to the classical idea that the economy historically tends to the stationary state.

Most of the theories of economic growth recently advanced by many economists such as Domar, 1946, Harrod, 1952, Hicks, 1950, Kalecki, 1954, and others are macroscopic, so that they cannot analyse any interindustrial relations in a dynamic process. There had been presented, however, multi-sectoral theories of economic growth, for instance, by Marx and Cassel. In the last section of this article we shall investigate the relations between Marx's and Harrod–Domar's theories of economic growth.

II Reconstruction of the Marxian reproduction scheme

2.1 It is well known that the Marxian system consists of two departments: the one that produces *constant capital* (or means of production), and the other that produces *consumption goods*. In this article, however, we shall consider an economy which is divided into n departments; the jth department producing the jth kind of constant capital ($j = 1, \ldots, m$) and the

[1] In this chapter we consider Marx's theory of reproduction in its relation to the multi-sectoral analysis of Leontief; Marx's theory of reproduction has hitherto been analysed by many economists such as Sweezy (1942), pp. 109–30, Peter (1953), Burchardt (1932), and others. The following is considerably different from any of them.

kth department producing the kth kind of consumption good ($k = m + 1, \ldots, n$).

For period t, we use the following notations: Let $Y_i(t)$ be the value of output produced in department $i(i = 1, \ldots, n)$, $C_{ji}(t)$ the value of constant capital j used up in department $i(j = 1, \ldots, m; i = 1, \ldots, n)$, $V_i(t)$ the value of variable capital employed in department $i(i = 1, \ldots, n)$, and $S_i(t)$ the surplus value created in department $i(i = 1, \ldots, n)$. All of them are assumed to be measured in terms of man-hours of labour time.[2] Needless to say, $\sum_{j=1}^{m} C_{ji}(t)/V_i(t)(= \sum_{j=1}^{m} c_{ji})$ represents the organic composition of capital of department $i, S_i(t)/V_i(t)$ $(= s_i)$ the rate of surplus value or the rate of exploitation of department i, and $V_i(t)/Y_i(t)(= v_i)$ the amount of variable capital per unit of output i. In what follows all of c_{ji}, s_i, and v_i are assumed constant over time.

2.2 As the value of output equals the sum of the cost of production (i.e., constant capital plus variable capital) and the profit (i.e., the surplus value), we have the following equation for each i:

$$\sum_{j=1}^{m} C_{ji}(t) + V_i(t) + S_i(t) = Y_i(t) \; (i = 1, \ldots, n)$$

Dividing both sides of the equation by $Y_i(t)$, then we have

$$\sum_{j=1}^{m} c_{ji}v_i + v_i + s_i v_i = 1 \; (i = 1, \ldots, n) \tag{1}$$

In Marxian economic theory, c_{ji}, s_i, and v_i are considered as the parameters whose values are determined by the technology and the social structure of the economic system in question. It is obvious from (1) that they are not all independent but dependent on each other.

2.3 Next we shall make the assumption that capitalists spend part of the surplus value on capital accumulation and the rest on consumption. If the rate of capital accumulation of department i is a_i, the capitalists of department i accumulate capital by the amount of $a_i S_i(t)$, which will be

[2] Constant capital is equivalent to outlay on materials plus depreciation, variable capital to outlay on wages and salaries, and surplus value to income available for distribution as interest and dividends or for reinvestment in the business. The value of output represents gross receipts from sales. Outlay on materials plus depreciation does not, in the process of production, undergo any quantitative alteration of value and is therefore called 'constant capital'. Outlay on wages and salaries does in a sense undergo an alteration of value in that it both reproduces the equivalent of its own value, and also produces an excess, a surplus value, which may itself vary and may be more or less according to circumstances. Outlay on wages and salaries is therefore called 'variable capital' (see Sweezy, (1942), pp. 62–3).

divided into variable capital and each constant capital in the proportion of $1:c_{1i}:c_{2i}:\ldots:c_{mi}$. Hence, for each department i, we find that the part of accumulation which goes to purchase additional constant capital j amounts to

$$\Delta C_{ji}(t) = \frac{c_{ji}}{\sum_{j=1}^{m} c_{ji} + 1} a_i S_i(t) \; (j = 1,\ldots,m; i = 1,\ldots,n)$$

and that the part of accumulation which serves to augment variable capital amounts to

$$\Delta V_i(t) = \frac{1}{\sum_{j=1}^{m} c_{ji} + 1} a_i S_i(t) \; (i = 1,\ldots,n)$$

Here, defining r_i as

$$r_i = \frac{a_i s_i}{\sum_{j=1}^{m} c_{ji} + 1} \; (i = 1,\ldots,n)$$

and taking into account the relations $C_{ji}(t) = c_{ji}v_i Y_i(t)$ and $S_i(t) = s_i v_i Y_i(t)$, we can show that the gross demand for constant capital j, – that is the sum of the amount $C_{ji}(t)$ spent on constant capital j which is just sufficient to maintain output i at its level in period t and the amount $\Delta C_{ji}(t)$ of additional purchase of constant capital j due to the accumulation of capital – is given by

$$C_{ji}(t) + \Delta C_{ji}(t) = c_{ji}v_i(1 + r_i)Y_i(t) \; (j = 1,\ldots,m; i = 1,\ldots,n) \quad (2)$$

and likewise that the gross demand for variable capital is given by

$$V_i(t) + \Delta V_i(t) = v_i(1 + r_i)Y_i(t) \; (i = 1,\ldots,n) \quad (3)$$

The community demand functions follow by summation over all departments; hence, if we write

$$h_{ji} = c_{ji}v_i(1 + r_i)$$
$$w_i = v_i(1 + r_i)$$

we find that the community demand for constant capital j is

$$D_j^{(1)}(t) = \sum_{i=1}^{n} h_{ji} Y_i(t) \; (j = 1,\ldots,m) \quad (4)$$

and the community demand for variable capital is

$$\sum_{i=1}^{n} w_i Y_i(t)$$

Now, let us assume that workers consume all their income and capitalists consume the rest of the surplus value after subtracting the portion to be spent on capital accumulation, and let β_k be the workers' propensity to consume good k and β'_k the ratio of the capitalists' consumption of the good to the capitalists' total consumption. Then we have

$$\sum_{k=m+1}^{n} \beta_k = 1, \quad \sum_{k=m+1}^{n} \beta'_k = 1 \tag{5}$$

and the community demand for consumption good k is given by

$$\beta_k\left[\sum_{i=1}^{n} w_i Y_i(t)\right] + \beta'_k\left[\sum_{i=1}^{n} (1 - a_i)s_i v_i Y_i(t)\right] \quad (k = m + 1,\ldots,n) \tag{6}$$

Hence if we write

$$h_{ki} = \beta_k w_i + \beta'_k(1 - a_i)s_i v_i \quad (k = m + 1,\ldots,n; i = 1,\ldots,n)$$

the community demand for consumption good k takes the form of

$$D_k^{(1)}(t) = \sum_{i=1}^{n} h_{ki} Y_i(t) \quad (k = m + 1,\ldots,n) \tag{7}$$

2.4 The linear expressions (4) and (7) can more concisely be written in the matrix form

$$D^{(1)}(t) = HY(t)$$

where H represents the square matrix $[h_{ji}]$ $(i,j = 1,\ldots,n)$, and $D^{(1)}(t)$ and $Y(t)$ are the n component column vectors whose elements are the $D_j^{(1)}(t)$ and $Y_j(t)$ respectively. It can easily be shown that the matrix H has the following properties; (i) all elements of H are non-negative, because all of c_{ji}, v_i, s_i, a_i, β_k, β'_k are non-negative and a_i is less than one, (ii) it follows from (1) and (5) that each of the columns of H adds up to one. The matrix H, therefore, has the same properties as the matrix of a finite Markov chain.

2.5 Let us now consider the inequality

$$D_i^{(1)}(t) \gtreqless Y_i(t) \quad (i = 1,\ldots,n) \tag{8}$$

If in (8) the sign $>$ holds, there is excess demand or underproduction in department i, while if in (8) the sign $<$ holds, there is excess supply or overproduction in the department. It goes without saying that department i is in equilibrium if and only if the equation $D_i^{(1)}(t) = Y_i(t)$ holds; but for the given set of outputs $Y_1(t),\ldots, Y_n(t)$, the simultaneous equations

$$D_i^{(1)}(t) = Y_i(t) \; (i = 1, \ldots, n)$$

do not necessarily hold. When in (8) the sign $>$ holds, the difference between $D_i^{(1)}(t)$ and $Y_i(t)$ is equal to the unexpected sales of output i, which are fulfilled by the reduction in the inventories of the department, and then the proceeds of the department will increase to $D_i^{(1)}(t)$. But, when in (8) the sign $<$ holds, the excess of $Y_i(t)$ over $D_i^{(1)}(t)$ is not sold and the proceeds of the department will be limited to $D_i^{(1)}(t)$.

Thus, when the proceeds of department i amount to $D_i^{(1)}(t)$ as a result of the excess supply of or the excess demand for the output of the department, the capitalists of department i will gain their income or the surplus value by the amount of $s_i v_i D_i^{(1)}(t)$; that is to say, when $D_i^{(1)}(t) > Y_i(t)$ [resp. $D_i^{(1)}(t) < Y_i(t)$], the actual surplus value $s_i v_i D_i^{(1)}(t)$ is more (resp. less) than the expected surplus value $s_i v_i Y_i(t)$.

When the surplus value is $s_i v_i D_i^{(1)}(t)$ but not $s_i v_i Y_i(t)$ the capitalists will accumulate capital by the amount of $a_i s_i v_i D_i^{(1)}(t)$, which will be divided into variable capital and each constant capital in the proportion of $1 : c_{1i} : c_{2i} : \ldots : c_{mi}$. Hence the additional purchase of constant capital j due to the capital accumulation $a_i s_i v_i D_i^{(1)}(t)$ is equal to

$$\frac{c_{ji}}{\sum_{i=1}^{m} c_{ji} + 1} a_i s_i v_i D_i^{(1)}(t)$$

and the additional purchase of variable capital due to the accumulation is

$$\frac{1}{\sum_{i=1}^{m} c_{ji} + 1} a_i s_i v_i D_i^{(1)}(t)$$

When the proceeds amount to $D_i^{(1)}(t)$, capitalists, on the other side, spend the amount $c_{ji} v_i D_i^{(1)}(t)$ on constant capital j in order to maintain output i at the level of $D_i^{(1)}(t)$. Therefore, the gross demand for constant capital j becomes

$$c_{ji} v_i (1 + r_i) D_i^{(1)}(t) \; (j = 1, \ldots, m; i = 1, \ldots, n)$$

and likewise the gross demand for variable capital becomes

$$v_i (1 + r_i) D_i^{(1)}(t) \; (i = 1, \ldots, n)$$

Thus we can easily find that when the proceeds of goods are $D_j^{(1)}(t), D_2^{(1)}(t), \ldots, D_n^{(1)}(t)$ the community demand for each good takes the value of

$$D_j^{(2)}(t) = \sum_{i=1}^{n} h_{ji} D_i^{(1)}(t) \; (j = 1, \ldots, n)$$

If we have inequality

$$D_i^{(2)}(t) \gtrless D_i^{(1)}(t)$$

in at least one department, then the same process will start again and again, and at last the economy will reach the state

$$D^{(u+1)}(t) = HD^{(u)}(t)$$

2.6 Now we shall introduce into consideration the notion of the degree of flexibility of demand schedules. All the demand schedules are said to be rigid if the demand schedules (2), (3), and (6) which are arranged at the beginning of period t are carried out though there exists any over or underproduction in the market, whereas the demand schedules are said to be perfectly flexible if they are changed so long as there exists any difference between *ex ante* community demand and *ex ante* community supply in the *market*. When demand schedules are flexible; groping or *tatonnement* takes place in the market; at the first step in the groping process the *ex ante* demand for good i is $D_i^{(1)}(t)$ and the *ex ante* supply is $Y_i(t)$ which equals the value of output i at the beginning of period t, and at the second step the *ex ante* demand becomes $D_i^{(2)}(t)$ and the *ex ante* supply becomes $D_i^{(1)}(t)$ and so on. When the process of groping continues until the *ex ante* demand and the *ex ante* supply become equal – that is, until $D_i^{(u)}(t) = D_i^{(u+1)}(t)\ (i = 1, \ldots, n)$ – the demand schedules are perfectly flexible; but they are said to be imperfectly flexible or to have degree u of flexibility when the groping process is truncated at the finite $(u + 1)$th step in the groping process in spite of the inequality $D_i^{(u)}(t) \gtrless D_i^{(u+1)}(t)$.

If all the schedules are rigid, all the productions are carried out according to the demand schedules arranged initially, but when the schedules are perfectly or imperfectly flexible, we assume that the productions are postponed up to the end of the groping process and carried out according to the demand schedules arranged at the end of the process. In order for the demand schedules to be rigid or to have degree u of flexibility, all those commodities i with $D_i^{(1)}(t) > Y_i(t)$ or $D_i^{(u+1)}(t) > D_i^{(u)}(t)$ must have enough inventories, now or at the end of the uth round of the groping process, which are sufficient for filling up the gaps between $D_i^{(1)}(t)$ and $Y_i(t)$, or those between $D_i^{(u+1)}(t)$ and $D_i^{(u)}(t)$ respectively. Furthermore, in the 'perfect flexibility' case we have to assume that infinitely many rounds of tatonnement may be carried out in a finite span of time.

III Dynamic process with rigid demand schedules

Assuming rigidity of the demand schedules, we shall analyse, in this section, the dynamic motion of the system in question. When all the schedules are rigid, capitalists in department i input constant capital j by the amount of

$$c_{ji}v_i(1 + r_i)Y_i(t) \; (j = 1, \ldots, m) \tag{2}$$

and variable capital by the amount of

$$v_i(1 + r_i)Y_i(t) \tag{3}$$

Under the assumption that the rate of surplus value is constant, this activity of production will produce the surplus value by the amount

$$s_i v_i(1 + r_i)Y_i(t) \tag{9}$$

Hence the value which is just equal to the sum of (2), (3) and (9) will be produced at the beginning of period $t + 1$. Taking into account (1), we find that the sum of (2), (3), and (9) equals

$$(1 + r_i)Y_i(t)$$

and thus we have

$$Y_i(t + 1) = (1 + r_i)Y_i(t) \; (i = 1, \ldots, n)$$

Since the rate of profit in department i is surplus value $S_i(t)$ over total capital $\sum_{i=1}^{m} C_{ji}(t) + V_i(t)$ of the department; i.e., $s_i / \sum_{i=1}^{m} c_{ji} + 1$, then we find that r_i which is the rate of growth of output i is equal to (the rate of accumulation of capital of department i) × (the rate of profit of department i).

Thus under the assumption that demand schedules are rigid, we can conclude as follows: Since all departments do not necessarily have the same rate of accumulation and the same rate of profit, the rate of growth of output may be different from one department to another. Since accumulation and exploitation are inseparable from capitalism, the rate of accumulation and the rate of profit are necessarily positive. Hence economic growth is warranted in the capitalist economy, and the state of 'simple reproduction' or the stationary state should be regarded as a mere fantasy.

IV Dynamic process with imperfectly flexible demand schedules

4.1 Now let us analyse the case of the imperfectly flexible demand schedules. Let u represent their degree of flexibility, and we have matrix equations

$$D^{(1)}(t) = HY(t)$$
$$D^{(x+1)}(t) = HD^{(x)}(t) \; (x = 1, \ldots, u)$$

By iteration we find

$$D^{(u)}(t) = H^u Y(t) \tag{10}$$

When the degree of flexibility of demand schedules is u, all productions in period t are carried out according to the demand schedules $D^{(u+1)}(t)$ arranged at the end of the groping process. Hence we get, at the beginning of the next period $t + 1$, output i whose value equals

$$Y_i(t+1) = (1 + r_i)D_i^{(u)}(t) \ (i = 1,\ldots,n) \tag{11}$$

Substituting the equation (10) into (11), we have

$$Y(t+1) = GH^u Y(t) \tag{12}$$

where G is a matrix whose diagonal elements are $1 + r_i$ and off-diagonal elements are all zero.

4.2 Next we shall assume that the degree of flexibility u is constant over time and that the matrix H is indecomposable[3] and has at least one diagonal element that is positive. Then from the last assumption which is very plausible, it follows that the matrix H is *primitive*.[4] Since H is a primitive Markov matrix, H^u also must be a primitive Markov matrix; i.e., H^u must have at least one positive diagonal element, every column adding up to one. Thus we can easily see that the matrix H^uG is non-negative and primitive, and that its ith column adds up to $1 + r_i$ $(i = 1,\ldots,n)$.

4.3 If we denote by $\lambda_1,\ldots,\lambda_n$ the latent roots of the equation $|\lambda I - H^uG| = 0$, then the λ_i's are shown to be the roots of the characteristic equation $|\lambda I - GH^u| = 0$, and the solution of equation system (12) can be written

[3] An n by n matrix A is said to be indecomposable if for no permutation matrix π does $\pi A \pi^{-1} = \begin{bmatrix} A_{11} & A_{12} \\ 0 & A_{22} \end{bmatrix}$ where A_{11}, A_{22} are square. See Solow (1952), and Debreu and Herstein, (1953).

[4] An indecomposable matrix $A \geq 0$ is said to be primitive if there is no permutation matrix π such that

$$\pi A \pi^{-1} = \begin{bmatrix} 0 & A_{12} & 0 & . & 0 \\ 0 & 0 & A_{23} & . & 0 \\ . & . & . & . & . \\ 0 & 0 & 0 & . & A_{k-1,k} \\ A_k & 0 & 0 & . & 0 \end{bmatrix}$$

with square submatrices on the diagonal. See Solow (1952) and Debreu and Herstein (1953). It is noted that where A is not primitive so that it can be transformed into the above cyclic form, we have multiple fixed-points of order k of the mapping: $y = A^k x/\Sigma A^k x$.

$$Y_i(t) = \sum_{j=1}^{n} b_{ij}\lambda_j^t \tag{13}$$

where b's depend upon the matrix $H^u G$ and the initial conditions. Since $H^u G$ is a non-negative matrix which is indecomposable and primitive, the Frobenius theorem tells us that $H^u G$ has a characteristic root λ_1 to which can be associated an eigenvector $Q > 0$, if λ_i is any characteristic root of $H^u G$ other than λ_1, $|\lambda_i| < \lambda_1$, and λ_1 is a simple root.

Therefore, the particular solution which corresponds to the root λ_1 becomes dominant in the general solution (13) when period t tends to infinity; and if at least one of $\lambda_2, \ldots, \lambda_n$ is negative or complex, the output $Y_i(t)$ may oscillate when initial conditions are taken suitably; all the oscillating terms in the general solution, however, become smaller and smaller *in the relative sense* when t tends to infinity.

Since

$$\lambda_1 Q = H^u G Q$$

and the sum of all elements of Q is one, we can easily show

$$\lambda_1 = \sum_{i=1}^{n} (1 + r_i)q_i = 1 + \sum_{i=1}^{n} r_i q_i$$

where q_i is the ith element of Q. Thus we know that the dominant solution $b_{i1}\lambda_1^t$ of (12), which is often called 'steady growth solution' or 'balanced growth solution', grows at the rate $\sum_{i=1}^{n} r_i q_i$ which is the weighted average of the products of each department's rate of accumulation and its rate of profit.

V Dynamic process with perfectly flexible demand schedules

5.1 In this section we shall assume perfect flexibility of demand schedules. Let the groping number u tend to infinity in

$$D^{(u+1)}(t) = HD^{(u)}(t)$$

Taking into account that H is an indecomposable and primitive Markov matrix, we can easily prove that $D^{(u)}(t)$ tends to

$$D^{(\infty)}(t) = HD^{(\infty)}(t) \tag{14}$$

Since all the productions are carried out according to the demand schedules $D^{(\infty)}(t)$ arranged finally, each department i will produce, at the beginning of the next period, output i by the amount of

$$Y_i(t + 1) = (1 + r_i)D_i^{(\infty)}(t) \quad (i = 1, \ldots, n) \tag{15}$$

5.2 Now let P be an n component vector such that

$$P = HP \tag{16}$$

where elements p_i of P are all positive and the sum of all p_i's is one. Since each column sum of H is one, it follows from $D^{(1)}(t) = HY(t)$ and $D^{(u+1)}(t) = HD^{(u)}(t)$ $(u = 1, 2, \ldots, \infty)$ that

$$\sum_{i=1}^{n} Y_i(t) = \sum_{i=1}^{n} D_i^{(1)}(t) = \sum_{i=1}^{n} D_i^{(2)}(t) = \ldots = \sum_{i=1}^{n} D_i^{(\infty)}(t)$$

From (14) and (16) we easily find that each element of $D^{(\infty)}(t)$ is proportional to its corresponding element in P. In fact it can be proved that

$$D_i^{(\infty)}(t) = p_i Y_0(t) \tag{17}$$

where $Y_0(t)$ denotes $\sum_{i=1}^{n} Y_i(t)$.. Introducing (17) into (15), we find

$$\sum_{i=1}^{n} Y_i(t+1) = \left[\sum_{i=1}^{n} (1 + r_i) p_i \right] Y_0(t)$$

i.e.

$$Y_0(t+1) = (1 + R) Y_0(t) \tag{18}$$

where $Y_0(t+1) = \sum_{i=1}^{n} Y_i(t+1)$ and $R = \sum_{i=1}^{n} r_i p_i$. Therefore, it follows from (15), (17), and (18) that

$$Y_i(t) = (1 + r_i) p_i Y_0(0)(1 + R)^{t-1} \quad (i = 1, \ldots, n)$$

5.3 Thus under the assumption that the demand schedules are perfectly flexible, output in each department grows in balance at the constant rate of growth R, and the mutual proportions of outputs remain constant. The economy changes only in scale, but not in composition, and there is no possibility of oscillation. The rate of growth R is the weighted average of the products of the rate of accumulation and the rate of profit in each department.

VI Unbalanced growth and decomposability of the system

6.1 So far we have assumed that the matrix H is indecomposable and arrived at the conclusion that from any arbitrary initial conditions, the economy eventually generates balanced growth when demand schedules are imperfectly flexible but not rigid, and that the economy necessarily grows in balance when demand schedules are perfectly flexible. In this section, however, we shall assume that H is decomposable.

6.2 *The case of imperfect flexibility of demand schedules* Let H be decomposable so that it may be partitioned in the form

$$\begin{bmatrix} H_{\mathrm{I}} & J \\ 0 & H_{\mathrm{II}} \end{bmatrix} \tag{19}$$

after the departments have been properly renumbered. In the expression (19) H_{I} and H_{II} are square. If H can be partitioned in the form (19), then the matrix GH^{u} can also be partitioned, after identical permutation of rows and columns, in the form

$$\begin{bmatrix} M_{\mathrm{I}} & N \\ 0 & M_{\mathrm{II}} \end{bmatrix}$$

where $M_{\mathrm{I}}(= G_{\mathrm{I}}H_{\mathrm{I}}^{u})$ and $M_{\mathrm{II}}(= G_{\mathrm{II}}H_{\mathrm{II}}^{u})$ are square, and M_{I}, M_{II}, and N are non-negative.

First we shall analyse the case in which each element of N is zero. In this case we can write (12) as

$$Y_{\mathrm{I}}^{(t+1)} = M_{\mathrm{I}}Y_{\mathrm{I}}^{(t)},$$
$$Y_{\mathrm{II}}^{(t+1)} = M_{\mathrm{II}}Y_{\mathrm{II}}^{(t)}$$

where $Y_{\mathrm{I}}(t)$ and $Y_{\mathrm{II}}(t)$ represent vectors, and the system is completely decomposed into two closed systems I and II.

Now let M_{I} and M_{II} be indecomposable and primitive. As was shown in the section IV, the closed system I may oscillate if the matrix M_{I} has at least one negative or complex characteristic root, but it will eventually generate balanced growth even though the system starts from any arbitrary initial condition. The closed system II will behave in the same way. Since, however, the rate of balanced growth of the system I (resp. II) is given by the weighted sum of r_is over all departments in the system I (resp. II) only, the rate of balanced growth of the system I is not necessarily equal to that of the system II. Hence the whole system starting from any arbitrary initial condition may possibly settle to the state of unbalanced growth in which there is balanced growth within each subsystem but not between the two subsystems.

Next let N contain at least one positive element. Then at least one column sum, say the ith column sum, of the matrix $H_{\mathrm{II}}^{u}G_{\mathrm{II}}$ is proved to be less than $1 + r_i$. Hence, if the ith column sum of $H_{\mathrm{II}}^{u}G_{\mathrm{II}}$ is sufficiently small, the maximal characteristic root λ_{II} of M_{II} may be less than one. If $\lambda_{\mathrm{II}} < 1$, each output of the departments in the subsystem II, decays and converges to the zero level of the output, but if λ_{II} is greater than or equal to one, it may grow or be stationary. As can be shown, however, the maximal root λ_{I} of the matrix M_{I} is necessarily greater than one, and therefore, each output of the departments in the subsystem I will necessarily grow through time. It can easily be proved that if $\lambda_I > \lambda_{II}$ the systems I and II will eventually grow in an unbalanced way, but that, in the case in which $\lambda_I \leq \lambda_{II}$, each output of all the n departments of the systems I and II will eventually grow in balance at the rate of growth $\lambda_{II} - 1$.

6.3 *The case of perfect flexibility of demand schedules.* Now let us assume that the matrix H may be partitioned in the form (19), and that each element of J is zero. Then both H_I and H_{II} are the Markov matrices which are assumed primitive, and hence there exist the demand schedules $D_I^{(\infty)}(t)$ and $D_{II}^{(\infty)}(t)$, such that

$$D_I^{(\infty)}(t) = H_I D_I^{(\infty)}(t)$$
$$D_{II}^{(\infty)}(t) = H_{II} D_{II}^{(\infty)}(t)$$

where $D_I^{(\infty)}(t)$ and $D_{II}^{(\infty)}(t)$ are vectors. By the same procedure as those shown in 5.1 and 5.2, we find that

$$Y_i(t) = (1 + r_i)p_i Y_0^I(0)(1 + R_I)^{t-1}$$

and

$$Y_j(t) = (1 + r_j)p_j Y_0^{II}(0)(1 + R_{II})^{t-1}$$

where department i (resp. j) belongs to the closed system I (resp. II), and $Y_0^I(0) = \Sigma Y_i(0)$ (resp. $Y_0^{II}(0) = \Sigma Y_j(0)$), and $R_I = \Sigma r_i p_i$ (resp. $R_{II} = \Sigma r_j p_j$); all the summations are taken over all the departments which belong to the system I (resp. II). Thus all the departments of the system I (resp. II) will grow in balance at the growth rate of R_I (resp. R_{II}) which is the weighted sum of r_is over all departments in the system I (resp. II). But since R_I is not necessarily equal to R_{II}, the systems I and II may move into the state of unbalanced growth. In other words, there may arise a balanced growth within each of the subsystems I and II, but an unbalanced growth between the two subsystems.

Suppose next that there exists at least one positive element in J. Then in the equation

$$\begin{bmatrix} D_I^{(\infty)}(t) \\ D_{II}^{(\infty)}(t) \end{bmatrix} = \begin{bmatrix} H_I & J \\ O & H_{II} \end{bmatrix} \begin{bmatrix} D_I^{(\infty)}(t) \\ D_{II}^{(\infty)}(t) \end{bmatrix}$$

each element of the vector $D_I^{(\infty)}(t)$ is proved to be positive and each element f $D_{II}^{(\infty)}(t)$ zero. We can easily show that each output of all the departments in the system II becomes zero, and that all departments in the system I will grow in balance at the rate given by the weighted sum of r_is over all the departments in the system I.

VII Relations between Marx's and Harrod–Domar's rates of growth

We have shown above that the rate of growth of output is determined by the rate of accumulation and the rate of profit. But Harrod, Domar, and others have recently argued that the rate of growth of the aggregate economy is equal to the average rate of saving divided by the capital coefficient. Then what relations are there between these two rates of growth?

Let $K_{ji}(t)$ be the stock of the jth capital good held by department i at period t, and adopting the idea of Bortkiewicz, 1951, p. 6, assume that there exists the following relations between $K_{ji}(t)$ and $C_{ji}(t)$

$$C_{ji}(t) = \alpha_{ji} K_{ji}(t) \; (j = 1, \ldots, m; i = 1, \ldots, n) \tag{20}$$

where α_{ji} is assumed constant.

If we denote the aggregate output by $Y(t)$, the aggregate capital stock by $K(t)$ and the aggregate investment by $I(t)$, then we have

$$Y(t) = \sum_{i=1}^{n} Y_i(t) \tag{21}$$

$$K(t) = \sum_{j=1}^{m} \sum_{i=1}^{n} K_{ji}(t),$$

$$I(t) = \sum_{j=1}^{m} \sum_{i=1}^{n} \Delta K_{ji}(t) \tag{22}$$

Denoting the aggregate saving by $S(t)$, we may derive from the aggregate equilibrium condition $I(t) = S(t)$ that

$$\frac{I(t)}{\Delta Y(t)} \frac{\Delta Y(t)}{Y(t)} = \frac{S(t)}{Y(t)}$$

Since $I(t)/\Delta Y(t)$ is the capital coefficient v and $S(t)/Y(t)$ is the average rate of saving s, we find immediately

$$\frac{\Delta Y(t)}{Y(t)} = \frac{s}{v}$$

which denotes Harrod–Domar's rate of growth of the aggregate economy.

On the other hand, if we denote the rate of growth of the ith output by R_i we find

$$\Delta Y_i(t) = R_i Y_i(t) \; (i = 1, \ldots, n) \tag{23}$$

Therefore it follows from (21) and (23) that

$$\Delta Y(t) = \sum_{i=1}^{n} R_i Y_i(t) \tag{24}$$

Since from (20)

$$\Delta K_{ji}(t) = \frac{c_{ji}v_i}{\alpha_{ji}} \Delta Y_i(t) = I_{ji}(t)$$

we find

$$I(t) = \sum_{j=1}^{m} \sum_{i=1}^{n} \frac{c_{ji}v_i}{\alpha_{ji}} \Delta Y_i(t)$$

Therefore, taking into account (23), we get

$$I(t) = \sum_{j=1}^{m} \sum_{i=1}^{n} \frac{c_{ji}v_i}{\alpha_{ji}} R_i Y_i(t) \tag{25}$$

Since from (20) and (22)

$$K(t) = \sum_{j=1}^{m} \sum_{i=1}^{n} \frac{c_{ji}v_i}{\alpha_{ji}} Y_i(t) \tag{26}$$

we can easily show that if each of the growth rates of all the departments is the same, i.e., if $R_1 = R_2 = \ldots = R_n = R$, we get from (21), (24), (25), and (26)

$$\frac{\Delta Y(t)}{Y(t)} = R; \; \frac{I(t)}{\Delta Y(t)} = \frac{K(t)}{Y(t)} = v \tag{27}$$

namely, if each of the growth rates of all the departments is the same, that is also equal to the rate of growth of the aggregate economy, and the marginal capital coefficient becomes equal to the average capital coefficient. As $I(t) = S(t)$, we have $I(t)/Y(t) = s$; so in view of (27) we obtain $R = s/v$. Thus we can say that, if all the departments in the economy grow in balance, the Harrod–Domar rate of growth is equal to the Marx rate of growth.

As was shown in this article, if all the departments have the same rate of accumulation and the same rate of profit, or if the demand schedules have the perfect flexibility and the whole system is indecomposable, the whole system will grow in balance. If the demand schedules have the imperfect flexibility and the whole system is indecomposable, the system will *eventually* grow in balance. Thus we can say that if one of these three is the case, the Marx rate becomes equal to the Harrod–Domar rate of growth. Otherwise the Harrod–Domar macroeconomic growth formula disagrees with the corresponding formula derived from Marx's multi-sectoral growth analysis. Nevertheless, it is true that neither Harrod nor Domar examined the conditions under which all sectors in the economy grow at a uniform rate.

Article III
A contribution to the non-linear theory of the trade cycle*

I Introduction

We have already two non-linear models of trade cycles which seek in non-linearities an explanation of the maintenance of trade cycles: that is, the Kaldor–Yasui[1] and the Hicks–Goodwin models.[2] The most controversial of the assumptions underlying these two models are those concerning the determinants of investment decisions. The rate of investment is assumed in the Kaldor–Yasui theory to depend on the level of income (the profit principle) and in the Hicks–Goodwin theory on the rate of change in income (the acceleration principle). But Dr Kalecki's analysis of the correlation between the rate of investment, the level of income, and the rate of change in income shows that a better approximation is obtained if investment is considered as a function, both of the level and of the rate of change in income, than of either of them only.[3] On this basis neither of the Kaldor–Yasui and the Hicks–Goodwin models can claim to be the best representation of actual cycles. In this article we shall be concerned with a more realistic model; namely, a synthesis of our predecessors.

II Assumption

To begin with, we state the Kaldor and the Hicks–Goodwin investment functions in precise terms. First, it is assumed by Dr Kaldor (a) that the rate of investment, I, depends positively on the level of income, Y, and negatively on the stock of capital, K, and (b) that the marginal propensity to invest,

*Published as Morishima, 1958.

[1] N. Kaldor, 1940. A mathematical formulation of Kaldor's graphical theory was first given by T. Yasui. See his article, 1953.

[2] J. R. Hicks, 1950 and R. M. Goodwin, 1951a. In spite of some important differences, both theories may be put in the same class because they both are based on the acceleration principle.

[3] M. Kalecki, 1949–50.

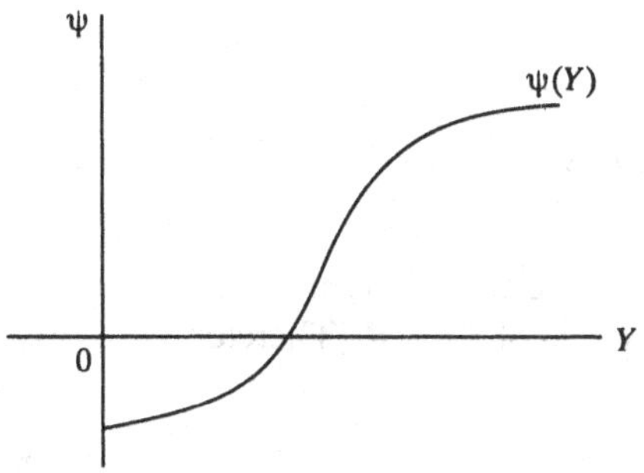

Figure A1

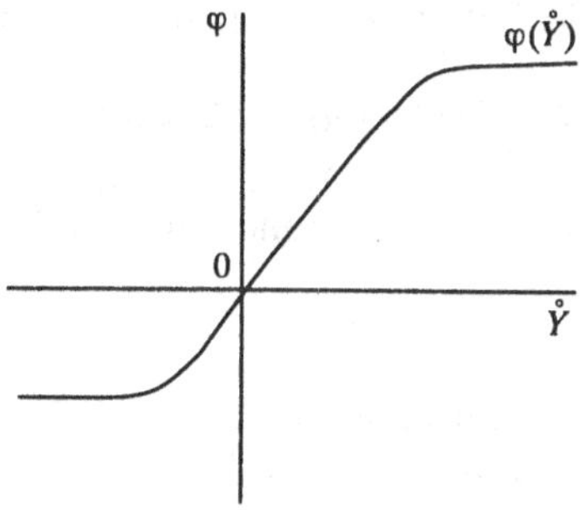

Figure A2

dI/dY, is small, both for low and for high levels of income, relative to its normal level;[4] this type of investment function is formulated by Professor Yasui as:[5]

$$I = \psi(Y) - \mu K$$

where $\psi(Y)$ deviates from linearity in an S-shaped fashion suggested in figure A1, and μ is positive.

Secondly, following Professor Goodwin,[6] we may assume (a) that the rate of investment is proportional to the difference between the ideal quantity of capital, Q, and the actual quantity, K, and (b) that the ideal investment, being the first derivative of the ideal quantity of capital, Q, depends positively on the rate of change in income, $\mathring{Y}$, over some middle range but passes to complete inflexibility at either extreme, as is shown in figure A2.[7] Then we have

[4] Kaldor, 1940. As is well known, this idea of Dr Kaldor is traceable to Dr Kalecki, 1937.
[5] Yasui, 1953.
[6] See R. M. Goodwin, 1948.
[7] See Goodwin, 1951a.

$$I = v(Q - K)\ (v > 0) \tag{1}$$

$$Q' = \phi(Y') \tag{2}$$

Differentiating (1) with respect to t, we obtain

$$K' + \theta I' = \phi(Y')$$

where $\theta = 1/v$. Since $K' = I$, the left-hand side of the above expression is the first two terms of the Taylor expansion of $I(t + \theta)$. Therefore we may say

$$I_{t+\theta} \approx \phi(Y'_t) \tag{3}$$

This expression is nothing else but the Hicks–Goodwin investment function which assumes the non-linear accelerator and the lag between investment decisions and the corresponding outlays.[8] Thus we may regard (1) and (2) as an alternative formulation of the Hicks–Goodwin type of investment function (3).

So far we are concerned with the case of no innovations. Now let L be capital stock required by the innovations. Since L has no negative effect on investment decisions, the Kaldor type of investment function may be reformulated as:[9]

$$I = \psi(Y') - \mu(K - L)$$

and since the ideal or desired stock of capital includes L, the Hicks–Goodwin type of investment function may be rewritten as[10]

$$I = v(Q + L - K),\ Q' = \phi(Y')$$

It is assumed in this article that the rate of investment is a linear combination of the Kaldor–Yasui and the Hicks–Goodwin investment functions; then we get

$$I = a[\psi(Y) - \mu(K - L)] + b[v(Q + L - K)] \tag{4}$$

where a and b are constant and positive.

Next we assume that consumption at time t is a linear function of the level of income at time $t - \tau$; accordingly we have

$$C_t = \alpha Y_{t-\tau} + \beta(t)$$

where $\beta(t)$ is the historically given upward drift of the consumption function. Expanding $Y_{t-\tau}$ in a Taylor series and dropping all but the first two terms of the expansion, we obtain

$$C = \alpha Y - \varepsilon Y' + \beta(t) \tag{5}$$

where $\varepsilon = \alpha\tau$.

[8] Goodwin, 1951a.
[9] Cf. Goodwin, 1951b.
[10] See Goodwin, 1948.

III The fundamental equation of the trade cycle theory

The fundamental equation of non-linear theory of trade cycles will be deduced as follows. Let $l(t)$ be autonomous or innovational investment; of course $l(t)$ is the first derivative of L. Since $Y = C + I + l(t)$, we get from (4) and (5)

$$Y = \alpha Y - \varepsilon Y' + a\psi(Y) + bvQ - (a\mu + bv)(K - L) + \beta(t) + l(t)$$

Differentiating this with respect to t and taking $Q' = \phi(Y')$ into account, we find

$$(1 - \alpha)Y' + \varepsilon Y'' - a\psi'(Y)Y' - bv\phi(Y') + (a\mu + bv)(K' - L')$$
$$= \beta'(t) + l'(t)$$

Because of $K' = I + l(t) = Y - C$ and $L' = l(t)$, this turns into

$$\varepsilon Y'' + [a\{\varepsilon\mu + (1 - \alpha) - \psi'(Y)\} + b\{\varepsilon v + (1 - \alpha)(1 - a)/b$$
$$- v\phi(Y')/Y'\}]Y' + (a\mu + bv)\{(1 - \alpha)Y - \beta(t) - l(t)\}$$
$$= \beta'(t) + l'(t)$$

For the moment we may take $\beta(t)$ and $l(t)$ to be constants, β^* and l^*, hence $\beta'(t)$ and $l'(t)$ are zeros. Then we may study deviations from the equilibrium income, $Y^* = (\beta^* + l^*)/(1 - \alpha)$, by substituting $z = Y - Y^*$, which gives[11]

$$\begin{aligned} &\varepsilon z'' + [a\{\varepsilon\mu + (1 - \alpha) - f'(z)\} \\ &+ b\{\varepsilon v + (1 - \alpha)(1 - a)/b - v\phi(z')/z'\}]z' \\ &+ (a\mu + bv)(1 - \alpha)z = 0 \end{aligned} \tag{6}$$

where $f(z) = \psi(Y) - \psi(Y^*)$. The equation (6) includes as special cases the Kaldor–Yasui and the Hicks–Goodwin equations; namely, if $a = 1$ and $b = 0$, (6) reduces to the former[12]

$$\varepsilon z'' + [\varepsilon\mu + (1 - \alpha) - f'(z)]z' + (1 - \alpha)\mu z = 0 \tag{7}$$

while, if $a = 0$ and $b = 1$, to the latter[13]

$$\varepsilon\theta z'' + [\varepsilon + (1 - \alpha)\theta - \phi(z')/z']z' + (1 - \alpha)z = 0 \tag{8}$$

[11] Dr Ichimura has tried to integrate the Kaldor and the Hicks–Goodwin theories and obtained a non-linear differential equation of the third order. He has offered a qualitative description by which one would expect periodic solutions of his equation. In any case, however, a mere qualitative discussion does not establish the existence of limit cycles at all. Cf. Ichimura, 1955, pp. 220–3.

[12] Professor Yasui states the Kaldor model in terms of gross investment and gross saving, whereas we use net aggregates only. His equation reads

$$\varepsilon z'' + [\varepsilon(\mu + \delta) + (1 - \alpha) - f'(z)]z' + (1 - \alpha)(\mu + \delta)z - \delta f(z) = 0$$

where δ is the ratio of the replacement investment to the existing capital stock. Putting $\delta = 0$, the above expression reduces to (7).

[13] Goodwin, 1951a.

where $\theta = 1/v$. These two equations are important and well known in the fields of physics and engineering; (7) is investigated in detail by van der Pol and (8) by Rayleigh. If $f'(z)$ is greater or less than $\varepsilon\mu + (1 - \alpha)$ according to whether $|z|$ is small or large, the equation (7) describes relaxation oscillations of the van der Pol type; similarly, if $\phi(z')/z'$ is greater or less than $\varepsilon + (1 - \alpha)\theta$ according to whether $|z'|$ is small or large, the equation (8) possesses periodic solutions of the Rayleigh type.[14]

Now let

$$m = \sqrt{(a\mu + bv)(1 - \alpha)/\varepsilon}$$
$$x = mz$$

and

$$t_1 = mt$$

Since $x' = dx/dt_1 = z'$ and $x'' = d^2x/dt_1^2 = z''/m$, the equation (6) can be written

$$x'' + [aF(x) + bG(x')]x' + x = 0 \tag{9}$$

where

$$F(x) = \{\varepsilon\mu + (1 - \alpha) - f'(x/m)\}/(\varepsilon m)$$
$$G(x') = \{\varepsilon v + (1 - \alpha) - v\phi(x')/x'\}/(\varepsilon m)$$

The equation (9) may be regarded as *the fundamental equation of non-linear theory of the trade cycle.*

IV The existence of cyclic solutions

Levinson and Smith have proved[15]

Theorem 1

The equation (9) *has at least one periodic solution if the following conditions are satisfied*:

(i) $aF(0) + bG(0) < 0$,
(ii) *there exists an* $M > 0$ *such that*

$$aF(x) + bG(x') \geqq -M \tag{10}$$

[14] By differentiating (8) with respect to t, the Rayleigh equation (8) is transformed into the van der Pol equation

$$\varepsilon\theta u'' + [\varepsilon + (1 - \alpha)\theta - \phi'(u)]u' + (1 - \alpha)u = 0$$

where $u = z'$. Thus the rate of change in income, u, in the Hicks–Goodwin model shows the same kind of oscillations as the level of income, z, in the Kaldor model.

[15] N. Levinson and O. K. Smith, 1942.

(iii) *there exists some* $x_0 > 0$ *such that* $aF(x) + bG(x') \geqq 0$ *for* $|x| \geqq x_0$,
(iv) *there exists some* $x_1 > x_0$ *such that*

$$\int_{x^0}^{x^1} [aF(x) + bG(x')]dx \geqq 10Mx_0$$

where $x' > 0$ *is an arbitrary decreasing positive function of* x *in the integration.*

As we shall prove in the next section, we have another theorem which is applicable to the converse case: that is,

Theorem 2

Let the requirements (i) *and* (ii) *of theorem 1 be satisfied. Moreover let there exist some* $x'_0 > 0$ *and some* $\delta_0 > 0$ *such that for* $x' \geqq x'_0$

$$aF(x) + bG(x') \geqq \delta_0 \tag{11}$$

Finally, let there exist some $x'_1 < 0$ *such that for* $x' \leqq x'_1$

$$aF(x) + bG(x') \geqq 0 \tag{12}$$

Under these conditions (9) *has at least one periodic solution.*

Let us assume therewith that, as in the Kaldor–Yasui model (7), the marginal propensity to invest, $f'(z)$, is greater or less than $\varepsilon\mu + (1 - \alpha)$ according to whether $|z|$ is small or large; and that, as in the Hicks–Goodwin model (8), the accelerator, $v\phi(z')/z'$, is greater or less than $\varepsilon v + (1 - \alpha)$ according to whether $|z'|$ is small or large. Then Theorem 1 is applicable to equation (9) if a/b is larger than some $(a/b)_0$, while Theorem 2 is if it is less than $(a/b)_1$. If $(a/b)_1 \geqq (a/b)_0$, Theorem 1 and/or Theorem 2 apply to every case. Hence the equation (9) possesses periodic solutions for any value of a/b. If $(a/b)_1 < (a/b)_0$, neither of our theorems is applicable to that case in which $(a/b)_1 < (a/b) < (a/b)_0$: to the writer's knowledge, there does not seem to be any established theorem which is true of the case $(a/b)_1 < (a/b) < (a/b)_0$.

Anyhow the equation (9) includes as extreme cases both the van der Pol equation (7) and the Rayleigh equation (8); thereby it is justified to call (9) a generalized equation for relaxation oscillations. Thus our model of the trade cycle may be regarded as a synthesis of the Kaldor–Yasui and the Hicks–Goodwin models.

V Proof of theorem 2

Since Levinson and Smith have proved Theorem 1, we shall demonstrate Theorem 2 only. The equation (9) can be written as a pair of first-order equations

$$dx/dt = v,\ dv/dt = -(aF(x) + bG(v))v - x \tag{13}$$

We introduce

$$\lambda(x, v) = x^2 + v^2$$

Clearly

$$\frac{d\lambda}{dt} = 2\left(x\frac{dx}{dt} + v\frac{dv}{dt}\right)$$

Or, using (13), this becomes

$$d\lambda/dt = -2v^2(aF(x) + bG(v))$$

If $aF(x) + bG(v) > 0$, then as t increases the integral curves of (13) in the (x, v)-plane cut inward across the circles $\lambda(x,v) = c$, while if $aF(x) + bG(v) < 0$ the integral curves cut outward across $\lambda(x, v) = c$. When $v > 0, x$ increases as t increases whereas, when $v < 0, x$ decreases as t increases. The slope of the integral curves sketched in figure A3 comes from the equation

$$dv/dx = -(aF(x) + bG(v)) - x/v \tag{14}$$

which follows from (13). Note that, since $aF(0) + bG(0) < 0$, around the origin the integral curves cut outward across $\lambda(x, v) = c$. Two dotted curves in figure A3 are the upper and lower boundaries of the domain in which $aF(x) + bG(v) < 0$.

From figure A3 we find that the solution of (13) which starts at the point $P_0(x_0, v_0)$ has the form sketched in figure A4. Let $\lambda(x_0, v_0) = \lambda_0$; $\lambda(x_1, 0) = \lambda_1$; $\lambda(x_2, v_1) = \lambda_2$; $\lambda(x_3, v_1) = \lambda_3$; $\lambda(x_4, 0) = \lambda_4$; $\lambda(x_5, v_0) = \lambda_5$; $\lambda(x_6, v_0) = \lambda_6$. Integrating

$$d\lambda/dx = -2v(aF(x) + bG(v)) \tag{15}$$

along the integral curve from $P_0(x_0, v_0)$ to $P_1(x_1, 0)$, it follows that

$$\lambda_1 - \lambda_0 = -2\int_{x_0}^{x_1} v(aF(x) + bG(v))dx$$

Taking (10) into account, we have

$$\lambda_1 - \lambda_0 \leqq 2M\int_{x_0}^{x_1} v dx \leqq 2M(x_1 - x_0)v_0 \tag{16}$$

Similarly, we obtain

$$\lambda_2 - \lambda_1 = -2\int_{x_1}^{x_2} v(aF(x) + bG(v))dx$$

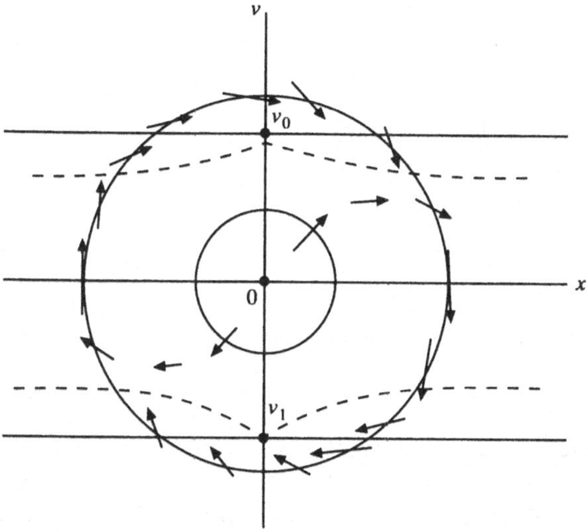

Figure A3

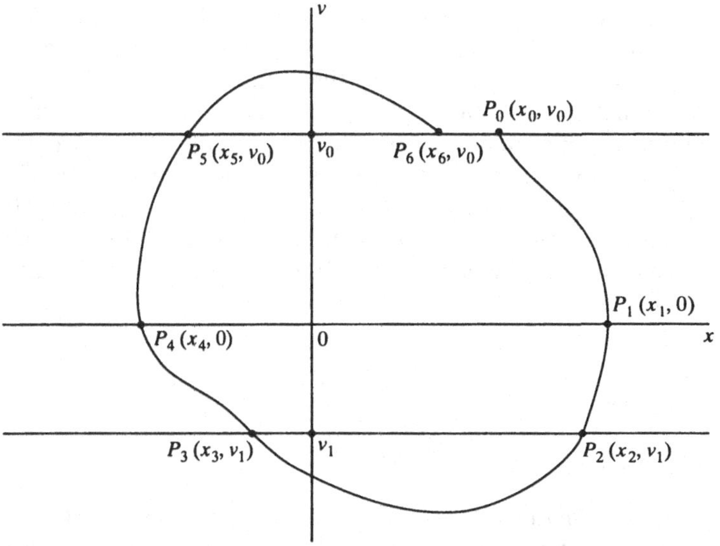

Figure A4

$$\leqq 2M \int_{x_2}^{x_1} (-v)dx \leqq 2M(x_2 - x_1)v_1 \tag{17}$$

$$\lambda_4 - \lambda_3 \leqq 2M(x_4 - x_3)v_1 \tag{18}$$

$$\lambda_5 - \lambda_4 \leqq 2M(x_5 - x_4)v_0 \tag{19}$$

Integrating (15) from P_2 to P_3

$$\lambda_3 - \lambda_2 = -2\int_{x_2}^{x_3} v(aF(x) + bG(v))dx$$

By (12) we find

$$\lambda_3 - \lambda_2 \leqq 0 \tag{20}$$

Finally, taking (11) into account, we obtain

$$\lambda_6 - \lambda_5 \leqq -2\delta_0(x_6 - x_5)v_0 \tag{21}$$

Now we can easily prove that if x_0 increases, then x_1, x_2, and x_6 increase and x_3, x_4, and x_5 decrease. It can also be proved that if x_0 is sufficiently large, then the differences $x_1 - x_0$, $x_1 - x_2$, $x_3 - x_4$, and $x_5 - x_4$ become sufficiently small; because it follows from (14) that if $|x_0|$, $|x_2|$, $|x_3|$, and $|x_5|$ are sufficiently large, the integral curve slopes very steeply at the points P_0, P_2, P_3, and P_5. Hence from (16) ~ (21) we find that $\lambda_0 > \lambda_6$ when x_0 is sufficiently large. Therefore P_6 lies to the left of P_0 as is shown in figure A4.

We now denote by R the region which is bounded on the outside by $P_0P_1P_2P_3P_4P_5P_6P_0$, and on the inside by the circle $\lambda(x, v) = r^2$, where r is chosen so small that in the interior of $\lambda(x, v) = r^2$, $aF(x) + bG(v)$ is negative. Then we can prove that no integral curve which starts in R will ever leave R as t increases; we can also prove that there is no singular point in R. (In equations (13) the only singular point in (x, v)-plane is $(0, 0)$. For dx/dt vanishes only if $v = 0$; once $v = 0$, dv/dt is zero only at $x = 0$.) Hence the region R satisfies the requirements of the following theorem of Bendixson:[16]

Theorem
If an integral curve of

$$dx/dt = X(x, y),\ dy/dt = Y(x, y)$$

lies in a finite region R for $t \to \infty$ and if there are no singular points in R, then the integral curve is either a closed curve or else it approaches nearer and nearer to a closed integral curve.

Therefore (9) has a least one closed integral curve which lies in R.

[16] Ivar Bendixson, 1901.

VI Another theorem for consolidating Kaldor–Yasui (van der Pol) and Hicks–Goodwin (Rayleigh) theories of oscillations

As far as we adopt the above approach, we have to show that the set of values of the ratio b/a for which Theorem 1 holds overlaps the corresponding set for Theorem 2, in order to establish the existence of limit cycles for the mixed van der Pol–Rayleigh equation. This is a hard task to be accomplished. In the following we take up an alternative approach, not pursuing the way developed by Levinson and Smith, but starting directly from the fundamental equation (9) above. We assume

(i′) $aF(0) + bG(0) < 0$.
(ii′) For all x there is an $\dot{x}_0$ such that

$$aF(x) + bG(\dot{x}) > 0 \text{ for all } |\dot{x}| \geqq |\dot{x}_0|.$$

(iii′) For all $\dot{x}$ there is an x_1 such that

$$aF(x) + bG(\dot{x}) > 0 \text{ for all } |x| \geqq |x_1|.$$

Comparing these with the assumptions made by Levinson and Smith, (i′) is the same as their (i), (ii′) is stronger than (ii), because the former restricts the values of the slope of the S-shaped investment function, $f'(xm)$, in the neighbourhood of the origin more severely than the latter does. On the other hand the restriction by (iii′) is only slightly stronger than that by (iii). But the following theorem is entirely free from their assumption (iv).

Theorem 3

The equation (9) *has at least one periodic solution, if* (i′), (ii′), *and* (iii′) *are all fulfilled.*

Proof: Consider a rectangular set of points $(x, \dot{x})$ with x's in the interval $[-x_1, x_1]$ and $\dot{x}$'s in $[-\dot{x}_0, \dot{x}_0]$. The equation (9) can be written in terms of two first-order equations (13). In the same way as we have derived from (13) in the proof of Theorem 2, we get

$$\frac{d\lambda}{dt} = -2v^2[aF(x) + bG(v)]$$

where $v = \dot{x}$. Therefore, it follows from (ii′) and (iii′) that $d\lambda/dt < 0$ in the outside of the rectangle as well as on its edge.

We now remove from the rectangle a small circle $\lambda(x, v) = r^2$, such that $aF(x) + bG(v) < 0$ for all x and v fulfilling $x^2 + v^2 \leqq r^2$, where r is a sufficiently small number. We denote the remaining part of the rectangle by R. As $d\lambda/dt > 0$ on the edge of the circle and $d\lambda/dt < 0$ on the edge of the

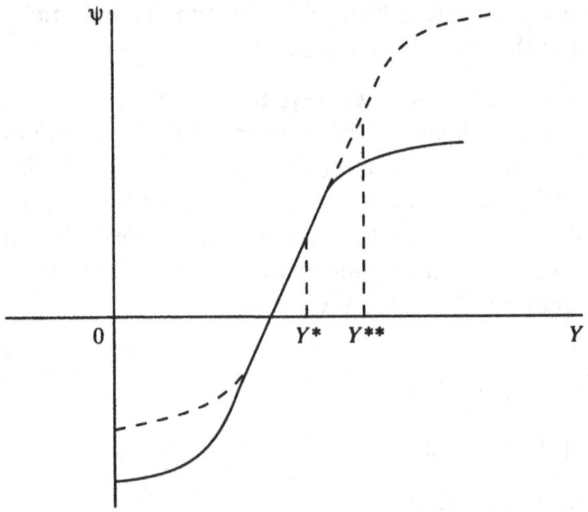

Figure A5

rectangle, no integral curve starting from any point in R will ever leave it as t increases. Also it is evident that there is no singular point in R. Hence by applying the Bendixson theorem we find that there is a limit cycle in R.

VII Oscillation and growth

So far we have been concerned with the pure trade cycle on the assumption that the autonomous outlays β and l are constant. An increase in $\beta^* + l^*$ to $\beta^{**} + l^{**}$ gives rise to an increase in the equilibrium income, Y^*, to Y^{**}. If Y^{**} is sufficiently large, the derivative of $\psi(Y)$ at the point Y^{**} may be so small as to make $F(0)$ positive. If a $F(0) + bG(0)$ is also positive, the requirement (i) of theorem 1 and of theorem 2 is not satisfied after the increase in $\beta + l$.

But we can avoid this difficulty by assuming[17] that an increase in autonomous outlays will enrich investment opportunities and, therefore, will push up both the ceiling and the floor of the function $\psi(Y)$ (see figure A5). After the upward shift of the ceiling of $\psi(Y)$ the derivative of $\psi(Y)$ at the point Y^{**} will be so large as to make $F(0)$ remain negative; accordingly the requirement (i) is satisfied. If the remaining requirements of the theorems are also satisfied, there exists at least one limit cycle after the increase in $\beta + l$.

[17] Professor Yasui assumes that innovations push up the ceiling of the Kaldor investment function. T. Yasui, 1954.

In a progressive society in which an increase in the autonomous outlays pushes up the ceiling and the floor of $\psi(Y)$, the origin for x and the limit cycle will shift to the right. It can be shown that the moving origin (or the shifting equilibrium point) will be followed by the limit cycle in a complicated spiral to the right so long as the shifting to the right is not too rapid.[18] Thus we obtain cyclical growth of income.

[18] Cf. Goodwin, 1951a.

Article IV
Stability, oscillations, and chaos*

1 When I was writing the original Japanese version of *DKR*, there was no work which used computers to solve differential equations, though just after its publication I saw Morehouse, Strotz, and Horwitz, 1950 in *Econometrica*, a report of an application of an analogue-computer to an inventory oscillation model. Economists' works were mainly confined to linear models, especially when they were concerned with systems containing many economic variables. At that time already, we knew basic mathematical properties concerning the stability of equilibrium, the existence of limit cycles, their stability and instability, and so on, which are valid for a fairly large class of non-linear systems. Once they are applied to general equilibrium models, however, they are not very fruitful. We have to be satisfied with rather limited analyses, as chapter 4 above evidences.

In my 1977 work, however, I have developed a simultaneous difference equation version of the model of tatonnement, which may be regarded as the prototype of the work discussed below in this article. The general equilibrium point of the economy is found to be a fixed point of the tatonnement process in terms of these difference equations. I have also observed that the model may have cyclic solutions, which are reduced to fixed points of the vertically integrated model if k elementary periods, where k stands for the period of the cycle, are aggregated into one period. We may refer to such points as fixed points of order k. Each of the k points on the course of one cycle forms a fixed point of order k, so that there are k connected fixed points belonging to one family.

Suppose a cycle of order k is globally stable. Then each fixed point on the course of the cycle is found to be an attracting periodic point (an attractor) in the terminology of the theory of chaos. Thus the picture obtained by plotting the last part of the sequence of tatonnement prices calculated by

* I wish to acknowledge the kind cooperation of Dr Ayumu Yasutomi of Kyoto University, especially in preparing figures A6, A7, A8.

the computer lists fixed points of order k only, with some remaining 'transient' points. The orbit diagram does not show any other fixed point. It is seen as if it does not exist. In this way I have obtained an attracting eight-period orbit (Morishima, 1977, p. 43).

The picture depends on the parameters of the model. In our case, they are the slope of the excess demand function, 1/a, the price flexibility, v, and the length of the elementary period h, as will be seen below. As the last two always appear in the form of a product, the essential parameters are two, a and $b = vh$. Our model which is non-linear may be structurally unstable with respect to either of the parameters. Therefore, if it changes, the picture may change drastically. As the following sections show, the eight-period attracting orbit may suddenly change into a sixteen-period or a four-period orbit if parameter a or b changes slightly. Moreover a slight movement of a parameter may generate chaotic behaviour of prices. It is chaotic in the sense that the movement is unpredictable and points on the orbit fill out an interval of the range of possible values of prices. However, such chaotic behaviour may suddenly disappear at a certain critical value of the parameter, because the model is structurally unstable there.

Chaos is an intrinsic phenomenon due to non-linearlity of the equation. But the diagram of a chaotic behaviour is drawn by use of a computer. As I have used a highly accurate computer, the results I have obtained are generally reliable. However, the results visualized by the use of a computer have to be carefully checked against the true results that would be obtained by the ideal computer with no inaccuracy. Unfortunately such an ideal computer is not available; any actual computer that we may use has its own limit of precision. This is a situation physicists often meet. The reality is always distorted by the tool they use. I cannot deal with this problem in this article properly and extensively; section 5 below merely shows how important it is to have a very accurate computer in the case of examining fluctuations around an unstable or structurally unstable equilibrium point.

2 Let us first summarize the procedure which enabled me to put the price adjustment equation in the form that I used in my work (1977)

$$q_j(t+h) = \frac{\max[q_j(t) + vhE_j(t), 0]}{\Sigma \max[q_k(t) + vhE_k(t), 0]}, j = 1, \ldots, n \tag{1}$$

where t is not the calendar time but a tatonnement time beginning at 0 and approaching infinity in each 'week'; h is time interval required for one round of tatonnement; the price adjustment factor is proportional to the length of the adjustment interval, so we may write the factor as vh. $q_j(t)$ is the price of j in terms of the composite commodity made up of one unit of every existing commodity, that is

$$q_j(t) = \frac{p_j(t)}{\Sigma p_i(t)}$$

where $p_k(t)$ is the price of j in terms of a certain arbitrarily chosen numeraire. To obtain (1) we assume that $p_k(t)$ is adjusted according to

$$p_k(t+h) = \max[p_k(t) + vh(\Sigma p_i(t))E_k(t), 0] \tag{2}$$

This equation differs from the corresponding one, $\dot{p}_k = F_k(E_k)$, in the text,[1] because (2) implies that the price adjustment depends not only on $E_k(t)$ but also the price level $(\Sigma p_i(t))$, while it is taken as being dependent solely on $E_k(t)$ in the text. This alteration is due to the consideration that if a unit of excess demand induces a price increase of v pence at the level of £100, so that we have either $\dot{p}_j = v(\Sigma p_i(t))E_j(t)$ or (2). From

$$\frac{p_j(t+h)}{\Sigma p_i(t)} = \max[q_j(t) + vhE_j(t), 0], \text{ for all } j = 1, \ldots, n$$

and

$$q_j(t+h)\left(\frac{\Sigma p_k(t+h)}{\Sigma p_i(t)}\right) = \max[q_j(t) + vhE_j(t), 0], \text{ for all } j$$

we obtain adjustment equations in terms of normalized prices q_js in the following form

$$q_j(t+h) = \frac{\max[q_j(t) + vhE_j(q(t)), 0]}{\Sigma \max[q_k(t) + vhE_k(q(t)), 0]} \tag{3}$$

where $q(t) = (q_1(t), \ldots, q_n(t))$.

Next we assume throughout the following that there are only two commodities, 1 and 2. Excess demand for commodity 1 is linear in terms of normalized prices q_1 and q_2

$$E_1 = -q_1 + \frac{1}{a}q_2 \tag{4}$$

Then, we have, in view of Walras' law

$$E_2 = -\frac{q_1}{q_2}\left(-q_1 + \frac{1}{a}q_2\right) \tag{5}$$

[1] To avoid that $p_k(t)$ becomes negative $F_k(E_k)$ is more precisely defined as

$$F_k(E_k) = \begin{cases} vE_k(p) & \text{if } p_k > 0, \\ \max[vE_k(p), 0] & \text{if } p_k = 0 \end{cases}$$

We then obtain equilibrium prices q_1^* and q_2^*

$$q_1^* = \frac{1}{1+a},$$

$$q_2^* = \frac{a}{1+a}$$

Therefore, we have

$$q_1^* E_1 + q_2^* E_2 = \frac{1}{a(1+a)} \frac{[1-(1+a)q_1]^2}{1-q_1} > 0 \text{ for } a > 0 \tag{6}$$

for all non-negative values of q_1, less than one. This means that the weak axiom of revealed preference holds between equilibrium price set (q_1^*, q_2^*) and any other set of normalized prices (q_1, q_2).

Where E_1 and E_2 are specified as (4) and (5), the adjustment function (3) for $j = 1$ and $n = 2$ may be written as

$$q(t+h) = \frac{A(t)}{A(t) + B(t)} \tag{7}$$

where

$$A(t) = \max\left[\frac{a}{b} q(t) + (1 - (1+a)q(t)), 0\right]$$

$$B(t) = \max\left[(1 - q(t))\left\{\frac{a}{b} - \frac{q(t)}{(1-q(t))^2}(1 - (1+a)q(t))\right\}, 0\right]$$

Note that in these q stands for q_1 and b for vh for simplicity.

Taking a and b as constant and using (7) as the formula for iteration, we can calculate numerically values of $q(h), q(2h), q(3h), \ldots$ starting from the initial value $q(0)$ specified arbitrarily. Putting $a = 0.6$ and $b = 1$, Morishima (1977) has shown that the economy has the fixed point of order 1, $q^* = 5/8$, as the equilibrium price and one of the fixed point of order 2, $q^* = 1/4$, from which a limit cycle of order 2, $q(0) = 1/4, q(h) = 3/4, q(2h) = 1/4, \ldots$ is generated. It has also shown that both of the equilibrium point and the two-period cycle are unstable; in fact, paths starting from within a small neighbourhood of either of them diverge from them and approach a limit cycle of order 8.[2] Between these two- and eight-period cycles, we can show that there exists a four-period cycle which is also unstable. All these are due to the normalization of prices which makes the system (that is otherwise linear) non-linear. I have furthermore pointed out that, as has been

[2] See Morishima, 1977, p. 42.

observed in the above mentioned book, the differential equation version of (3) is always stable because the weak axiom of revealed preference (6) is assumed. All these will be more systematically explained below.

3 In spite of these observations and the finding of the concepts, such as fixed points of various (higher) orders, and the structural instability that has appeared even in *DKR*, I was unable, at the time of writing my 1977 book, to connect the above argument with the theory of chaos.[3] It is true that for the parameter combination, $(a, b) = (0.6, 1)$, the sequence of $q(t)$ generated by (7) does not trace out any chaotic movement. But we obtain a more general picture systematically showing the results of repeated calculations of $q(t)$ by varying the values of one of the parameters, a and b.

First, fixing a at 0.6 and varying b from 0 to 2 we obtain the orbit diagram of $q(t)$ of (7) with b plotted horizontally. (See figure A6.) This is a picture of the asymptotic behaviour of $q(t)$ for a variety of different values of b. For each b we compute the first 25,000 values generated by the iteration formula (7) for the same b. We only plot the last 5,000 on the diagram whose vertical coordinate measures the value of $q(t)$ in the normalized price interval [0, 1]; thus the early transient behaviour is not recorded. The bifurcation diagram for (7) obtained shows that $q(t)$ eventually traces out an eight-period cycle. In fact we have eight points on the vertical line through $b = 1$, $q(t)$ visiting these points repeatedly in a certain definite order.

With b being small $q(t)$ converges on a single point which is the equilibrium point, $q^* = 5/8$; for b in a middle range we have a two-period cycle, then a four-period cycle, and then an eight-period cycle. This clearly shows that (7) undergoes a series of period-doublings as b increases. However, for still more greater bs, $q(t)$ traces out a four-period cycle[4] and then a two-period cycle. For further greater values of b, the fraction a/b becomes insignificant in the formulas $A(t)$ and $B(t)$. Wherever $q(0)$ is set such that $(1 + a)q(0) < 1$, we obtain from (7) $q(h) = 1$, so that $(1 + a)q(h) > 1$. Then we get $q(2h) = 0$, which yields $q(3h) = b/(a + b)$. Afterwards we have $q(4h) = 0$, $q(5h) = b/(a + b)$, and so on. Similarly, where $q(0)$ is set such that $(1 + a)q(0) > 1$, we obtain the sequence, $q(h) = 0$, $q(2h) = b/(a + b)$, $q(3h) = 0, \ldots$. In any case we get a two-period cycle having $b/(a + b)$ and 0 as the peak and the trough. In the event of b tending to infinity the sequence oscillates between the maximum and the minimum value of $q(t)$, 1 and 0.

These observations enable us to derive the following three conclusions. (i)

[3] I did not know, at that time, even the now standard literature, Li, T. Y. and Yorke, J. A., 1975, which is followed by Baumol, W. J. and Benhabib, J., 1989, Devaney, R. L., 1989 and Goodwin, R. M., 1990 among many others.

[4] For b in the interval (1.18, 1.76), note that the fourth fixed point of the cycle is $q(t) = 0$.

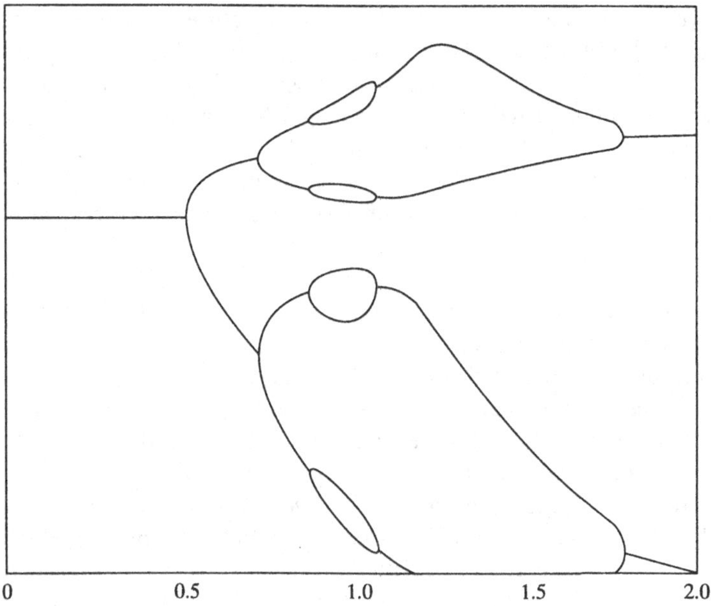

Figure A6 The orbit diagram of $q(t)$ with $0 < b < 2.0$ plotted horizontally but a fixed at 0.6

As the parameter b increases, the sequence of the price $q(t)$ generated by (7) first undergoes a series of period-doublings which later turns to a series of period-halvings. (ii) Where b is sufficiently small, the sequence $q(t)$ converges to the equilibrium value as the excess demand functions fulfil the weak axiom of revealed preference between the equilibrium price set and any other set of prices. (This is consistent with the result already obtained for the differential equation system; in fact, it may be regarded as the limiting case of (7) with h tending to 0.) Finally (iii) on the limit of b tending to infinity $q(t)$ follows a path of a two-period cycle swinging between the two extreme values of q, that is, 1 and 0. (This is not surprising at all but almost self-evident. With h being fixed, infinitely large b implies infinitely large v. If $q(0)$ is set below the equilibrium value, E_1 is positive, so that we have a big increase in q because it is infinitely sensitive to a positive excess demand E_1; thus q hits at its ceiling, $q = 1$. Conversely, if $q(0)$ is set above the equilibrium value, we obtain a big fall in q, reaching its floor, $q = 0$. It is thus seen that an extreme price flexibility creates instability, whereas it is known that a moderate one serves as a stabilizer.) From these results we see that no chaotic movement of $q(t)$ arises for any value of b as far as parameter a is set at 0.6.

Similar to figure A6, figure A7 measures b along the horizontal axis, but the value of a is set at 0.5. Comparing these two figures it is immediately suggested that there must be a big change in the structure of the model, i.e., structural instability, while a is in the interval $(0.5, 0.6)$. Within the bands which are darkened by numerous dots we observe chaotic behaviour of prices as will be explained in the next section regarding figure A8. Next to the bands we see an area in which a few smears of dots only are visible. In this area the 'max' operation applied to $A(t)$ or $B(t)$ is effective, so that $q(t+h)$ takes on the value 1 (the ceiling) or 0 (the floor); there is no attractor between them.

4 Next we fix b at 1 and change a from 0 to 2. We have figure A8; its horizontal axis measures the value of a, while the vertical axis shows the calculated value of $q(t)$. It is easily observed that as parameter a changes, $q(t)$ undergoes a sequence of period-halving bifurcations. The vertical line through the point of $a = 0.6$ cuts the 'windows' of the orbit diagram eight times; this means, as has been explained in the previous section, that the path generated by (7) converges to an eight-period cycle at $b = 1$, if a is set at 0.6. By magnifying the diagram we find that there are eight small windows which are on the left-hand side of the vertical line through $a = 0.6$ but very close to it. That is to say, for a in the interval $(0.5909, 0.5952)$, $q(t)$ traces a sixteen-period cycle.

As has been seen in section 3 above, period-doubling or halving bifurcations do not necessarily lead to chaotic phenomena, but in this case of b fixed at 1 and a changed, chaotic behaviour of $q(t)$ may arise after the period-doubling or -halving regime is terminated. For smaller values of a but above 0.5, we have a band in which dots representing the results of computation of $q(t)$ are scattered at various heights. Let V_a be an area corresponding to a given value, a, of abscissa of figure A8 that is darkened by scattered dots. Although it is difficult to determine whether these dots really represent chaotic behaviour, it is highly probable that they satisfy the following conditions of chaotic movement. (i) The $q(t)$ of (7) is 'topologically transitive' in V_a in the sense that $q(t)$ initiating at an arbitrary point in the set $[0, 1]$ becomes very near, at some point in time, to any point in V_a. (ii) The $q(t)$ has the property of 'sensitive dependence' on initial conditions, in the sense that two dynamic paths starting from two close initial positions, however close they may be, will eventually be separated from each other by at least some positive distance during the course of iteration.

If these two conditions are fulfilled, the sequence of dots traced out in V_a is unpredictable. Because of the sensitive dependence on initial conditions two paths which are very close at the start will later diverge substantially, so that the future cannot be predicted from the initial state of affairs. Also, because of the topological transitivity, the path from an initial point will visit every point in V_a sooner or later. However, in the case of $q(t)$ being not

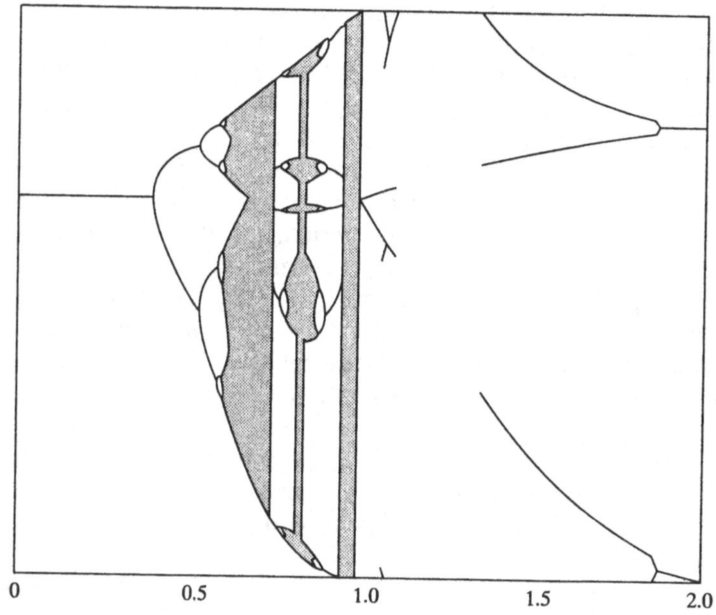

Figure A7 The orbit diagram of $q(t)$ with $0 < b < 2.0$ plotted horizontally but a fixed at 0.5

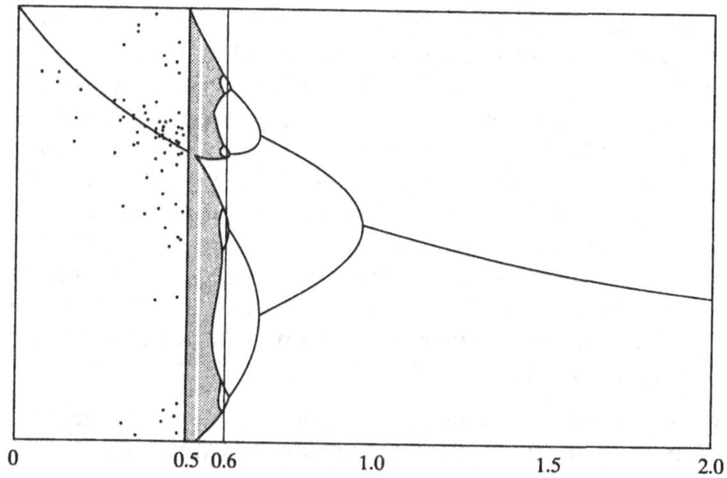

Figure A8 The orbit diagram of $q(t)$ with $0 < a < 2.0$ plotted horizontally but b fixed at 1

topologically transitive over the whole region of V_a, $q(t)$ may never visit some part of V_a; thus V_a contains a blank range with no dot plotted. The path leaps over this range and moves from either side of the range to the other. Even though V_a is separated by the range into two parts, they are stitched together by the thread connecting points $q(t), t = 0, h, 2h, \ldots$.

Through the left quarter part of figure A8 runs a tail of the bifurcation diagram rising from right to left. In association with any a in the part, there is a point on the tail which represents the equilibrium price that corresponds to a, that is $q^* = 1/(1 + a)$. Similarly, through the right half of the figure A8 set is an 'antenna', points on which represent equilibria corresponding to as. Dots that are off the tail in the left quarter of the figure are transient dots, which appear on the way towards respective equilibrium points. In any case figure A8 reveals that the equilibrium is stable for both very small and very large as as long as b is set at 1.

But the nature of stability is entirely different between these two areas. First in the left quarter, the equilibrium point is unstable in the small, so that $q(t)$ having started from a point in a neighbourhood of the equilibrium point diverges from it and finally hits, say at t, the ceiling, $q(t) = 1$. Then, in the next period, $q(t + h)$ takes on the value 0, because $A(t)$ and $B(t) = \infty$. (Note that b is fixed at 1.) Where $q(t + h) = 0$, we have $A(t + h) = 1$ and $B(t + h) = a$. Hence $q(t + 2h) = 1/(1 + a)$, which is the equilibrium point corresponding to a.[5] It is at once seen from the above that the factor which eventually stabilizes the path $q(t)$ so far diverging from the equilibrium point is the 'max' operations which the terms A and B must subject themselves to. On the other hand, equilibria standing side by side on the 'antenna' in the right half of figure A8 have all local stability; $q(t)$ which has been initiated with a point in the region [0, 1] converges to respective equilibria which correspond to specified values of a, with hitting neither ceiling nor floor during the course.

As figures A7 and A8 show, the darkened area within which the price $q(t)$ moves about in a chaotic manner does not usually stretch itself over the whole price domain [0, 1] but limits itself in a certain proper subset S in it. This means that the price movement eventually settles in S, though it endlessly fluctuates within S. Thus as all the paths converge to the region S, it may be said to be stable. In this way the concept of stability of a point (an equilibrium point) is extended to the one of stability of a region, in non-linear systems by means of the theory of chaos.

5 Finally, I show that the computer that is used for depicting the orbit diagram of, for example, tatonnement movement of prices may present sheer

[5] $q(t)$ may directly reach the floor 0 without hitting the ceiling 1. Then at the end of the next round of tatonnement $q(t)$ of course settles at the equilibrium price.

illusions as if they are new fact findings. Consider the price adjustment mechanism which has one and only one fixed point of order 1, say, $q^* = 0.65162$. Suppose it is unstable.

Also now suppose there are three types of computer available: (1) accurate, (2) approximate, and (3) rough. Let us assume that the initial price $q(0)$ for iteration is given at 0.65162 exactly. The economist who uses the computer 'accurate' at once finds that it is the fixed point. However, the one who uses the computer 'approximate' or 'rough' takes the initial price as 0.6516 or 0.652 respectively, because the former can only calculate down to the fourth decimal place, while the latter only to the third place. As 0.6516 is below the fixed point, the economist who uses the 'approximate' obtains an orbit diverging downwards, while the user of the 'rough' will get an orbit diverging upwards. We thus acquire three different orbit diagrams by three different kinds of computer. The first plots only one dot that is the fixed point. The second and third plot many dots below and above the fixed point, respectively. Only the first is free from error; it gives us exactly what should be obtained from the model. On the other hand, the phenomena of divergence should not have happened within the framework of this model when the initial position of the price were set at 0.65162 exactly. They are illusions created by the inaccuracy of the computer. Moreover, they illustrate that different illusions may be obtained according as computers are different in accuracy.

This example suggests that the orbit diagrams obtained by the use of computer must be carefully examined. Any computer has its own limited precision. Especially, at the point where the model is structurally unstable, the path generated from the model may be radically wrong. It must be further noted that small errors in computation which are introduced by rounding-off may be magnified in the process of iterations. In any case, especially in the case of the diagram showing chaotic behaviour, it is important to distinguish the behaviour caused by pure economic logics of the model from that caused by the logics of imprecision due to the use of the computer.

We now conclude this article with the following comment. In case of the adjustment of prices being described in terms of differential equations, the equilibrium is stable, provided that the excess demand functions satisfy the weak axiom of revealed preference. But where an approach in terms of difference equations is taken as more appropriate, stability is not a necessary conclusion. Prices may diverge from equilibrium, or show a periodic motion, or even continue to change in an unpredictable way. Thus the stability analysis based on differential equations of price adjustment is already very much in favour of concluding stability. Such an approach, of course, should carefully be avoided if we want to make a rigorous and precise examination of whether prices are really stable or not. Furthermore, we cannot regard the computer as a neutral helper of the analysis; it may mislead us by producing illusions at a certain degree, because of its unavoidable inaccuracy.

Article V
A generalization of the gross substitute system*

I Introduction

It is my pleasure to see that a system which attracted me more than ten years ago (1952a, 1957), has recently been revived by such economists as Bassett, Habibagahi, and Quirk, 1967, Bassett, Maybee and Quirk, 1968, Karlin, 1959, Kennedy, 1970, Kuenne, 1970, Quirk and Saposnik, 1968, and others. The system is referred to as the Morishima system by Arrow and Hurwicz, 1958, pp. 549–50 but the idea was suggested to me by Hicks, 1946, pp. 73–5.

In the famous stability chapter of *Value and Capital*, Hicks showed that the laws of comparative statics are simple if those goods which are substitutes of substitutes, or complements of complements, for good i are direct substitutes for i, and if those goods which are complements of substitutes, or substitutes of complements, for good i are direct complements with i. In terms of gross substitutability and gross complementarity, such a system is characterized by the following complementarity–substitutability chain

$$\text{(CS)}\ \operatorname{sign}(\partial E_i/\partial p_k) = \operatorname{sign}\left(\frac{\partial E_i}{\partial p_j}\frac{\partial E_j}{\partial p_k}\right) \text{ for } i, j, k \text{ distinct}$$

where E_i denotes the excess demand for good i and p_i its price in terms of numeraire.[1] I applied the condition (CS) only to the non-numeraire goods

* Published as Morishima, 1970.

[1] The condition (CS) implies sign symmetry. Suppose $\partial E_i/\partial p_j$ is positive. From (CS) we have $\operatorname{sign}(\partial E_i/\partial p_k) = \operatorname{sign}(\partial E_j/\partial p_k)$, and from (CS) written in the form

$$\operatorname{sign}(\partial E_i/\partial p_j) = \operatorname{sign}\left(\frac{\partial E_i}{\partial p_k}\frac{\partial E_k}{\partial p_j}\right)$$

we obtain $\operatorname{sign}(\partial E_i/\partial p_k) = \operatorname{sign}(\partial E_k/\partial p_j)$. Hence $\operatorname{sign}(\partial E_j/\partial p_k) = \operatorname{sign}(\partial E_k/\partial p_j)$. Similarly for the case where $\partial E_i/\partial p_j$ is negative.

1, 2,..., n, in my paper, 1952a, throughout except for its last section, but Kennedy, like Arrow and Hurwicz, is interested in a system where the condition (CS) holds for all commodities including the numeraire. Arrow and Hurwicz used the term, 'Morishima case', to distinguish this system from my own system, but now Kennedy calls it the 'Morishima system' to distinguish it from the Morishima case proper. It is the conclusion of Kennedy, and also of Arrow and Hurwicz, that some sorts of dilemma are inevitable in the extended Morishima system, if the equilibrium is to be stable.[2]

I cannot, however, agree with Kennedy, and Arrow and Hurwicz, on such an inflexionless extension of the condition (CS), originally intended to be applied to non-numeraire goods, to the entire economy including the numeraire. In order to preserve stability, it must be carefully extended such that it does not contradict other properties, such as homogeneity and the Walras identity, which should have priority over (CS) in characterizing the system.[3]

In this article, it is assumed that (CS) holds only for non-numeraire goods. Then the non-numeraire goods, 1,..., n, can be divided, after suitable relabelling of goods, into two non-overlapping groups, $R = \{1,\ldots,m\}$ and $S = \{m+1,\ldots,n\}$, such that any two goods belonging to the same group are substitutes for each other and any two goods belonging to different groups are complementary with each other;[4] in other words

$$\text{(M)}\begin{cases}\partial E_h/\partial p_j > 0, h \neq j; h, j \in R, & \partial E_h/\partial p_k < 0, h \in R, k \in S, \\ \partial E_i/\partial p_j < 0, j \in R, i \in S, & \partial E_i/\partial p_k > 0, i \neq k; i, k \in S\end{cases}$$

Next, excess demand functions (including that of numeraire, i.e., good 0)

[2] Quirk and Saposnik obtained the same results.

[3] I accept Kennedy's instability theorem for the extended Morishima system as a logical exercise, but I prefer a different approach. Imagine an economy consisting of tea, coffee, cocoa, sugar, saccharine, and gold. The reader will agree that the condition (CS) does *not* hold for gold (numeraire), although it holds for the other goods. Similarly, in a stable economy consisting of tea, coffee, cocoa, sugar, and saccharine (now gold is not a member) and having one of them, say sugar, as numeraire, the condition (CS) will no more hold for sugar because of homogeneity and the Walras law which claim prior consideration. This may be likened to the parliamentary procedure that if an MP becomes the Speaker, he must, during his period of office, be independent of the party he has belonged to.

[4] See my 1952 paper, 1952a. The postulate (CS) can be weakened so as to include zero elements. If $\partial E_i/\partial p_j = 0$ for $i \neq j, i, j \in R$ (or $i, j \in S$), then goods i and j are called quasi-substitutive, while if it holds for $i \in R$ and $j \in S$ (or $i \in S$ and $j \in R$), they are called quasi-complements. When the system is 'indecomposable', two goods which are quasi-substitutes (or quasi-complements) according to one grouping cannot be quasi-complements (or quasi-substitutes) by any other grouping. For this see appendix below. The results of this paper, though they are obtained on the assumption of the absence of zero elements, are true in indecomposable, weak Morishima systems as well.

are postulated to be homogeneous of degree zero in non-normalized prices. Then, by Euler's formula

$$\text{(H)}\frac{\partial E_i}{\partial p_0}p_0 + \sum_{j\in R}\frac{\partial E_i}{\partial p_j}p_j + \sum_{k\in S}\frac{\partial E_i}{\partial p_k}p_k = 0,\ i = 0, 1, 2, \ldots, n,$$

which can be rewritten as follows

$$\sum_{j\in R}\frac{\partial E_h}{\partial p_j}p_j + \sum_{k\in S}\left(-\frac{\partial E_h}{\partial p_k}\right)p_k = -\left(\frac{\partial E_h}{\partial p_0}p_0 + 2\sum_{k\in S}\frac{\partial E_h}{\partial p_k}p_k\right), h\in R,$$

$$\sum_{j\in R}\left(-\frac{\partial E_i}{\partial p_j}\right)p_j + \sum_{k\in S}\frac{\partial E_i}{\partial p_k}p_k = -\left(\frac{\partial E_i}{\partial p_0}p_0 + 2\sum_{k\in R}\frac{\partial E_i}{\partial p_j}p_j\right), i\in S,$$

For the first expression we assume that the part in the brackets on the right-hand side is positive, and for the second, that it is greater than $-E_i$; namely

$$\text{(N)}\begin{cases}\dfrac{\partial E_h}{\partial p_0}p_0 + 2\displaystyle\sum_{k\in S}\frac{\partial E_h}{\partial p_k}p_k > 0, h\in R,\\[2ex] \dfrac{\partial E_i}{\partial p_0}p_0 + 2\displaystyle\sum_{j\in R}\frac{\partial E_i}{\partial p_j}p_j + E_i > 0, i\in S\end{cases}$$

It is evident that when there is no complementarity, i.e., S is empty, the condition (M) is reduced to the gross substitutability of non-numeraire goods for one another and (N) to the gross substitutability of them for the numeraire. A system which postulates (M) for the non-numeraire subeconomy and (N) for the numeraire may thus be regarded as a generalization of the gross substitute system. On the other hand, the Arrow–Hurwicz–Kennedy system postulating the condition (CS) or (M) for the entire economy is inconsistent with the condition (N) for the numeraire (unless S is empty). Consequently, it would not be surprising to find that their system (unlike the gross substitute system) is definitely unstable.

Other assumptions which we will use later are rather customary. First, excess demand functions are bounded from below (B). Second, they are continuous on the non-negative orthant of the $(n + 1)$-dimensional price space, (C). Third, the excess demand for good 0 is always positive if its price is null, so that good 0 cannot be free, (D). Therefore, we may normalize prices such that $p_0 = 1$. Fourth, if the price of good i in group R is taken sufficiently large, then its excess demand becomes negative, (E). Finally, the excess demand functions satisfy Walras' law

$$\text{(W)} \sum_{i=0}^{n} p_i E_i(p_0, p_1, \ldots, p_n) = 0 \text{ for all } p \geqq 0$$

where $p = (p_0, p_1, \ldots, p_n)$.

Remark 1 It is now well known that under (C) and (W) there exists an equilibrium price set, at which we have

$$E_i(p) \leqq 0 \quad i = 0, 1, 2, \ldots, n$$

In the case of a gross substitute economy, there is no free good. However, in the case of our more general system fulfilling (M) and (N), it is possible that some goods in group R may be free; but there is no free good in group S.[5]

II The uniqueness of equilibrium

We first establish:

Theorem 1

The conditions (M) and (N), in addition to other conventional assumptions, (B)–(E), (H), and (W), imply uniqueness of the equilibrium price ray.

Remark 2 If we strengthen the second inequality of (N) into

$$\frac{\partial E_i}{\partial p_0} + 2\sum_{j \in R} \frac{\partial E_i}{\partial p_j} p_j + \min(E_i, 0) > 0, \quad i \in S$$

we have from (H)

$$-\sum_{j \in R} \frac{\partial E_i}{\partial p_j} p_j + \sum_{k \in S} \frac{\partial E_i}{\partial p_k} p_k < 0, \quad i \in S$$

(H) and (N) also imply

$$\sum_{j \in R} \frac{\partial E_h}{\partial p_j} p_j - \sum_{k \in S} \frac{\partial E_h}{\partial p_k} p_k < 0, \quad h \in R$$

Under (M), these two sets of inequalities imply that the $n \times n$ Jacobian $A(p)$

[5] Suppose a good, say i, in S were free. We would have from (H) and (N)

$$\sum_{k \in S} \frac{\partial E_i}{\partial p_k} p_k < \sum_{j \in R} \frac{\partial E_i}{\partial p_j} p_j + E_i$$

for good i. Because of (M), we have $\partial E_i/\partial p_j < 0$ for $j \in R$. On the other hand, we have $p_i = 0$ and $E_i \leqq 0$, since good i is free. Hence, from the above inequality we obtain

$$\sum_{\substack{k \in S \\ k \neq i}} \frac{\partial E_i}{\partial p_k} p_k < 0$$

Evidently, this contradicts the last set of inequalities of (M).

of excess demand functions $E_i(1, p), i = 1, \ldots, n$, is Hicksian everywhere.[6] Hence the equilibrium price ray is unique by virtue of a theorem due to Gale and Nikaido (1965). However, under (N) the Jacobian is not necessarily Hicksian when $E_i > 0$ for some i in the group S. Therefore, we cannot apply their theorem directly to our case.

Proof: Imitating Hahn (1968), we reduce the original $(n + 1)$-goods economy to an $(m + 1)$-goods economy by fixing the price of goods $m + 1$, $m + 2, \ldots$ n, in terms of good 0 at $\alpha_{m+1}, \alpha_{m+2}, \ldots, \alpha_n$ and consolidating goods $0, m + 1, m + 2, \ldots, n$ into a composite commodity μ. Write

$$E_h^* = E_h(p_0, p_1, \ldots, p_m, \alpha_{m+1}p_0, \ldots, \alpha_n p_0),\ h \in R,$$

$$E_\mu^* = E_0(p_0, p_1, \ldots, p_m, \alpha_{m+1}p_0, \ldots, \alpha_n p_0)$$

$$+ \sum_{i \in S} \alpha_i E_i(p_0, p_1, \ldots, p_m, \alpha_{m+1}p_0, \ldots, \alpha_n p_0)$$

It follows from (B) and (D) that $E_\mu^* = \infty$ when $p_0 = 0$. Therefore, good μ cannot be a free good in the $(m + 1)$-goods economy and may be taken as the numeraire as we will do in the following.

Because of (N), *a fortiori* we have

$$\frac{\partial E_h^*}{\partial p_0} = \frac{\partial E_h}{\partial p_0} + \sum_{k \in S} \frac{\partial E_h}{\partial p_k} \alpha_k > 0,\ h \in R$$

This, together with (H), implies

$$\sum_{j \in R} \frac{\partial E_h^*}{\partial p_j} p_j < 0,\ h \in R$$

Hence the $m \times m$ Jacobian $[\partial E_h^*/\partial p_j]$ is Hicksian everywhere, so that the Gale–Nikaido theorem ensures uniqueness of the equilibrium price ray to the $(m + 1)$-goods economy.

Next consider an $(m + 2)$-goods economy, where the prices of goods $1, 2, \ldots, m + 1$ are flexible and the other goods, $0, m + 2, \ldots, n$, are aggregated into a good μ which serves as the numeraire. We now write

$$E_h^{**} = E_h(p_0, p_1, \ldots, p_{m+1}, \alpha_{m+2}p_0, \ldots, \alpha_n p_0)\ h = 1, \ldots, m + 1,$$

$$E_\mu^{**} = E_0(p_0, p_1, \ldots, p_{m+1}, \alpha_{m+2}p_0, \ldots, \alpha_n p_0)$$

$$+ \sum_{i=m+2}^{n} \alpha_i E_i(p_0, p_1, \ldots, p_{m+1}, \alpha_{m+2}p_0, \ldots, \alpha_n p_0)$$

[6] That is to say, the principal minors of $A(p)$ alternate in sign, those of order 1 being negative, those of order 2 positive, and so on.

Then

$$\frac{\partial E_h^{**}}{\partial p_0} = \frac{\partial E_h}{\partial p_0} + \sum_{k=m+2}^{n} \frac{\partial E_h}{\partial p_k}\alpha_k, \frac{\partial E_h^{**}}{\partial p_j} = \frac{\partial E_h}{\partial p_j}, j = 1, 2, \ldots, m+1$$

As $\partial E_h/\partial p_k < 0$, $h \in R$ and $k \in S$ and $\partial E_{m+1}/\partial p_k > 0, k \neq m+1, k \in S$, we obtain from (N)

$$\frac{\partial E_h^{**}}{\partial p_0} p_0 + 2\frac{\partial E_h^{**}}{\partial p_{m+1}} p_{m+1} > 0,\ h \in R,$$
$$\frac{\partial E_{m+1}^{**}}{\partial p_0} p_0 + 2\sum_{j\in R} \frac{\partial E_{m+1}^{**}}{\partial p_j} p_j + \sum_{k=m+2}^{n} \frac{\partial E_{m+1}^{**}}{\partial p_k} p_k + E_{m+1}^{**} > 0 \quad (1)$$

Subtracting (1) from the respective equations of (H), we have

$$\sum_{j\in R} \frac{\partial E_h^{**}}{\partial p_j} p - \frac{\partial E_h^{**}}{\partial p_{m+1}} p_{m+1} < 0,\ h \in R,$$
$$-\sum_{j\in R} \frac{\partial E_{m+1}^{**}}{\partial p_j} p_j + \frac{\partial E_{m+1}^{**}}{\partial p_{m+1}} p_{m+1} - E_{m+1}^{**} < 0 \quad (2)$$

Let us now take $\alpha_{m+2}, \ldots, \alpha_n$ such that they are common to the $(m+1)$-goods and the $(m+2)$-goods economies. Denote by $P(\alpha_{m+1}) = (p_1(\alpha_{m+1}), \ldots, p_m(\alpha_{m+1}))$ the vector of equilibrium prices of goods $1, \ldots, m$ which prevail in the $(m+1)$-goods economy when the price of good $m+1$ is set at α_{m+1}. As they are not necessarily equilibrium prices in the $(m+2)$-goods economy, $E_{m+1}(1, P(\alpha_{m+1}), \alpha_{m+1}, \ldots, \alpha_n)$ may be positive. But if it equals zero by any chance,[7] then the $(m+2)$-goods economy is in equilibrium at prices $P(\alpha_{m+1})$ and α_{m+1}. If inequalities (2) hold with $E_{m+1}^{**} = 0$ at $(P(\alpha_{m+1}), \alpha_{m+1})$, then the $(m+1) \times (m+1)$ Jacobian of E_i $(i = 1, \ldots, m+1)$ is Hicksian at $(P(\alpha_{m+1}), \alpha_{m+1})$, because of the assumption (M).

If the general equilibrium of the $(m+2)$-goods economy were not unique, there should be a number of α_{m+1}s, at each of which the $(m+1) \times (m+1)$ Jacobian is of the Hicksian type. Let α_{m+1}^1 be the smallest among them. We then have

$$E_{m+1}(1, P(\alpha_{m+1}^1), \alpha_{m+1}^1, \alpha_{m+2}, \ldots, \alpha_n) = 0,$$
$$\frac{dE_{m+1}}{d\alpha_{m+1}} = \sum_{j\in R} \frac{\partial E_{m+1}}{\partial p_j} \frac{dp_j}{d\alpha_{m+1}} + \frac{\partial E_{m+1}}{\partial p_{m+1}} < 0 \quad (3)$$

[7] One might at first think that there is a possibility of $E_{m+1}(1, P(\alpha_{m+1}), \alpha_{m+1}, \ldots, \alpha_n)$ being negative. But if it were so, good $m+1$ should be free at the equilibrium prices, $P(\alpha_{m+1})$ and α_{m+1}, of the $(m+2)$-goods economy. We have, however, shown that in the group S, to which good $m+1$ belongs, there can be no free good. See Remark 1 above.

the last inequality, which is to hold at the equilibrium price set $(P(\alpha^1_{m+1}), \alpha^1_{m+1})$ and in a small neighbourhood of it, being a consequence of the fact that the $(m+1) \times (m+1)$ Jacobian is Hicksian. Similarly, at $(P(\alpha^2_{m+1}), \alpha^2_{m+1})$ which is another equilibrium price set, we should have

$$E_{m+1} = 0 \text{ and } dE_{m+1}/d\alpha_{m+1} < 0$$

Since (C) is assumed, these contradict (3) unless there is, between α^1_{m+1} and α^2_{m+1}, a third α_{m+1}, at which

$$E_{m+1} = 0 \text{ and } dE_{m+1}/d\alpha_{m+1} \geqq 0$$

However, there exists no such α_{m+1}, because at every point fulfilling

$$E_{m+1}(1, P(\alpha_{m+1}), \alpha_{m+1}, \ldots, \alpha_n) = 0$$

the $(m+1) \times (m+1)$ Jacobian should be Hicksian, so that $dE_{m+1}/d\alpha_{m+1}$ must be negative. Hence the equilibrium of the $(m+2)$-goods economy is unique.

The above argument can *mutatis mutandis* be applied to the $(m+3)$-goods economy to show that it has a unique equilibrium. The mathematical induction can be continued until the composite numeraire μ is completely disaggregated into the original $n - m + 1$ goods $0, m+1, m+2, \ldots, n$. Hence the $(n+1)$-goods economy, where good 0 serves as numeraire and the prices of all other goods are flexible, has a unique equilibrium.

III The main stability theorem

Let us now proceed to the main subject of this article. We assume that if excess demand for good i is positive (or negative), the price of that good (in terms of numeraire, good 0) is increased (or decreased), with the exception of the case of excess demand for good i being negative at $p_i = 0$, in which the price of good i cannot fall and, therefore, remains unchanged. By a suitable choice of units of measurement for each of the $n+1$ commodities, this process of pricing can be described by the following differential equations

$$\text{(A)}\quad dp_i/dt = \begin{cases} 0 & \text{if } p_i = 0 \text{ and } E_i < 0 \\ E_i(1, p_1, \ldots, p_n) & \text{otherwise} \end{cases}$$

We can then prove

Theorem 2

If excess demand functions satisfy (M) and (N) in addition to (B)–(E), (H), and (W), then all paths generated by the dynamic system (A) eventually lead prices to their equilibrium values.

Proof: Let us define V as

$$V = \max_{j\in R, k\in S} (E_j/p_j, -E_k/p_k, 0)$$

Suppose the markets are, at the start, not in general equilibrium; V may be 0 but we begin with the case of $V > 0$.

If $V = E_h/p_h$ for some $h \in R$, we have

$$\frac{dV}{dt} = \frac{(dE_h/dt)p_h - E_h(dp_h/dt)}{p_h^2} = \frac{(dE_h/dt)p_h - E_h^2}{p_h^2}$$

because of (A). Assumptions (N) and (H), together with (M), imply

$$0 > \left(\sum_{j\in R} \frac{\partial E_h}{\partial p_j} p_j - \sum_{k\in S} \frac{\partial E_h}{\partial p_k} p_k\right) \frac{E_h}{p_h}$$

$$\geq \sum_{j\in R} \frac{\partial E_h}{\partial p_j} p_j \frac{E_j}{p_j} - \sum_{k\in S} \frac{\partial E_h}{\partial p_k} p_k \left(-\frac{E_k}{p_k}\right)$$

because $\partial E_h/\partial p_j > 0$ for all $j \neq h, j \in R$, and $-\partial E_h/\partial p_k > 0$ for all $k \in S$ by (M); and

$$E_h/p_h = \max_{j\in R, k\in S} (E_j/p_j, -E_k/p_k, 0) > 0$$

Therefore

$$\frac{dE_h}{dt} = \sum_{j=1}^{n} \frac{\partial E_h}{\partial p_j} \frac{dp_j}{dt} = \sum_{j=1}^{n} \frac{\partial E_h}{\partial p_j} E_j < 0$$

Hence

$$dV/dt < 0 \tag{4}$$

On the other hand, if $V = -E_i/p_i$ for some $i \in S$, we obtain

$$dV/dt = \frac{-(dE_i/dt)p_i + E_i(dp_i/dt)}{p_i^2} = -\frac{(dE_i/dt)p_i - E_i^2}{p_i^2}$$

(H) and (N) imply, in this case, the following inequality

$$0 > \left[\sum_{j\in R}\left(-\frac{\partial E_i}{\partial p_j}\right)p_j + \sum_{k\in S} \frac{\partial E_i}{\partial p_k} p_k - E_i\right]\left(-\frac{E_i}{p_i}\right)$$

the right-hand side of which is not less than

$$\sum_{j\in R}\left(-\frac{\partial E_i}{\partial p_j}\right)p_j \frac{E_j}{p_j} + \sum_{k\in S} \frac{\partial E_i}{\partial p_k} p_k \left(-\frac{E_k}{p_k}\right) + \frac{E_i^2}{p_i}$$

because $-\partial E_i/\partial p_j > 0$ for all $j \in R$ and $\partial E_i/\partial p_k > 0$ for all $k \neq i, k \in S$, by (M) and

$$-E_i/p_i = \max_{j \in R, k \in S} (E_j/p_j, -E_k/p_k)$$

Hence

$$\sum_{j \in R} \frac{\partial E_i}{\partial p_j} E_j + \sum_{k \in S} \frac{\partial E_i}{\partial p_k} E_k > \frac{E_i^2}{p_i}$$

Since the left-hand side of this expression is seen to equal dE_i/dt as $dp_j/dt = E_j$ for all j, we finally obtain

$$(dE_i/dt)p_i - E_i^2 > 0$$

Hence $dV/dt < 0$.

Thus V is decreasing in either case, so that V approaches 0 as t tends to infinity.[8] This means that for a small positive number ε arbitrarily taken, there is a large t_ε such that for all $t \geqq t_\varepsilon$, the inequalities

$$E_j(1, p(t))/p_j(t) \leqq \varepsilon \; j \in R \tag{5}$$

$$E_k(1, p(t))/p_k(t) \geqq -\varepsilon \; k \in S \tag{6}$$

By taking ε very small, we can see from (5) and (A) that, when t becomes very large, there is no substantial increase in prices of the goods in group R.

Let us now define U as $\min_{j \in R} E_j/p_j$. If U tends to zero as t tends to infinity, then we find, in view of the boundedness of $p_j(t)$ from above that we have just established, the relationship

$$\lim_{t \to \infty} E_j(1, p(t)) = 0, j \in R$$

Therefore, from (W), we obtain

$$\lim_{t \to \infty} \sum_{k \in S} E_k(1, p(t))p_k(t) = 0 \tag{7}$$

Next, suppose that U does not converge to zero and remains negative when t tends to infinity. Then there must be a good h whose E_h/p_h is as small as a negative number δ at $t = t_1, t_2, \ldots,$ *ad infinitum* such that $\lim_{v \to \infty} t_v = \infty$. As $dp_h/dt < 0$ at these points of time (because $E_h \leqq \delta p_h < 0$), and the rise in p_h, if at all, is negligible throughout the semi-open period $[t_\varepsilon, \infty]$, $p_h(t)$ will eventually approach 0. Hence $\lim_{v \to \infty} E_h(1, p(t_v))p_h(t_v) = 0$. (Note that such a

[8] See, for example, Morishima, 1964, p. 30, footnote. Note that when V reaches 0 at some stage of development, it remains at zero thereafter.

good is 'free' in equilibrium.)

For all other non-free goods in R, $\lim_{t \to \infty} E_j/p_j = 0$ and p_j is bounded from above, so that $\lim_{t \to \infty} E_j(1, p(t)) = 0$. Therefore, we find

$$\lim_{v \to \infty} \sum_{j \in R} E_j(1, p(t_v))p_j(t_v) = 0$$

Because of (W), it yields

$$\lim_{v \to \infty} \sum_{j \in S} E_k(1, p(t_v))p_k(t_v) = 0 \tag{7'}$$

Suppose now there is a good i in group S whose excess demand satisfies with some positive number θ

$$E_i(1, p(t))/p_i(t)) \geqq \theta \text{ for all } t \geqq t_\theta$$

Then, from (A)

$$dp_i/dt = E_i > \theta p_i(t)$$

so that $\lim_{v \to \infty} p_i(t) = \infty$. Hence $\lim_{v \to \infty} E_i(1, p(t))p_i(t) > \theta p_i(t)^2 = \infty$. This contradicts (7) or (7'), because there is no good in S whose $E_k(1, p(t))p_k(t)$ tends to $-\infty$ when t tends to infinity. Hence, if t is taken sufficiently large, inequalities

$$\theta \geqq E_k(1, p(t))/p_k(t) \geqq -\varepsilon, \; k \in S$$

must hold for all positive θ and ε.

The above argument establishes

$$\lim_{v \to \infty} E_j(1, p(t)) \leqq 0, \; j \in R,$$

$$\lim_{v \to \infty} E_k(1, p(t)) = 0, \; k \in S$$

These relationships show that the adjustment process (A) eventually brings the economy into a state of equilibrium.

When the pricing starts from a point at which $V = 0$, V continues to be zero forever. (5) and (6) hold with $\varepsilon = 0$ for all $t \geqq 0$. The same argument as above proves stability.

IV Other stability results

We have so far dealt with a system which satisfies (N), together with (M) and other conventional assumptions. As is easily recognized, (N) is not symmetric between R and S, because the inequalities of (N) for $i \in S$ contain E_i as the last term, whereas those for $h \in R$ do not. If one does not like such an asymmetry, one might remove term E_i from the second group of inequalities of (N). But is seems to me that such a revised version of (N), referred to as (N′) below, is not sufficient for global stability, so that I introduce the notions of 'regularity' and 'weak symmetry' of the Jacobian $[\partial E(p)/\partial p]$, which are to be defined below, although I am not happy to have such addenda. We can establish the following two theorems:

Theorem 3

If the normalized system (A) obeying (M) and (N′) is regular, then the (unique) equilibrium is globally stable.

Theorem 4

If the normalized system (A) obeying (M) and (N′) is weakly symmetric, then the (unique) equilibrium is globally stable.

Let us write $[\partial E(p)/\partial p]$ simply as $A(p)$, and partition it in the form

$$A(p) = \begin{bmatrix} A_{RR}(p) & A_{RS}(p) \\ A_{SR}(p) & A_{SS}(p) \end{bmatrix}$$

where $A_{RR}(p)$ and $A_{SS}(p)$ with positive off-diagonal elements are square and $A_{RS}(p) < 0$, $A_{SR}(p) < 0$. Let the inverse of $A(p)$ be also partitioned into the form

$$B(p) = \begin{bmatrix} B_{RR}(p) & B_{SR}(p) \\ B_{RS}(p) & B_{SS}(p) \end{bmatrix}$$

Evidently, all off-diagonal elements of

$$A^*(p) = \begin{bmatrix} A_{RR}(p) & -A_{RS}(p) \\ -A_{SR}(p) & A_{SS}(p) \end{bmatrix}$$

are positive, and

$$B^*(p) = \begin{bmatrix} B_{RR}(p) & -B_{SR}(p) \\ -B_{RS}(p) & B_{SS}(p) \end{bmatrix}$$

is the inverse of $A^*(p)$.

Obviously, the structure, $A(p)$, at p is identical with the equilibrium structure $A(p^0)$ if and only if $B^*(p) = B^*(p^0)$, while $A(p)$ is symmetric if and only if $B^*(p)$ is symmetric. The condition that $c(p)B^*(p) = c^0B^*(p^0)$ for some positive row vectors $c(p)$ and c^0 is weaker than the condition for the identical structure $B^*(p) = B^*(p^0)$, and the condition that $c(p)B^*(p) = d(p)B^*(p)'$ for some positive row vectors $c(p)$ and $d(p)$ is weaker than the condition for the symmetric structure, $B^*(p) = B^*(p)'$.[9] We call the system

[9] The prime denotes transposition.

regular if $c(p)B^*(p) = c^0B^*(p^0)$ holds between any price set p and the equilibrium price set p^0 with positive vectors $c(p)$ and c^0, and *weakly symmetric* if $c(p)B^*(p) = d(p)B^*(p)'$ holds everywhere with some positive vectors $c(p)$ and $d(p)$. Note that $c(p)$ and $d(p)$ depend on p, and c^0 is independent of p. We can now prove the theorems.

Proof of Theorem 3: From (H) and (N′) we obtain

$$\sum_{j\in R} \frac{\partial E_h}{\partial p_j} p_j + \sum_{k\in S}\left(-\frac{\partial E_h}{\partial p_k}\right) p_k < 0,\ h \in R$$

$$\sum_{j\in R}\left(-\frac{\partial E_i}{\partial p_j}\right) p_j + \sum_{k\in S} \frac{\partial E_i}{\partial p_k} p_k < 0,\ i \in S$$

These inequalities imply that $A^*(p)$ is Hicksian everywhere.

As $B^*(p)A^*(p) = I$, we have $c(p)B^*(p)A^*(p) = c(p)$. By regularity

$$-c(p)B^*(p) = -c^0B^*(p^0) = v^0$$

so that we obtain $v^0A^*(p) = -c(p) < 0$. On the other hand, we have $-B^*(p^0) > 0$ because $A^*(p)$ is a Hicksian matrix with positive off-diagonal elements. Hence $v^0 > 0$ because $c^0 > 0$. Thus $A(p)$ is dominant diagonal. Therefore, the equilibrium point p^0 is stable.[10]

Proof of Theorem 4: We have

$$-c(p)B^*(p)A^*(p) = -c(p) \text{ and } -d(p)B^*(p)'A^*(p)' = -d(p)$$

In view of the weak symmetry and the positiveness of $c(p)$ and $d(p)$ we obtain $v(p)A^*(p) < 0$ and $v(p)A^*(p)' < 0$, where $v(p) = -c(p)B^*(p) = -d(p)B^*(p)'$. Hence

$$v(p)(A^*(p) + A^*(p)') < 0$$

On the other hand, $v(p) > 0$, because $c(p) > 0$ and $-B^*(p) > 0$, the latter following from the fact that $A^*(p)$ is Hicksian everywhere because of (H) and (N′). Thus the above inequality holds with $v(p) > 0$ for the matrix, $A^*(p) + A^*(p)'$, with positive off-diagonal elements. Therefore, $A^*(p) + A^*(p)'$, which is symmetric, is a Hicksian matrix. Hence $A(p) + A(p)'$ is negative definite, so that there is global stability.[11]

Finally, in case of the adjustment of prices being described by

$$(\text{A}')\ (dp_i/dt)/p_i = E_i(p_1, \ldots, p_n),\ i = 1, \ldots, n$$

instead of (*A*), the general equilibrium is shown to be stable under (N′) without the additional assumption of regularity or weak symmetry. In fact, put $z_i = \log p_i$; then (A′) can be written as

[10] Karlin, 1959, pp. 320–3.

[11] Arrow and Hurwicz, 1950, p. 536.

$$dz_i/dt = F_i(z_1,\ldots,z_n),\ i = 1,\ldots,n$$

As $\partial F_i/\partial z_j = (\partial E_i/\partial p_j)p_j$, we obtain from (N′) and (H)

$$\sum_{j\in R}\frac{\partial F_h}{\partial z_j} + \sum_{k\in S}\left(-\frac{\partial F_h}{\partial z_k}\right) < 0,\ h\in R,$$

$$\sum_{j\in R}\left(-\frac{\partial F_i}{\partial z_j}\right) + \sum_{k\in S}\frac{\partial F_i}{\partial z_k} < 0,\ i\in S$$

Therefore, when (M) holds, the z system is dominant diagonal, and hence the equilibrium is globally stable.[12]

Appendix

Theorem

Let $E_{ij} = \partial E_i/\partial p_j$ *and* $E = (E_{ij})$. *Suppose matrix* E *is indecomposable and satisfies, for two non-overlapping groups,* $R = \{1,\ldots,m\}$ *and* $S = \{m+1,\ldots,n\}$, *the following (CS) conditions*

$$(\mathrm{M})\begin{cases} E_{hj} \geqq 0, h \neq j; h,j\in R;\ E_{hk} \leqq 0, h\in R, k\in S; \\ E_{ij} \leqq 0, j\in R, i\in S, \qquad E_{ik} \geqq 0, i \neq k; i,k\in S \end{cases}$$

Then there is no second set of groups, R' *and* S', *for which*

$$(\mathrm{M}')\begin{cases} E_{hj} \geqq 0, h \neq j; h,j\in R';\ E_{hk} \leqq 0, h\in R', k\in S'; \\ E_{ij} \leqq 0, j\in R', i\in S', \qquad E_{ik} \geqq 0, i \neq k; i,k\in S' \end{cases}$$

Proof: Suppose the contrary. We then may assume that there is a second set of groups $R' = \{R_1, S_1\}$ and $S' = \{S_2, R_2\}$, where $R_1 = \{1,\ldots,s\}$, $s \leqq m$, $R_2 = \{s+1,\ldots,m\}$, $S_1 = \{m+1,\ldots,u\}$, $u \leqq n$, and $S_2 = \{u+1,\ldots,n\}$. If $s = m$, then $u < n$ and if $u = n$, then $s < m$; otherwise $R = R'$ and $S = S'$, a contradiction to the existence of two distinct sets of groups. Then the grouping in terms of $R = \{R_1, R_2\}$ and $S = \{S_1, S_2\}$ enables us to write matrix E as

$$\begin{array}{c} \\ E = \\ \\ \end{array}
\begin{array}{cccc} R_1 & R_2 & S_1 & S_2 \end{array}$$

$$E = \begin{bmatrix} A_{11} & A_{12} & A_{13} & A_{14} \\ A_{21} & A_{22} & A_{23} & A_{24} \\ A_{31} & A_{32} & A_{33} & A_{34} \\ A_{41} & A_{42} & A_{43} & A_{44} \end{bmatrix} \begin{matrix} R_1 \\ R_2 \\ S_1 \\ S_2 \end{matrix}$$

[12] Inada, 1968, pp. 343–4.

On the other hand, for the grouping in terms of R' and S', E is arranged as

$$E' = \begin{array}{c} \begin{matrix} R_1 & S_1 & S_2 & R_2 \end{matrix} \\ \left[\begin{matrix} A_{11} & A_{13} & A_{14} & A_{12} \\ A_{31} & A_{33} & A_{34} & A_{32} \\ A_{41} & A_{43} & A_{44} & A_{42} \\ A_{21} & A_{23} & A_{24} & A_{22} \end{matrix}\right] \begin{matrix} R_1 \\ S_1 \\ S_2 \\ R_2 \end{matrix} \end{array}$$

As $A_{12} \geqq 0$ and $\leqq 0$ from (M) and (M′), respectively, we have $A_{12} = 0$. Similarly, $A_{21} = 0$. In exactly the same way we find that both A_{24} and A_{42} vanish, and both A_{3i} and A_{i3} ($i = 1,4$) vanish too. Then E (or E') may be transformed, by identical permutation of rows and columns, into

$$\left[\begin{array}{cc|cc} A_{11} & A_{14} & & \\ A_{41} & A_{44} & \multicolumn{2}{c}{0} \\ \hline & & A_{22} & A_{23} \\ \multicolumn{2}{c|}{0} & A_{32} & A_{33} \end{array}\right]$$

which is obviously decomposable, a contradiction.

If $s = m, R_2$ is empty, while if $u = n, S_2$ is empty. In either case we can show that E is decomposable, a contradiction again. Thus in every possible case the set of groups R and S is unique, wherever E is indecomposable.

In the economy consisting of two commodities a and b which are competitive, factors, $f_1,\ldots,f_m$ are combined with each other to produce a, while $f_{m+1},\ldots,f_m$ are used to produce b. Then, at the level of factors $f_1,\ldots,f_n$, complementarity prevails within each of the groups $R = \{f_1,\ldots,f_m\}$ and $S = \{f_{m+1},\ldots,f_n\}$, but we have substitutability between groups R and S. As I have pointed out before, such complementarity–substitutability relationships are characterized as

$$\text{(CS*)}\ \operatorname{sign} E_{ik} = -\operatorname{sign}(E_{ij}, E_{jk}) \text{ for } i, j, k \text{ distinct}$$

This economy may be referred to as an 'anti-M' system. It can be extended so as to include zero elements but two goods cannot be quasi-complements and quasi-substitutes simultaneously, as long as the system is indecomposable, because a theorem parallel to the one established above *mutatis mutandis* holds for indecomposable 'anti-M' systems.

Article VI
The laws of the working of the quasi-Frobenian system*

I Introduction

The stability of multiple markets was first discussed by Professor J. R. Hicks; and he derived from his stability conditions the following three rules about changes in the price system: (1) If the demand for a commodity is increased, then its price rises necessarily. (2) If all commodities are substitutes for one another, then all prices will rise whenever the demand for one of them increases. (3) Further, on the same assumption that all commodities are substitutes for one another, it can be proved that an increased demand for a commodity raises the prices of all the other commodities proportionately less than the price of the commodity. But, since the Hicksian method of stability analysis is but an implicit form of dynamic analysis and therefore imperfect or incorrect, we must reexamine what conditions are necessary and sufficient in order that a system of multiple exchange should be stable dynamically; and this has been done by P. A. Samuelson and O. Lange.

Samuelson, 1948, has tried to show how the problem of stability of equilibrium is intimately tied up with the problem of deriving the rules about the way in which the price system will react to changes in various data or parameters. But, if the system consists of many variables, we cannot derive any definite rule from his stability conditions that the real parts of the latent roots of the system are all negative. Hence many economists have investigated under what conditions Samuelson's true dynamic stability conditions are equivalent to the Hicksian conditions from which we can derive the three rules mentioned above. First, it is shown by Samuelson, 1948, p. 271 and Lange, 1944, pp. 97–8, that the true dynamic stability conditions are equivalent to the Hicksian conditions for stability when the matrix of the system is symmetric, i.e., when the marginal effect of a change in the price p_i upon the rate of change of the price of p_j over time equals the

* Written in 1954 but remained unpublished until now.

marginal effect of a change in the price p_j upon the rate of change of the price p_i over time. Second, Samuelson, 1948, p. 438, and Sono, 1944, pp. 47–9, have independently proved that, if the matrix of the system is a negative quasi-definite matrix, then the system is stable dynamically and the Hicksian conditions are satisfied too. Thirdly, Metzler, 1945, has proved that (I) the Hicksian conditions are necessary (but not sufficient) if the system is to be stable for all possible (non-negative) rates of adjustment in different markets and that (II) the Hicksian conditions are necessary and sufficient for dynamic stability if no complementarity is present in the system. Needless to say, these four cases, in which the Hicksian conditions follow from the dynamic stability, obey the above-mentioned Hicksian Rule 1; and further, it can be shown that the Metzler's case II, in which no complementarity is present, obeys Rules 2 and 3 too.

In Metzler's case II, all of Rules 1, 2, and 3 are derived from the following theorem of Frobenius, 1908.

If A is a non-negative, indecomposable matrix, then it has a characteristic root v which is simple, real, positive and not less in absolute value than any other root, and if $\rho \geq v$, then the cofactor of each element in the characteristic determinant $|\rho I_n - A|$ is positive. I_n stands for the identity matrix of order n.

Then we may call the system, in which no complementarity is present, the Frobenian system.

Since we had not yet any rule about changes in the prices of the complementary commodities, I (1952a), inquired, in an issue of *Osaka Economic Papers*, into the problem of the working of a system that if substitutes of substitutes, and complements of complements are direct substitutes, and if complements of substitutes and substitutes of complements, are direct complements, then the system must obey the following rules: (1) The dynamic stability conditions are identical with the Hicksian conditions for stability. (2) If the demand for a commodity is increased, then its price rises necessarily. (3) An increased demand for a commodity raises the prices of those commodities which are substitutes for the commodity and lowers the prices of those commodities which are complements with the commodity. (4) If two commodities are extremely substitutive or extremely complementary, then the system is unstable.

But I assumed in the paper the complete absence of independency and therefore any relation between pairs of commodities was assumed to be either substitution or complementarity. In this article I abandon this assumption and analyse a system of multiple exchange which contains not only substitutes but also complements and independent goods.

II The quasi-Frobenian system

Let there be n commodities (excluding the numeraire) in the economy and let $E_i(p_1, \ldots, p_n)$ be the excess demand function of the ith commodity, where p_j denotes the price of the jth commodity. Good 0 is the numeraire and hence its price is identically unity. The excess demand function may be or may not be linear. But, for simplicity, we shall assume here that the excess demand function of each commodity is a linear function of $p_1, \ldots, p_n$. Therefore we have

$$E_i = \sum_{j=1}^{n} a_{ij}(p_j - p_j^0) \; (i = 1, 2, \ldots, n)$$

where p_j^0 is the equilibrium price and all of the coefficients and a_{ij} are constants. It follows from the definition of substitution and complementarity that a_{ij} is positive (resp. negative) when the jth commodity is a substitute for (resp. a complement with) the ith one; the jth commodity is said to be independent of the ith one when a_{ij} is zero.

Next suppose that excess demand causes the price to rise and excess supply causes it to fall. Then we have, as a first approximation, the following dynamical system

$$\frac{dp_i}{dt} = k_i \sum_{j=1}^{n} a_{ij}(p_j - p_j^0) \; (i = 1, 2, \ldots, n) \tag{1}$$

where k_i is assumed to be constant and positive and is called the speed of adjustment in the ith market. By the familiar procedure we can easily determine the general solutions of the system (1); and we can show that, in order for the system to be stable, the real part of each root of the characteristic equation

$$f(v) = |v\delta_{ij} - k_j a_{ij}| = 0 \tag{2}$$

must be negative.

Now denote the n by n matrix $(k_i a_{ij})$ by H and the n by n unit matrix by I_n. Let α be a positive number which is greater than the greatest modules of $k_1 a_{11}, k_2, a_{22}, \ldots, k_n, a_{nn}$. Throughout this article we assume that the matrix $(H + \alpha I_n)$ can be partitioned, after identical permutation of rows and columns in the form

$$\begin{vmatrix} A_{11} & A_{12} \\ A_{21} & A_{22} \end{vmatrix} \tag{3}$$

where A_{11} and A_{22} are square non-negative matrices and A_{12} and A_{21} are non-positive. Since properties of the matrix (3) can be derived from those of the non-negative matrix

$$\begin{vmatrix} A_{11} & -A_{12} \\ -A_{21} & A_{22} \end{vmatrix}$$

we call the system, whose matrix is (3), the quasi-Frobenian system. The system which consists of black tea, green tea, coffee, cocoa, sugar, saccharine, and honey, may be an example of the quasi-Frobenian system. Another example is the system which consists of sugar produced in Cuba, Java, and India and coffee produced in Brazil, Colombia, and Java. Thus the actual economy contains many quasi-Frobenian subsystems.

Let the ith commodity be independent of the jth one, viz., $a_{ij} = 0$. If $k_i a_{ij}$ is an element of the non-negative submatrix A_{11} or A_{22}, we call the ith commodity a quasi-substitute for the jth one, while if $k_i a_{ij}$ is an element of the non-positive submatrix A_{12} or A_{21}, the ith commodity is called a quasi-complement with the jth one. We can prove

Theorem 1

If the matrix $(H + \alpha I_n)$ *is indecomposable, a commodity cannot be both a quasi-complement and a quasi-substitute of a given commodity in two different permutations of the matrix.* (Proof is omitted. See the appendix of Article V above.) We can also prove

Theorem 2

If the system (1) *is quasi-Frobenian, then the true dynamic stability conditions are identical with the Hicksian conditions for perfect stability, i.e., the quasi-Frobenian system is stable if and only if all principle minors of the determinant* $|a_{ij}|$ *alternate in sign as follows*

$$a_{ij} < 0, \begin{vmatrix} a_{ii} & a_{ij} \\ a_{ji} & a_{jj} \end{vmatrix} > 0, \begin{vmatrix} a_{ii} & a_{ij} & a_{ik} \\ a_{ji} & a_{jj} & a_{jk} \\ a_{ki} & a_{kj} & a_{kk} \end{vmatrix} < 0, \ldots, (i \neq j \neq k \neq i) \quad (4)$$

(Proof is omitted, as I have discussed it in Article V.)

III Comparative statics

(i) Effects of an increase in demand. Let β_i be the parameter with respect to which the demand for the ith commodity increases. Then if we differentiate the equilibrium system $E_j(p_1, p_2, \ldots, p_n, \beta_j) = 0$ $(j = 1, \ldots, n)$ partially with respect to β_i, we obtain

$$\sum_{r=1}^{n} a_{jr} \frac{\partial p_r}{\partial \beta_i} = 0 \; (j \neq i)$$

$$\sum_{r=1}^{n} a_{ir}\frac{\partial p_r}{\partial \beta_i} = -a_{i\beta} \tag{5}$$

where $a_{i\beta} = \partial a_i/\partial \beta_i > 0$. Solving

$$\frac{\partial p_i}{\partial \beta_i} = -a_{i\beta}\frac{J_{ii}}{J} \tag{6}$$

$$\frac{\partial p_r}{\partial \beta_i} = -a_{i\beta}\frac{J_{ir}}{J} \tag{7}$$

where J denotes the determinant $|a_{ij}|$ and J_{ii} (or J_{ir}) represents the cofactor of a_{ii} (or a_{ir}) in J. It follows directly from Theorem 2 that J_{ii}/J is necessarily negative in the stable system (1). Hence we have proved the following.

Theorem 3

The price of the ith commodity rises when its demand is increased.

In the following we assume that the system (1) is indecomposable. Then it is uniquely determined whether a commodity is a quasi-complement with, or a quasi-substitute of, a given commodity by Theorem 1.

Let $k_i a_{ih} + \alpha\delta_{ih}$ be an element of the m by m matrix A_{11} or the $n-m$ by $n-m$ matrix A_{22} and $k_i a_{il} + \alpha\delta_{il}$ be an element of A_{12} or A_{21}. Since, if $\rho \geq \nu$, the cofactor of each element in the quasi-Frobenian determinant

$$\begin{vmatrix} \rho I_m - A_{11} & A_{12} \\ A_{21} & \rho I_{n-m} - A_{22} \end{vmatrix}$$

is positive, then it follows that if $\rho \geq \nu$, the cofactor of $\rho\delta_{ih} - k_i a_{ih} - \alpha\delta_{ih}$ in the quasi-Frobenian determinant $|\rho I_n - (H + \alpha I_n)|$ is positive and the cofactor of $\rho\delta_{il} - k_i a_{il} - \alpha\delta_{il}$ is negative. Therefore if the system is stable, that is to say, if $\nu < \alpha$, it can be proved that sign $(-1)^{n-1}J_{ih} > 0$ and $\text{sign}(-1)^{n-1}J_{il} < 0$. As sign $J = \text{sign}(-1)^n$ by the stability condition for the quasi-Frobenian system, we have

$$\text{sign}(-J_{ih}/J) > 0$$
$$\text{sign}(-J_{il}/J) < 0$$

Together with (7), these lead to the following.

Theorem 4

An increased demand for a commodity raises the prices of those commodities which are substitutes or quasi-substitutes for the commodity and lowers the prices of those commodities which are complements or quasi-complements with the commodity.

According to Mosak, 1944, p. 46, the ith commodity is said to be a (gross) substitute for the rth commodity *in the inverse sense* if a rise in the quantity of the ith commodity leads to a lower demand-price for the rth commodity (i.e., if $\partial p_r/\partial E_i = J_{ir}/J < 0$) and is said to be a (gross) complement of the rth commodity in the inverse sense if it leads to an increase in the demand-price for the rth commodity (i.e., if $\partial p_r/\partial E_i = J_{ir}/J > 0$). Hence, in the case of the system being quasi-Frobenian, Theorem 4 is equivalent to:

Theorem 5

When two commodities are substitutive or quasi-substitutive, they are substitutive in the inverse sense and when they are complementary or quasi-complementary, they are complementary in the inverse sense too.

(ii) Let us now examine the effect of a_{sj} on $\partial p_r/\partial \beta_i$. Differentiating $\partial p_r/\partial \beta_i$ with respect to a_{ss}, we have

$$\frac{\partial}{\partial a_{ss}}\left(\frac{\partial p_r}{\partial \beta_i}\right) = \frac{\partial}{\partial_{ss}}\left(-\frac{J_{ir}}{J}\right) = \frac{J_{ir}J_{ss}}{J^2}\ (s = i, r) \tag{8}$$

$$\frac{\partial}{\partial a_{ss}}\left(\frac{\partial p_r}{\partial \beta_i}\right) = \frac{J_{ir}J_{ss} - J_{irss}J}{J^2} = \frac{J_{is}J_{sr}}{J^2}\ (s \neq i, r) \tag{9}$$

Since the system is quasi-Frobenian, it can be easily proved that sign $(-J_{ir}/J) = \text{sign}(J_{is}J_{sr}/J^2)$. Hence it follows from (8) and (9) that $\frac{\partial}{\partial a_{ss}}\left(\frac{\partial p_r}{\partial \beta_i}\right) > 0 (s = 1, \ldots, n)$ when the rth commodity is a substitute or a quasi-substitute for the ith one, and that $\frac{\partial}{\partial a_{ss}}\left(\frac{\partial p_r}{\partial \beta_i}\right) < 0 (s = 1, \ldots, n)$ when the rth commodity is a complement or a quasi-complement with the ith one; and putting $r = i$ in (8) and (9), we find $\frac{\partial}{\partial a_{ss}}\left(\frac{\partial p_i}{\partial \beta_i}\right) > 0 (s = 1, \ldots, n)$. Consequently we may say as follows:

Theorem 6

All prices will be less sensitive with respect to a change in demand, according as an excess demand curve becomes more downwards sloping.

Similarly, differentiating $\partial p_r/\partial \beta_i$ with respect to a_{sj}, we have

$$\frac{\partial}{\partial a_{sj}}\left(\frac{\partial p_r}{\partial \beta_i}\right) = \left(\frac{J_{ir}J_{sj}}{J^2}\right)\ (s = i \text{ or } j = r) \tag{10}$$

$$\frac{\partial}{\partial a_{sj}}\left(\frac{\partial p_r}{\partial \beta_i}\right) = \left(\frac{J_{ij}J_{sr}}{J^2}\right)\ (s = i \text{ and } j \neq r) \tag{11}$$

Since sign $(J_{ij}/J) = \text{sign}(J_{ir}J_{rj}/J^2)$, we obtain $\text{sign}(J_{ij}J_{sr}/J^2) = \text{sign}(-J_{ir}J_{rj}J_{sr}/J^3) = \text{sign}(J_{ir}J_{sj}/J^2)$. Therefore we get from (10) and (11)

$$\text{sign} = \frac{\partial}{\partial a_{sj}}\left(\frac{\partial p_r}{\partial \beta_i}\right) = \text{sign}\left(\frac{J_{ir}J_{sj}}{J^2}\right) \; (s,j = 1,\ldots,n) \tag{12}$$

Hence if the jth commodity is a substitute for the sth one, it follows from (12) that $\frac{\partial}{\partial a_{sj}}\left(\frac{\partial p_r}{\partial \beta_i}\right) > 0$ (resp. <0) when the rth commodity is a substitute or a quasi-substitute for (resp. a complement or a quasi-complement with) the ith one and that $\frac{\partial}{\partial a_{sj}}\left(\frac{\partial p_i}{\partial \beta_i}\right) > 0$, while if the jth commodity is a complement with the sth one, we find that $\frac{\partial}{\partial a_{sj}}\left(\frac{\partial p_r}{\partial \beta_i}\right) < 0$ (resp. > 0) when the rth commodity is a substitute or a quasi-substitute for (resp. a complement or a quasi-complement with) the ith one and that $\frac{\partial}{\partial a_{sj}}\left(\frac{\partial p_i}{\partial \beta_i}\right) < 0$. Therefore we have the following.

Theorem 7

A given rise in demand affects all prices more, the more substitutability or the more complementarity there is between a pair of commodities in the system.

(iii) Now let the rth commodity be a substitute or a quasi-substitute for the ith commodity. It follows from (6) and (7) that

$$\frac{p_i}{p_r}\frac{\dfrac{\partial p_r}{\partial \beta_i}}{\dfrac{\partial p_i}{\partial \beta_i}} = \frac{p_i J_{ir}}{p_r J_{ii}} \tag{13}$$

which we may call the elasticity of reaction of the price p_r to a change in the price p_i. We shall analyse, in the following, the effect of a_{sj} on (13).

Suppose a_{sr} or a_{si} to vary, other coefficients a_{hk} remaining unchanged. Then we have

$$\begin{aligned}
&\frac{\partial}{\partial a_{sr}}\left(\frac{J_{ir}}{J_{ii}}\right) = -\frac{J_{ir}J_{iisr}}{J_{ii}^2} \; (s \neq i),\\
&\frac{\partial}{\partial a_{ir}}\left(\frac{J_{ir}}{J_{ii}}\right) = 0,\\
&\frac{\partial}{\partial a_{si}}\left(\frac{J_{ir}}{J_{ii}}\right) = \frac{J_{irsi}}{J_{ii}} = -\frac{J_{iisr}}{J_{ii}} \; (s \neq i),
\end{aligned} \tag{14}$$

$$\frac{\partial}{\partial a_{ii}}\left(\frac{J_{ir}}{J_{ii}}\right) = 0$$

The system obtained by omission of the ith commodity is also quasi-Frobenian, which might be decomposable. And if A is a Frobenian matrix which is decomposable, the cofactor of each element in the determinant $|\rho I - A|$ is non-negative (see Debreu and Herstein, 1953, pp. 5–6). Therefore we can easily prove that J_{iisr}/J_{ii} is non-positive [resp. non-negative] when the rth commodity is a substitute for [resp. a complement with] the sth one. From (14) we get the following theorems.

Theorem 8

If the rth commodity becomes more substitutive for or more complementary with a commodity other than the ith one, or if the ith commodity becomes more substitutive for or more complementary with a commodity other than the rth one, then the elasticity of reaction of the prices p_r to a change in the price p_i increases or remains unchanged, respectively.

Theorem 9

The elasticity (13) is increased when the ith commodity becomes more substitutive for the rth one, while it remains unchanged if the rth commodity becomes more substitutive for the ith one.

Theorem 10

The elasticity (13) is increased when the excess demand curve of the rth commodity becomes more downward sloping, while it remains unchanged when the excess demand curve of the ith commodity becomes more downward sloping.

IV Comparative dynamics

Denote the root $\nu - \alpha$ of the characteristic equation (2) by λ_1. Since λ_1 has been shown to be greater than the real part of each other root of (2), the sum of all the particular solutions other than $p_i^0 + C_i e^{\lambda_1 t}$ can be neglected at a time sufficiently distant from the initial point in time. We may refer to the particular solution corresponding to λ_1 as the steady-state solution and to the other as the solutions which represent transient states. The steady-state solution increases or decreases in the constant ratio $1:e^{\lambda_1}$ per unit of time, which expresses the damping ratio of the steady-state solution defined by T. Koopmans, 1940, p. 80. In the following, we shall analyse the effects of changes in a_{ii}. Differentiating the characteristic equation (2) partially with respect to a_{ii}

$$\sum_{r=1}^{n} |\lambda I_{n-1} - H_{rr}| \frac{d\lambda}{da_{ii}} - k_i |\lambda I_{n-1} - H_{ii}| = 0$$

solving

$$\frac{d\lambda}{da_{ii}} = \frac{k_i |\lambda I_{n-1} - H_{ii}|}{\sum_{r=1}^{n} |\lambda I_{n-1} - H_{rr}|}$$

since all of $|\lambda I_{n-1} - H_{rr}|$ are positive when $\lambda = \nu - \alpha$, $d\lambda/da_{ii}$ is necessarily positive in the vicinity of the point $\lambda = \lambda_1$. Hence we have the following.

Theorem 11

The damping ratio of the steady-state solution increases when any excess demand curve becomes more downward sloping, that is to say, the system is more stable when a demand curve is more downward sloping.

Next we shall analyse the effect of a_{ij} $(i \neq j)$. Differentiating (2) with respect to a_{ij}, we have

$$\frac{d\lambda}{da_{ij}} = \frac{k_i |(\lambda I_n - H)_{ij}|}{\sum_{r=1}^{n} |\lambda I_{n-1} - H_{rr}|} \tag{15}$$

where $|(\lambda I - H)_{ij}|$ represents the cofactor of $\lambda\delta_{ij} - k_i a_{ij}$ in the determinant $|\lambda I_n - H|$. Since, when $\lambda = \nu - \alpha$, $|(\lambda I_n - H)_{ij}|$ is positive (resp. negative) if the jth commodity is a substitute or a quasi-substitute for (resp. a complement or a quasi-complement with) the ith commodity, it follows from (15) that, in the vicinity of the point $\lambda = \lambda_1$, $d\lambda/da_{ij}$ is positive (resp. negative) when the jth commodity is a substitute or a quasi-substitute for (resp. a complement or a quasi-complement with) the ith one. Hence we have proved

Theorem 12

The damping ratio of the steady- state is greater, the less substitutability or the less complementarity there is between any pair of commodities in the system, and, hence, if two commodities are extremely substitutive or extremely complementary, then the system is necessarily unstable.

V Pattern of signs in the marginal-rate matrix

In this section we shall assume that income effects are sufficiently small. Then the gross effect of a price change upon the excess demand for a commodity is in the same direction as the true 'compensated' substitution effect which the second term X_{ij} of the aggregate Slutsky equation represents. Hence the pattern of signs in the gross effect matrix (a_{ij}) is the same as the one in the true-substitution-effect matrix $M = (X_{ij})$. Consequently, the matrix $(M + \sigma I_n)$ is also quasi-Frobenian, where σ is a positive number which is greater than the greatest modulus of $X_{11}, X_{22}, \ldots, X_{nn}$.

Next, we shall define a representative man as a man so constituted that if all members of the community were representative men, the community would act as it does in fact act. Then, if we denote the second term of the Slutsky equation of a representative man by x_{ij}, we have relations

$$X_{ij} = \theta x_{ij} \; (i,j = 1,2,\ldots,n) \tag{16}$$

where θ is the number of consumers in the system.

Since $(M + \sigma I_n)$ is quasi-Frobenian, the matrix $(N + \tau I_n)$ is also quasi-Frobenian, where $N = (x_{ij})$ $(i,j = 1,\ldots,n)$ $\tau = \sigma/\theta$. Consequently, the matrix $(N + \tau I_n)$ can be partitioned, after identical permutations of rows and columns, in the form:

$$\begin{vmatrix} N_{11} & N_{12} \\ N_{21} & N_{22} \end{vmatrix}$$

where N_{11} and N_{22} are square non-negative matrices and N_{12} and N_{21} are non-positive.

Let the representative man's marginal rate of substitution of the jth commodity for the numeraire be $R^j = R^j(x_0, x_1, \ldots, x_n)$. According to Hicks, 1946, p. 44, the jth commodity is said to be a substitute for [resp. complementary with] the ith commodity if the marginal rate of substitution of the jth commodity for the numeraire is diminished [resp. increased] when the ith commodity is substituted for the numeraire in such a way as to leave the consumer no better off than before. That is to say, the jth commodity is a substitute for [resp. complementary with] the ith one from the point of view of the representative man, if and only if

$$R_i^j - R^i R_0^j < 0 \text{ (resp. } >0)$$

where subscripts denote partial differentiation. In order to avoid any confusion, we shall refer to this definition of substitute and complement as Hicks' literary definition.

Now we shall consider what relation exists between his mathematical and literary definitions: x_{ij} and $R_i^j - R^i R_0^j$. By the familiar subjective stability conditions of the representative man, i.e., by the principle of diminishing marginal rate of substitution, the determinant $|x_{ij}|$ $(i,j = 1,\ldots,n)$ is Hicksian. Therefore the greatest positive characteristic root μ of the quasi-Frobenian equation $|\rho I_n - (N + \tau I_n)| = 0$ is less than τ.

If $\rho \geq \mu$, then the cofactor of $\rho\delta_{ji} - x_{ji} - \tau\delta_{ji}$ in $|\rho I_n - (N + \tau I_n)|$ is positive (resp. negative) when $x_{ji} + \tau\delta_{ji}$ is an element of N_{11} or N_{22} (resp. N_{12} or N_{21}). Consequently we find that the cofactor of $-x_{ji}$ $(j \neq i)$ in $|-N|$ is positive [resp. negative] when x_{ji} is an element of N_{11} or N_{22} [resp. N_{12} or N_{21}].

Since we can easily prove that the cofactor of $-x_{ji}$ in $|-N|$ is equal to $-(R_i^j - R^i R_0^j)|-N|$ and since $|-N| > 0$ from the subjective stability conditions of the representative man, hence we find that the sign of the cofactor of $-x_{ji}$ in $|-N|$ is identical with the sign of $-(R_i^j - R^i R_0^j)$. Therefore $R_i^j - R^i R_0^j$ is negative (resp. positive) if x_{ji} is an element of N_{11} or N_{22} (resp. N_{12} or N_{21}). Consequently we have:

Theorem 13

Let our system be an indecomposable quasi-Frobenian system in which income effects are sufficiently small. If two goods are substitutes or quasi-substitutes (resp. complements or quasi-complements) in terms of X_{ij} then they are substitutes (resp. complements) for the representative man, by Hicks' literary definition.

Article VII
The Cournot–Walras arbitrage, resource consuming exchange, and competitive equilibrium*

I Introduction

In recent years new lights have been shed upon the theory of perfect competition from the viewpoint of the theory of the core. With the intention of making some contributions in more or less similar directions we begin by summarizing some of the recent developments in a non-technical way.

Consider an economy E consisting of m agents, each owning an initial endowment of n commodities. The agents are interested in obtaining through exchange, commodity bundles that make them better off according to their individual preferences. The *initial endowment* of agent i is a non-negative n-vector $\bar{x}_i = (\bar{x}_{1i}, \ldots, \bar{x}_{ji}, \ldots, \bar{x}_{ni})$ and his *preferences* are represented by a real-valued *utility function* U_i defined on the non-negative orthant of R^n. The outcome of exchange is an allocation $x = (x_1, \ldots, x_i, \ldots, x_m)$, or simply (x_i), which is a redistribution of the initial endowments $(\bar{x}_i)$ which satisfies

$$\sum_{i=1}^{m} x_i = \sum_{i=1}^{m} \bar{x}_i \tag{1.1}$$

It is reasonable to argue that an allocation (x_i) that is *feasible* in the sense of satisfying (1.1) must satisfy at least two basic properties to be an admissible outcome of a realistic exchange process. First, in addition to (1.1) one must have

$$U_i(x_i) \geq U_i(\bar{x}_i) \text{ for all } i = 1, 2, \ldots, m \tag{1.2}$$

The second property is that an allocation (x_i) satisfying (1.1) is not admissible if there exists another allocation (x_i') satisfying (1.1) such that for all i

$$U_i(x_i') \geq U_i(x_i) \tag{1.3}$$

with strict inequality for some i.

* Published as Morishima and Majumdar, 1978.

Two sets of admissible outcomes or solutions to the exchange problem have been studied in considerable depth. First, in the Walrasian equilibrium analysis, attention is focused on a class of allocations attainable by using a price system which each agent accepts as given. Without aiming at generality, let us make the following assumptions on the endowments and utility functions of our agents:

A.1.1 *For each i,* $\bar{x}_i \gg 0$
A.1.2 U_i *is a continuous function on the non-negative orthant of* R^n
A.1.3 *For any non-negative* x, $x' \geq x$ *implies* $U_i(x') > U_i(x)$
A.1.4 *Let* x *and* x' *be distinct non-negative vectors and* α_1, α_2 *be positive real numbers adding up to* 1. *If* $U_i(x) \geq U_i(x')$ *then* $U_i(\alpha_1 x + \alpha_2 x') > U_i(x')$

The assumptions guarantee the existence of a *Walrasian equilibrium* which consists of a strictly positive price vector $p = (p_j) \gg 0$ and an allocation (x_i') satisfying

$$\text{(a)} \quad \sum_{i=1}^{m} x_i' = \sum_{i=1}^{m} \bar{x}_i \tag{1.4}$$

$$\text{(b) for each } i,\ U_i(x_i') \geq U_i(x) \text{ for all } x \geq 0 \text{ satisfying } px \leq p\bar{x}_i \tag{1.5}$$

The price vector $p = (p_j)$ defines the *exchange ratio* between any pair of commodities. Besides the two basic properties (1.2) and (1.3) stated earlier, a *competitive allocation* has the interesting *equal treatment property.* Two agents are said to be of the same *type* when they have the same utility function and the same initial endowment. It is easy to verify that a competitive allocation assigns the same commodity bundle to agents of the same type.

Once an equilibrium price vector p is found, a Walrasian auctioneer can easily perform the necessary redistribution of the initial resources to attain the equilibrium allocation by using the exchange rates defined by p. A basic problem is that such an equilibrium price vector need not be known to start with, and unless much stronger assumptions are made, the Walrasian tatonnement directed by an auctioneer need not lead to an equilibrium. One possibility is for the auctioneer to obtain the relevant demand functions of the agents and the initial endowments and compute the equilibrium price vector directly by using some algorithm of the type discussed by Scarf, 1967. Of course, such computation or any other adjustment process may be costly. For the moment the important thing to remember is that once an equilibrium price vector is found, the agents need not communicate with one another to attain their final allocation. Their decisions or plans can be made completely independently, and yet they will be consistent and realizable.

A second conceptual problem is the justification of the price-adopting behaviour assumed in Walrasian theory. It has long been recognized that such an assumption is tenable only when there are 'many' agents. For, in this case, the demand and supply of a single agent is negligible relative to the aggregate demand and supply, and it does not seem unnatural to assume that he believes that he does not have any influence on the terms of transactions, i.e., the exchange ratios at all. Even in the case of many agents, however, one may wonder about the possibility of a collection of agents acting together to gain some monopolistic advantage and to improve their situation relative to a competitive allocation.

Actually, the last idea is at the basis of an alternative approach that singles out a collection of allocations satisfying (1.1). A proposed allocation (x_i) satisfying (1.1) is said to be *blocked* by a (non-empty) coalition S of agents if there exists $(z_i)_{i \in S}$, such that

$$U_i(z_i) \geq U_i(x_i)$$

for all i in S with strict inequality for some i in S

$$\sum_{i \in S} z_i = \sum_{i \in S} x_i$$

The *core* of an economy consists of all allocations satisfying (1.1) that *cannot* be blocked. A proposed allocation not in the core cannot be a possible outcome of an exchange process where agents are allowed to form coalitions without costs, since there will be a group of agents not interested in the transactions involved in the proposal.

A competitive equilibrium is in the core, i.e., is unblocked. It was Edgeworth's conjecture that in an economy with many agents the core shrinks to the set of competitive allocations. Verification of this conjecture engaged the attention of a number of mathematical economists following Debreu and Scarf (1963). Since we need their result in Section 3, we state it precisely. Suppose that there are *m types* of agents and let E_r be an economy with exactly r agents of each type. Debreu and Scarf showed that under assumptions A.1.1 through A.1.3 *an allocation in the core of E_r assigns the same commodity vector to all agents of the same type*, i.e., an allocation in the core of E_r has the equal treatment property. *If (x_i) is in the core of E_r for all r, then it is competitive.*

This basic result of Debreu–Scarf for the 'replicated' economies E_r was subsequently extended to more general economies in which the size of the economy can be increased in a less restrictive way. The most definitive results seem to be those of Bewley, 1973 who pointed out the weak points of the limit theorems in Hildenbrand, 1970 and Kannai, 1970. Using quite technical arguments Bewley was able to prove that in a large economy in which there are sufficiently many agents similar to any particular one, every allocation is close to a competitive allocation. Since it is known that in general an economy has only a finite number of competitive equilibria (Debreu, 1970), the core decomposes into disjoint clusters of allocations, the allocations in a given cluster being very similar.

A different approach to study the relation between the core and the set of competitive equilibria was developed by Aumann, 1964. Instead of analysing finite economies growing in size, Aumann considered a model in which the set of agents was uncountable – an atomless measure space. In this formulation, the core turns out to be *exactly* equal to the set of competitive equilibria. Hildenbrand (1970) showed how one could consider an economy with uncountably many agents to be the 'limit' (in a precise sense) of a sequence of finite economies.

While the behaviour of the core with 'sufficiently many' agents has been the primary object of analysis, Green, 1972, showed that if different economies of a given finite size are considered, by allowing the preferences and endowments to vary, one obtains the equal treatment property rather rarely.

However, the Debreu–Scarf replication is not the only alternative way to attain a competitive equilibrium. While in a finite economy the core could be much larger than the set of competitive allocations, it is a subset of the set of Pareto optimal allocations. In section II we consider an exchange economy where agents are able to find a Pareto optimal allocation with no cost. In addition we follow Cournot and Walras in assuming that a proposed exchange will not take place when the ratio between some particular pair of commodities is not equal to the ratio of exchange rates of these commodities in terms of some third commodity. We show that if there exists an 'indecomposable' group of price-takers then the final allocations must necessarily be competitive.

In this argument we do not use the idea of 'replication' at all; the number of agents is fixed throughout. Moreover we do not assume that some of the agents will form a coalition to block a Pareto optimum allocation whenever they find that they can attain a more favourable outcome by doing so; instead, we merely assume that the agents are able to rule out those allocations which are not Pareto optimal. In this respect the model of section II is weaker or more general than the models of the core theory of exchange. On the other hand, in comparison with the usual Walrasian model of perfect competition it may be emphasized that our model does not assume that every and each agent is a price taker; we merely assume the existence of an 'indecomposable' group of price takers, which may be reduced to a single agent if it feels a sufficiently large marginal utility for any commodity which is available only in a small amount. In this respect, our model is greatly weaker than the conventional Walrasian model, but stronger than the models of the core theory which assume nothing about price-adapting behaviour. It is interesting to see that if Cournot–Walras arbitrage prevails in such an economy, Pareto optimal allocations except the competitive equilibria are all blocked and eliminated, irrespective of the number of the agents.

In the preceding discussion and the literature cited above no attention was paid to the costs involved in forming coalition. Perhaps the simplest way of capturing the idea that coalition formation may itself be resource consuming would be to specify a vector ε of goods that is used up whenever a group of agents attempts to block a proposed allocation. Thus, if $x = (x_i)$ is a proposed allocation satisfying (1.1), a coalition S of agents will block it only if it is possible to find commodity vectors $(y_i)_{i\in S}$ such that

$$\sum_{i\in S} y_i = \sum_{i\in S} \bar{x}_i - \varepsilon \text{ and } U_i(y_i) \geq U_i(x_i)$$

for all i in S with strict inequality holding for some i. Alternatively one might suppose that blocking costs depend on the size of the coalition. In the context of transferable utilities, these two variants were introduced by Shapley and Subik, 1966, in their discussion of ε cores. It is plain that the introduction of coalition costs of this type increases the size of the core, since, roughly speaking, blocking is made more difficult. A somewhat different approach is that of Vind, 1972, Grodal, 1972, and Schmeidler, 1972, who considered the model with an atomless measure space of agents and showed that the core remains unchanged if coalitions smaller than a pre-assigned size are costless to form, whereas coalitions of a larger size are impossible to form.

One may wonder, however, whether size alone is relevant in estimating the costs involved in coalition formation. Psychological factors aside, the preferences and the nature of initial endowments may well determine whether some group of agents may engage in a serious dialogue. Owners of the same commodity, or commodities complementary to each other may find it easier to communicate and may try to form a cartel to assert monopolistic power. This point has been recognized in Arrow and Hahn, 1971, p. 186. It is difficult to conjecture what general formal results can be obtained if one allows for coalition costs to vary from one group of agents to another of the same size. It is possible that quite different qualitative results may hold. As an example, suppose that in the Debreu–Scarf model one superimposes the restriction that a given semi-positive vector of commodities must be expended whenever agents of different types attempt to form a coalition to block a proposed allocation. In this case even if such costs do not increase with the size of the coalition and agents of the same type can form a costless coalition, *it is easy to construct examples in which there are allocations in the core of replicated economies violating the equal treatment property.*

Typically direct exchange involves considerable exchange of information and bargaining. Starting from the initial endowments, the agents note the gains from trade – and conflicting interests are reconciled through a sequence of offers and counteroffers. Verification of whether an allocation is acceptable – for example whether it belongs to the core – actually requires examination of alternative redistributions of the initial resources of the various groups of agents. All these may be termed 'costs of direct exchange' or costs of finding an equilibrium through direct exchange. It is reasonable to assume that such costs increase with the number of participants engaged in bargaining, perhaps more than proportionately. On the other hand, setting up a competitive market and computing an equilibrium price vector are also expensive. Whether it is preferable to engage in direct bargaining or to use prices naturally depends on the relative magnitude of these costs. The point has also been recognized by Arrow and Hahn, 1971, p. 186, who observed that 'the competitive price system may be expected to prevail when all costs of bargaining are high relative to the costs of price-directed markets'. In section III we suggest an analytical framework for a precise and formal discussion of such intuitive ideas. Throughout, the exposition is kept particularly simple by making strong assumptions. Our discussion of the elementary cases seems to indicate that more general results should be obtainable if one is prepared to use more technical arguments.

II The Cournot–Walras arbitrage

We now consider an exchange economy of a given size – there being m agents and n goods. Let h and i be indices for representing agents and j and k be those for goods. The agent i has his initial endowment $\bar{x}_i = (\bar{x}_{li}, \ldots, \bar{x}_{ni})$ and his utility function U_i, a real valued function on the non-negative orthant of R^n. In addition to assumption A.1.1 through A.1.4 we assume in this section that for agent i the following A.2.1.

A.2.1 U_i is differentiable

We specify the rules of exchange as follows. First, it is assumed that the agents reject a proposed reallocation $x^1 = (x_i^1)$ of the initial allocation $\bar{x} = (\bar{x}_i)$ unless

$$x_i^1 \gtrsim \bar{x}_i \text{ for all } i \text{ and } x_i^1 \succ \bar{x}_i \text{ for some } i$$

An eligible allocation x^1 is further compared with another eligible x^2; if $x_i^2 \succsim x_i^1$ for all i and $x_i^2 \succ x_i^1$ for some i, x^1 will be replaced by x^2, which will in turn be compared with another possible allocation. This process of monotonic replacement of x^1 by x^2, x^2 by x^3, and so on will finally settle at a Pareto optimum reallocation x, so that x has no other x' such that

$$x_i' \succsim x_i \text{ for all } i \text{ and } x_i' \succ x_i \text{ for some } i$$

At the start of the process x^1 is socially preferred to $\bar{x}$ unless $x^1 \neq \bar{x}$, and the process is monotonic. Therefore, if the preferences are assumed to be transitive, the final allocation x must dominate the initial endowment $\bar{x}$; thus, unless $x \neq \bar{x}$, we have

$$x_i \succsim \bar{x}_i \text{ for all } i \text{ and } x_i' \succ x_i \text{ for some } i$$

Throughout this section we assume that a Pareto optimum can be found without cost.

Secondly, we follow Walras (and Cournot) in assuming that agents do not agree to the final allocation unless the price, i.e., the exchange ratio of one of any two commodities in terms of the other, is equal to the ratio of the prices of these two commodities in terms of any third commodity. For, if this chain rule of exchange ratios is violated by some triplets of goods, then a direct exchange of one of the goods against another will be replaced by an indirect exchange of them through the third. Moreover, the rule tacitly pre-supposes that the prices or exchange ratios should be independent of the agents involved. Otherwise, all buyers (or sellers) will rush to the most generous sellers (or buyers).

Let $x_{ji,kh}$ be the quantity of good j that i acquires from h in exchange for good k. Quantities of goods which an agent offers to some other agent are taken as negative, so that

$$x_{ji,kh} = -x_{jh,ki} \tag{2.1}$$

Also, we have identities

$$x_{ji} = \bar{x}_{ji} + \sum_{h \neq i} \sum_{k} x_{jh,ki} \text{ for all } j \text{ and all } i \tag{2.2}$$

Now let p_{kj} be the quantity of good j acquired in exchange for one unit of good k which is independent of agents involved, so that

$$p_{kj} = \frac{x_{jh,ki}}{x_{ki,jh}} \text{ for all } h \text{ and all } i$$

This, together with (2.1) implies

$$x_{jh,ki} + p_{kj} x_{kh,ji} = 0$$

which may be put in the form

$$p_{j1}x_{jh,ki} + p_{k1}x_{kh,ji} = 0$$

because the Cournot–Walras condition of no further arbitrage requires

$$p_{kj} = \frac{p_{k1}}{p_{j1}}$$

provided that good 1 is not a free good. Hence

$$\sum_j \sum_{h \neq i} \sum_k p_{j1}x_{jh,ki} + \sum_j \sum_{h \neq i} \sum_k p_{k1}x_{kh,ji} = 0 \tag{2.3}$$

Since the first term on the left-hand side of this expression is identical with the second term, (2.3) implies that

$$2\sum_j p_{j1}\left(\sum_{h \neq i} \sum_k x_{jh,ki}\right) = 0$$

so that we obtain from (2.2)

$$\sum_j p_{j1}x_{ji} = \sum_j p_{j1}\bar{x}_{ji}, \text{ for all } i \tag{2.4}$$

that is to say, in any state where no further arbitrage is possible, goods are allocated such that the budget equation holds for each agent.

The third rule is stated as follows. Let x_i be the final allocation to agent i; it satisfies (2.2). When each i carries out only $t \times 100$ per cent of those transactions which bring it from $\bar{x}_i$ to x_i, its allocation after the trade will be $x_i(t)$ with components

$$x_{ji}(t) = \bar{x}_{ji} + t\left(\sum_{h \neq i} \sum_k x_{jh,ki}\right) \text{ for all } j \text{ and all } i$$

Obviously

$$x_i(t) = tx_i + (1 - t)\bar{x}_i \text{ for all } i$$

and

$$\sum_j p_{j1}x_{ji}(t) = \sum_j p_{i1}\bar{x}_{ji} \text{ for all } i$$

As x_i is at worst as preferable as $\bar{x}_i$, we have by A.1.4

$$x_i(t) \succ \bar{x}_i \text{ for all } i$$

so that all agents prefer to the initial allocation $\bar{x}$ an allocation $x(t) = (x_i(t))$, *which lies on the way from* $\bar{x}$ to x. This holds for all positive t less than one. But it does not necessarily imply that they prefer $x(t)$ to the final allocation x. The third rule which is required in order for the transition from $\bar{x}$ to x not to be obstructed states that

$$x_i \succsim x_i(t) \text{ for all } i \text{ and } x_i \succ x_i(t) \text{ for some } i$$

for all values of t between 0 and 1; otherwise someone would not agree, at some point on the way from $\bar{x}$ to x, to carry out exchange any further. In Walras' own words, this rule implies that 'all of the piecemeal exchange transactions, without exception and including the final one however small that may be, are advantageous, though the advantage diminishes progressively from the first to the [final] transaction' (Walras, 1954, p. 124).

Let us now prove the Identity Theorem that the final allocation satisfying the above three rules is identical with the general competitive exchange equilibrium which is established when agents maximize their own utilities subject to the respective budget equations, by taking prices as given. For the sake of simplicity we prove the theorem on the assumption that each agent retains some quantity of every good after the transactions. The proof *mutatis mutandis* holds true without this assumption, though it becomes more complicated.

As the final allocation $x = (x_i)$ is a Pareto optimum by Rule 1, the agents' indifference surfaces are tangent to each other at x. Suppose now that they are not all tangent to their budget planes; that is to say, there is an agent whose budget plane cuts its indifference surface. If it cuts from below for agent i, we have

$$x_i(t) \prec x_i \prec x_i(t') \qquad (2.5)$$

for all t and t' sufficiently close to 1 from below and above respectively. If

$$x_h(t') \succsim x_h \text{ for all } h \neq i$$

for the same t', then the x cannot be a Pareto optimum; it is dominated by $x(t')$. This is a contradiction, so that there must be an agent r for whom

$$x_r(t') \prec x_r \text{ for all } t' \text{ sufficiently close to 1 from above} \qquad (2.6)$$

If we also have $x_r \precsim x_r(t)$ for some $t < 1$, then by A.1.4 we have $x_r \prec x_r(t'')$ for some t'' such that $t < t'' < 1$. Therefore, agent r does not agree to those transactions which result in x_r, but will only agree to carrying them out partly. This is a contradiction to Rule 3; hence $x_r \succ x_r(t)$ for all t. This, together with (2.6), implies that $U_r(x_r)$ takes on a maximum at x_r subject to agent r's budget equation; therefore r's indifference curve is tangent to its budget equation. Under the assumption for simplicity that each agent retains some positive amounts of all goods, we can show that once an agent's indifference surface is tangent to its budget plane at the final allocation which is a Pareto optimum, then the same is true for all other agents. Hence, the indifference surfaces of all agents are tangent to their respective budget planes; this is obviously a contradiction to the assumption that agent *i's* budget plane cuts its indifference surface from below.

Therefore, if an agent's budget plane cuts its indifference surface, it should do so from above; that is

$$x_i(t) \succ x_i \succ x_i(t')$$

for all $t < 1$ and $t' > 1$, both being sufficiently close to 1. In this case agent i does not carry out all the transactions that result in x_i, because it reaches before x_i an $x_i(t)$ which is more preferable to x_i; thus Rule 3 is violated. Hence we have a contradiction in any case unless we accept that at the final allocation x, all agents' indifference surfaces are tangent to their respective budget planes.

We have thus seen that at the allocation x each $U_i(x_i)$ is maximized subject to the budget equation (2.4). Moreover, we have (1.1); that is, the total demand for each commodity equals its total supply at the same x. Therefore, the final allocation x satisfying our three rules is a competitive exchange equilibrium.

III Costs of finding an equilibrium

In the second section we completely ignored the costs of finding out whether a proposed allocation is a Pareto optimum, as well as the costs for the Cournot–Walras arbitrage. Similarly, in the core theory of exchange we usually ignore the costs of finding out whether an allocation is in the core, or whether it can be blocked so that it cannot be an acceptable stable outcome of the exchange process. This of course is quite unrealistic. A satisfactory treatment of this problem requires that we develop a model describing how the agents arrive at a final reallocation of the initial endowments through a succession of bilateral and multilateral exchanges. The total cost of transactions is likely to depend on various factors like the amount of search needed for agents whose preferences and endowments are such that a transaction is possible, the total number of actual transactions made or contracts executed and so on. Thus, the cost will vary from one particular path of exchanges from the initial endowments to a final reallocation to another. If such direct exchange involves expenditure of resources in amounts larger than the cost of finding a competitive equilibrium by setting up the Walrasian market, it may well be in the interest of the agents to choose the latter option and achieve a reallocation by using a price system. Instead of attempting to introduce all the conceptual difficulties at the same time, we show how some interesting results can be obtained if the standard model is modified in a simple manner.

We start with the Debreu–Scarf framework. To take the simplest example, assume that the ith agent must spend a semi-positive vector $c_i \succ 0$ to participate in the exchange process where we have

A.3.1

$$\bar{x}_i - c_i = x_i^* \gg 0$$

Next, we rule out a 'no trade outcome' of exchange, since a discussion of a resource-consuming exchange process is not meaningful unless actual transfer of commodities takes place.

A.3.2 *There exists a set of m semi-positive vectors*

$$(\tilde{x}_1, \ldots, \tilde{x}_m)$$

such that

$$\sum_{i=1}^{m} \tilde{x}_i = \sum_{i=1}^{m} x_i^*$$

and

$$U_i(\tilde{x}_i) \succ U_i(\bar{x}_i) \text{ for all } i$$

In other words, A.3.2 guarantees that although exchange is resource consuming, it pays the agents to participate in it, since it is possible for them to be better off through a redistribution of the 'net' initial endowments.

For this exchange process, an allocation (x_i) is a feasible outcome if it satisfies

$$\sum_{i=1}^{m} x_i = \sum_{i=1}^{m} x_i^* \tag{3.1}$$

Consider a hypothetical economy E^* consisting of m agents where the agent i has the utility function U_i (same as in E) and the initial endowment x_i^*. Now, any feasible allocation satisfying (3.1) that is not in the core of E^* (defined by (1.5)) can clearly be blocked by a set of agents.

Suppose that we allow for the possibility of the agents setting up a market and achieve a competitive equilibrium allocation. Typically, setting up such a market and arriving at an equilibrium will also involve expenditure of resources. Extending the notion of blocking, we say that a feasible allocation (x_i) (satisfying (3.1)) will be blocked if there is an allocation (y_i) which is a competitive equilibrium of E relative to a price system p such that for all i, $U_i(y_i - d_i) \geq U_i(x_i)$ with strict inequality for some i, where d_i is the contribution of the agent i for setting up the market, etc. Obviously $\sum_{i=1}^{m} d_i$ must be enough to cover the total cost of setting up the market and finding the equilibrium price vector. For an economy of a given size, say m, we cannot say whether an allocation satisfying (3.1) that is actually in the core of E^* can be blocked by a 'market allocation' in the sense just specified. It obviously will depend on what the total cost of setting up the market and finding out the equilibrium price vector is as compared with the total resource consumption of direct exchange $\left(\text{given by } \sum_{i=1}^{m} c_i\right)$.

With some further assumptions, definitive statements can, however, be made for the case of the sequence of replicated economies studied in Debreu–Scarf, 1963.

The first assumption is not restrictive at all in view of the recent results obtained by a number of mathematical economists following Debreu (1970).

A.3.3

Both the economies E and E have finite sets of competitive equilibria. We index the distinct equilibrium price-allocations of E and E* as* $(p^1, x^1), \ldots, (p^k, x^k), \ldots, (p^q, x^q)$ *and* $(p^{*1}, x^{*1}), \ldots, (p^{*k'}, x^{*k'}), \ldots, (p^{*q'}, x^{*q'})$ *respectively*

It has been shown by Debreu *et al.* (1970) that A.3.3 typically holds with probability one as we consider all possible endowments and for sufficiently small c_i, the number of equilibrium price vectors does not change, i.e., $q = q'$.

The next assumption is more restrictive, although the motivation behind it can be explained easily.

A.3.4

For any $k'(=1, 2, \ldots, q')$ *there is some* $k(=1, 2, \ldots, q)$ *such that for all* $i(=1, 2, \ldots, m)$ *one has* $U_i(x_i^k) \succ U_i(x_i^{*k'})$

A.3.4 is a rather strong assumption and it might be of some interest to characterize the preferences and endowments of the agents that guarantee A.3.4 since examples violating A.3.4 can be constructed. But this will be an unnecessary digression from our main theme, since our main arguments will soon be put in a framework completely independent of A.3.3 or A.3.4. At this point we go back to the sequence of replicated resource consuming economies just to note a strong and interesting implication of our assumptions that can be derived relatively easily by using the limit theorem of Debreu and Scarf.

It is useful to recall that once the competitive equilibria for E (or E^*) is known, no further calculation is needed as we increase the size of the economy in the Debreu–Scarf manner. If E_r (or E_r^*) is the economy consisting of r agents of type $i(=1,2,\ldots,m)$, then the competitive equilibria for E_r (or E_r^*) are obtained by taking each of the q competitive equilibria (p^k, x^k) for E_r and assigning to every agent of type i the same allocation $x_i, i=1,\ldots,m$.

Given our assumptions, by using the continuity of U_i it is easy to see that we can find $\varepsilon \succ 0$ such that if a non-negative vector z satisfies $\| z - x_i^{*k'} \| \prec \varepsilon$ for some $x_i^{*k'}$, it is true that $U_i(z) \prec U_i(x_i^k)$ for some x_i^k. Applying the Debreu–Scarf theorem to the sequence E_r^* of replicated economies we conclude that given $\varepsilon \succ 0$, there is some $r^0(\varepsilon)$ such that for all $r \geq r^0(\varepsilon)$ if $x^0 = (x_i^0)$ is in the core of E_r^*, then there is some competitive allocation $(p^{*k'}, x^{*k'})$ having the property that $\| x_i^{*k'} - x_i^0 \| \prec \varepsilon$ for all i. This implies that for all i, $U_i(x_i^0) \prec U_i(x_i^k)$ for some competitive equilibrium (p^k, x^k) of the economy E_r. Continuity of U_i guarantees that there are semi-positive vectors (d_i) such that $U_i(x_i^k - d_i) \succ U_i(x_i^0)$.

Suppose that the set-up costs for the markets and costs of attaining a competitive equilibrium are bounded above as the number of agents goes up. This assumption may be quite reasonable, particularly in the case of replicated economies for which the set of equilibrium price allocations of E_r (for all r) are all known, once they are computed for E. But with all these assumptions, the arguments sketched above lead precisely to the following conclusion: *when the cost of direct exchange increases 'proportionately' with* $r\left(\textit{i.e., for } E_r, \textit{ the total cost is given by } r\sum_{i=1}^{m} c_i\right)$, *then under the assumptions listed above, only 'unblocked' allocations are competitive allocations in a Walrasian market, for a sufficiently large (finite) r.* The exact value of r will, of course, depend on the behaviour of total set-up costs for the markets and the c_is.

While the arguments above were presented in the context of the replicated economies of Debreu–Scarf, they can be modified to apply to a more general framework. We assumed previously that the per capita cost of direct exchange does not depend on 'r', the common number of agents of each type. Actually, the case in which the per capita cost of direct exchange varies with the total number of agents is also interesting, if not more realistic. Suppose that the two costs discussed above – the cost of obtaining a final unblocked allocation after transactions and the set-up costs of the markets and attaining a competitive equilibrium with the help of auctioneers – are both incurred or paid for in terms of the same commodity (say, commodity 1) by the agents in proportion to their initial holdings of commodity 1. This, of course, is a rather strong assumption – such a particular commodity need not exist at all. But the assumption brings out the significance of the existence of these costs in the theory of trade in a particularly simple and intuitive manner.

At the risk of abusing the notation, let E_r denote an economy in which there are 'r' agents. The amount of commodity 1 is $c'(r)$ for finding an allocation in the core without auctioneers, and $d'(r)$ represents the cost of attaining an equilibrium allocation in a competitive market. Their allocations to agent $i(=1,2,\ldots,r)$ are denoted by $c_i'(r)$ and $d_i'(r)$ respectively. Let $c(r)$ (resp. $d(r)$) be the n vector for which the first element is $c'(r)$ (resp. $d'(r)$), others being zero. Similarly we define $c_i(r)$ and $d_i(r)$. Thus $\bar{x}_i^*(r) = \bar{x}_i - c_i(r)$ and $\bar{x}_i^{**} = \bar{x}_i - d_i(r)$ represent the net endowment of agent i after the payment of the respective costs. Let $W^*(r) = \sum_{i=1}^{r} \bar{x}_i^*(r)$ and $W^{**}(r) = \sum_{i=1}^{r} \bar{x}_i^{**}(r)$. Assume that $d'(r)$ is bounded above as r changes, and, in fact, for all r, $d_i'(r) < x_i$ where x_i is the initial endowment of the first commodity that i possesses. Thus, $\bar{x}_i^{**}(r)$ is always strictly positive (since, according to A.1 $\bar{x}_i \gg 0$) for all r. That is to say, after paying the cost of finding a competitive equilibrium, each agent i has a semi-positive initial endowment $\bar{x}_i^{**}(r)$, so that a competitive equilibrium for such an economy always exists. On the other hand, it is possible that $c'(r)$ increases monotonically with r at such a rate that for all sufficiently large $r, c'(r) > \sum_{i=1}^{r} \bar{x}_{1i}$ so that the amount of commodity 1 available is simply short of what is essential to pay for the costs of direct reallocations or transactions in an economy of such a size. Thus, the set of all feasible reallocations becomes empty and the agents are left with their initial endowments. If in the competitive equilibria attainable for these economies each agent is better off relative to the 'no-trade situation', then the only viable outcomes are the reallocations achieved in the competitive markets.

Suppose that there exists some critical value r_0 such that for all $r < r_0$ one has $c'(r) < d'(r)$ and for all $r > r_0, c'(r) > d'(r)$ with equality holding for r_0. In this case, for all $r < r_0$, $W^*(r) > W^{**}(r)$. If (x_i^{**}) is any competitive market allocation $\left(\text{satisfying } \sum_{i=1}^{r} x_i^{**} = W^{**}(r)\right)$ for the economy $E_r(r \prec r_0)$, then

$x_i^{**} + \frac{1}{r}[W^*(r) - W^{**}(r)]$ is a feasible reallocation for *direct exchange* among the r agents. With a strong monotonicity assumption on U_i, the agents will clearly 'block' (x_i^{**}) and reject the idea of a price-guided reallocation in a market and engage in direct exchange. In this case, the set-up costs for markets being too high, the competitive allocations are no longer in the admissible set of unblocked reallocations. Thus, as long as $r \prec r_0$, there is a basic qualitative difference even in this simple framework due to the difference in the behaviour of costs.

We may conclude by summarizing some of the basic ideas. Introduction of costs involved in direct trading or in setting up a market and achieving equilibrium may lead to some interesting problems and new qualitative results. In an economy where the agents have the options of either setting up a competitive market or bargaining directly, the concept of 'blocking' can be modified. A proposed reallocation will be rejected if, after taking into account the appropriate costs, a better reallocation is possible either by using the price system or direct negotiation. In such a context, the set of competitive equilibria need not be 'unblocked' in small economies, if costs of achieving the equilibria are too high relative to the costs of direct exchange. Under some plausible conditions on the nature of these costs, the only unblocked allocations in large economies must necessarily be competitive allocations. The last statement is *prima facie* similar to the Edgeworth conjecture that the core approximates the competitive equilibria in large economies, but the reasons are entirely different.

Article VIII
The dilemma of durable goods

1 Under the slogan of the 'neoclassical synthesis' the neoclassical general equilibrium theory and Keynesian economics have both been taught in parallel in two classrooms. In one it is taught that the price mechanism works; a general equilibrium exists at which labour is fully employed and the economy is in a state of Pareto-optimum, while in the other, full employment is taught to be impossible and the market has to be supported and supplemented by conscious and conscientious economic policy activities of the government. These two views should of course be incompatible. As Keynes has pointed out, there must be a hidden hypothesis of 'Say's law' behind the neoclassical world; where it is rejected, the theory has to abdicate and be replaced by a new regime in which unemployment is recognized as a long-standing, unremovable state of affairs, that is inevitable. The mechanism of self-regulation of the market does not work where Say's law of the market is negated. It is deeply disappointing particularly for the author that he has to complete this volume with the final section of the Addendum which establishes a thesis that no general equilibrium of full employment is possible unless the equalization of rates of profits between capital goods is ruled out.

I call this thesis the 'dilemma of durable goods' that is very much consistent with Keynes' view of 'Say's law'. It may be regarded as a microeconomic version of the law which Keynes put in macroeconomic terms. Although Walras seriously but unsuccessfully faced the dilemma (as will be seen in section 2 below), it has been a tradition of the general equilibrium theory since Hicks to avoid the dilemma by ignoring durable goods or treating them in the same way as we deal with non-durable goods. I have to say that my *DKR* is not an exception to this tradition. I now fully acknowledge the weakness of the volume in this respect, but this is because of a development of the theory which has happened during the forty-five years after the publication of *DKR*. Moreover, the 'dilemma' has not yet been solved unfortunately, or fortunately, so that it remains still to be challenged.

Let us be concerned with an economy with m kinds of durable capital goods, in addition to n kinds of non-durable goods for which the price mechanism works in the sense that the price of each non-durable good changes such that its demand is adjusted to its supply. Each durable capital good has three markets: a market for the new good, another for the second-hand good, and a third for capital services. The problem related to the second-hand goods will be discussed in the final section of this article. Until then, we are only concerned with the remaining two markets.

Let us assume that new capital goods which are bought in the market for the new capital goods in the current period will be installed in the buyer's factory in the same period, so that they are available for production from the next period. The total amount of capital good i which is available for production in the current period, K_i, is the sum of capital good i installed in the past. We assume all capital goods never deteriorate in their productivity; technological improvements are ignored. These enable us to remain unconcerned with vintages and ages of capital goods. K_i is a simple sum of outputs of i in the past.

Thus, for each capital good there are a pair of markets: one for newly produced capital good i and the other for the capital services which are brought forth by capital good i produced in the past. We then have $2m$ markets in total. Of course, there are a pair of supply and demand to each of them. The supply of new capital good i is its output which is just produced and made available in the market for sale in the current period, while its demand is the one for investment for the purpose of production in the future. These are designated X_i and D_i, respectively. On the other hand, as for capital services, we assume that one unit of the stock of capital good i yields one unit of capital service i, for the sake of simplicity. Then the supply of capital service i amounts to K_i, which is constant, while its demand F_i is the sum of the firms' demands for the purpose of producing capital goods, $X_1,\ldots,X_m$ and non-durable goods $X_{m+1},\ldots,X_{m+n}$; we thus have

$$F_i = H_{i1} + \ldots + H_{im} + H_{im+1} + \ldots + H_{im+n}$$

where $H_{ij}, j = 1,\ldots,m+n$, is the demand for factor i that is needed for producing X_j (durable capital good or non-durable good).

2 Walras is concerned with the case of all production functions being subject to constant returns to scale and the firms choosing production coefficients so as to minimize the unit cost of production. Then the coefficients are obtained as functions of the prices of the factors of production. Let a_{ij} be the amount of factor i which is used for producing one unit of good j. Then

$$H_{ij} = a_{ij}X_j$$

where the production coefficient a_{ij} is a function of the prices of factors of production. The price of the product j is determined so as to be equal to its unit cost, that is also a function of factor prices. We have such an equation for each product.

We assume only labour is an exogenous (non-producible) factor, so that we have $m + n$ price–cost equations taken altogether. On the left-hand side of the equations we have the prices of products, $p_1, \ldots, p_m, p_{m+1}, \ldots, p_{m+n}$, while on the right-hand side prices of factors of production including the price of labour, p_{m+n+1}. As we assume no production yielding an excess profit, the price of capital service i is the income of the capitalist who owns one unit of capital good i. Remembering that depreciations are all ignored and that the rates of profits are equalized through all capital goods, we see that prices of products, the rate of profits, and the wage rate are ultimate variables on the right-hand side of the price–cost equations. The theorems 1 and 2 of chapter III of Morishima (1964, p. 66) together imply that once the value of the real wage rate is specified, then the equilibrium prices of commodities and the equilibrium rate of profits (which I called the 'long-run equilibrium' prices and rate of interest, respectively, in the book) are determined. The correspondence between the rate of profits and the real wage rate is, in particular, referred to by Samuelson as the factor price frontier. A similar 'frontier' can be traced out between the equilibrium price of commodity i and the real wage rate w, for all $i = 1, \ldots, m + n$. The remaining price element, the real wage rate, will be determined such that full employment is realized in the labour market. Then the prices of all products and the rate of profits (and therefore the prices of capital services too) are determined by the frontier for each commodity (or the equation for the cost of production).

Thus, contrary to the usual view of Walras, the prices of commodities produced are determined, in his own system, by the price–cost equations, rather than the equations of supply = demand; only the prices of the primary factors of production (in our present case, labour being the single factor) are set so as to make their supplies equal their respective demands. Once the prices are given, the demands for non-capital goods, $D_i(p, w), i = m + 1, \ldots, m + n$, are determined, then the outputs of these commodities, X_i, are fixed such that they are equal to their demands, $X_i = D_i(p, w), i = m + 1, \ldots, m + n$. Then the equilibrium conditions for capital services, $i = 1, \ldots, m$, are written

$$\begin{aligned} a_{11}X_1 + \ldots + a_{1m}X_m + a_{1m+1}X_{m+1} + \ldots + a_{1m+n}X_{m+n} &= K_1, \\ a_{21}X_1 + \ldots + a_{2m}X_m + a_{2m+1}X_{m+1} + \ldots + a_{2m+n}X_{m+n} &= K_2, \\ a_{m1}X_1 + \ldots + a_{mm}X_m + a_{mm+1}X_{m+1} + \ldots + a_{mm+n}X_{m+n} &= K_m \end{aligned} \tag{1}$$

In each of these equations the last n terms, $a_{im+1}X_{m+1}, \ldots, a_{im+n}X_{m+n}$, are already fixed, so that these m equations contain m unknowns, $X_1, \ldots, X_m$. The markets for capital services are cleared by adjusting quantities of outputs rather than the prices of capital services. It must be remembered that in the treatment of the markets of capital services, the real Walras is again very much contrary to the conventional, accepted view of him.

Finally, we have the markets of newly produced capital goods. Obviously their outputs that have been determined above so as to make full employment of the existing stocks of capital goods are supplied to the demanders. It is implied implicity that there are in the market the same amounts of demand which are enough to buy out all of the new capital goods supplied. Walras did not state this fact explicitly, but the existence of such demands is an implicit but necessary assumption for his system to be a complete system of general equilibrium. Thus he has tacitly assumed that for each capital good there is enough demand that is as large as its supply, however large the latter may be. That is to say, the equations

$$D_i = X_i \tag{2}$$

always hold for all $i = 1, \ldots, m$, regardless of the values of X_i fixed. Of course, there is no economic justification for them, but once we assume an aggregate identity

$$p_1X_1 + p_2X_2 + \ldots + p_mX_m \equiv p_1D_1 + p_2D_2 + \ldots + p_mD_m, \tag{2'}$$

then the equations (2) needed for the equilibrium of the markets of the new capital goods immediately follow from (2′), because investors are indifferent to the markets since the profitability is the same among these capital goods. (2′) is referred to as Say's law because it implies that the total supply of capital goods creates exactly the same amount of the total demand for them. We may then conclude that Walras' general equilibrium of capital formation exists only under the unrealistic assumption of Say's law.

3 After Hicks, theorists have been concerned with the economy where each of the firms is provided with a production function which is subject to diminishing returns. With given prices it determines its output so as to maximize its profits. Then the firm's output X_i, inputs $H_{ji}, j = 1, \ldots, m$, and labour input H_{m+n+1i} are obtained as functions of the prices of factors of production as well as the price of output p_i. We have three kinds of markets: They are for (1) the non-durable products, (2) the factors of production, and (3) the durable capital goods. In the market for the first kind, prices of non-durable goods are determined such that their supplies equal their respective demands

$$D_i = X_i, \ i = m + 1, \ldots, m + n \tag{3}$$

The prices of capital services and the price of labour (the wage rate) are determined by

$$H_{j1} + \ldots + H_{jm+n} = K_j, j = 1, \ldots, m \tag{4}$$

$$H_{m+n+1,1} + \ldots + H_{m+n+1,m+n} = N \tag{5}$$

respectively, where N stands for the supply of labour. Finally, the price of capital goods are determined by

$$D_i = X_i, i = 1, \ldots, m \tag{6}$$

Equations (3), (4), (5), (6) together give us prices $p_1, \ldots, p_m, p_{m+1}, \ldots, p_{m+n}, p_{m+n+1}$, and $q_1, \ldots, q_m$, where q_i are prices of capital services.[1]

Thus the 'price mechanism' works perfectly as is claimed by the mainline economists. We have full employment of labour (5), together with full utilization of capital stocks (4), in the state of general equilibrium. It is nevertheless true that it is not a state of genuine equilibrium, because the system has no endogenous mechanism which makes the rates of profits equal through all capital goods. In fact, unless some exceptionally favourable circumstances prevail, we do not have

$$q_1/p_1 = q_2/p_2 = \ldots = q_m/p_m$$

where q_i is the price of capital service i. It is also obvious that there is no mechanism which equates the rates of profits to each other through firms. These mean that this type of equilibrium is established only in a state where the circulation of capital is not perfect but limited. It is a state where the competition in terms of the profitability is obstructed by certain barriers; once they are removed, that equilibrium is vacated and the economy is trapped in a state with some of the equations, (3)–(6), being violated. Thus it is at least clear that contemporary general equilibrium theory does not carefully examine the consequences of the inequality in the rate of profits.

4 Garegnani (1960) offered another view of Walras in his book published in 1960, which contrasts with my article that appeared in the same year (M. Morishima, 1960, pp. 238–43). By mixing a part of Walras' general equilibrium equation system with a part of his system of tatonnement algorithm, Garegnani makes up a new mixed Walrasian model consisting of a part determined by equilibrium equations and a part to be adjusted by the tatonnement procedure. In particular, he views that prices are determined by the price–cost equations, while the market for capital

[1] In (3)–(6) D_is are given as function of prices. Of course, strictly speaking, only relative prices are determined, because one of the equations (3)–(6) follows from the rest, according to the usual business. Also, in (3)–(6) the equation is replaced by an inequality '$\leqq$' if we allow for a free good.

services is adjusted according to the rule for tatonnement: the price of capital service *i* rises, or falls, wherever there is an excess demand for, or supply of, the service, respectively. Therefore, roughly speaking, we may say that Garegnani's model is a mixture of section 2 and section 3 above, that is, the price determination sector of section 2 and the capital service markets of section 3.

Garegnani then insists that the prices of capital services are doubly determined, once by the unit costs of production of capital goods assuring the prices of capital services in proportion to the prices of capital goods and then twice by the scarcity of the services obtained from historically given capital stocks. And he concludes that this double determination implies overdeterminacy. This is, however, a totally wrong conclusion.[2]

This is seen in the following way. It is true that there are double specifications of a state of general equilibrium in Walras' *Elements*, one in terms of equations (or more accurately, in terms of inequalities) and the other as a state to be obtained at the end of the tatonnement process. But it is also true that the double specifications neither mean overspecification nor overdeterminacy. They may, in fact, be consistent with each other, as they actually are in Walras' own model which implicitly assumes Say's law. This is the essence of my article in 1960. Starting with a mapping of prices and quantities into themselves which accords with tatonnement adjustments, I have obtained a fixed point at which Walras' general equilibrium conditions (equations or inequalities) are all satisfied, so that it is a point of general equilibrium. It is now evident that Walras' tatonnement (i.e., price adjustment according to scarcity and quantity adjustments according to profitability) leads the economy to a state where the price–cost equations are all held. By Say's law each D_i adjusts itself to the corresponding X_i thus determined. Garegnani did not see this connection between the equation approach and the adjustment approach through Say's law in Walras. It is more unfortunate that the so-called neo-Ricardians' (such as Eatwell's) attacks on Walras are based on this short-sighted view of him by Garegnani. This seems also to imply that the latter did not properly appreciate the fact that outputs of new capital goods are regarded by Walras as perfectly flexible. Thus he missed to point out Walras' weak point that the true demand functions of new capital goods are absent in Walras' economy, so that if they are explicitly introduced to avoid Say's law, the

[2] Unfortunately, on the basis of this false statement, Lord Eatwell magnified the scale of falsification in his Ph.D thesis by saying that Walras can avoid the Garegnani overdeterminacy *only* when only one good is produced, others being not produced because they are less profitable than the one produced. Of course, this statement is entirely wrong. Whereas Garegnani too gave some consideration to the inequality approach, it did not lead him to the correct understanding of Walras. See chapter 2 (written in 1962) of P. Garegnani, 1989.

system has to suffer from another kind of overdeterminacy as I have discussed in section 2 above, that is totally different from the one alleged by Garegnani.

5 For those neo-classical economists who see general equilibrium theory from the point of view of its interpretation as is presented in the section above, the von Neumann theory of economic equilibrium is very different. But for those who correctly take Walras as we have seen him in section 2, it is clear that von Neumann's view of economic equilibrium does not greatly differ from Walras'. Of course there are obvious differences between them: (1) von Neumann was concerned with a state of balanced growth, while Walras did not make such a restriction upon capital accumulation. (2) The former ruled out consumers' choice, while it was a main concern of the latter. (3) The former allowed for joint production, while the latter ruled it out. As for labour, as discussed before and will be repeated later, the former made some peculiar assumptions, but they may be replaced by usual assumptions on demand for and supply of labour which are acceptable for the latter. Removing these von Neumann assumptions from his model, I tried to reduce it to a Walrasian model in my (1969) *Theory of Economic Growth*, chapters VI–VIII. In the following I deal with this version, but the same argument *mutatis mutandis* holds for the original von Neumann model too.

Such a von Neumann–Walras model consists of two sets of conditions (or inequalities): (1) Price–cost inequalities and supply–demand inequalities. The former implies that the total prices obtained from a unit operation of an activity does not exceed the unit cost including the normal profits. The latter implies that the demand for a good does not exceed its supply. This condition holds not only for products but also for the goods used for production, including labour and land, though I neglect land throughout the following.

These sets of conditions are not independent from, but coupled with, each other. That is to say, if the price–cost condition holds for an activity with strict inequality, then it is not utilized for production at all. Secondly, if the supply–demand condition holds for a commodity with strict inequality, it cannot have a positive price and should be a free good. These two relations, which I call the rule of profitability (stating that an unprofitable activity should not be employed) and the rule of free goods (stating that the commodity supplied in excess should not have a positive price), hold together only in the state of general equilibrium. In other disequilibrium states, as well as the equilibrium state, however, the following powerful identity holds:

$$\Sigma X_i E_i + \Sigma F_j p_j + Gw + (I - A) + (S - I) \equiv 0 \qquad (7)$$

where E_i = excess profits of an activity i, X_i = its level of activity, F_j = excess demand for commodity j, p_j = its price, G = excess demand for labour, w = the wage rate, A = the increase in the stocks of goods from the current period to the next, I = the total amount of investment demand, and S = savings. I call this identity the (extended) Walras' law.[3]

Identity (7) is derived in the following way. Let T be the total purchasing power available in the society which consists of the total supply of labour *plus* the profits obtained from the production activities in the previous period. The former equals the total amount of the excess supply of labour *plus* the total wages for labour to be paid by the firms, while the latter equals the income earned by selling outputs that have been produced by the activities in the past and just become available in the market at the beginning of the current period (this part being designated by (a)) *minus* costs spent for production in the past (designated by (b)). Then (a) is equal to the excess supply of commodities *plus* the total consumption and the total amount of commodities demanded for production. This last, together with the wage payment, gives the costs spent for production in the present period, that is equal to the value of output left over to the next period *minus* the excess profits. The former may exceed the value of output left over to the present from the past. This last is shown to be equal to the part (b) above defined in terms of the cost prices, as we assume that the rule of profitability prevailed in the previous period.

Now we may summarize the above, rather tedious description of accounting relations into the following equation

$T \equiv$ the excess supply of commodities and labour − the excess profits + consumption + the increase in the stocks of goods from the current period to the next

Hence

The excess demand for commodities and labour + the excess profits + T − consumption − the increase in the stocks of goods $\equiv 0$

The term, T − consumption, represents savings. Therefore, the above identity can be put, in symbols, in the form (7); that is the extended Walras law. In the usual case which assumes the excess profits to be included in T, that term constitutes a part of S, and (7) reduces to the usual form as is given by (19) on page 92 of my *Walras' Economics*.

The state of general equilibrium is defined as

(i) no process yielding excess profits, $E_i \leq 0$,

[3] See Morishima, 1969, p. 139.

(ii) no excess demand for any commodity, $F_j \leqq 0$,
(iii) no excess demand for labour, $G \leqq 0$,
(iv) the stocks of goods increased in the current period being equal to investment demands for use in the future, $A = I$.

By the rule of profitability, $X_i = 0$ if $E_i < 0$ in (i), while by the rule of free goods $p_j = 0$ if $F_j < 0$ in (ii) and $w = 0$ if $G < 0$ in (iii). Therefore we have $X_iE_i = 0$, $F_jp_j = 0$ and $Gw = 0$ in the state of general equilibrium, so that it follows from (7) that $S = I$ (savings = the total amount of investment demands) holds in equilibrium.

We can show that the von Neumann equilibrium is a special case of the general equilibrium analysis of this type. In fact, we obtain his model of balanced growth where $X_j = (1 + g)X_{j,-1}$ ($X_{i,-1}$ is the level of activity in the previous period and g is the common rate of growth), at stationary prices, i.e., $p_j = p_{j,-1}$ and $w = w_{-1}$ ($p_{j,-1}$ and w_{-1} are the price and wage rate in the previous period), there is no consumer choice for the workers and the capitalists, and finally there is neither excess supply nor excess demand for labour as he assumes that labour is exported or imported as soon as we find an excess supply of excess demand in the labour market.[4]

The conditions (i), (ii), (iii), (iv) above correspond to the equations in section 2 above; that is, (i) to Walras' price–cost equations and (ii) to (1). Consequently, a state of general equilibrium is obtained in the same way as Walras found solutions to his system of equilibrium of capital formation.[5] First, we find a price–wage system which satisfies (i) and (iii) above. As the normal profits may be included in the cost of production in the form of the prices paid for capital services, the conditions for an equal rate of profits by von Neumann are equivalent to Walras' price–cost equations. Secondly, X_is are adjusted so as to fulfil (ii), i.e., (1) in section 2. We note that as the present system of the von Neumann–Walras type allows for joint production, the number of activities is not necessarily equal to the number of goods. Consequently, all the conditions (i), (ii), (iii) are put in inequality forms, rather than the equation forms in section 2; therefore, the activity levels X_i, the prices p_j, and the wage rate w have to be adjusted so as to fulfil the rule of profitability and the rule of free goods. Finally, (iv) corresponds to (2′). Where all these conditions are realized, it follows from Walras' law that savings equal investment demand, $S = I$. On this point we need rather careful comments.

The most fundamental assumption of the von Neumann model is that it

4 For more detailed argument, see Morishima, 1969, chapter VIII.

5 We may therefore say that Walras is a legitimate precursor of von Neumann. I do not understand that Joan Robinson was hostile to Walras, whereas she was rather sympathetic to von Neumann.

takes one period to complete any production activity. This means that the outputs of current activities appear only in the beginning of the next period. Their prices are therefore determined in the markets of the next period, so that we can only make expectations of them in the current period. Of course the people buy the same kinds of commodities in the current period, but they are the products of the activities carried out in the previous period. To avoid expected prices, von Neumann assumes that the prices prevailing in the current markets will continue to hold in the next period. We have, however, no economic rationale for the neglect of expected prices.

Once expectations are allowed for, the profitability is calculated on the basis of outputs evaluated in terms of expected prices and inputs in terms of current prices. It is evident that the choice of techniques is affected by more or less precarious elements of price expectations. Also the levels of current production activities depend on the demands which we may expect in the next period when outputs become available. The outputs of the next period are evaluated at their expected prices in this period. Their total sum is discounted by 1 + the rate of normal profits (because it is equal to the rate of interest). This is compared with the same sum for the previous period, and the difference between them gives the increase in the stocks of goods in the current period, denoted by A. In this difference, the first part is devoted for replacement of the existing stocks and the rest provides a net increase in the stocks.

Let D_j be the investment demand for commodity j and ϕ_j its expected price that is formed on the basis of the current prices. The total of investment demand amounts to

$$I = \Sigma\phi_j D_j$$

In order for A to be accepted and useful in the next period, A should be equal to I as is required by (iv). If this holds, together with other conditions (i), (ii), (iii) satisfying the rules of profitability and free goods, we obtain $S = I$ from (7). This means that investment demands D_j are sufficiently flexible; otherwise I does not equal A and, therefore, I does not reach S, a gap remaining between them. Then, even though techniques are chosen in an efficient way, that is to say, condition (i) satisfies the rule of profitability, (ii) and (iii) violate the rule of free goods wherever $S = A > I$. Thus, there must be either unemployment of labour at a positive wage rate, or a commodity which is in excess supply at a positive price.

This is the conclusion obtained by Keynes; it occurs when investment demands D_j cease to be flexible at some levels, so that I does not reach S. When Say's law prevails, D_js are created flexibly, so that there is no barrier for the aggregate demand to reach S. This Keynesian case is obtained only where Say's law does not hold. We obtain this conclusion because we deal with an economy with capital goods and are confronted with the 'dilemma of durable goods'. We have first to take account of the equalization of rates of profits of all capital goods; then a capital good and the capital service from it have no two prices which can change independently. We have only one price to clear two markets, the market for a new capital good *k* and the market for the capital service offered by the existing stock of the capital good *k*. If the latter is cleared by adjusting the price of the capital service, then the price of the corresponding capital good is also fixed, so that the market for a new capital good is cleared only by changing the quantity of the capital good produced. If there is enough demand for them, both markets are cleared. In order to have this we must assume Say's law. Where we negate it because of its implausibility, we have markets of capital goods left uncleared. In such circumstances it is highly likely that there will be unemployment of labour too.

It is ironic to see that this conclusion has similar effects to Garegnani's rejective view of Walras' capital theory which he derived by reasoning wrongly. Rejecting his argument, I have instead found that the equal rate of profits hinders the economy from settling at a state of general equilibrium with full employment of labour and full use of stocks of goods, unless Say's law whose unrealistic character is obvious is accepted.[6] Keynes accepted the equal rate of profits[7] and rejected Say's law. It is seen from the above that I have also made the same choice. Then the Walrasian full-employment and full-use equilibrium is impossible and should accordingly be replaced by a weaker one that allows for unemployment and other disequilibrium elements. This might perhaps be the change that Garegnani wanted to have, when he wrongly declared an internal inconsistency or 'overdeterminacy' of Walras' theory of capital.

Anyhow, the concept of general equilibrium of full employment of labour and full use of resources and capital stocks produced in the past, whether Walras' one equalizing the rates of profits or Hicks', Arrow's and Hahn's or Patinkin's leaving the rates unequal, is not a concept useful to examine the actual state of the economy with a big magnitude of unemployment. The general equilibrium theory should deal with less restrictive states of equilibrium, or disequilibrium. There is a good reason why Walras would not oppose but rather accept this change. As has been seen in article I above, Walras drafted a programme of analysis of economic fluctuations in a form of sequential analysis of disequilibrium states which are obtained by truncating the tatonnement process in its middle. We may well conceive of

[6] M. Morishima, 1977, p. 95; 1989. With regard to Hicks' stance towards this problem see Morishima, 1994.

[7] Keynes accepts that marginal efficiencies of capital goods are equalized throughout. This is his version of the equal rate of profits.

him agreeing to truncate the process at a point where investment demands reach the ceiling set by the anti-Say's law. Of course, there is no such analysis by Walras but the disequilibrium is not entirely foreign to him.

6 Before moving to the problem of second-hand markets for durable capital goods, two comments are made on sections 2 and 3, respectively. First, it has been said that constant returns to scale are assumed for the production of each commodity in section 2. But the constancy of returns to scale is not necessary for the approach there. Even though the case of diminishing returns that has been discussed in section 3 may alternatively be dealt with as in section 2. We may minimize the unit cost of production for each given level of output; then the production coefficients are determined as functions of prices and the output, and the price of output is determined so as to be equal to the minimum unit costs (which already include normal profits). In solving simultaneous equations (or inequalities) of prices and costs, outputs are regarded as parameters. On the other hand, in solving the demand–supply equations (or inequalities) concerning capital services, (1) above, we notice that input coefficients a_{ij} are functions of prices and outputs. Since prices are functions of outputs as we have just seen above, and outputs of non-durable goods are determined so as to equal their demand, outputs of durable capital goods may be obtained so that (1) is fulfilled.

In the neo-classical approach discussed in section 3 one might say that even though temporary equilibrium prices established there do not satisfy the condition of equal rate of profits, this would be considered to be legitimate enough because the period needed for establishing a temporary equilibrium, for example Hicks' 'week', is too short for realizing a state of equal rate of profits. This state would be obtained through a long process of capital movement over a considerable number of weeks. Capital would desert inefficient firms and move towards more efficient ones. Finally, capital is allocated among most efficient firms for which rates of profits are equalized. However, neo-classical general equilibrium theorists have never been concerned with explaining the process of the rise and fall of firms as a result of immigration and emigration of capital. In the Hicks–Arrow–Debreu model, for example, in any period firms with production possibility sets exogenously given are provided with an amount of capital that is enough for achieving its maximum profits.

Finally, some comments on the second-hand markets on durable capital goods: first, let k be a capital good of t years old and $k + 1$ be the same capital good of $t + 1$ years old. Von Neumann distinguishes $k + 1$ from k and treats them as different commodities. But $k + 1$ is produced only by k. A process, which produces commodity j by using one unit of capital good k

and other factors of production in appropriate units, makes not only one unit of commodity j but also one unit of the one year older capital good, $k+1$, left over, available in the markets of the next period. Thus he regards $k+1$ as the joint output of j. Let l_j be the use of labour per unit operation of this process. Then the profitability of the process is calculated by

$$\phi_j + \phi_{k+1} - \beta(\Sigma^* a_{ji}p_i + p_k + wl_j)$$

where ϕ_j and ϕ_{k+1} are expected prices of the respective goods, Σ^* is the summation over all goods used for production of j and $k+1$, and $\beta = 1 +$ the rate of normal profits (or the rate of interest). Where the above expression takes on a positive value, the process brings forth excess profits; if it is zero, it yields only normal profits. We assume this in the following.

Let us write

$$\beta p_k - \phi_{k+1} = \beta p_k - p_k + p_k - \phi_{k+1} = rp_k + \delta p_k$$

where $r =$ the rate of normal profits and $\delta = (p_k - \phi_{k+1})/p_k =$ the rate of depreciation. Then the profitability equation

$$\phi_j + \phi_{k+1} - \beta(\Sigma^* a_{ji}p_i + p_k + wl_j) = 0$$

may be put in the form

$$\phi_j = \Sigma^* a_{ji}p_i + \delta p_k + wl_j + r \text{ (the total unit cost including the cost of using capital good } k\text{)}$$

As far as this price–cost equation is concerned, von Neumann's accounting that treats the older capital good $k+1$ as joint output is not different from the conventional one. It distinguishes various second-hand capital goods according to their ages as well as their kinds; and hence we have many second-hand markets. Then we have the expected prices $\phi_{k+1}, \phi_{k+2}, \ldots$ of old capital goods. If enough demand is not expected for $k+h$ old capital good, it would become free and would therefore be discarded. We arrive at the conclusion that investment demands concerning old capital goods are crucial in deciding their economic lifetime. Indeed, to discard or not to discard old capital goods is a very important part of the problem of investment. This important problem is not dealt with properly by von Neumann, since he is only concerned with the state of balanced growth equilibrium.

Secondly, let X_k be the output of capital good k. If there is enough demand for k, however large X_k may be, we say that Say's law holds in the market of k. Since it can be shown that the total value of X_k, $\Sigma p_k X_k$, for all capital goods equals the aggregate savings, the total value of demand for capital goods, i.e., the aggregate investment, equals the aggregate savings, where Say's law prevails in every market. Thus we see that the law holds macroeconomically in exactly the same sense as Keynes, wherever it prevails microeconomically, i.e., in every capital good market.

Next we show that the converse is also true. To see this, the total amount of investment, that is equal to the aggregate savings because of the macroeconomic Say's law, is allocated among capital goods according to the order of their rates of profits. Then, where these rates are equalized, investors are indifferent among capital goods, so that $S \equiv \Sigma p_k X_k$ is distributed such that $X_k = D_k$ for every k because $I \equiv \Sigma p_k D_k$ and $S \equiv I$ by Say's law. We thus obtain microeconomic Say's law.

Thirdly, we have so far been concerned with the problem of the 'dilemma of durable goods', on the assumption that these are all real (non-monetary) commodities. However, it is evident that money is also a durable commodity, so that it has two markets: rental and stock markets. What I have called the securities market in this volume is the lending and borrowing market, or the buying and selling market of money services for one week. That is to say, it is the rental market of money. On the other hand, the money market, where the demand for cash balances is equated to the existing amount of money, is the stock market of money.

As we have seen in this volume Hicks wanted to show the equivalence of the loanable fund theory of interest based on the rental market of money and the liquidity preference theory based on the stock market of money. I have reviewed his argument and reached the conclusion that although they are not equivalent from the genetical-causal point of view, they obtain the same level of the rate of interest in the state of temporary general equilibrium. Like Hicks, I have, however, neglected in this analysis, the problem of the dilemma of durable goods entirely.

In the event of the rate of profits being equalized, we have to conclude differently. Let us assume, for simplicity's sake, that there is no non-durable commodity. Let E_0 be the excess demand for money, E_1 the excess demand for securities, E_i, $i = 2, \ldots, n$, the excess demand for i in its rental market, E_j, $j = i + n - 1$, where $i = 2, \ldots, n$, the excess demand for j in the stock market j. We may then put Walras' law in the form

$$E_0 + E_1 + \Sigma p_i E_i + \Sigma p_j E_j = 0$$

If we assume the equal rate of profits for good $i = 2, \ldots, n$, that is, if

$$\frac{p_2}{p_{n+1}} = \frac{p_3}{p_{n+2}} = \ldots = \frac{p_n}{p_{2n-1}} \tag{8}$$

then the price mechanism cannot work perfectly because of the dilemma of durable goods; so we cannot have

$$E_i = 0, i = 2, \ldots, 2n - 1$$

simultaneously. In the case of the price mechanism working in the rental markets and investment demand being insufficient for new capital goods, we would have

$$E_i = 0, i = 2, \ldots, n; \; E_j < 0, j = n + 1, \ldots, 2n - 1$$

so that

$$E_0 + E_1 > 0$$

by virtue of Walras' law.

Now we assume, according to the liquidity preference theory, that the rate of interest r is determined such that $E_0 = 0$.[8] Then the rates of profits listed in (8) all adjust themselves so as to equal the r thus determined. The insufficiency of effective demand that is represented by $\sum_{n+1}^{2n-1} p_j E_j$ is also determined correspondingly. The government will then try and fill up the shortage at least partly. Let β_j, $j = n + 1, \ldots, 2n - 1$, be the demand for good j of the government. To make the expenditure of the amount $\Sigma p_j \beta_j$, the government must raise the same amount of money; to do so it must issue securities of the same amount. Let the government's supply of securities be S_1^G which is

$$S_1^G = \Sigma p_j \beta_j \tag{9}$$

This equation assumes that the amount of money the government acquires by issuing securities is immediately spent for buying commodities of the amount β_j, so that there is no change in the government's balance of money.

Adding (9) to Walras' identity, we obtain

$$E_0 + (E_1 - S_1^G) + \Sigma p_i E_i + \Sigma p_j (E_j + \beta_j) = 0$$

In this we have $E_0 = 0$ and $E_i = 0$, $i = 2, \ldots, n$ because the interest rate and the rental markets are adjusted such that the corresponding markets are cleared. However, $E_j + \beta_j$ may still be negative wherever the government demand β_j is insufficient. The remaining negative excess demands are 'rationed' according to some rule of quantity adjustment. This may disturb E_0 and $E_1 - S_1^G$. If an excess demand or supply appears in either market, then the rationing is carried out in the monetary sectors too. Thus, where Say's law does not hold, both the price–interest mechanism and quantity adjustment mechanism must work in order to establish an equilibrium under insufficient effective demand. I regard these rationings as a part of the whole adjustment process that is crucially needed for synthesizing general

[8] Alternatively we may take the loanable fund theory; then r is set at the value making $E_1 = 0$. This value is different from that making $E_0 = 0$, because of the inequality above. Thus the two interest theories are not equivalent under anti-Say's law.

equilibrium theory and Keynesian economics. It would perhaps be very different from what Paul Samuelson calls the neoclassical synthesis.

7 Finally, the above argument concerning the dilemma of durable goods is compared with the conventional story that non-competitive behaviour creates market failure. In order to view the dilemma from this angle it is first stated that market success in the sense that a Pareto optimum is realized in the state of equilibrium happens in the Hicks–Arrow–Debreu type of economy in which firms behave so as to maximize their profits taking prices as given. In this sort of equilibrium model, as I have seen, the rates of profits are not equalized throughout firms; that is to say, there is no competition with respect to profit rates. Therefore, if we regard competition in this economy as the standard of competitiveness among firms, then Walras' own model of capital formation has to be taken as an excessively competitive one because competition is made there with regard to rates of profits also.

Thus market failure would happen in those cases of firms behaving either less or more competitively. This is because in order to realize a state of Pareto optimum at equilibrium, firms should not compete with each other in terms of the rate of profits; also, durable (capital) goods should not compete with others in terms of their profitability. Where capital moves from one firm to another in pursuit of a higher rate of profits, capital will evacuate a number of production facilities. In the case of effective demand being created, however small the creation may be, it will be distributed among efficient firms only, so that deserted production facilities will be closed down – both unemployed workers and capital goods will consequently appear in the economy. Obviously such a state cannot be a Pareto optimum.

It is further noted that throughout the above we tacitly assume all capital goods newly produced being sold at their production prices. This implies Say's law for capital goods, because if it does not hold, their market prices may deviate from the respective production prices. Then the equal rates of profits would not be established for capital goods, because the firms producing these goods would acquire additional sales profits which are not necessarily at an equal rate. In this way we must say that the dilemma of durable goods cannot be solved unless we give up the condition of equal rates of profits. But this solution is not a solution to the dilemma.

References

The items with * are those cited in the original Japanese version of *DKR*. Some of them are also referred to in the part of Addendum, those which are cited in this part only carrying no *.

Andronow, A. A. and C. E. Chaikin, 1949*, *Theory of Oscillations*, Princeton University Press.

Arrow, K. J., 1951, 'Alternative Proof of the Substitution Theorem for Leontief Model in the General Case', in T. C. Koopmans ed., *Activity Analysis of Production and Allocation*, John Wiley and Sons.

Arrow, K. J. and G. Debreu, 1954, 'Existence of an Equilibrium for a Competitive Economy', *Econometrica*, 22.

Arrow, K. J. and F. H. Hahn, 1971, *General Competitive Analysis*, North-Holland Publ. Co.

Arrow, K. J. and L. Hurwicz, 1958, 'On the Stability of the Competitive Equilibrium', *Econometrica*, 26.

Arrow, K. J. and M. McManus, 1958, 'A Note on Dynamic Stability', *Econometrica*, 26.

Aumann, R. J., 1964, 'Markets with a Continuum of Traders', *Econometrica*, 34.

Bassett, L., H. Habibagahi and J. Quirk, 1967, 'Qualitative Economics and Morishima Matrices', *Econometrica*, 35.

Bassett, L., J. Maybee and J. Quirk, 1968, 'Qualitative Economics and the Scope of the Correspondence Principle', *Econometrica*, 36.

Baumol, W. J. and J. Benhabib, 1989, 'Chaos, Significance, Mechanism and Economic Applications', *The Journal of Economic Perspective*, 3.

Bendixson, I., 1901, 'Sur les courbes définies par les équations differentielles', *Acta Mathematica*, 24.

1962, 'New Concepts and Techniques for Equilibrium Analysis', *International Economic Review*, 3.

Bewley, T., 1973, 'Edgeworth's Conjecture', *Econometrica*, 41.

Bortkiewicz von, L., 1951, 'Value and Price in the Marxian System', *International Economic Papers*, No. 2.

Burchardt, F., 1932, 'Die Schemata des stationaren Kreislaufs bei Böhm-Bawerk

und Marx', *Weltwirtschaftliches Archiv*, 35.
Chipman, J. S., 1950, 'The Multi-Sector Multiplier', *Econometrica*, 18.
1951, *The Theory of Inter-Sectoral Money Flows and Income Formation*, The Johns Hopkins Press.
Debreu, G., 1970, 'Economies with a Finite Set of Equilibria', *Econometrica*, 38.
Debreu, G. and I. N. Herstein, 1953, 'Nonnegative Square Matrices', *Econometrica*, 21.
Debreu, G. and H. Scarf, 1963, 'A Limit Theorem on the Core of an Economy', *International Economic Review*, 4.
Devaney, R. L., 1989, *An Introduction to Chaotic Dynamical Systems*, Addison-Wesley.
Domar, E. D., 1946, 'Capital Expansion, Rate of Growth, and Employment', *Econometrica*, 14.
Frobenius, G., 1908, 'Über Matrizen aus positiven Elementen', Sitzungberichte der königlich preussischen Akademie der Wissenschaften.
Furuya, H., 1949*, 'Keizai Kinko no Antei Bunseki (Stability Conditions for Economic Equilibrium)', Tokyo University, *Riron Keizaigaku no Shomondai.*
Gale, D. and H. Nikaido, 1965, 'The Jacobian Matrix and Global Univalence of Mappings', *Mathematische Annalen*, 159.
Garegnani, P., 1960, *Il Capital nelle Teorie della Distribuzione*, Milano.
1989, *Kapital, Einkommenversteilung und Effective Nachfrage*, Marburg.
Georgescu-Roegen, N., 1951, 'Some Properties of a Generalized Leontief Model', in T. C. Koopmans ed., *Activity Analysis of Production and Allocation*, John Wiley and Sons.
Goodwin, R. M., 1948, 'Secular and Cyclical Aspects of the Multiplier and the Accelerator', in *Income, Employment and Public Policy, Essays in Honor of Alvin Hansen*, W. W. Norton.
1950, 'Does the Matrix Multiplier Oscillate?', *The Economic Journal*, 60.
1951a, 'Nonlinear Accelerator and the Persistence of Business Cycle', *Econometrica*, 19.
1951b, 'Econometrics in Business-Cycle Analysis', in A. H. Hansen, *Business Cycles and National Income*, W. W. Norton.
1990, *Chaotic Economic Dynamics*, Oxford University Press.
Green, J., 1972, 'On the Inequitable Nature of Core Allocations', *Journal of Economic Theory*, 4.
Grodal, B., 1972, 'A Second Remark on the Core of an Atomless Economy', *Econometrica*, 40.
Hahn, F. H., 1958, 'Gross Substitutes and the Dynamic Stability of General Equilibrium', *Econometrica*, 26.
1968, 'On Some Propositions of General Equilibrium Analysis', *Econometrica*, 35.
Hahn, F. H. and T. Negishi, 1962, 'A Theorem on Non-Tatonnement Stability', *Econometrica*, 30.
Harrod, R. F., 1952, *Towards a Dynamic Economics*, Macmillan.
Hawkins, D. and H. A. Simon, 1949, 'Note: Some Conditions of Macroeconomic Stability', *Econometrica*, 17.

Hicks, J.R., 1946*, *Value and Capital*, Oxford University Press.
1950, *A Contribution to the Theory of Trade Cycle*, Oxford University Press.
1979, *Causality in Economics*, Blackwell.
Hildenbrand, W., 1970, 'On Economies with Many Agents', *Journal of Economic Theory*, 2.
Hirsch, M.A. 1902, 'Sur les racines d'une équation fondamentale', *Acta Mathematica*, 25.
Ichimura, S., 1955, 'Towards a General Nonlinear Macrodynamic Theory of Economic Fluctuations', in K.K. Kurihara ed., *Post-Keynesian Economics*, George Allen and Unwin.
Inada, K., 1968, 'On Stability of the Golden Rule Path in the Hayekian Process Case', *Review of Economic Studies*, 35.
Kaldor, N., 1940, 'A Model of Trade Cycle', *The Economic Journal*, 50.
Kalecki, M., 1937, 'A Theory of Business Cycle', *The Review of Economic Studies*, 5.
1949–50, 'A New Approach to the Problem of Business Cycles', *The Review of Economic Studies*, 16.
1954, *Theory of Economic Dynamics*, George Allen and Unwin.
Kannai, Y., 1970, 'Continuity Properties of the Core of a Market', *Econometrica*, 38.
Karlin, S., 1959, *Mathematical Methods and the Theory in Games, Programming and Economics*, Vol. I, Pergamon Press.
Kennedy, C.M., 1970, 'The Stability of the "Morishima System"', *The Review of Economic Studies*, 37.
Keynes, J.M., 1921*, *A Treatise on Probability*, Macmillan.
1936*, *The General Theory of Employment, Interest and Money*, Macmillan.
Klein, L.R., 1946*, 'Macro-Economics and the Theory of Rational Behavior', *Econometrica*, 14.
1947, *The Keynesian Revolution*, Macmillan.
Koopmans, T.C., 1940, 'The Degree of Damping in Business Cycles', *Econometrica*, 8.
Kuenne, R.E., 1963, *The Theory of General Economic Equilibrium*, Princeton University Press.
Kuhn, H. and A. Tucker, 1950, 'Nonlinear Programming', in *Proceedings of the Second Berkeley Symposium on Mathematical Statistics and Probability*, Berkeley.
Lange, O., 1940, 'Complementarity, and Inter-Relations of Shifts in Demand', *Review of Economic Studies*, 8.
1942*, 'Say's Law: A Restatement and Criticism', in O. Lange *et al.* eds., *Studies in Mathematical Economics and Econometrics*, University of Chicago Press.
1944*, *Price Flexibility and Employment*, Indiana: The Principia Press.
La Volpe, G., 1993, *Studies on the Theory of General Dynamic Economic Equilibrium*, Macmillan: the original Italian version was published in 1936.
Leser, C.C.V., 1943, 'The Consumer's Demand for Money', *Econometrica*, 14.
Levinson, N. and O.K. Smith, 1942, 'A General Equation for Relaxation Oscillation', *Duke Mathematical Journal*, 9.

Lewis, E. E., 1938, 'Intercommodity Relationship in Stable Demand', *Econometrica*, 11.

Li, T. Y. and J. A. Yorke, 1975, 'Period Three Implies Chaos', *American Mathematical Monthly*, 82.

Liapounoff, A. M., 1907*, 'Problème général de la stabilité du mouvement', *Annales de la Faculté des Sciences de l'Université de Toulouse*, 2nd series, Vol. 9.

Lindahl, E., 1939, *Studies in the Theory of Money and Capital*, London: George Allen and Unwin.

Marschak, J., 1950, 'Rational Behaviour, Uncertain Prospects, and Measurable Utility', *Econometrica*, 18.

McManus, M., 1958, 'Transformations in Economic Theories', *Review of Economic Studies*, 25.

Metzler, L. A., 1945*, 'Stability of Multiple Markets: The Hicksian Conditions', *Econometrica*, 13.

1950, 'A Multiple-Region Theory of Income and Trade', *Econometrica*, 18.

Morehouse, N. F., R. H. Strotz and S. J. Horwitz, 1950, 'An Electro-Analog Method for Investigating Problems in Economic Dynamics: Inventory Oscillations', *Econometrica*, 18.

Morishima, M., 1948*, 'Shohisha Katsudo to Kigyosha Katsudo (Consumer Behaviour and Producer Behaviour)', *Keizai Ronso*, 61–2.

1949*, 'Seigakuteki Antei Jyoken to Dogakuteki Antei Jyoken (On Static and Dynamic Stability Conditions)', *Shakai Kagaku Hyoron*, No. 3.

1952a, 'On the Laws of Change of the Price System in an Economy which Contains Complementary Commodities', *Osaka Economic Papers*, 1.

1952b, 'Consumer Behaviour and Liquidity Preference', *Econometrica*, 20.

1956, 'An Analysis of the Capitalist Process of Reproduction', *Metroeconomica*, 8.

1957, 'Notes on the Theory of Stability of Multiple Exchange', *Review of Economic Studies*, 24.

1958a, 'Related Goods and Global Stability of Equilibrium', ISER Discussion Paper, No. 4, Osaka University, unpublished.

1958b, 'A Contribution to the Nonlinear Theory of the Trade Cycle', *Zeitschrift fur Nationalokonomie*, 18.

1960, 'Existence of Solution to the Walrasian System of Capital Formation', *Zeitschrift fur Nationalokonomie*, 20.

1964, *Equilibrium, Stability and Growth*, Oxford University Press.

1969, *Theory of Economic Growth*, Oxford University Press.

1970, 'A Generalization of the Gross Substitute System', *Review of Economic Studies*, 37.

1973, *Marx's Economics*, Cambridge University Press.

1977, *Walras' Economics*, Cambridge University Press.

1989, *Ricardo's Economics*, Cambridge University Press.

1992, *Capital and Credit*, Cambridge University Press.

1994, 'Capital and Growth', in O. F. Hamounda ed., *The Legacy of Hicks*, Routledge.

Morishima, M. and T. Fujimoto, 1974, 'The Frobenius Theorem, Its Solow–Samuelson Extension and the Kuhn–Tucker Theorem', *Journal of Mathematical Economics*, 1.

Morishima, M. and M. Majumdar, 1978, 'The Cournot–Walras Arbitrage, Resource Consuming Exchange, and Competitive Equilibrium', *Hommage A François Perroux*, Presses Universitaires de Grenoble.

Morishima, M. *et al.*, 1973, *Theory of Demand: Real and Monetary*, Oxford University Press.

Mosak, J. L., 1944, *General Equilibrium Theory of International Trade*, The Principia Press.

Murata, Y., 1972, 'An Alternative Proof of the Frobenius Theorem', *Journal of Economic Theory*, 5.

Nataf, A., 1948*, 'Sur la possibilité de construction de certains macromodeles', *Econometrica*, 15.

Neumann von, J., 1945–6, 'A Model of General Economic Equilibrium', *Review of Economic Studies*, 8.

Nikaido, H., 1956, 'On the Classical Multilateral Exchange Problem', *Metroeconomica*, 8.

1969, *Convexity Structure and Economic Theory*, Academic Press.

Okamoto, T. and M. Morishima, 1950*, 'Shohingun no Riron to Kigyogun no Riron (Aggregations with Respect to Group of Commodities and Group of Firms)', *Kikan Riron Keizaigaku*, 1.

Okishio, N., 1950*, 'Shuren Jyoken to Working no Mondai (Conditions for Convergence and the Problem of Working)', *Kindai Keizai Riron Kenkyu*, 1.

Patinkin, D., 1948*, 'Relative Prices, Say's Law and the Demand for Money', *Econometrica*, 16.

1949*, 'Indeterminacy of Absolute Prices in Classical Economics', *Econometrica*, 17.

1949–50, 'A Reconsideration of the General Equilibrium Theory for Money', *Review of Economic Studies*, 18.

1955, *Money, Interest and Prices*, Row, Peterson and Company.

Peter, H., 1953, 'A Comparison of Marxian and Keynesian Dynamics', *International Economic Papers*, No. 3.

Quirk, J. and R. Saposnik, 1968, *Introduction to General Equilibrium Theory and Welfare Economics*, McGraw-Hill.

Rutmann, M. A., 1938, 'Sur une classe spécielle d'opérateurs linéaires totalement continus', *Comptes Rendus (Doklady) de l'Académie des Sciences de l'URSS*, 58.

1940, 'Sur les opérateurs totalement continus linéaires laissant invariant un certain cone', *Matematičeshiĭ Sbornik*, 8.

Samuelson, P. A., 1948*, *Foundations of Economic Analysis*, Harvard University Press.

1953–4, 'Price of Factors and Goods in General Equilibrium', *Review of Economic Studies*, 21.

Scarf, H., 1967, 'On the Computation of Equilibrium Prices', in W. Fellner ed., *Ten Economic Studies in the Tradition of Irving Fisher*, John Wiley.

Schmeidler, D., 1972, 'A Remark on the Core of an Atomless Economy', *Econometrica*, 40.

Shapley, L. and M. Subik, 1966, 'Quasi-Cores in a Monetary Economy with Non-convex Preferences', *Econometrica*, 34.

Solow, R. M., 1952, 'On the Structure of Linear Models', *Econometrica*, 20.

Solow, R. M. and P. A. Samuelson, 1953, 'Balanced Growth under Constant Returns to Scale', *Econometrica*, 21.

Sono, M., 1943*, 'Kakaku Hendo ni tomonau Bunri Kano Zai no Jukyu Hendo (The Effect of Price Changes on the Demand and Supply of Separable Goods)', *Kokumin Keizai Zasshi*, 74; English translation, *International Economic Review*, 1961, vol. 2.

1944*, 'Shijyo Kinko no Antei Jyoken (Stability Conditions for Market Equilibrium)', *Keizai Ronso*, 58.

Steindl, J., 1952, *Maturity and Stagnation in American Capitalism*, Blackwell.

Sweezy, P. M., 1942, *The Theory of Capitalist Development*, Oxford University Press.

Takata, Y., 1948*, *Saikin Rishiron Kenkyu (Studies in Contemporary Theory of Interest)*, Nihon Keizai Hyoronsha.

Uzawa, H., 1957, 'A Note on the Stability of Equilibrium', Stanford University, Technical Report.

Vind, K., 1972, 'A Third Remark on the Core of an Atomless Economy', *Econometrica*, 40.

Walras, L., 1954, *Elements of Pure Economics*, Richard D. Irwin.

Watanabe, T., 1950*, 'Toransufa Mondai to Hi-Keynesian Riron (The Transfer Problem and Non-Keynesian Theory)', *Keizaigaku*, 17–18.

Wielandt, H., 1950, 'Unzerlegbare, nicht-negative Matrizen', *Mathematische Zeitschrift*, 52.

Yasui, T., 1940*, 'Kinko Bunseki to Katei Bunseki (Equilibrium Analysis and Process Analysis)', *Keizaigaku Ronshu*, 10.

1944, 'Sultsky-Riron ni okeru Bunrikano no Shiso to Dojisei no Katei (Relation between Homogeneity Postulate and Separability Notion in Slutsky Theory)', *Keizai oyobi Keizaigaku no Sai-shuppatsu.*

1950*, 'Antei no Ippan Riron (A General Theory of Stability)', *Kikan Riron Keizaigaku*, 1.

1953, 'Self-Excited Oscillations and Business Cycles', *Cowles Commission Discussion Paper*, Economics, No. 2065.

1954, 'Junkanteki Seicho ni kansuru Ichi Shiron (A Preliminary Essay in Cyclical Growth)', *Keizai Kenkyu*, 5.

Yokoyama, T., 1950*, 'Senkei Taikei no Antei Jyoken (Stability Conditions for Linear Economic System)', *Kindai Keizai Riron Kenkyu*, 1.

Index